AZ GR BRITAIN NORTHERN IRELAND
Handy Road Atlas

EDITION 31   2023

Motorway
Autoroute
Autobahn
≡**M1**≡

Motorway Under Construction
Autoroute en construction
Autobahn im Bau

Motorway Proposed
Autoroute prévue
Geplante Autobahn

Motorway Junctions with Numbers
Autoroute échangeur numéroté
Beschränkter Fahrtrichtungswechsel

Unlimited Interchange   **4**   Limited Interchange   **5**
Echangeur complet   Echangeur partiel
Autobahnanschlußstelle mit Nummer   Unbeschränkter Fahrtrichtungswechsel

Motorway Service Area   ≡**S**
with access from one carriageway only
Aire de services d'autoroute   Rastplatz oder Raststätte   **S**
accessible d'un seul côté   Einbahn

Major Road Service Areas with 24 hour facilities
Aire de services sur route prioritaire ouverte 24h sur 24
Raststätte durchgehend geöffnet

Primary Route   ≡**S**≡   Class A Road   ≡**S**≡
Route à grande circulation   Route de type A
Hauptverkehrsstraße   A- Straße

Truckstop (selection of)   **T**
Sélection d'aire pour poids lourds
Auswahl von Fernfahrerrastplatz

Major Road Junctions
Jonctions grands routiers
Hauptverkehrsstrasse Kreuzungen

           Other   Autre   Andere

Primary Route
Route à grande circulation   **A40**
Hauptverkehrsstraße

Primary Route Junction with Number
Echangeur numéroté   **4**
Hauptverkehrsstraßenkreuzung mit Nummer

Primary Route Destination
Route prioritaire, direction   **DOVER**
Hauptverkehrsstraße Richtung

Dual Carriageways (A & B roads)
Route à double chaussées séparées (route A & B)
Zweispurige Schnellstraße (A- und B- Straßen)

Class A Road
Route de type A   **A129**
A-Straße

Class B Road
Route de type B   **B177**
B-Straße

Narrow Major Road (passing places)
Route prioritaire étroite (possibilité de dépassement)
Schmale Hauptverkehrsstraße (mit Überholmöglichkeit)

Major Roads Under Construction
Route prioritaire en construction
Hauptverkehrsstraße im Bau

Major Roads Proposed
Route prioritaire prévue
Geplante Hauptverkehrsstaße

Gradient 1:7 (14%) **& steeper**   »
(Descent in direction of arrow)
Pente égale ou supérieure à 14% (dans le sens de la descente)
14% Steigung und steiler (in Pfeilrichtung)

Toll   *Toll*
Barrière de péage
Gebührenpflichtig

Dart Charge   **C**
www.gov.uk/pay-dartford-crossing-charge

Park & Ride   **P+R**
Parking avec Service Navette
Parken und Reisen

Mileage between markers   8
Distence en miles entre les flèches
Strecke zwischen Markierungen in Meilen

Airport   ✈
Aéroport
Flughafen

Railway and Station
Voie ferrée et gare
Eisenbahnlinie und Bahnhof

Level Crossing and Tunnel
Passage à niveau et tunnel
Bahnübergang und Tunnel

River or Canal
Rivière ou canal
Fluß oder Kanal

County or Unitary Authority Boundary
Limite de comté ou de division administrative
Grafschafts- oder Verwaltungsbezirksgrenze

National Boundary
Frontière nationale
Landesgrenze

Built-up Area
Agglomération
Geschloßene Ortschaft

Town, Village or Hamlet
Ville, Village ou hameau
Stadt, Dorf oder Weiler

Wooded Area
Zone boisée
Waldgebiet

Spot Height in Feet   · 813
Altitude (en pieds)
Höhe in Fuß

Height Above Sea Level   1,400'-2000'   427m-610m
Altitude par rapport au niveau de la mer   2000'+   610m+
Höhe über Meeresspiegel

National Grid Reference (kilometres)   100
Coordonnées géographiques nationales (Kilomètres)
Nationale geographische Koordinaten (Kilometer)

Page Continuation
Suite à la page indiquée   **24**
Seitenfortsetzung

Scale to Map Pages   1:316,800 = 5 miles to 1 inch / 3.1 km to 1 cm

| 0 | 1 | 2 | 3 | 4 | 5 | | 10 | | 15 | | 20 Miles |

| 0 | 1 | 2 | 3 | 4 | 5 | | 10 | 15 | 20 | 25 | 30 Kilometres |

Airfield +
Terrain d'aviation
Flugplatz

Heliport (H)
Héliport
Hubschrauberlandeplatz

Abbey, Church, Friary, Priory +
Abbaye, église, monastère, prieuré
Abtei, Kirche, Mönchskloster, Kloster

Animal Collection
Ménagerie
Tiersammlung

Aquarium
Aquarium
Aquarium

Arboretum, Botanical Garden
Jardin Botanique
Botanischer Garten

Aviary, Bird Garden
Volière
Voliere

Battle Site and Date
Champ de bataille et date   1066
Schlachtfeld und Datum

Blue Flag Beach
Plage Pavillon Bleu
Blaue Flagge Strand

Bridge
Pont
Brücke

Castle (open to public)
Château (ouvert au public)
Schloß / Burg (für die Öffentlichkeit zugänglich)

Castle with Garden (open to public)
Château avec parc (ouvert au public)
Schloß mit Garten (für die Öffentlichkeit zugänglich)

Cathedral +
Cathédrale
Kathedrale

Cidermaker
Cidrerie (fabrication)
Apfelwein Hersteller

Country Park
Parc régional
Landschaftspark

Distillery
Distillerie
Brennerei

Farm Park, Open Farm
Park Animalier
Bauernhof Park

Ferry (vehicular, sea)
(vehicular, river)
(foot only)
Bac (véhicules, mer)
(véhicules, rivière)
(piétons)
Fähre (auto, meer)
(auto, fluß)
(nur für Personen)

Fortress, Hill Fort
Château Fort
Festung

Garden (open to public)
Jardin (ouvert au public)
Garten (für die Öffentlichkeit zugänglich)

Golf Course
Terrain de golf
Golfplatz

Historic Building (open to public)
Monument historique (ouvert au public)
Historisches Gebäude (für die Öffentlichkeit zugänglich)

Historic Building with Garden (open to public)
Monument historique avec jardin (ouvert au public)
Historisches Gebäude mit Garten (für die Öffentlichkeit zugänglich)

Horse Racecourse
Hippodrome
Pferderennbahn

Industrial Monument
Monument Industrielle
Industriedenkmal

Leisure Park, Leisure Pool
Parc d'Attraction, Loisirs Piscine
Freizeitpark, Freizeit pool

Lighthouse
Phare
Leuchtturm

Mine, Cave
Mine, Grotte
Bergwerk, Höhle

Monument
Monument
Denkmal

Motor Racing Circuit
Circuit Automobile
Automobilrennbahn

Museum, Art Gallery (M)
Musée
Museum, Galerie

National Park
Parc national
Nationalpark

National Trust Property
National Trust Property
National Trust- Eigentum

Natural Attraction ★
Attraction Naturelle
Natürliche Anziehung

Nature Reserve or Bird Sanctuary
Réserve naturelle botanique ou ornithologique
Natur- oder Vogelschutzgebiet

Nature Trail or Forest Walk
Chemin forestier, piste verte
Naturpfad oder Waldweg

Place of Interest   *Craft Centre* •
Site, curiosité
Sehenswürdigkeit

Prehistoric Monument
Monument Préhistorique
Prähistorische Denkmal

Railway, Steam or Narrow Gauge
Chemin de fer, à vapeur ou à voie étroite
Eisenbahn, Dampf- oder Schmalspurbahn

Roman Remains
Vestiges Romains
Römischen Ruinen

Theme Park
Centre de loisirs
Vergnügungspark

Tourist Information Centre [i]
Office de Tourisme
Touristeninformationen

Viewpoint (180 degrees)   (360 degrees)
Vue panoramique (180 degrés)   (360 degrés)
Aussichtspunkt (180 Grade)   (360 Grade)

Vineyard
Vignoble
Weinberg

Visitor Information Centre [V]
Centre d'information touristique
Besucherzentrum

Wildlife Park
Réserve de faune
Wildpark

Windmill
Moulin à vent
Windmühle

Zoo or Safari Park
Parc ou réserve zoologique
Zoo oder Safari-Park

Please note: symbols have been enlarged for clarity

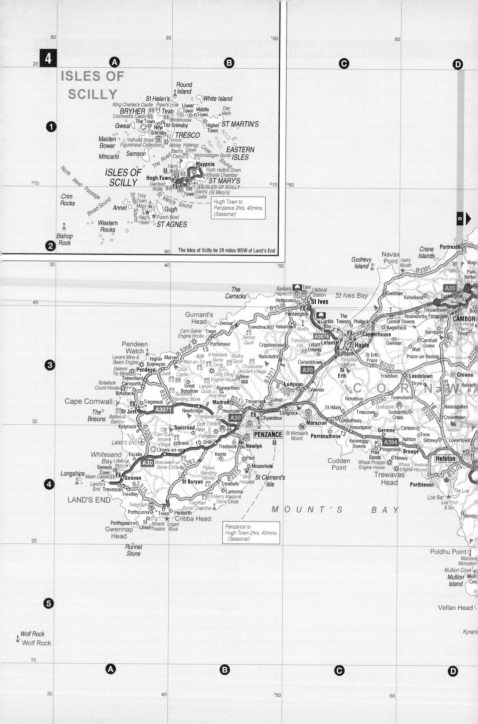

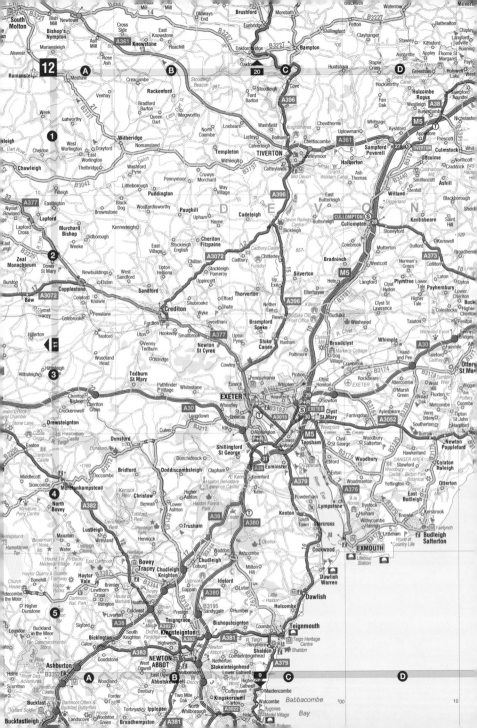

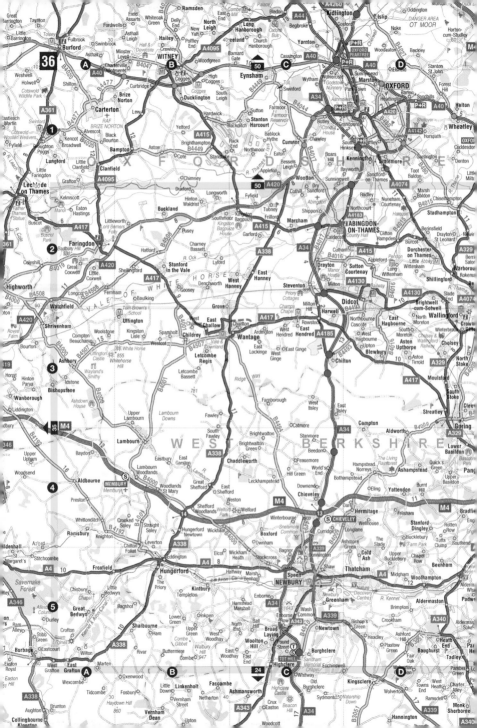

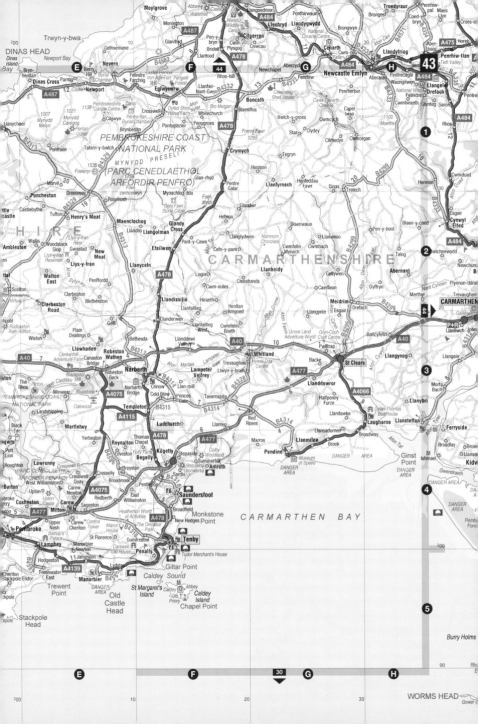

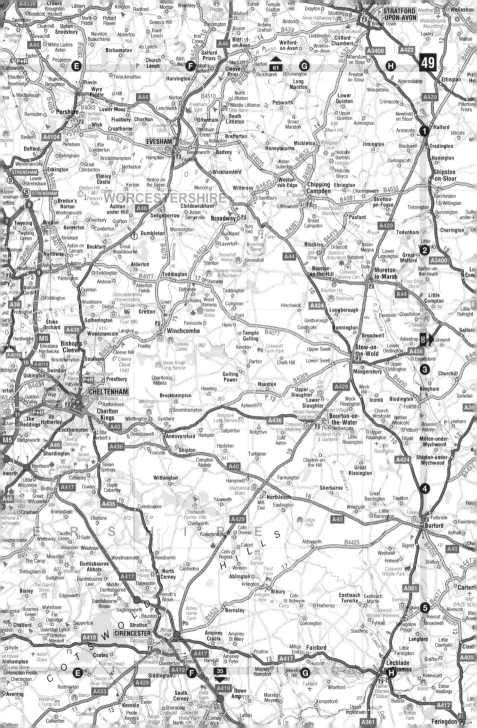

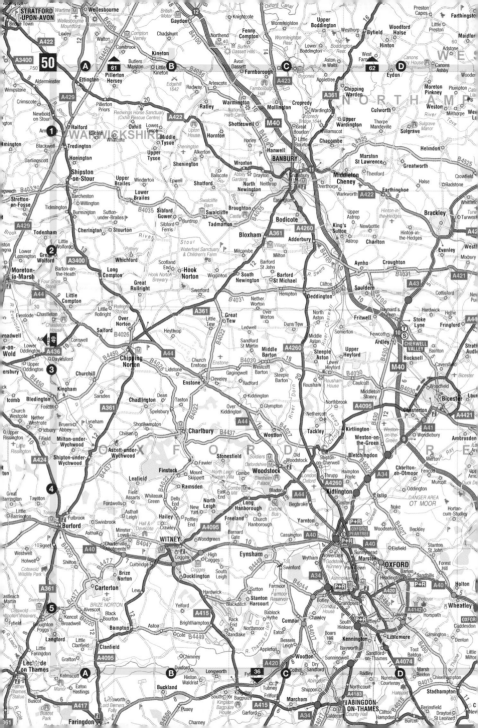

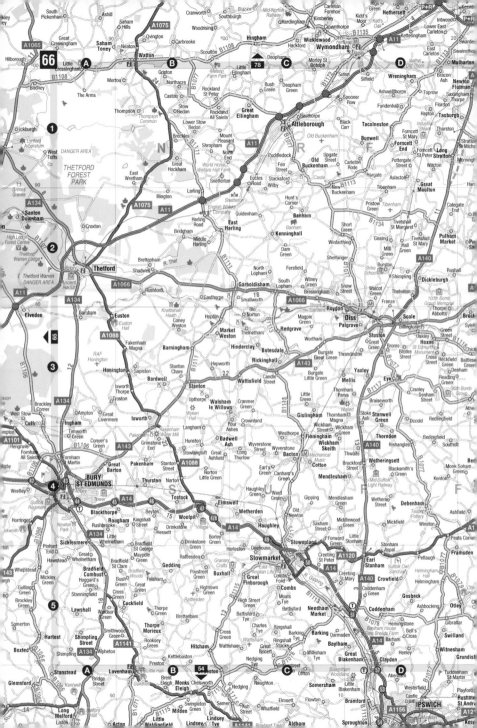

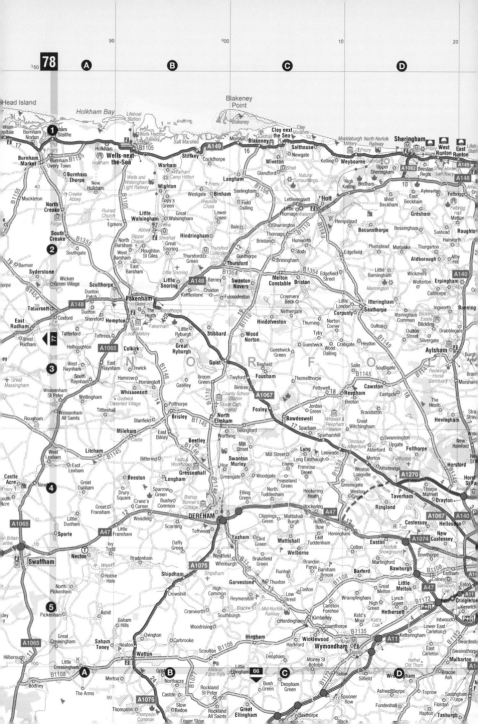

The Skerries

West Mouse

Carmel Head

Middle Mouse

Cemaes Bay
Llanbadrig
Porth Wen
Bull Bay
Bull Bay
East Mo

Cemlyn Bay
Penrhyn
Wylfa

Cemaes
Tregele
A5025

Burwen

B5111
Amlwch
Amlwch Port
Pengorl

Llanfairynghornwy

Llanfechell
Bodewryd

Parys Mountain
Penysarn
Gadfa

Thomas Mon

Mynydd Mechell
Rhosgoch

Penygraigwen
City Dulas

Church Bay
Llanrhyddiad
Llanfflewyn

Llyn Llygeirian
Llanfaethlu

Carreglefn
Rhosybol

A N G L E S E Y
Llandyfrydog
Bachau
Magne

Holyhead to:
Dublin 3hrs. 15mins.
Dublin 1hr. 50mins.
(Fast Ferry)

HOLYHEAD BAY

A5025

Llanddeusant

Llyn Alaw

Llanerchymedd

Melin Hywel

Gwredog

Llanbabo

Llanfair-yn-neubwll

Llaneuddog
Pen-llyn
Standing Stone

Carmel

Bryngwran

Llannerchymedd Station

Llanwyllog

Llyn Cefni

Llynfaes

Tryfil

Capel Mawr

Pentre Be

Llangwyfan-isaf

Aberffraw

St Cwyfan's
'The Church in the Sea'

Aberffraw Bay

Malltraeth Sands

Hermon

Llangadwaladr

Bodorgan

A4080

Malltraeth

Llanfaelog

Rhosneigr

Maelog

Barclodiad Y Gawres Grave

Llyn Coron

Bethel

Bodedern
Valley
A5

Gwaenabwyn
B5109

Trefor

A5

Gwalchmai

Mona
Bodffordd

Heneglwys
Rhostrehwfa

Cerrigceinwen

Din Dryfol
Chambered Tomb

Soar

Dothan
A4080

Pencarnisiog

Bryn Du

Treddraeth

Capel Coron

Capel Mawr

Dwyran

Newborough
Model Village

Foel Fa Park

Newborough
Forest

Newborough
Bay

Llanddwyn Island

Llanddwyn Bay

Abermenai Point

Foryd Bay

Caernarfon Bay

Airworld

Dinas Dinlle

Llandwrog

A499

Penygro

Llanil

Pontllyfni

Aberdesach

Clynnog-fawr

St Beuno

Capel Uchaf

Tai'n Lon

D

Trefor

St Beuno's Well
1671
Bwlch Mawr

Gyrn Ddu

Yr Eifl

A
68
B
C
D

Trwyn y Gorlech

Tre'r Cein

Bwlchde

HOLYHEAD
Salt Island
Breakwater

Caer y Twr Hillfort
Porth-y-felin
Fort
Gogarth Bay
Yr Y Llaingoch
Ellins Tower

Holyhead Mountain Hut Circles

HOLY
ISLAND

Strydoer
A5
Kingsland
Penrhos

Penrhos Feilw Standing Stones

Datarch Ancient Huts

Porth Dafarch

Standing Stone

Trearddur

Four Mile Bridge

Llyn Dinam

Llanfihangel yn Nhowyn

Ty Newydd Burial Chamber

RAF Valley

Cymyran Bay

Rhoscolyn

St Gwenfaen's Well

Maltraeth Bay

Ty Croes

E   F   G   H

❶

N O R T H

S E A

❷

80

❸

70

❹

60

❺

350

E   F   77   G   H

550   60   70   80

Scolt Head Island

Holkham Bay

Holme Dunes   Brancaster Bay

550   60   70   80   90

Addlethorpe St Helen
Seal Sanctuary & Wildlife Centre
Meers Bridge   Lifeboat Station
Mablethorpe   Ye Olde Curiosity
Trusthorpe
104
Thorpe   **Sutton on Sea**
          Sandilands
A1111
          Hannah
Markby   A52
Huttoft   Anderby Creek
Thurlby   Anderby   Drainage
49
          Mumby   On Your Marques
Cumberworth   Authorpe Row
sthorpe   Helsey
thorpe   **Chapel St Leonards**
oughby   **Hogsthorpe**
Sloothby   A52   Ashley's Field   Field's Animal Farm
          Slackholme End
Hasthorpe   Addlethorpe   **Ingoldmells**
Orby   Ingoldmells Point
          Skegness (Ingoldmells)   Butlin's
A158   Orby Marsh   Water Leisure Park
          Winthorpe   **Seathorne**
Burgh le Marsh   Natureland Seal Sanctuary
7   Church Farm   Bottons Pleasure Beach
          SKEGNESS   Model Village
Croft   Croft
Thorpe St Peter   A52   Seacroft
          Croft Marsh
          Magdalen   Gibraltar
Wainfleet All Saints   Gibraltar Point
ntleet Mary   Key's Toft
DANGER AREA
Deeps
Boston

108

POINT OF AYRE

Rue Point

The Ayres

A16

The Ayres
Cranstal

The
Lhen

A10

B6
Dhoon
B13
A19
B3
Bride
A17

Jurby Head
Jurby West
Jurby
Jurby East
A19
B1
Andreas
A10

Ballasalla
B5
Sandygate
Civil War Fort
A9
Regaby

Shellag Point

The Cronk
A13
St Judes
A17
B13
Dhoon Grove
B14

Ramsey Bay

Orrisdale
A14
Sulby
Curragh
6
B8

Ramsey
Lhergy Cristal
Manx Electric Railway
Port e Vullen

Orrisdale Head
Ballaugh
Churchtown
Glen Auldyn

Glen Wyllin
A3
Ravensdale
Bishopscourt Glen

A14

Elfin
Lewaigue
A15
Maughold
Crosses

Kirk Michael
Ballaleigh
A18
Corrany
1854
North Barrule

Maugh.
B19
Ballajora
Port Moar

Glen Mooar
Sleau Dhoo
1601
SNAEFELL
Clagh Ouyr
A2
Cornaa
Cashtal Yn Ard
Port Cornaa

Gob y Deigan
Ballacarnane Beg
Barregarrow
B10
Sulby Resr.
21
14
Glen Mona
Dhoon

Knocksharry
A4
Cronk-y-Voddy
B10
Snaefell Mountain
Great Laxey Wheel Laxey Mine
Dhoon Glen
Bulgham Bay

St Patrick's Isle
Leece Ballagyr
A3
Rhenass Waterfall
Colden 1599
Laxey Glen
Laxey
Old Laxey Head

House of Manannan
A20
ISLE
Glen Helen
Injebreck Resr.
A18
B12
Ballabeanragh
Laxey

Peel
A1
Tynwald
Ballig
Sleau Ruy 1570
OF
MAN
Ballacannell

Patrick
A30
Greeba Castle
B22
Baldwin
B21
Baldrine

Contrary Head
St John's
A1
Crosby
Hillberry
A2
Clay Head

Glen Maye
Glen Maye
A3
Lower Foxdale
11
Glen Vine
Strang
Willaston
Onchan
Groudle
Laxey Bay

Dalby Point
A27
Dalby
Foxdale
A24
Garth
Union Mills
A6
DOUGLAS
Groudle Railway
Port Groudle

Niarbyl Bay
A36
South Barrule Hill 1586 Fort
B35
Braaid
A24
Kewaigue
Onchan Head
A11

Stroin Vuigh
A36
Close Clark
B30
St Mark's
Newtown
Spring Valley
Douglas Bay

Fleshwick Bay
A27
Ballamodha
B22
A25
Quine's Hill
Douglas Head

Lingague
Ronague
Grenaby
A3
Keristal
Little Ness

Bradda Head
Surby
Colby
B42
Ballabeg
Rushen
Port Soderick

Bradda Glen
Port Erin
A7
A5
Ballasalla
B25
Isle of Man Steam
Santon Head

Railway
Chambered Cairn
The Howe
Port St Mary
A5
ISLE OF MAN
A12
Derby Fort
St Michael's Island

The Cregneash
Kitterland
A31
B18
Castletown
Derbyhaven
Rushen
Keys

SPANISH HEAD
National Folk
Scarlett
Nautical

Calf of Man
Dreswick Point

Douglas to:
Belfast 2hrs. 45mins.
(Fast Ferry, Seasonal)
Birkenhead 4hrs. 15mins.
(Seasonal)
Heysham 3hrs. 30mins.
Dublin 2hrs. 45mins.
(Fast Ferry, Seasonal)
Liverpool 2hrs. 30mins.
(Fast Ferry, Seasonal)

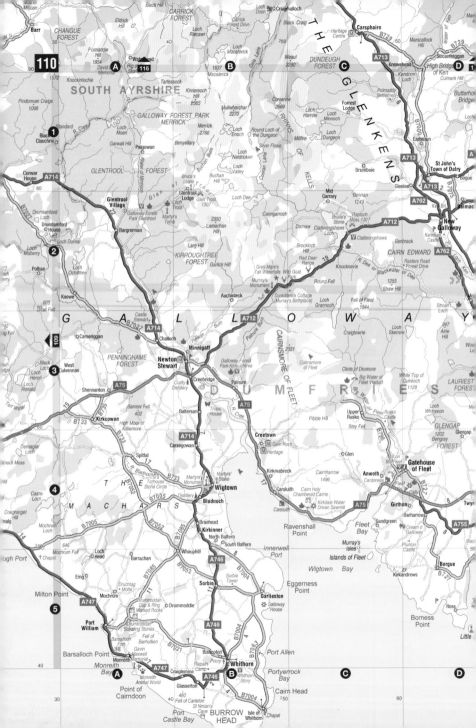

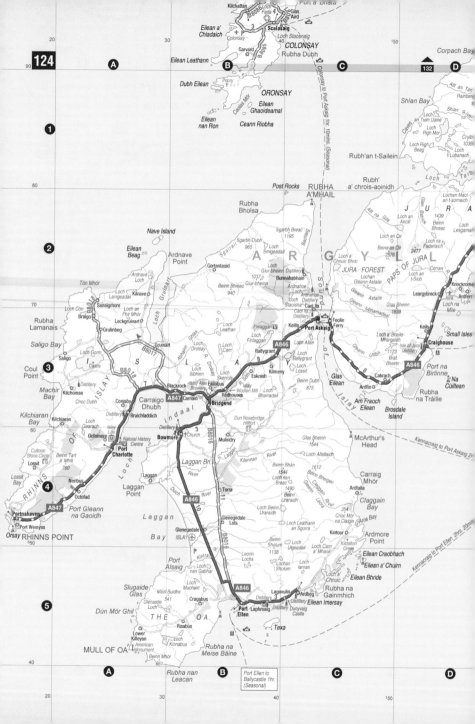

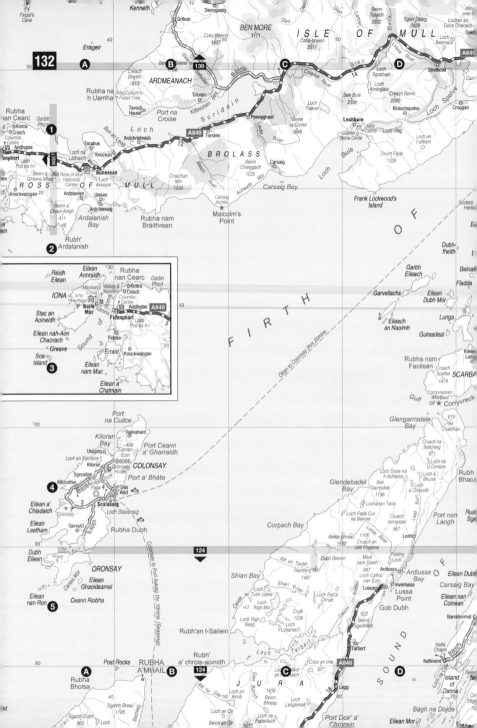

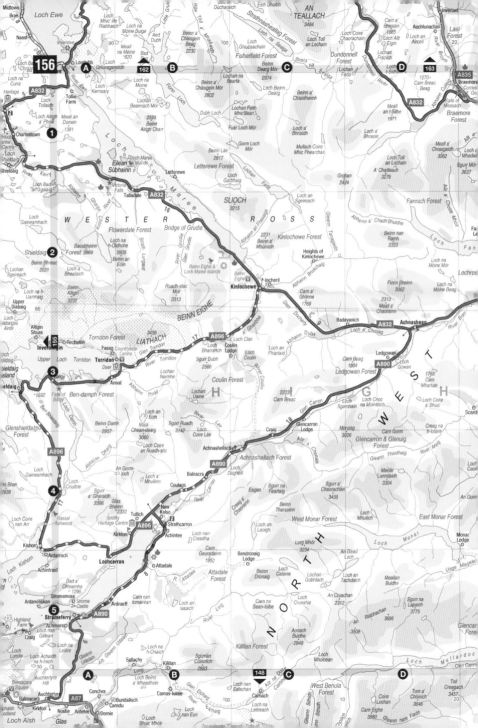

Seisiadar

60   70   80   90

30
A   B   C   D

1

20

2

10

171

3

°00

4

90

5

80

A   B   C   D

60   70   90

Camas Eilean Ghlais
Reiff

Eilean Mullagrach

Isle Rist

Glas-leac Mór

Tanera Beg

Ulapool to Stornoway 2hrs. 40mins.

Summe

Glas-leac Beag

Eilean Dubh

Priest Island

Bottle Island

Greenstone Point

Rubha Beag

Loch na Doire Duinne

Opinan   Mellon Udrigle

Stattic Point

Loch nan Clachan Geala

Loch a' Chore

Gruinard Island

Eilean Furadh Mór

Slaggan Bay

Loch an t-Slagain

Beinn Dearg Mhór 513

Achgarve

Gruinard Bay

Mungasdale

Rubha Reidh

Camas Mór

Rubha nan Sasan

Mellon Charles

Laide

Gruinard House

Cove

Ormiscaig

Sand

Second Coast

An Cuaidh 972

Loch an Draing

Mellangaun

A832

First Coast

Loch Airigh na Eilean

Aultbea

Loch na Bì

Beinn Dearg Bad Challeach 897

Melvaig

Loch Sguod

Drumchork

Aultgrishan

Isle of Ewe

Loch a' Bhaid-luachraich

Loch Fada

Seana Chamas

Cnoc Breac 962

Midtown

Brae

Loch Ewe

Beinn Mhic ile Riabhaich

Loch na Móine Buige

Aird Dubh

Peterburn

Naast

Meall na Mèine 620

Beinn a' Chàisgei Beag 2230

Port Erradale

Loch nan Liagh

Inverewe

Bad Bog

North Erradale

Loch Bad a' Chreamh

Poolewe

Londubh

Loch Ghiuragarstidh

Loch na Moine

155

Big S

River Sand

Loch na Curra

A832

C

Loch Kernsary

D

Longa Island

Caolas Beag

Lonemore

Mial

Heritage

Tollie Farm

Loch Tollaigh

Loch na Beannach Mór

Smithstown

B8021

Strath

Loch Airigh a' Phuill

Meall an Doirein

2595 Beinn

Gairloch

Loch Gairloch

Eilean

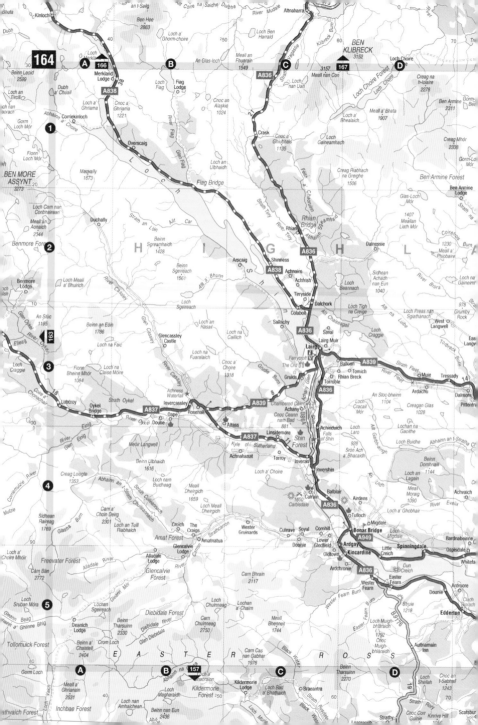

E   F   G   H

250   60   70   80

1

STRATHY
POINT

Eilean
Hoan

Whiten Head
or An Ceann Geal

Eilean
Clùimhrig

Port Allt
a' Mhuilinn
Totegan

Port
Vasgo

Aultivullin
Brawl

ongobeg

Rispond

Ben Hutig
1338

Achininver
Midfield
Lubinvullin
Achinahuagh
West
Strathan

Strathan

Eilean
nan Ron

Achanahuagh
Talmine

Neave or
Coombe Island

Farr
Point

Kirtomy
Point

Ardmore
Point

Armadale
Bay

Auttiphurst
Strathy

Strathy
Bay

rtnancon

Loch
Eriboll

Loch a'
Mhuillinn

Skinnet
Midtown

Rabbit
Islands

Raineach
Strathan
Skerray

Clasheddy

Skerray

Bay of
Swordly

Farr

Clerkhill
Crask

Swordly
Kirtomy

F M
Bettyhill

Armadale

18
Lednagullin

Strathy
Forest

Loch
Gaineimh

Bowside
Lodge

Eriboll

756
Ben
Arnaboll

Hope

30

Loch
Macovally

Achuvoldrach

Coldbackie
Blandy

Rhitongue

Dalcharn

Achtoty Bay
Torrisdale
Modsarie
Torrisdale

Clachan
Invernaver

A836
10

Borgie

Leckfurin

Coille na Borgie
Chambered Tomb

Clachan

Buidhe
Beag

Loch
Meadie

Benn
nam Bo
751

168

Strathy Forest

Loch
Buidhe Mòr

Tongue
Braetongue

A838

Castèal
Bharraich

Beinn Bhreac
1018

Caol
Cormaic

Skelpick

Ben
Hope

3040

Ribigill

Loch
Fhionnaich

Loch a'
Mhuillinn

Drum nan Clàr

Kinloch
Lodge

A836

Cnoc
Craggie
1943

Loch
Hakel

Borgie
Forest

Na Caol
Lochan

Loch
Stephan

Archargary

Loch Mòr
na Caorach

Loch
nan Clach

Cnoc Badi
na Gaoi
698

Loch na
Seilg

Loch
Craggie

Loch nan
Ealachan

Meallan
Liath
1962

Kinloch
River

River Borgie

Carnachy

Dunviden
Lochs

950

Cashel Dhu

Beinn
Stumanadh
1728

Rhifail

Loch
Meleag

Loch
Strathy

Loch
nam Breac

L   A   N   D

Ben Loyal
2509

Loch
nam Breac

1519
einne-
sheinn
Mhòr

Alltnacaillich
Dun Domaigil

Ben an
Dherue

Loch Haluim

Loch an
Dherue

Rough
Haugh

Beinn
Rifa-gil

963

Loch
na Sadhaiche

Loch Loyal
Lodge
1828
Cnoc nan
Cuilean

Loch Loyal

Skail Chambered
Cairn

Skail

Caol-loch
Mòr
1133

Cnoc nan
Tri-chlach

Loch
na Cròcach

Skail

Loch Syre

Caol-loch
Mòr
1133

Loch Druim
a' Chliabhain
1902

bernuisgach
Lodge

Loch nan
Ealachan

Loch
Coulside

Loch
Meadie

A836

Loch
Bad na Gallaig

Syre

Rhifail
Loch

Rimsdale
Loch

Ben
Griam Beg
1938

40

lee

Allt a'
Chraois

Pole Hill
965

Rosal
Clearance
Village

Navar
Forest

Rimsdale

Garvault

Ben
Griam Mòr
1938

Acfi

Loch Coire na
Saidhe Duibhe

Grumbeg
Settlement

B871

16

Badanloch
Forest

Loch Coire na
Saidhe Duibhe

Allt an
Cràisg

River Mudale

Grummore

B873

Loch Navar

Loch
Rimsdale

Loch
nan Clàr

Badanloch
Lodge

B871

Loch
a' Ghorm-choire

Mudale

Altnaharra

Meavaig Burn

Loch Ben
Harrald

Klibreck Burn

BEN
KLIBRECK
3152

Loch Choire
Lodge

Loch
Truderscaig

Loch nan Alltan Fhearna

Loch
Badanloch

Loch
Achnamoine

River Helms

Fiag
Lodge

An Glas-loch

Meall an
Fhuarain
1549

Vagastie

A836

164

F

Meall nan Con
3157
Loch
nan Uan

Loch Choire Forest

Creag na
h-Iolaire
2278

Loch Choire

Ben Armine
2311

Gorm-Loch
Beag

H

an Liath
d Mhòir
1423

165

Alt nan Abhainn

30

Crai'50tt
Alaskie
1024

Meall a' Bhata
1907

Loch a'
Bhealaich

Allt an Eallaig

Altnaduin

River A

Borrobol Forest

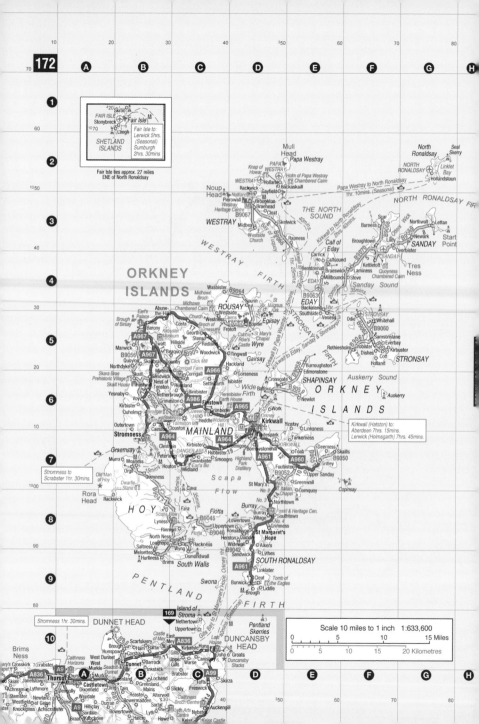

SHETLAND
ISLANDS

ST MAGNUS BAY

MAINLAND

Scale 10 miles to 1 inch   1:633,600

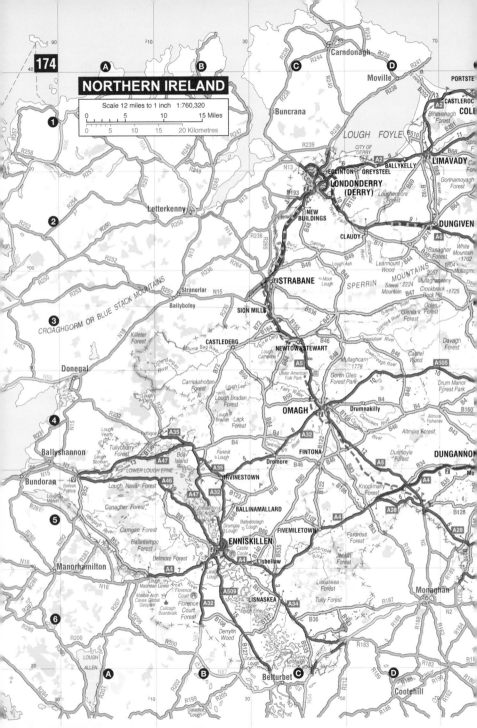

REFERENCE

MOTORWAY WITH NUMBER   M4   S   Service Area

MOTORWAY
(Under Construction / Proposed)

MOTORWAY JUNCTIONS   Limited

PRIMARY ROUTE   A6

A ROAD   A272

NATIONAL BOUNDARY

TOWNS SHOWN IN
THE MILEAGE CHART   **NORWICH**

SCALE

0   10   20   30 Miles

0   10   20   30   40 Kilometres

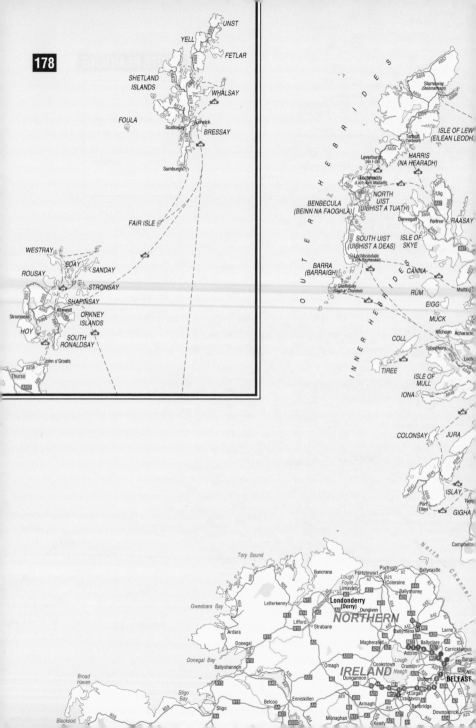

UNST

YELL

FETLAR

SHETLAND
ISLANDS

WHALSAY

FOULA

Scalloway

Lerwick

BRESSAY

Sumburgh

FAIR ISLE

WESTRAY

EDAY

ROUSAY   SANDAY

STRONSAY

SHAPINSAY

Stromness   Kirkwall   ORKNEY
ISLANDS

HOY

SOUTH
RONALDSAY

John o'Groats

Thurso

A836   A832

ISLE OF LEW
(EILEAN LEODH

Stornoway
(Steòrnabhagh)

Tarbert
(Tairbeart)

HARRIS
(NA HEARADH)

Leverburgh
(An t-Ob)

Lochmaddy
(Loch nam Madadh)

NORTH
UIST
(UIBHIST A TUATH)

BENBECULA
(BEINN NA FAOGHLA)

Uig

Dunvegan   Portree   RAASAY

SOUTH UIST
(UIBHIST A DEAS)

ISLE OF
SKYE

BARRA
(BARRAIGH)

Lochboisdale
(Loch Baghasdail)

Castlebay
(Bàgh a' Chaisteil)

CANNA

RÙM   EIGG

MALLAIG

MUCK

COLL   Kilchoan   Acharacle

Tobermory   Loch

TIREE

ISLE OF
MULL

IONA

COLONSAY   JURA

ISLAY

Port
Ellen   Tayn

GIGHA

North   Channel

Campbelto

OUTER HEBRIDES

INNER HEBRIDES

Tory Sound

Buncrana   Portstewart   Portrush   Ballycastle

Lough
Foyle   Coleraine

Letterkenny   Limavady   Ballymoney

Gweebara Bay

Londonderry
(Derry)   Dungiven

Lifford   NORTHERN

Ardara   Strabane

Donegal

Ballymena   Larne

Magherafelt   Ballyclare   Carrickfergus

Donegal Bay   Antrim

Ballyshannon   Cookstown   Lough
Neagh   Crumlin   BELFAST

Broad
Haven   Omagh   Dungannon   IRELAND   Lisburn

Lurgan   Bangu

Sligo
Bay   Belcoo   Enniskillen   Lurgan   Craigavon

Armagh   Banbridge   Downpatrick

Sligo   Monaghan

Blacksod   Keady

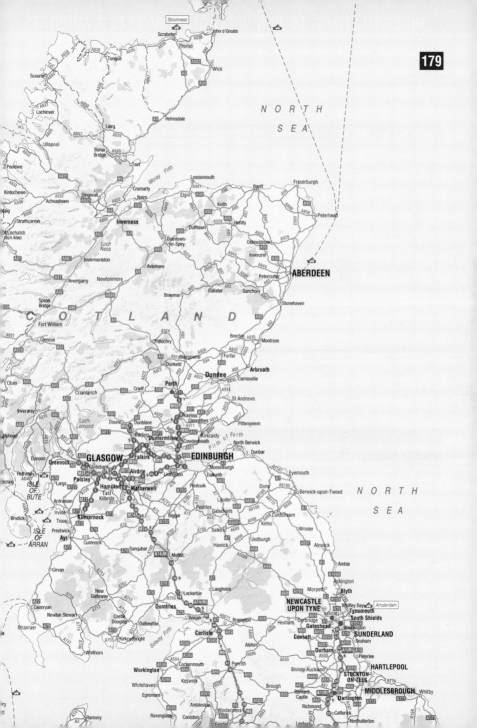

INDEX TO CITIES, TOWNS, VILLAGES, HAMLETS & AIRPORTS

(1) A strict alphabetical order is used e.g. An Dùnan follows Andreas but precedes Andwell.

(2) The map reference given refers to the actual map square in which the town spot or built-up area is located and not to the place name.

(3) Where two or more places of the same name occur in the same County or Unitary Authority, the nearest large town is also given; e.g. Achiemore. High nr. Durness . . . .2D **166** indicates that Achiemore is located in square 2D on page **166** and is situated near Durness in the Unitary Authority of Highland.

(4) Only one reference is given although due to page overlaps the place may appear on more than one page.

(5) Major towns and destinations are shown in bold, i.e. **Aberdeen**. Aber 3G **153**

COUNTIES and UNITARY AUTHORITIES with the abbreviations used in this index

Aberdeen : *Aber*
Aberdeenshire : *Abers*
Angus : *Ang*
Antrim & Newtownabbey : *Ant*
Ards & North Down : *Ards*
Argyll & Bute : *Arg*
Armagh, Banbridge & Craigavon : *Arm*
Bath & N E Somerset : *Bath*
Bedford : *Bed*
Belfast : *Bel*
Blackburn with Darwen : *Bkbn*
Blackpool : *Bkpl*
Blaenau Gwent : *Blae*
Bournemouth : *Bour*
Bracknell Forest : *Brac*
Bridgend : *B'end*
Brighton & Hove : *Brig*
Bristol : *Bris*
Buckinghamshire : *Buck*
Caerphilly : *Cphy*
Cambridgeshire : *Cambs*
Cardiff : *Card*
Carmarthenshire : *Carm*
Causeway Coast & Glens : *Caus*
Central Bedfordshire : *C Beds*
Ceredigion : *Cdgn*
Cheshire East : *Ches E*
Cheshire West & Chester : *Ches W*
Clackmannanshire : *Clac*
Conwy : *Cnwy*
Cornwall : *Corn*
Cumbria : *Cumb*

Darlington : *Darl*
Denbighshire : *Den*
Derby : *Derb*
Derbyshire : *Derbs*
Derry & Strabane : *Derr*
Devon : *Devn*
Dorset : *Dors*
Dumfries & Galloway : *Dum*
Dundee : *D'dee*
Durham : *Dur*
East Ayrshire : *E Ayr*
East Dunbartonshire : *E Dun*
East Lothian : *E Lot*
East Renfrewshire : *E Ren*
East Riding of Yorkshire : *E Yor*
East Sussex : *E Sus*
Edinburgh : *Edin*
Essex : *Essx*
Falkirk : *Falk*
Fermanagh & Omagh : *Ferm*
Fife : *Fife*
Flintshire : *Flin*
Glasgow : *Glas*
Gloucestershire : *Glos*
Greater London : *G Lon*
Greater Manchester : *G Man*
Gwynedd : *Gwyn*
Halton : *Hal*
Hampshire : *Hants*
Hartlepool : *Hart*
Herefordshire : *Here*
Hertfordshire : *Herts*

Highland : *High*
Inverclyde : *Inv*
Isle of Anglesey : *IOA*
Isle of Man : *IOM*
Isle of Wight : *IOW*
Isles of Scilly : *IOS*
Kent : *Kent*
Kingston upon Hull : *Hull*
Lancashire : *Lanc*
Leicester : *Leic*
Leicestershire : *Leics*
Lincolnshire : *Linc*
Lisburn & Castlereagh : *Lis*
Luton : *Lutn*
Medway : *Medw*
Merseyside : *Mers*
Merthyr Tydfil : *Mer T*
Mid & East Antrim : *ME Ant*
Middlesbrough : *Midd*
Midlothian : *Midl*
Mid Ulster : *M Ulst*
Milton Keynes : *Mil*
Monmouthshire : *Mon*
Moray : *Mor*
Neath Port Talbot : *Neat*
Newport : *Newp*
Newry, Mourne & Down : *New M*
Norfolk : *Norf*
Northamptonshire : *Nptn*
North Ayrshire : *N Ayr*
North East Lincolnshire : *NE Lin*
North Lanarkshire : *N Lan*

North Lincolnshire : *N Lin*
North Somerset : *N Som*
Northumberland : *Nmbd*
North Yorkshire : *N Yor*
Nottingham : *Nott*
Nottinghamshire : *Notts*
Orkney : *Orkn*
Oxfordshire : *Oxon*
Pembrokeshire : *Pemb*
Perth & Kinross : *Per*
Peterborough : *Pet*
Plymouth : *Plym*
Poole : *Pool*
Portsmouth : *Port*
Powys : *Powy*
Reading : *Read*
Redcar & Cleveland : *Red C*
Renfrewshire : *Ren*
Rhondda Cynon Taff : *Rhon*
Rutland : *Rut*
Scottish Borders : *Bord*
Shetland : *Shet*
Shropshire : *Shrp*
Slough : *Slo*
Somerset : *Som*
Southampton : *Sotn*
South Ayrshire : *S Ayr*
Southend-on-Sea : *S'end*
South Gloucestershire : *S Glo*
South Lanarkshire : *S Lan*
South Yorkshire : *S Yor*
Staffordshire : *Staf*

Stirling : *Stir*
Stockton-on-Tees : *Stoc* T
Stoke-on-Trent : *Stoke*
Suffolk : *Suff*
Surrey : *Surr*
Swansea : *Swan*
Swindon : *Swin*
Telford & Wrekin : *Telf*
Thurrock : *Thur*
Torbay : *Torb*
Torfaen : *Torf*
Tyne & Wear : *Tyne*
Vale of Glamorgan, The : *V Glam*
Warrington : *Warr*
Warwickshire : *Warw*
West Berkshire : *W Ber*
West Dunbartonshire : *W Dun*
Western Isles : *W Isl*
West Lothian : *W Lot*
West Midlands : *W Mid*
West Sussex : *W Sus*
West Yorkshire : *W Yor*
Wiltshire : *Wilts*
Windsor & Maidenhead : *Wind*
Wokingham : *Wok*
Worcestershire : *Worc*
Wrexham : *Wrex*
York : *York*

INDEX

A

Abbas Combe. *Som*..............4C **22**
Abberley. *Worc*................4B **60**
Abberley Common. *Worc*......4B **60**
Abberton. *Essx*................4D **54**
Abberton. *Worc*................5D **61**
Abberwick. *Nmbd*.............3F **121**
Abbess Roding. *Essx*........4F **53**
Abbey. *Devn*...................1E **13**
Abbeydale. *S Yor*.............2H **85**
Abbeydale Park. *S Yor*.......2H **85**
Abbey Dore. *Here*............2G **47**
Abbey Gate. *Devn*............3F **13**
Abbey Hulton. *Stoke*.........1D **72**
Abbey St Bathans. *Bord*.....3D **130**
Abbeystead. *Lanc*............4E **97**
Abbeytown. *Cumb*............4C **112**
Abbey Village. *Lanc*..........2E **91**
Abbey Wood. *G Lon*.........3F **39**
Abbots Bickington. *Devn*.....1D **11**
Abbots Bromley. *Staf*........3E **73**
Abbotsbury. *Dors*............4A **14**
Abbotsham. *Devn*.............4E **19**
Abbotskerswell. *Devn*........2E **9**
Abbots Langley. *Herts*.......5A **52**
Abbots Leigh. *N Som*........4A **34**
Abbotsley. *Cambs*............5B **64**
Abbots Morton. *Worc*........5E **61**
Abbots Ripton. *Cambs*.......3B **64**

Abbot's Salford. *Warw*.......5E **61**
Abbotstone. *Hants*...........3D **24**
Abbots Worthy. *Hants*.......3C **24**
Abbots Ann. *Hants*...........2B **24**
Abcott. *Shrp*..................3F **59**
Abdon. *Shrp*..................2H **59**
Abenhall. *Glos*...............4B **48**
Aber. *Cdgn*...................1E **45**
Aberaeron. *Cdgn*.............4D **56**
Aberafan. *Neat*..............3G **31**
Aberaman. *Rhon*.............5D **46**
Aberangell. *Gwyn*...........4H **69**
Aberarad. *Carm*..............1H **43**
Aberarder. *High*..............1A **150**
Aberargie. *Per*...............2D **136**
Aberarth. *Cdgn*..............4D **57**
Aberavon. *Neat*..............3G **31**
Aber-banc. *Cdgn*............1D **44**
Aberbargoed. *Cphy*..........2E **33**
Aberbechan. *Powy*...........1D **58**
Aberbeeg. *Blae*...............5F **47**
Aberbran. *Powy*..............3C **46**
Abercanaid. *Mer T*...........5D **46**
Abercarn. *Cphy*..............2F **33**
Abercastle. *Pemb*............1C **42**
Abercegir. *Powy*.............5H **69**
Aberchalder. *High*............3F **149**
Aberchirder. *Abers*...........3D **160**
Aberchwiler. *Den*.............4C **82**
Abercorn. *W Lot*.............2D **129**
Abercraf. *Powy*...............4B **46**

Abercregan. *Neat*............2B **32**
Abercrombie. *Fife*............3H **137**
Abercwmboi. *Rhon*...........2D **32**
Abercych. *Pemb*..............1C **44**
Abercynon. *Rhon*............2D **32**
Aber-Cywarch. *Gwyn*........4A **70**
Aberdalgie. *Per*..............1C **136**
Aberdar. *Rhon*..............5C **46**
Aberdare. *Rhon*.............5C **46**
Aberdaron. *Gwyn*............3A **68**
Aberdaugleddau. *Pemb*......4D **42**
Aberdeen. *Aber*.............3G **153**
Aberdeen International
Airport. *Aber*..................2F **153**
Aberdesach. *Gwyn*...........5D **80**
Aberdour. *Fife*...............1E **129**
Aberdovey. *Gwyn*............1F **57**
Aberdulais. *Neat*.............5A **46**
Aberdyfi. *Gwyn*..............1F **57**
Abereiddy. *Pemb*.............1B **42**
Abererch. *Gwyn*..............2C **68**
Aberfan. *Mer T*...............5D **46**
Aberfeldy. *Per*...............4F **143**
Aberffraw. *IOA*...............4C **80**
Aberffrwd. *Cdgn*.............3F **57**
Aberford. *W Yor*.............1E **93**
Aberfoyle. *Stir*...............3E **135**
Abergarw. *B'end*.............3C **32**
Abergarwed. *Neat*............5B **46**
Abergavenny. *Mon*...........4G **47**
Abergele. *Cnwy*..............3B **82**

Aber-Giâr. *Carm*..............1F **45**
Abergorlech. *Carm*...........2F **45**
Abergwaun. *Pemb*...........1D **42**
Abergwesyn. *Powy*...........5A **58**
Abergwili. *Carm*..............3E **45**
Abergwynfi. *Neat*............2B **32**
Abergwyngregyn. *Gwyn*.....3F **81**
Abergynolwyn. *Gwyn*........5F **69**
Aberhafesp. *Powy*............1C **58**
Aberhonddu. *Powy*...........3D **46**
Aberhosan. *Powy*.............1H **57**
Aberkenfig. *B'end*............3B **32**
Aberlady. *E Lot*..............1A **130**
Aberlemno. *Ang*.............3E **145**
Aberllefenni. *Gwyn*..........5G **69**
Abermaw. *Gwyn*.............4F **69**
Abermeurig. *Cdgn*...........5E **57**
Aber-miwl. *Powy*.............1D **58**
Abermule. *Powy*..............1D **58**
Abernant. *Carm*..............2H **43**
Abernant. *Rhon*..............5D **46**
Abernethy. *Per*...............2D **136**
Abernyte. *Per*................5B **144**
Aber-oer. *Wrex*..............1E **71**
Aberpennar. *Rhon*...........2D **32**
Aberporth. *Cdgn*.............5B **56**
Aberriw. *Powy*...............5D **70**
Abersoch. *Gwyn*.............3C **68**
Abersychan. *Torf*.............5F **47**
Abertawe. *Swan*............3F **31**
Aberteifi. *Cdgn*..............1B **44**
Aberthin. *V Glam*............4D **32**

Abertillery. *Blae*.............5F **47**
Abertridwr. *Cphy*............3E **32**
Abertyleri. *Blae*............5F **47**
Abertysswg. *Cphy*...........5E **47**
Aberuthven. *Per*.............2B **136**
Aber Village. *Powy*..........3E **46**
Aberwheeler. *Den*...........4C **82**
Aberyscir. *Powy*.............3C **46**
Aberystwyth. *Cdgn*........2E **57**
Abhainn Suidhe. *W Isl*......7C **171**
Abingdon-on-Thames.
Oxon.........................2C **36**
Abinger Common. *Surr*......1C **26**
Abinger Hammer. *Surr*......1B **26**
Abington. *S Lan*.............2B **118**
Abington Pigotts. *Cambs*....1D **52**
Ab Kettleby. *Leics*..........3E **74**
Ab Lench. *Worc*.............5E **61**
Ablington. *Glos*.............5G **49**
Ablington. *Wilts*............2G **23**
Abney. *Derbs*...............3F **85**
Aboyne. *Abers*..............4C **152**
Abram. *G Man*.............4E **90**
Abriachan. *High*.............5H **157**
Abridge. *Essx*...............1F **39**
Abronhill. *N Lan*............2A **128**
Abson. *S Glo*................4C **34**
Abthorpe. *Nptn*.............1E **51**
Acaster-Hill. *Orkn*..........5B **172**
Aby. *Linc*....................3D **88**
Acairseid. *W Isl*.............8C **170**
Acaster Malbis. *York*........5H **99**

Acaster Selby – Alpraham

Acaster Selby. N Yor 5H 99
Accott. Devn 3G 19
Accrington. Lanc 2F 91
Acha. Arg 3C 138
Achachork. High 4D 155
Achadh a' Chuirn. High 1E 147
Achahoish. Arg 2F 125
Achaleven. Arg 5D 140
Achallader. Arg 4H 141
Acha Mor. W Isl 5F 171
Achanalt. High 2E 157
Achandunie. High 1A 158
Ach' an Todhair. High 1E 141
Achany. High 3C 164
Achaphubuil. High 1E 141
Acharacle. High 2A 140
Acharn. Ang 1B 144
Acharn. Per 4E 143
Acharole. High 3E 169
Achateny. High 2G 139
Achavanich. High 4D 169
Achdalieu. High 1E 141
Achduart. High 3E 163
Achentoul. High 5A 168
Achfary. High 5C 166
Achfrish. High 2C 164
Achgarve. High 4C 162
Achiemore. High
nr. Durness 2D 166
nr. Thurso 3A 168
A' Chill. High 3A 146
Achiltibuie. High 3E 163
Achina. High 2H 167
Achinahuagh. High 2F 167
Achindarroch. High 3E 141
Achinduich. High 3C 164
Achinduin. Arg 5C 140
Achininver. High 2F 167
Achintee. High 4B 156
Achintraid. High 5H 155
Achleck. Arg 4F 139
Achlorachan. High 3F 157
Achluachrach. High 5E 149
Achlyness. High 3C 166
Achmelvich. High 1E 163
Achmony. High 5H 157
Achmore. High
nr. Stromeferry 5A 156
nr. Ullapool 4E 163
Achnacarnin. High 1E 163
Achnacarry. High 5D 148
Achnaclerach. High 2G 157
Achnacloich. High 3D 147
Ach na Cloiche. High 3D 147
Achnaconeran. High 2G 149
Achnacroish. Arg 4C 140
Achnafalnich. Arg 1B 134
Achnagarron. High 1A 158
Achnagoul. Arg 3H 133
Achnaha. High 2F 139
Achnahanat. High 4C 164
Achnahannet. High 1D 151
Achnairn. High 2C 164
Achnamara. Arg 1F 125
Achnanellan. High 5C 148
Achnasheen. High 3D 156
Achnashellach. High 4C 156
Achosnich. High 2F 139
Achow. High 5E 169
Achranich. High 4B 140
Achreamie. High 2C 168
Achriabhach. High 2F 141
Achriesgill. High 3C 166
Achrimsdale. High 3G 165
Achscrabster. High 2C 168
Achtoty. High 2G 167
Achurch. Nptn 2H 63
Achuvoldrach. High 3F 167
Achvaich. High 4E 164
Achvoan. High 3E 165
Ackenthwaite. Cumb 1E 97
Ackergill. High 3F 169
Ackergillshore. High 3F 169
Acklam. Midd 3B 106
Acklam. N Yor 3B 100
Ackleton. Shrp 1B 60
Acklington. Nmbd 4G 121
Ackton. W Yor 2E 93
Ackworth Moor Top
W Yor 3E 93
Acle. Norf 4G 79
Acocks Green. W Mid 2F 61
Acol. Kent 4H 41
Acomb. Nmbd 3C 114
Acomb. York 4H 99
Aconbury. Here 2A 48
Acre. G Man 4H 91
Acre. Lanc 2F 91
Acrefair. Wrex 1E 71
Acrise. Kent 1F 29
Acton. Ches E 5A 84
Acton. Dors 5E 15
Acton. G Lon 2C 38
Acton. Shrp 2F 59
Acton. Staf 1C 72
Acton. Suff 1B 54
Acton. Worc 4C 60
Acton. Wrex 5F 83
Acton Beauchamp. Here 5A 60
Acton Bridge. Ches W 3H 83
Acton Burnell. Shrp 5H 71
Acton Green. Here 5A 60
Acton Pigott. Shrp 5H 71
Acton Round. Shrp 1A 60
Acton Scott. Shrp 2G 59
Acton Trussell. Staf 4D 72
Acton Turville. S Glo 3D 34
Adabroc. W Isl 1H 171
Adam's Hill. Worc 3D 60
Adbaston. Staf 3B 72
Adber. Dors 4B 22
Adderbury. Oxon 2C 50
Adderley. Shrp 2A 72
Adderstone. Nmbd 1F 121
Addiewell. W Lot 3C 128
Addingham. W Yor 5C 98
Addington. Buck 3F 51
Addington. G Lon 4E 39
Addington. Kent 5A 40
Addinston. Bord 4B 130
Addiscombe. G Lon 4E 39
Addlestone. Surr 4B 38
Addlethorpe. Linc 4E 89
Adeney. Telf 4B 72
Adfa. Powy 5C 70
Adforton. Here 3G 59
Adgestone. IOW 4D 16
Adisham. Kent 5G 41
Adlestrop. Glos 3H 49
Adlingfleet. E Yor 2B 94
Adlington. Ches E 2D 84
Adlington. Lanc 3E 90
Admaston. Staf 3E 73
Admaston. Telf 4A 72
Admington. Warw 1H 49
Adpar. Cdgn 1D 44
Adsborough. Som 4F 21
Adstock. Buck 2F 51
Adstone. Nptn 5C 62
Adversane. W Sus 3B 26
Advie. High 5F 159
Adwalton. W Yor 2C 92
Adwell. Oxon 2E 37
Adwick le Street. S Yor 4F 93
Adwick upon Dearne
S Yor 4E 93
Adziel. Abers 3G 161
Ae. Dum 1A 112
Affleck. Abers 1F 153
Affpuddle. Dors 3D 14
Affric Lodge. High 1D 148
Afon-wen. Flin 3D 82
Agglethorpe. N Yor 1C 98
Aglionby. Cumb 4F 113
Ahoghill. ME Ant 2F 175
Aigburth. Mers 2F 83
Aiginis. W Isl 4G 171
Aike. E Yor 5E 101
Aikers. Orkn 8D 172
Aiketgate. Cumb 5F 113
Aikhead. Cumb 5D 112
Aikton. Cumb 4D 112
Ailey. Here 1G 47
Ailsworth. Pet 1A 64
Ainderby Quernhow. N Yor 1F 99
Ainderby Steeple. N Yor 5A 106
Aingers Green. Essx 3E 54
Ainsdale. Mers 3B 90
Ainsdale-on-Sea. Mers 3B 90
Ainstable. Cumb 5G 113
Ainsworth. G Man 3F 91
Ainthorpe. N Yor 4E 107
Aintree. Mers 1F 83
Aird. Arg 3E 133
Aird. Dum 3F 109
Aird. High
nr. Port Henderson 1G 155
nr. Tarskavaig 3D 147
Aird. W Isl
on Benbecula 3C 170
on Isle of Lewis 4H 171
The Aird. High 3D 154
Àird a Bhasair. High 3E 147
Aird a Mhachair. W Isl 4C 170
Aird a Mhulaidh. W Isl 6D 171
Aird Asaig. W Isl 7D 171
Aird Dhail. W Isl 1G 171
Airdens. High 4D 164
Airdeny. Arg 1G 133
Aird Mhidhinis. W Isl 8C 170
Aird Mhighe. W Isl
nr. Ceann a Bhaigh 8D 171
nr. Fionnsabhagh 9C 171
Aird Mhor. W Isl on Barra 8C 170
on South Uist 4D 170
Airdrie. N Lan 3A 128
Aird Shleibhe. W Isl 9D 171
Aird Thunga. W Isl 4G 171
Aird Uig. W Isl 4C 171
Airedale. W Yor 2E 93
Airidh a Bhruaich. W Isl 6E 171
Airies. Dum 3E 109
Airmyn. E Yor 2H 93
Airntully. Per 5H 143
Airor. High 3F 147
Airth. Falk 1C 128
Airton. N Yor 4B 98
Aisby. Linc
nr. Gainsborough 1F 87
nr. Grantham 2H 75
Aisgernis. W Isl 6C 170
Aish. Devn
nr. Buckfastleigh 2C 8
nr. Totnes 3E 9
Aisholt. Som 3E 21
Aiskew. N Yor 1E 99
Aislaby. N Yor
nr. Pickering 1B 100
nr. Whitby 4F 107
Aislaby. Stoc T 3B 106
Aisthorpe. Linc 2G 87
Aith. Shet
on Fetlar 3H 173
on Mainland 6E 173
Aithsetter. Shet 8F 173
Akeld. Nmbd 2D 120
Akeley. Buck 2F 51
Akenham. Suff 1E 55
Albaston. Corn 5E 11
Alberbury. Shrp 4F 71
Albert Town. Pemb 3D 42
Albert Village. Leics 4H 73
Albourne. W Sus 4D 26
Albrighton. Shrp
nr. Shrewsbury 4G 71
nr. Telford 5C 72
Alburgh. Norf 2E 67
Albury. Herts 3E 53
Albury. Surr 1B 26
Albyfield. Cumb 4G 113
Alby Hill. Norf 2D 78
Alcaig. High 3H 157
Alcaston. Shrp 2G 59
Alcester. Warw 5E 61
Alciston. E Sus 5G 27
Alcombe. Som 2C 20
Alconbury. Cambs 3A 64
Alconbury Weston. Cambs 3A 64
Aldborough. Norf 2D 78
Aldborough. N Yor 3G 99
Aldbourne. Wilts 4A 36
Aldbrough. E Yor 1F 95
Aldbrough St John. N Yor 3F 105
Aldbury. Herts 4H 51
Aldcliffe. Lanc 3D 96
Aldclune. Per 2G 143
Aldeburgh. Suff 5G 67
Aldeby. Norf 1G 67
Aldenham. Herts 1C 38
Alderbury. Wilts 4G 23
Aldercar. Derbs 1B 74
Alderford. Norf 4D 78
Alderholt. Dors 1G 15
Alderley. Glos 2C 34
Alderley Edge. Ches E 3C 84
Aldermaston. W Ber 5D 36
Aldermaston Soke. Hants 5E 36
Aldermaston Wharf. W Ber 5E 36
Alderminster. Warw 1H 49
Alder Moor. Staf 3G 73
Aldersey Green. Ches W 5G 83
Aldershot. Hants 1G 25
Alderton. Glos 2F 49
Alderton. Nptn 1F 51
Alderton. Shrp 3G 71
Alderton. Suff 1G 55
Alderton. Wilts 3D 34
Alderton Fields. Glos 2F 49
Alderwasley. Derbs 5H 85
Aldfield. N Yor 3E 99
Aldford. Ches W 5G 83
Aldgate. Rut 5G 75
Aldham. Essx 3C 54
Aldham. Suff 1D 54
Aldingbourne. W Sus 5A 26
Aldingham. Cumb 2B 96
Aldington. Kent 2E 29
Aldington. Worc 1F 49
Aldington Frith. Kent 2E 29
Aldochlay. Arg 4C 134
Aldon. Shrp 3G 59
Aldoth. Cumb 5C 112
Aldreth. Cambs 3D 64
Aldridge. W Mid 5E 73
Aldringham. Suff 4G 67
Aldsworth. Glos 4G 49
Aldsworth. W Sus 2F 17
Aldwark. Derbs 5G 85
Aldwark. N Yor 3G 99
Aldwick. W Sus 3H 17
Aldwincle. Nptn 2H 63
Aldworth. W Ber 4D 36
Alexandria. W Dun 1E 127
Aley. Som 3E 21
Aley Green. C Beds 4A 52
Alfardisworthy. Devn 1C 10
Alfington. Devn 3E 12
Alfold. Surr 2B 26
Alfold Bars. W Sus 2B 26
Alfold Crossways. Surr 2B 26
Alford. Abers 2C 152
Alford. Linc 3D 88
Alford. Som 3B 22
Alfreton. Derbs 5B 86
Alfrick. Worc 5B 60
Alfrick Pound. Worc 5B 60
Alfriston. E Sus 5G 27
Algarkirk. Linc 2B 76
Alhampton. Som 3B 22
Aline Lodge. W Isl 6D 171
Alkborough. N Lin 2B 94
Alkerton. Oxon 1B 50
Alkham. Kent 1G 29
Alkington. Shrp 2H 71
Alkmonton. Derbs 2F 73
Alladale Lodge. High 5B 164
Allaleigh. Devn 3E 9
Allanbank. N Lan 4B 128
Allanton. N Lan 4B 128
Allanton. Bord 4E 131
Allaston. Glos 5B 48
Allbrook. Hants 4C 24
All Cannings. Wilts 5F 35
Allendale Town. Nmbd 4B 114
Allen End. Warw 1F 61
Allenheads. Nmbd 5B 114
Allensford. Dur 5D 115
Allen's Green. Herts 4E 53
Allensmore. Here 2H 47
Allenton. Derb 2A 74
Aller. Som 4H 21
Allerby. Cumb 1B 102
Allercombe. Devn 3D 12
Allerford. Som 2C 20
Allerston. N Yor 1C 100
Allerthorpe. E Yor 5B 100
Allerton. Mers 2G 83
Allerton. W Yor 1B 92
Allerton Bywater. W Yor 2E 93
Allerton Mauleverer. N Yor 4G 99
Allesley. W Mid 2G 61
Allestree. Derb 2H 73
Allet. Corn 4B 6
Allexton. Leics 5F 75
Allgreave. Ches E 4D 84
Allhallows. Medw 3C 40
Allhallows-on-Sea. Medw 3C 40
Alligin Shuas. High 3H 155
Allimore Green. Staf 4C 72
Allington. Kent 5B 40
Allington. Linc 1F 75
Allington. Wilts
nr. Amesbury 3H 23
nr. Devizes 5F 35
Allithwaite. Cumb 2C 96
Alloa. Clac 4A 136
Allonby. Cumb 5B 112
Allostock. Ches W 3B 84
Alloway. S Ayr 3C 116
Allowenshay. Som 1G 13
All Saints South Elmham
Suff 2F 67
Allscott. Shrp 1B 60
Allscott. Telf 4A 72
All Stretton. Shrp 1G 59
Allt. Carm 5F 45
Alltami. Flin 4E 83
Alltgobhlach. N Ayr 5G 125
Alltmawr. Powy 1D 46
Alltnacaillich. High 4E 167
Allt na h' Airbhe. High 4F 163
Alltour. High 5E 148
Alltsigh. High 2G 149
Alltwalis. Carm 2E 45
Alltwen. Neat 5H 45
Alltyblacca. Cdgn 1F 45
Allt-y-goed. Pemb 1B 44
Almeley. Here 5F 59
Almeley Wootton. Here 5F 59
Almer. Dors 3E 15
Almholme. S Yor 4F 93
Almington. Staf 2B 72
Alminstone Cross. Devn 4D 18
Almodington. W Sus 3G 17
Almondbank. Per 1C 136
Almondbury. W Yor 3B 92
Almondsbury. S Glo 3B 34
Alne. N Yor 3G 99
Alness. High 2A 158
Alnessferry. High 2A 158
Alnham. Nmbd 3D 121
Alnmouth. Nmbd 3G 121
Alnwick. Nmbd 3F 121
Alphamstone. Essx 2B 54
Alpheton. Suff 5A 66
Alphington. Devn 3C 12
Alpington. Norf 5E 79
Alport. Derbs 4G 85
Alport. Powy 1E 59
Alpraham. Ches E 5H 83

Alresford. Essx....3D 54
Alrewas. Staf....4F 73
Alsager. Ches E....5B 84
Alsagers Bank. Staf....1C 72
Alsop en le Dale. Derbs....5F 85
Alston. Cumb....5A 114
Alston. Devn....2G 13
Alstone. Glos....2E 49
Alstone. Som....2G 21
Alstonefield. Staf....5F 85
Alston Sutton. Som....1H 21
Alswear. Devn....4H 19
Altandhu. High....2D 163
Altanduin. High....1F 165
Altarnun. Corn....4C 10
Altass. High....3B 164
Alterwall. High....2E 169
Altgaltraig. Arg....2B 126
Altham. Lanc....1F 91
Althorne. Essx....1D 40
Althorpe. N Lin....4B 94
Altnabreac. High....4C 168
Altnacealgach. High....2G 163
Altnafeadh. High....3G 141
Altnaharra. High....5F 167
Altofts. W Yor....2D 93
Alton. Derbs....4A 86
Alton. Hants....3F 25
Alton. Staf....1E 73
Alton Barnes. Wilts....5G 35
Altonhill. E Ayr....1D 116
Alton Pancras. Dors....2C 14
Alton Priors. Wilts....5G 35
Altrincham. G Man....2B 84
Altrua. High....4E 149
Alva. Clac....4A 136
Alvanley. Ches W....3G 83
Alvaston. Derb....2A 74
Alvechurch. Worc....3E 61
Alvecote. Warw....5G 73
Alvediston. Wilts....4E 23
Alveley. Shrp....2B 60
Alverdiscott. Devn....4F 19
Alverstoke. Hants....3D 16
Alverstone. IOW....4D 16
Alverthorpe. W Yor....2D 92
Alverton. Notts....1E 75
Alves. Mor....2F 159
Alvescot. Oxon....5A 50
Alveston. S Glo....3B 34
Alveston. Warw....5G 61
Alvie. High....3C 150
Alvingham. Linc....1C 88
Alvington. Glos....5B 48
Alwalton. Cambs....1A 64
Alweston. Dors....1B 14
Alwington. Devn....4E 19
Alwinton. Nmbd....4D 120
Alwoodley. W Yor....5E 99
Alyth. Per....4B 144
Amatnatua. High....4B 164
Am Baile. W Isl....7C 170
Ambaston. Derbs....2B 74
Ambergate. Derbs....5H 85
Amber Hill. Linc....1B 76
Amberley. Glos....5D 48
Amberley. W Sus....4B 26
Amble. Nmbd....4G 121
Amblecote. W Mid....2C 60
Ambler Thorn. W Yor....2A 92
Ambleside. Cumb....4E 103
Ambleston. Pemb....2E 43
Ambrosden. Oxon....4E 50
Amcotts. N Lin....3B 94
Amersham. Buck....1A 38
Amerton. Staf....3D 73
Amesbury. Wilts....2G 23
Amisfield. Dum....1B 112
Amlwch. IOA....1D 80
Amlwch Port. IOA....1D 80
Ammanford. Carm....4G 45
Amotherby. N Yor....2B 100
Ampfield. Hants....4B 24
Ampleforth. N Yor....2H 99

Ampleforth College. N Yor....2H 99
Ampney Crucis. Glos....5F 49
Ampney St Mary. Glos....5F 49
Ampney St Peter. Glos....5F 49
Amport. Hants....2A 24
Ampthill. C Beds....2A 52
Ampton. Suff....3A 66
Amroth. Pemb....4F 43
Amulree. Per....5G 143
Anaheilt. High....2C 140
An Aird. High....3D 147
Antrobus. Ches W....3A 84
An Camus Darach. High....4E 147
Ancaster. Linc....1G 75
Anchor. Shrp....2D 58
Anchorsholme. Lanc....5C 96
Anchor Street. Norf....3F 79
An Cnoc. W Isl....4G 171
An Cnoc Ard. W Isl....1H 171
An Coroghon. High....3A 146
Ancroft. Nmbd....5G 131
Ancrum. Bord....2A 120
Ancton. W Sus....5A 26
Anderby. Linc....3E 89
Anderby Creek. Linc....3E 89
Anderson. Dors....3D 15
Anderton. Ches W....3A 84
Andertons Mill. Lanc....3D 90
Andover. Hants....2B 24
Andover Down. Hants....2B 24
Andoversford. Glos....4F 49
An Dùnan. High....1D 147
Andwell. Hants....1E 25
Anelog. Gwyn....3A 68
Anfield. Mers....1F 83
Angarrack. Corn....3C 4
Angelbank. Shrp....3H 59
Angersleigh. Som....1E 13
Angerton. Cumb....4D 112
Angle. Pemb....4C 42
An Gleann Ur. W Isl....4G 171
Angmering. W Sus....5B 26
Angmering-on-Sea. W Sus....5B 26
Angram. N Yor
    nr. Keld....5B 104
    nr. York....5H 99
Anick. Nmbd....3C 114
Ankerbold. Derbs....4A 86
Ankerville. High....1C 158
Anlaby. E Yor....2D 94
Anlaby Park. Hull....2D 94
An Leth Meadhanach. W Isl....7C 170
Anmer. Norf....3G 77
Anmore. Hants....1E 17
Annahilt. Lis....5G 175
Annalong. New M....6H 175
An Mam. Dum....3D 112
Annaside. Cumb....1A 96
Annat. Arg....1H 133
Annat. High....3A 156
Annathill. N Lan....2A 128
Anna Valley. Hants....2B 24
Annbank. S Ayr....2D 116
Anneley. Notts....5C 86
Annesley Woodhouse. Notts....5C 86
Annfield Plain. Dur....4E 115
Annscroft. Shrp....5G 71
An Sailean. High....2A 140
Ansdell. Lanc....2B 90
Ansford. Som....3B 22
Ansley. Warw....1G 61
Anslow. Staf....3G 73
Anslow Gate. Staf....3F 73
Ansteadbrook. Surr....2A 26
Anstey. Herts....2E 53
Anstey. Leics....5C 74
Anston. S Lan....5D 128
Anstruther Easter. Fife....3H 137
Anstruther Wester. Fife....3H 137
Ansty. Warw....2A 62
Ansty. W Sus....3D 27
Ansty. Wilts....4E 23
An Taobh Tuath. W Isl....1E 170

An t-Aodann Ban. High....3C 154
An t Ath Leathann. High....1E 147
An Teanga. High....3E 147
Anthill Common. Hants....1E 17
Anthorn. Cumb....4C 112
Antingham. Norf....2E 79
An t-Ob. W Isl....9C 171
Anton's Gowt. Linc....1B 76
Antony. Corn....3A 8
An t-Òrd. High....2E 147
Antrim. Ant....3G 175
Antrobus. Ches W....3A 84
Anvil Corner. Devn....2D 10
Anwick. Linc....5A 88
Anwoth. Dum....4C 110
Apethorpe. Nptn....1H 63
Apeton. Staf....4C 72
Apley. Linc....3A 88
Apperknowle. Derbs....3A 86
Apperley. Glos....3D 48
Apperley Dene. Nmbd....4D 114
Appersett. N Yor....5B 104
Appin. Arg....4D 140
Appleby. N Lin....3C 94
Appleby-in-Westmorland
    Cumb....2H 103
Appleby Magna. Leics....5H 73
Appleby Parva. Leics....5H 73
Applecross. High....4G 155
Appledore. Devn
    nr. Bideford....3E 19
    nr. Tiverton....1D 12
Appledore. Kent....3D 28
Appledore Heath. Kent....2D 28
Appleford. Oxon....2D 36
Applegarthtown. Dum....1C 112
Applemore. Hants....2B 16
Appleshaw. Hants....2B 24
Applethwaite. Cumb....2D 102
Appleton. Hal....2H 83
Appleton. Oxon....5C 50
Appleton-le-Moors. N Yor....1B 100
Appleton-le-Street. N Yor....2B 100
Appleton Roebuck. N Yor....5H 99
Appleton Thorn. Warr....2A 84
Appleton Wiske. N Yor....4A 106
Appletree. Nptn....1C 50
Appletreehall. Bord....3H 119
Appletreewick. N Yor....3C 98
Appley. Som....4D 20
Appley Bridge. Lanc....3D 90
Apse Heath. IOW....4D 16
Apsley End. C Beds....2B 52
Apuldram. W Sus....2G 17
Arabella. High....1C 158
Arasaig. High....5E 147
Arbeadie. Abers....4D 152
Arberth. Pemb....3F 43
Arbirlot. Arg....4F 145
Arborfield. Wok....5F 37
Arborfield Cross. Wok....5F 37
Arborfield Garrison. Wok....5F 37
Arbourthorne. S Yor....2A 86
Arbroath. Arg....4F 145
Arbuthnott. Abers....1H 145
Arcan. High....3H 157
Archargary. High....3H 167
Archdeacon Newton. Darl....3F 105
Archiestown. Mor....4G 159
Arclid. Ches E....4B 84
Arclid Green. Ches E....4B 84
Ardachu. High....3D 164
Ardalanish. Arg....2A 132
Ardaneaskan. High....5H 155
Ardarroch. High....5H 155
Ardbeg. Arg
    nr. Dunoon....1C 126
    on Islay....5C 124
    on Isle of Bute....3B 126
Ardcharnich. High....5F 163
Ardchiavaig. Arg....2A 132
Ardchonnell. Arg....2G 133
Ardchrishnish. Arg....1B 132
Ardchronie. High....5D 164

Ardchullarie. Stir....2E 135
Ardchyle. Stir....1E 135
Ard-dhubh. High....4G 155
Arddleen. Powy....4E 71
Arddlin. Powy....4E 71
Ardechive. High....4D 148
Ardeley. Herts....3D 52
Ardelve. High....1A 148
Arden. Arg....1E 127
Ardendrain. High....5H 157
Arden Hall. N Yor....5C 106
Ardens Grafton. Warw....5F 61
Ardentinny. Arg....1C 126
Ardeonaig. Stir....5D 142
Ardersier. High....3B 158
Ardery. High....2B 140
Ardessie. High....5E 163
Ardfern. Arg....3F 133
Ardfernal. Arg....2D 124
Ardfin. Arg....3C 124
Ardgartan. Arg....3B 134
Ardgay. High....4D 164
Ardglass. New M....6J 175
Ardgour. High....2E 141
Ardheslaigh. High....3G 155
Ardindrean. High....5F 163
Ardingly. W Sus....3E 27
Ardington. Oxon....3C 36
Ardlamont House. Arg....3A 126
Ardleigh. Essx....3D 54
Ardler. Per....4B 144
Ardley. Oxon....3D 50
Ardlui. Arg....2C 134
Ardlussa. Arg....1E 125
Ardmair. High....4F 163
Ardmay. Arg....3B 134
Ardminish. Arg....5E 125
Ardmolich. High....1B 140
Ardmore. High
    nr. Kinlochbervie....3C 166
    nr. Tain....5E 164
Ardnacross. Arg....4G 139
Ardnadam. Arg....1C 126
Ardnagrask. High....4H 157
Ardnamurach. High....4G 147
Ardnarff. High....5A 156
Ardnastang. High....2C 140
Ardoch. Per....5H 143
Ardochy House. High....3E 148
Ardpatrick. Arg....3F 125
Ardrishaig. Arg....1G 125
Ardroag. High....4B 154
Ardross. High....1A 158
Ardrossan. N Ayr....5D 126
Ardshealach. High....2A 140
Ardslignish. High....2G 139
Ardtalla. Arg....4C 124
Ardtalnaig. Per....5E 142
Ardtoe. High....1A 140
Arduaine. Arg....2E 133
Ardullie. High....2H 157
Ardvasar. High....3E 147
Ardvorlich. Per....1F 135
Ardwell. Dum....5G 109
Ardwell. Mor....5A 160
Arean. High....1A 140
Areley Common. Worc....3C 60
Areley Kings. Worc....3C 60
Arford. Hants....3G 25
Argoed. Cphy....2E 33
Argoed Mill. Powy....4B 58
Aridhglas. Arg....2B 132
Arinacrinachd. High....3G 155
Arinagour. Arg....3D 138
Arisaig. High....5E 147
Ariundle. High....2C 140
Arivegaig. High....2A 140
Arkendale. N Yor....3F 99
Arkesden. Essx....2E 53
Arkholme. Lanc....2E 97
Arkle Town. N Yor....4D 104
Arkley. G Lon....1D 38
Arksey. S Yor....4F 93

Arkwright Town. Derbs....3B 86
Arlecdon. Cumb....3B 102
Arlescote. Warw....1B 50
Arlesey. C Beds....2B 52
Arleston. Telf....4A 72
Arley. Ches E....2A 84
Arlingham. Glos....4C 48
Arlington. Devn....2G 19
Arlington. E Sus....5G 27
Arlington. Glos....5G 49
Arlington Beccott. Devn....2G 19
Armadail. High....3E 147
Armadale. High
    nr. Isleornsay....3E 147
    nr. Strathy....2H 167
Armadale. W Lot....3C 128
Armagh. Arm....5E 175
Armathwaite. Cumb....5G 113
Arminghall. Norf....5E 79
Armitage. Staf....4E 73
Armitage Bridge. W Yor....3B 92
Armley. W Yor....1C 92
The Arms. Norf....1A 66
Armscote. Warw....1H 49
Armston. Nptn....2H 63
Armthorpe. S Yor....4G 93
Arncliffe. N Yor....2B 98
Arncliffe Cote. N Yor....2B 98
Arncroach. Fife....3H 137
Arne. Dors....4E 15
Arnesby. Leics....1D 62
Arnicle. Arg....2B 122
Arnisdale. High....2G 147
Arnish. High....4E 155
Arniston. Midl....3G 129
Arnol. W Isl....3F 171
Arnold. E Yor....5F 101
Arnold. Notts....1C 74
Arnprior. Stir....4F 135
Arnside. Cumb....2D 96
Aros Mains. Arg....4G 139
Arpafeelie. High....3A 158
Arrad Foot. Cumb....1C 96
Arram. E Yor....5E 101
Arras. E Yor....5D 100
Arrathorne. N Yor....5E 105
Arreton. IOW....4D 16
Arrington. Cambs....5C 64
Arrochar. Arg....3B 134
Arrow. Warw....5E 61
Arscaig. High....2C 164
Artafallie. High....4A 158
Arthington. W Yor....5E 99
Arthingworth. Nptn....2E 63
Arthog. Gwyn....4F 69
Arthrath. Abers....5G 161
Arthurstone. Per....4B 144
Artington. Surr....1A 26
Arundel. W Sus....5B 26
Asby. Cumb....2B 102
Ascog. Arg....3C 126
Ascot. Wind....4A 38
Ascott-under-Wychwood
    Oxon....4B 50
Asenby. N Yor....2F 99
Asfordby. Leics....4E 74
Asfordby Hill. Leics....4E 74
Asgarby. Linc
    nr. Horncastle....4C 88
    nr. Sleaford....1A 76
Ash. Devn....4E 9
Ash. Dors....1D 14
Ash. Kent
    nr. Sandwich....5G 41
    nr. Swanley....4H 39
Ash. Som....4H 21
Ash. Surr....1G 25
Ashampstead. W Ber....4D 36
Ashbocking. Suff....5D 66
Ashbourne. Derbs....1F 73
Ashbrittle. Som....4D 20
Ashbrook. Shrp....1G 59
Ashburton. Devn....2D 8
Ashbury. Devn....3F 11

Ashbury – Badachro

Ashbury. Oxon 3A 36
Ashby. N Lin 4B 94
Ashby by Partney. Linc 4D 88
Ashby cum Fenby. NE Lin 4F 95
Ashby de la Launde. Linc 5H 87
Ashby-de-la-Zouch. Leics 4A 74
Ashby Folville. Leics 4E 74
Ashby Magna. Leics 1C 62
Ashby Parva. Leics 2C 62
Ashby Puerorum. Linc 3C 88
Ashby St Ledgars. Nptn 4C 62
Ashby St Mary. Norf 5F 79
Ashchurch. Glos 2E 49
Ashcombe. Devn 5C 12
Ashcott. Som 3H 21
Ashdon. Essx 1F 53
Ashe. Hants 2D 24
Asheldham. Essx 5C 54
Ashen. Essx 1H 53
Ashendon. Buck 4F 51
Ashey. IOW 4D 16
Ashfield. Hants 1B 16
Ashfield. Here 3A 48
Ashfield. Shrp 2H 59
Ashfield. Stir 3G 135
Ashfield. Suff 4E 66
Ashfield Green. Suff 3E 67
Ashfold Crossways. W Sus 3D 26
Ashford. Devn
nr. Barnstaple 3F 19
nr. Kingsbridge 4C 8
Ashford. Hants 1G 15
Ashford. Kent 1E 28
Ashford. Surr 3B 38
Ashford Bowdler. Shrp 3H 59
Ashford Carbonel. Shrp 3H 59
Ashford Hill. Hants 5D 36
Ashford in the Water
Derbs 4F 85
Ashgill. S Lan 5A 128
Ash Green. Warw 2H 61
Ashgrove. Mor 2G 159
Ashill. Devn 1D 12
Ashill. Norf 5A 78
Ashill. Som 1G 13
Ashingdon. Essx 1C 40
Ashington. Nmbd 1F 115
Ashington. W Sus 4C 26
Ashkirk. Bord 2G 119
Ashleworth. Glos 3D 48
Ashley. Cambs 4F 65
Ashley. Ches E 2B 84
Ashley. Dors 2G 15
Ashley. Glos 2E 35
Ashley. Hants
nr. New Milton 3A 16
nr. Winchester 3B 24
Ashley. Kent 1H 29
Ashley. Nptn 1E 63
Ashley. Staf 2B 72
Ashley. Wilts 5D 34
Ashley Green. Buck 5H 51
Ashley Heath. Dors 2G 15
Ashley Heath. Staf 2B 72
Ashley Moor. Here 4G 59
Ash Magna. Shrp 2H 71
Ashmanhaugh. Norf 3F 79
Ashmansworth. Hants 1C 24
Ashmansworthy. Devn 1D 10
Ashmead Green. Glos 2C 34
Ash Mill. Devn 4A 20
Ashmill. Devn 3D 11
Ashmore. Dors 1E 15
Ashmore Green. W Ber 5D 36
Ashorne. Warw 5H 61
Ashover. Derbs 4A 86
Ashow. Warw 3H 61
Ash Parva. Shrp 2H 71
Ashperton. Here 1B 48
Ashprington. Devn 3E 9
Ash Priors. Som 4E 21
Ashreigney. Devn 1G 11
Ash Street. Suff 1D 54
Ashtead. Surr 5C 38
Ash Thomas. Devn 1D 12
Ashton. Corn 4D 4
Ashton. Here 4H 59
Ashton. Inv 2D 126
Ashton. Nptn
nr. Oundle 2H 63
nr. Roade 1F 51
Ashton. Pet 5A 76
Ashton Common. Wilts 1D 23
Ashton Hayes. Ches W 4H 83
Ashton-in-Makerfield
G Man 1H 83
Ashton Keynes. Wilts 2F 35
Ashton under Hill. Worc 2E 49
Ashton-under-Lyne. G Man 1D 84
Ashton upon Mersey
G Man 1B 84
Ashurst. Hants 1B 16
Ashurst. Kent 2G 27
Ashurst. Lanc 4C 90
Ashurst. W Sus 4C 26
Ashurst Wood. W Sus 2F 27
Ash Vale. Surr 1G 25
Ashwater. Devn 3D 11
Ashwell. Herts 2C 52
Ashwell. Rut 4F 75
Ashwellthorpe. Norf 1D 66
Ashwick. Som 2B 22
Ashwicken. Norf 4G 77
Ashwood. Staf 2C 60
Askam in Furness. Cumb 2B 96
Askern. S Yor 3F 93
Askerswell. Dors 3A 14
Askett. Buck 5G 51
Askham. Cumb 2G 103
Askham. Notts 3E 87
Askham Bryan. York 5H 99
Askham Richard. York 5H 99
Askrigg. N Yor 5C 104
Askwith. N Yor 5D 98
Aslackby. Linc 2H 75
Aslacton. Norf 1D 66
Aslockton. Notts 1E 75
Aspatria. Cumb 5C 112
Aspenden. Herts 3D 52
Asperton. Linc 2B 76
Aspley Guise. C Beds 2H 51
Aspley Heath. C Beds 2H 51
Aspull. G Man 4E 90
Asselby. E Yor 2H 93
Assington. Suff 2C 54
Assington Green. Suff 5G 65
Astbury. Ches E 4C 84
Astcote. Nptn 5D 62
Asterby. Linc 3B 88
Asterley. Shrp 5F 71
Asterton. Shrp 1F 59
Asthall. Oxon 4A 50
Asthall Leigh. Oxon 4B 50
Astle. High 4E 165
Astley. G Man 4F 91
Astley. Shrp 4H 71
Astley. Warw 2H 61
Astley. Worc 4B 60
Astley Abbotts. Shrp 1B 60
Astley Bridge. G Man 3F 91
Astley Cross. Worc 4C 60
Aston. Ches E 1A 72
Aston. Ches W 3H 83
Aston. Derbs
nr. Hope 2F 85
nr. Sudbury 2F 73
Aston. Flin 4F 83
Aston. Here 4G 59
Aston. Herts 3C 52
Aston. Oxon 5B 50
Aston. Shrp
nr. Bridgnorth 1C 60
nr. Wem 3H 71
Aston. S Yor 2B 86
Aston. Staf 1B 72
Aston. Telf 5A 72
Aston. W Mid 1E 61
Aston. Wok 3F 37
Aston Abbotts. Buck 3G 51
Aston Botterell. Shrp 2A 60
Aston-by-Stone. Staf 2D 72
Aston Cantlow. Warw 5F 61
Aston Clinton. Buck 4G 51
Aston Crews. Here 3B 48
Aston Cross. Glos 2E 49
Aston End. Herts 3C 52
Aston Eyre. Shrp 1A 60
Aston Fields. Worc 4D 60
Aston Flamville. Leics 1B 62
Aston Ingham. Here 3B 48
Aston juxta Mondrum
Ches E 5A 84
Astonlane. Shrp 1A 60
Aston le Walls. Nptn 5B 62
Aston Magna. Glos 2G 49
Aston Munslow. Shrp 2H 59
Aston on Carrant. Glos 2E 49
Aston on Clun. Shrp 2F 59
Aston-on-Trent. Derbs 3B 74
Aston Pigott. Shrp 5F 71
Aston Rogers. Shrp 5F 71
Aston Rowant. Oxon 2F 37
Aston Sandford. Buck 5F 51
Aston Somerville. Worc 2F 49
Aston Subedge. Glos 1G 49
Aston Tirrold. Oxon 3D 36
Aston Upthorpe. Oxon 3D 36
Astrop. Nptn 2D 50
Astwick. C Beds 2C 52
Astwood. Mil 1H 51
Astwood Bank. Worc 4E 61
Aswarby. Linc 2H 75
Aswardby. Linc 3C 88
Atcham. Shrp 5H 71
Atch Lench. Worc 5E 61
Athelhampton. Dors 3C 14
Athelington. Suff 3E 66
Athelney. Som 4G 21
Athelstaneford. E Lot 2B 130
Atherfield Green. IOW 5C 16
Atherington. Devn 4F 19
Atherington. W Sus 5B 26
Athersley. S Yor 4D 92
Atherstone. Warw 1H 61
Atherstone on Stour. Warw 5G 61
Atherton. G Man 4E 91
Ath-Tharracail. High 2A 140
Atlow. Derbs 1G 73
Attadale. High 5B 156
Attenborough. Notts 2C 74
Atterby. Linc 1G 87
Atterley. Shrp 1A 60
Atterton. Leics 1A 62
Attleborough. Norf 1C 66
Attleborough. Warw 1A 62
Attlebridge. Norf 4D 78
Atwick. E Yor 4F 101
Atworth. Wilts 5D 34
Auberrow. Here 1H 47
Aubourn. Linc 4G 87
Aucharnie. Abers 4D 160
Auchattie. Abers 4D 152
Auchavan. Ang 2A 144
Auchbreck. Mor 1G 151
Auchenback. E Ren 4G 127
Auchenblae. Abers 1G 145
Auchenbrack. Dum 5G 117
Auchenbreck. Arg 1B 126
Auchencairn. Dum
nr. Dalbeattie 4E 111
nr. Dumfries 1A 112
Auchencarroch. W Dun 1F 127
Auchencrow. Bord 3E 131
Auchendennan. Arg 1E 127
Auchendinny. Midl 3F 129
Auchengray. S Lan 4C 128
Auchenhalrig. Mor 2A 160
Auchenheath. S Lan 5B 128
Auchenlochan. Arg 2A 126
Auchenmade. N Ayr 5E 127
Auchenmalg. Dum 4H 109
Auchentiber. N Ayr 5E 127
Auchenvennel. Arg 1D 126
Auchindrain. Arg 3H 133
Auchininna. Abers 4D 160
Auchinleck. Dum 2B 110
Auchinleck. E Ayr 2E 117
Auchinloch. N Lan 2H 127
Auchinstarry. N Lan 2A 128
Auchleven. Abers 1D 152
Auchlochan. S Lan 1H 117
Auchlunachan. High 5F 163
Auchmillan. E Ayr 2E 117
Auchmithie. Ang 4F 145
Auchmuirbridge. Fife 3E 136
Auchmull. Ang 1E 145
Auchnacree. Ang 2D 144
Auchnafree. Per 5F 143
Auchnagallin. High 5E 159
Auchnagatt. Abers 4G 161
Aucholzie. Abers 4H 151
Auchreddie. Abers 4F 161
Auchterarder. Per 2B 136
Auchteraw. High 3F 149
Auchterderran. Fife 4E 136
Auchterhouse. Ang 5C 144
Auchtermuchty. Fife 2E 137
Auchterneed. High 3G 157
Auchtertool. Fife 4E 136
Auchtertyre. High 1G 147
Auchtubh. Stir 1E 135
Auckengill. High 2F 169
Auckley. S Yor 4G 93
Audenshaw. G Man 1D 84
Audlem. Ches E 1A 72
Audley. Staf 5B 84
Audley End. Essx 2F 53
Audmore. Staf 3C 72
Auds. Abers 2D 160
Aughertree. Cumb 1D 102
Aughton. E Yor 1H 93
Aughton. Lanc
nr. Lancaster 3E 97
nr. Ormskirk 4B 90
Aughton. S Yor 2B 86
Aughton. Wilts 1H 23
Aughton Park. Lanc 4C 90
Auldearn. High 3D 158
Aulden. Here 5G 59
Auldgirth. Dum 1G 111
Auldhouse. S Lan 4H 127
Ault a' chruinn. High 1B 148
Aultbea. High 5C 162
Aultdearg. High 2E 157
Aultgrishan. High 5B 162
Aultguish Inn. High 1F 157
Ault Hucknall. Derbs 4B 86
Aultibea. High 1H 165
Aultiphurst. High 2A 168
Aultivullin. High 2A 168
Aultmore. Mor 3B 160
Aultnamain Inn. High 5D 164
Aunby. Linc 4H 75
Aunsby. Linc 2H 75
Aust. S Glo 3A 34
Austerfield. S Yor 1D 86
Austin Fen. Linc 1C 88
Austrey. Warw 5G 73
Austwick. N Yor 3G 97
Authorpe. Linc 2D 88
Authorpe Row. Linc 3E 89
Avebury. Wilts 5G 35
Avebury Trusloe. Wilts 5F 35
Aveley. Thur 2G 39
Avening. Glos 2D 35
Averham. Notts 5E 87
Aveton Gifford. Devn 4C 8
Avielochan. High 2D 150
Aviemore. High 2C 150
Avington. Hants 3D 24
Avoch. High 3B 158
Avon. Hants 3G 15
Avonbridge. Falk 2C 128
Avon Dassett. Warw 5B 62
Avonmouth. Bris 4A 34
Avonwick. Devn 3D 8
Awbridge. Hants 4B 24
Awliscombe. Devn 2E 13
Awre. Glos 5C 48
Awsworth. Notts 1B 74
Axbridge. Som 1H 21
Axford. Hants 2E 24
Axford. Wilts 5H 35
Axminster. Devn 3G 13
Axmouth. Devn 3F 13
Aycliffe Village. Dur 2F 105
Aydon. Nmbd 3D 114
Aykley Heads. Dur 5F 115
Aylburton. Glos 5B 48
Aylburton Common. Glos 5B 48
Ayle. Nmbd 5A 114
Aylesbeare. Devn 3D 12
Aylesbury. Buck 4G 51
Aylesby. NE Lin 4F 95
Aylescott. Devn 1G 11
Aylesford. Kent 5B 40
Aylesham. Kent 5G 41
Aylestone. Leic 5C 74
Aylmerton. Norf 2D 78
Aylsham. Norf 3D 78
Aylton. Here 2B 48
Aylworth. Glos 3G 49
Aymestrey. Here 4G 59
Aynho. Nptn 2D 50
Ayot Green. Herts 4C 52
Ayot St Lawrence. Herts 4B 52
Ayot St Peter. Herts 4C 52
Ayr. S Ayr 2C 116
Ayres of Selivoe. Shet 7D 173
Ayreville. Torb 2E 9
Aysgarth. N Yor 1C 98
Ayshford. Devn 1D 12
Ayside. Cumb 1C 96
Ayston. Rut 5F 75
Ayton. Bord 3F 131
Aywick. Shet 3G 173
Azerley. N Yor 2E 99

B

Babbacombe. Torb 2F 9
Babbinswood. Shrp 2F 71
Babbs Green. Herts 4D 53
Babcary. Som 4A 22
Babel. Carm 2B 46
Babell. Flin 3D 82
Babingley. Norf 3F 77
Bablock Hythe. Oxon 5C 50
Babraham. Cambs 5E 65
Babworth. Notts 2D 86
Bac. W Isl 3G 171
Bachau. IOA 2D 80
Bacheldre. Powy 1E 59
Bachymbyd Fawr. Den 4C 82
Backaland. Orkn 4E 172
Backaskaill. Orkn 2D 172
Backbarrow. Cumb 1C 96
Backe. Carm 3G 43
Backfolds. Abers 3H 161
Backford. Ches W 3G 83
Backhill. Abers 5E 161
Backhill of Clackriach
Abers 4G 161
Backies. High 3F 165
Backmuir of New Gilston
Fife 3G 137
Back of Keppoch. High 5E 147
Back Street. Suff 5G 65
Backwell. N Som 5H 33
Backworth. Tyne 2G 115
Bacon End. Essx 4G 53
Baconsthorpe. Norf 2D 78
Bacton. Here 2G 47
Bacton. Norf 2F 79
Bacton. Suff 4C 66
Bacton Green. Norf 2F 79
Bacup. Lanc 2G 91
Badachonacher. High 1A 158
Badachro. High 1G 155

Bishopdown – Bolton Abbey

Bishopdown. *Wilts* 3G 23
Bishop Middleham. *Dur* 1A 106
Bishopmill. *Mor* 2G 159
Bishop Monkton. *N Yor* 3F 99
Bishop Norton. *Linc* 1G 87
Bishopsbourne. *Kent* 5F 41
Bishops Cannings. *Wilts* 5F 35
Bishop's Castle. *Shrp* 2F 59
Bishop's Caundle. *Dors* 1B 14
Bishop's Cleeve. *Glos* 3E 49
Bishop's Down. *Dors* 1B 14
Bishop's Frome. *Here* 1B 48
Bishop's Green. *Essx* 4G 53
Bishop's Green. *Hants* 5D 36
Bishop's Hull. *Som* 4F 21
Bishop's Itchington. *Warw* 5A 62
Bishops Lydeard. *Som* 4E 21
Bishop's Norton. *Glos* 3D 48
Bishop's Nympton. *Devn* 4A 20
Bishop's Offley. *Staf* 3B 72
Bishop's Stortford. *Herts* 3E 53
Bishop's Sutton. *Hants* 3E 24
Bishop's Tachbrook. *Warw* 4H 61
Bishop's Tawton. *Devn* 3F 19
Bishopsteignton. *Devn* 5C 12
Bishopstoke. *Hants* 1C 16
Bishopston. *Swan* 4E 31
Bishopstone. *Buck* 4G 51
Bishopstone. *E Sus* 5F 27
Bishopstone. *Here* 1H 47
Bishopstone. *Swin* 3H 35
Bishopstone. *Wilts* 4F 23
Bishopstrow. *Wilts* 2D 23
Bishop Sutton. *Bath* 1A 22
Bishop's Waltham. *Hants* 1D 16
Bishops Wood. *Staf* 5C 72
Bishopswood. *Som* 1F 13
Bishopsworth. *Bris* 5A 34
Bishop Thornton. *N Yor* 3E 99
Bishopthorpe. *York* 5H 99
Bishopton. *Darl* 2A 106
Bishopton. *Dum* 5B 110
Bishopton. *N Yor* 2E 99
Bishopton. *Ren* 2F 127
Bishopton. *Warw* 5F 61
Bishop Wilton. *E Yor* 4B 100
Bishton. *Newp* 3G 33
Bishton. *Staf* 3E 73
Bisley. *Glos* 5E 49
Bisley. *Surr* 5A 38
Bispham. *Bkpl* 5C 96
Bispham Green. *Lanc* 3C 90
Bissoe. *Corn* 4B 6
Bisterne. *Hants* 2G 15
Bisterne Close. *Hants* 2H 15
Bitchfield. *Linc* 3G 75
Bittadon. *Devn* 2F 19
Bittaford. *Devn* 3C 8
Bittering. *Norf* 4B 78
Bitterley. *Shrp* 3H 59
Bitterne. *Sotn* 1C 16
Bitteswell. *Leics* 2C 62
Bitton. *S Glo* 5B 34
Bix. *Oxon* 3F 37
Bixter. *Shet* 6E 173
Blaby. *Leics* 1C 62
Blackawton. *Devn* 3E 9
Black Bank. *Cambs* 2E 65
Black Barn. *Linc* 3D 76
Blackborough. *Devn* 2D 12
Blackborough. *Norf* 4F 77
Blackborough End. *Norf* 4F 77
Black Bourton. *Oxon* 5A 50
Blackboys. *E Sus* 3G 27
Blackbrook. *Derbs* 1H 73
Blackbrook. *Mers* 1H 83
Blackbrook. *Staf* 2B 72
Blackbrook. *Surr* 1C 26
Blackburn. *Abers* 2F 153
Blackburn. *Bkbn* 2E 91
Blackburn. *W Lot* 3C 128
Black Callerton. *Tyne* 3E 115
Black Carr. *Norf* 1C 66
Black Clauchrie. *S Ayr* 1H 109
Black Corries. *High* 3G 141
Black Crofts. *Arg* 5D 140
Black Cross. *Corn* 2D 6
Blackden Heath. *Ches E* 3B 84
Blackditch. *Oxon* 5C 50
Black Dog. *Devn* 2B 12
Blackdog. *Abers* 2G 153
Blackdown. *Dors* 2G 13
Blackdyke. *Cumb* 4C 112
Blacker Hill. *S Yor* 4D 92
Blackfen. *G Lon* 3F 39
Blackfield. *Hants* 2C 16
Blackford. *Cumb* 3E 113
Blackford. *Per* 3A 136
Blackford. *Shrp* 2H 59
Blackford. *Som*
nr. Burnham-on-Sea 2H 21
nr. Wincanton 4B 22
Blackfordby. *Leics* 4H 73
Blackgang. *IOW* 5C 16
Blackhall. *Edin* 2F 129
Blackhall. *Ren* 3F 127
Blackhall Colliery. *Dur* 1B 106
Blackhall Mill. *Tyne* 4E 115
Blackhall Rocks. *Dur* 1B 106
Blackham. *E Sus* 2F 27
Blackheath. *Essx* 3D 54
Blackheath. *G Lon* 3E 39
Blackheath. *Suff* 3G 67
Blackheath. *Surr* 1B 26
Blackheath. *W Mid* 2D 61
Black Heddon. *Nmbd* 2D 115
Black Hill. *Warw* 5G 61
Blackhill. *Abers* 4H 161
Blackhill. *High* 3C 154
Blackhills. *Abers* 2G 161
Blackhills. *High* 3D 158
Blackjack. *Linc* 2B 76
Blackland. *Wilts* 5F 35
Black Lane. *G Man* 4F 91
Blackleach. *Lanc* 1C 90
Blackley. *G Man* 4G 91
Blackley. *W Yor* 3B 92
Blacklunans. *Per* 2A 144
Blackmill. *B'end* 3C 32
Blackmoor. *G Man* 4E 91
Blackmoor. *Hants* 3F 25
Blackmoor Gate. *Devn* 2G 19
Blackmore. *Essx* 5G 53
Blackmore End. *Essx* 2H 53
Blackmore End. *Herts* 4B 52
Black Mount. *Arg* 4G 141
Blackness. *Falk* 2D 128
Blacknest. *Hants* 2F 25
Blackney. *Dors* 3H 13
Blacknoll. *Dors* 4D 14
Black Notley. *Essx* 3A 54
Blacko. *Lanc* 5A 98
Black Pill. *Swan* 3F 31
Blackpool. *Bkpl* 1B 90
Blackpool. *Devn* 4E 9
Blackpool Corner. *Dors* 3G 13
Blackpool Gate. *Cumb* 2G 113
Blackridge. *W Lot* 3B 128
Blackrock. *Arg* 3B 124
Blackrock. *Mon* 4F 47
Blackrod. *G Man* 3E 90
Blackshaw. *Dum* 3B 112
Blackshaw Head. *W Yor* 2H 91
Blackshaw Moor. *Staf* 5E 85
Blacksmith's Green. *Suff* 4D 66
Blacksnape. *Bkbn* 2F 91
Blackstone. *W Sus* 4D 26
Black Street. *Suff* 2H 67
Black Tar. *Pemb* 4D 43
Blackthorn. *Oxon* 4E 50
Blackthorpe. *Suff* 4B 66
Blacktoft. *E Yor* 2B 94
Blacktop. *Aber* 3F 153
Black Torrington. *Devn* 2E 11
Blacktown. *Newp* 3F 33
Blackwall Tunnel. *G Lon* 2E 39
Blackwater. *Corn* 4B 6
Blackwater. *Hants* 1G 25
Blackwater. *IOW* 4D 16
Blackwater. *Som* 1F 13
Blackwaterfoot. *N Ayr* 3C 122
Blackwell. *Darl* 3F 105
Blackwell. *Derbs*
nr. Alfreton 5B 86
nr. Buxton 3F 85
Blackwell. *Som* 4D 20
Blackwell. *Warw* 1H 49
Blackwell. *Worc* 3D 61
Blackwood. *Cphy* 2E 33
Blackwood. *Dum* 1G 111
Blackwood. *S Lan* 5A 128
Blackwood Hill. *Staf* 5D 84
Blacon. *Ches W* 4F 83
Bladnoch. *Dum* 4B 110
Bladon. *Oxon* 4C 50
Blaenannerch. *Cdgn* 1C 44
Blaenau Dolwyddelan
Cnwy 5F 81
Blaenau Ffestiniog. *Gwyn* 1G 69
Blaenavon. *Torf* 5F 47
Blaenawey. *Mon* 4F 47
Blaen Celyn. *Cdgn* 5C 56
Blaen Clydach. *Rhon* 2C 32
Blaencwm. *Rhon* 2C 32
Blaendulais. *Neat* 5B 46
Blaenffos. *Pemb* 1F 43
Blaengarw. *B'end* 2C 32
Blaen-geuffordd. *Cdgn* 2F 57
Blaengwrach. *Neat* 5B 46
Blaengwynfi. *Neat* 2B 32
Blaenllechau. *Rhon* 2C 32
Blaenpennal. *Cdgn* 4F 57
Blaenplwyf. *Cdgn* 3E 57
Blaenporth. *Cdgn* 1C 44
Blaenrhondda. *Rhon* 5C 46
Blaenwaun. *Carm* 2G 43
Blaen-y-coed. *Carm* 2H 43
Blagdon. *N Som* 1A 22
Blagdon. *Torb* 2E 9
Blagdon Hill. *Som* 1F 13
Blagill. *Cumb* 5A 114
Blaguegate. *Lanc* 4C 90
Blaich. *High* 1E 141
Blain. *High* 2A 140
Blaina. *Blae* 5F 47
Blair Atholl. *Per* 2F 143
Blair Drummond. *Stir* 4G 135
Blairgowrie. *Per* 4A 144
Blairhall. *Fife* 1D 128
Blairingone. *Per* 4B 136
Blairlogie. *Stir* 4H 135
Blairmore. *Abers* 5B 160
Blairmore. *Arg* 1C 126
Blairmore. *High* 3B 166
Blairquhanan. *W Dun* 1F 127
Blaisdon. *Glos* 4C 48
Blakebrook. *Worc* 3C 60
Blakedown. *Worc* 3C 60
Blake End. *Essx* 3H 53
Blakemere. *Here* 1G 47
Blakeney. *Glos* 5B 48
Blakeney. *Norf* 1C 78
Blakenhall. *Ches E* 1B 72
Blakeshall. *Worc* 2C 60
Blakesley. *Nptn* 5D 62
Blanchland. *Nmbd* 4C 114
Blandford Camp. *Dors* 2E 15
Blandford Forum. *Dors* 2D 15
Blandford St Mary. *Dors* 2D 15
Bland Hill. *N Yor* 4E 98
Blandy. *High* 2G 167
Blanefield. *Stir* 2G 127
Blankney. *Linc* 4H 87
Blantyre. *S Lan* 4H 127
Blarmachfoldach. *High* 2E 141
Blarnalearoch. *High* 4F 163
Blashford. *Hants* 2G 15
Blaston. *Leics* 1F 63
Blatchbridge. *Som* 2C 22
Blathaisbhal. *W Isl* 1D 170
Blatherwycke. *Nptn* 1G 63
Blawith. *Cumb* 1B 96
Blaxhall. *Suff* 5F 67
Blaxton. *S Yor* 4G 93
Blaydon. *Tyne* 3E 115
Bleadney. *Som* 2H 21
Bleadon. *N Som* 1G 21
Blean. *Kent* 4F 41
Bleary. *Arm* 5F 175
Bleasby. *Linc* 2A 88
Bleasby. *Notts* 1E 74
Bleasby Moor. *Linc* 2A 88
Blebocraigs. *Fife* 2G 137
Bleddfa. *Powy* 4E 58
Bledington. *Glos* 3H 49
Bledlow. *Buck* 5F 51
Bledlow Ridge. *Buck* 2F 37
Blencarn. *Cumb* 1H 103
Blencogo. *Cumb* 5C 112
Blendworth. *Hants* 1F 17
Blennerhasset. *Cumb* 5C 112
Bletchingdon. *Oxon* 4D 50
Bletchingley. *Surr* 5E 39
Bletchley. *Mil* 2G 51
Bletchley. *Shrp* 2A 72
Bletherston. *Pemb* 2E 43
Bletsoe. *Bed* 5H 63
Blewbury. *Oxon* 3D 36
Blickling. *Norf* 3D 78
Blidworth. *Notts* 5C 86
Blindburn. *Nmbd* 3C 120
Blindcrake. *Cumb* 1C 102
Blindley Heath. *Surr* 1E 27
Blindmoor. *Som* 1F 13
Blisland. *Corn* 5B 10
Blissford. *Hants* 1G 15
Bliss Gate. *Worc* 3B 60
Blists Hill. *Telf* 5A 72
Blisworth. *Nptn* 5E 63
Blithbury. *Staf* 3E 73
Blitterlees. *Cumb* 4C 112
Blockley. *Glos* 2G 49
Blofield. *Norf* 5F 79
Blofield Heath. *Norf* 4F 79
Blo' Norton. *Norf* 3C 66
Bloomfield. *Bord* 2H 119
Blore. *Staf* 1F 73
Blount's Green. *Staf* 2E 73
Bloxham. *Oxon* 2C 50
Bloxholm. *Linc* 5H 87
Bloxwich. *W Mid* 5D 73
Bloxworth. *Dors* 3D 15
Blubberhouses. *N Yor* 4D 98
Blue Anchor. *Som* 2D 20
Blue Anchor. *Swan* 3E 31
Blue Bell Hill. *Kent* 4B 40
Blue Row. *Essx* 4D 54
Bluetown. *Kent* 5D 40
Blundeston. *Suff* 1H 67
Blunham. *C Beds* 5A 64
Blunsdon St Andrew
Swin 3G 35
Bluntington. *Worc* 3C 60
Bluntisham. *Cambs* 3C 64
Blunts. *Corn* 2H 7
Blurton. *Stoke* 1C 72
Blyborough. *Linc* 1G 87
Blyford. *Suff* 3G 67
Blymhill. *Staf* 4C 72
Blymhill Lawns. *Staf* 4C 72
Blyth. *Nmbd* 1G 115
Blyth. *Notts* 2D 86
Blyth. *Bord* 5E 129
Blyth Bank. *Bord* 5E 129
Blyth Bridge. *Bord* 5E 129
Blythburgh. *Suff* 3G 67
The Blythe. *Staf* 3E 73
Blythe Bridge. *Staf* 1D 72
Blythe Marsh. *Staf* 1D 72
Blyton. *Linc* 1F 87
Boarhills. *Fife* 2H 137
Boarhunt. *Hants* 2E 16
Boar's Head. *G Man* 4D 90
Boarshead. *E Sus* 2G 27
Boars Hill. *Oxon* 5C 50
Boarstall. *Buck* 4E 51
Boasley Cross. *Devn* 3F 11
Boath. *High* 1H 157
Boat of Garten. *High* 2D 150
Bobbing. *Kent* 4C 40
Bobbington. *Staf* 1C 60
Bobbingworth. *Essx* 5F 53
Bocaddon. *Corn* 3F 7
Bocking. *Essx* 3A 54
Bocking Churchstreet
Essx 3A 54
Boddam. *Abers* 4H 161
Boddam. *Shet* 10E 173
Boddington. *Glos* 3D 49
Bodedern. *IOA* 2C 80
Bodelwyddan. *Den* 3C 82
Bodenham. *Here* 5H 59
Bodenham. *Wilts* 4G 23
Bodewryd. *IOA* 1C 80
Bodfari. *Den* 3C 82
Bodffordd. *IOA* 3D 80
Bodham. *Norf* 1D 78
Bodiam. *E Sus* 3B 28
Bodicote. *Oxon* 2C 50
Bodieve. *Corn* 1D 6
Bodinnick. *Corn* 3F 7
Bodle Street Green. *E Sus* 4A 28
Bodmin. *Corn* 2E 7
Bodnant. *Cnwy* 3H 81
Bodney. *Norf* 1H 65
Bodorgan. *IOA* 4C 80
Bodrane. *Corn* 2G 7
Bodsham. *Kent* 1F 29
Boduan. *Gwyn* 2C 68
Bodymoor Heath. *Warw* 1F 61
The Bog. *Shrp* 1F 59
Bogallan. *High* 3A 158
Bogbrae Croft. *Abers* 5H 161
Bogend. *S Ayr* 1C 116
Boghall. *Midl* 3F 129
Boghall. *W Lot* 3C 128
Boghead. *S Lan* 5A 128
Bogindollo. *Ang* 3D 144
Bogmoor. *Mor* 2A 160
Bogniebrae. *Abers* 4C 160
Bognor Regis. *W Sus* 3H 17
Bograxie. *Abers* 2E 152
Bogside. *N Lan* 4B 128
Bogton. *Abers* 3D 160
Bogue. *Dum* 1D 110
Bohenie. *High* 5E 149
Bohortha. *Corn* 5C 6
Boirseam. *W Isl* 9C 171
Bokiddick. *Corn* 2E 7
Bolam. *Dur* 2E 105
Bolam. *Nmbd* 1D 115
Bolberry. *Devn* 5C 8
Bold Heath. *Mers* 2H 83
Boldon. *Tyne* 3G 115
Boldon Colliery. *Tyne* 3G 115
Boldre. *Hants* 3B 16
Boldron. *Dur* 3D 104
Bole. *Notts* 2E 87
Bolehall. *Staf* 5G 73
Bolehill. *Derbs* 5G 85
Bolenowe. *Corn* 5A 6
Boleside. *Bord* 1G 119
Bolham. *Devn* 1C 12
Bolham Water. *Devn* 1E 13
Bolingey. *Corn* 3B 6
Bollington. *Ches E* 3D 84
Bolney. *W Sus* 3D 26
Bolnhurst. *Bed* 5H 63
Bolshan. *Ang* 3F 145
Bolsover. *Derbs* 3B 86
Bolsterstone. *S Yor* 1G 85
Bolstone. *Here* 2A 48
Boltachan. *Per* 3F 143
Boltby. *N Yor* 1G 99
Bolton. *Cumb* 2H 103
Bolton. *E Lot* 2B 130
Bolton. *E Yor* 4B 100
Bolton. *G Man* 4F 91
Bolton. *Nmbd* 3F 121
Bolton Abbey. *N Yor* 4C 98

Bolton-by-Bowland. Lanc 5G 97
Boltonfellend. Cumb 3F 113
Boltongate. Cumb 5D 112
Bolton Green. Lanc 3D 90
Bolton-le-Sands. Lanc 3D 97
Bolton Low Houses
Cumb 5D 112
Bolton New Houses
Cumb 5D 112
Bolton-on-Swale. N Yor 5F 105
Bolton Percy. N Yor 5H 99
Bolton Town End. Lanc 3D 97
Bolton upon Dearne
S Yor 4E 93
Bolton Wood Lane
Cumb 5D 112
Bolventor. Corn 5B 10
Bomarsund. Nmbd 1F 115
Bomere Heath. Shrp 4G 71
Bonar Bridge. High 4D 164
Bonawe. Arg 5E 141
Bonby. N Lin 3D 94
Boncath. Pemb 1G 43
Bonchester Bridge. Bord 3H 119
Bonchurch. IOW 5D 16
Bond End. Staf 4F 73
Bondleigh. Devn 2G 11
Bonds. Lanc 5D 97
Bonehill. Devn 5H 11
Bonehill. Staf 5F 73
Bo'ness. Falk 1C 128
Boney Hay. Staf 4E 73
Bonham. Wilts 3C 22
Bonhill. W Dun 2E 127
Boningale. Shrp 5C 72
Bonjedward. Bord 2A 120
Bonkle. N Lan 4B 128
Bonnington. Ang 5E 145
Bonnington. Edin 3E 129
Bonnington. Kent 2E 29
Bonnybank. Fife 3F 137
Bonnybridge. Falk 1B 128
Bonnykelly. Abers 3F 161
Bonnyrigg. Midl 3G 129
Bonnyton. Ang 5C 144
Bonnytown. Fife 2H 137
Bonsall. Derbs 5G 85
Bont. Mon 4G 47
Bontddu. Gwyn 4F 69
Bont Dolgadfan. Powy 5A 70
Y Bont-Faen. V Glam 4C 32
Bontgoch. Cdgn 2F 57
Bonthorpe. Linc 3D 89
Bont Newydd. Gwyn 1G 69
Bont-newydd. Cnwy 3C 82
Bontnewydd. Cdgn 4F 57
Bontnewydd. Gwyn 4D 81
Bontuchel. Den 5C 82
Bonvilston. V Glam 4D 32
Bon-y-maen. Swan 3F 31
Booker. Buck 2G 37
Booley. Shrp 3H 71
Boorley Green. Hants 1D 16
Boosbeck. Red C 3D 106
Boot. Cumb 4C 102
Booth. W Yor 2A 92
Boothby Graffoe. Linc 5G 87
Boothby Pagnell. Linc 2G 75
Booth Green. Ches E 2D 84
Booth of Toft. Shet 4F 173
Boothstown. G Man 4F 91
Boothville. Nptn 4E 63
Bootle. Cumb 1A 96
Bootle. Mers 1F 83
Booton. Norf 3D 78
Booze. N Yor 4D 104
Boquhan. Stir 1G 127
Boraston. Shrp 3A 60
Borden. Kent 4C 40
Borden. W Sus 4G 25
Bordlands. Bord 5E 129
Bordley. N Yor 3B 98
Bordon. Hants 3F 25

Boreham. Wilts 2D 23
Boreham Street. E Sus 4A 28
Borehamwood. Herts 1C 38
Boreland. Dum 5D 118
Boreston. Devn 3D 8
Borestone Brae. Stir 4G 135
Boreton. Shrp 5H 71
Borgh. W Isl
on Barra 8B 170
on Benbecula 3C 170
on Berneray 1E 170
on Isle of Lewis 2G 171
Borghasdal. W Isl 9C 171
Borghastan. W Isl 3D 171
Borgh na Sgiotaig. High 1C 154
Borgie. High 3G 167
Borgue. Dum 5D 110
Borgue. Dum 1H 165
Borley. Essx 1B 54
Borley Green. Essx 1B 54
Borley Green. Suff 4B 66
Borlum. High 1H 149
Bornais. W Isl 6C 170
Bornesketaig. High 1C 154
Boroughbridge. N Yor 3F 99
Borough Green. Kent 5H 39
Borreraig. High 3A 154
Borrobol Lodge. High 1F 165
Borrodale. High 4A 154
Borrowash. Derbs 2B 74
Borrowby. N Yor
nr. Northallerton 1G 99
nr. Whitby 3E 107
Borrowston. High 4F 169
Borrowstonehill. Orkn 7D 172
Borrowstoun. Falk 1C 128
Borstal. Medw 4B 40
Borth. Cdgn 2F 57
Borthwick. Midl 4G 129
Borth-y-Gest. Gwyn 2E 69
Borve. High 4D 154
Borwick. Lanc 2E 97
Bosbury. Here 1B 48
Boscastle. Corn 3A 10
Boscombe. Bour 3G 15
Boscombe. Wilts 3H 23
Boscoppa. Corn 3E 7
Bosham. W Sus 2G 17
Bosherston. Pemb 5D 42
Bosley. Ches E 4D 84
Bossall. N Yor 3B 100
Bossiney. Corn 4A 10
Bossingham. Kent 1F 29
Bossington. Som 2B 20
Bostadh. W Isl 3D 171
Bostock Green. Ches W 4A 84
Boston. Linc 1C 76
Boston Spa. W Yor 5G 99
Boswarthen. Corn 3B 4
Boswinger. Corn 4D 6
Botallack. Corn 3A 4
Botany Bay. G Lon 1D 39
Botcheston. Leics 5B 74
Botesdale. Suff 3C 66
Bothal. Nmbd 1F 115
Bothampstead. W Ber 4D 36
Bothamsall. Notts 3D 86
Bothel. Cumb 1C 102
Bothenhampton. Dors 3H 13
Bothwell. S Lan 4A 128
Botley. Buck 5H 51
Botley. Hants 1D 16
Botley. Oxon 5C 50
Botloe's Green. Glos 3C 48
Botolph Claydon. Buck 3F 51
Botolphs. W Sus 5C 26
Bottacks. High 2G 157
Bottesford. Leics 2F 75
Bottesford. N Lin 4B 94
Bottisham. Cambs 4E 65
Bottlehill. Wilts 1G 23
Bottomcraig. Fife 1F 137
Bottom o' th' Moor
G Man 3E 91

Botton. N Yor 4D 107
Botton Head. Lanc 3F 97
Bottreaux Mill. Devn 4B 20
Botus Fleming. Corn 2A 8
Botwnnog. Gwyn 2B 68
Bough Beech. Kent 1F 27
Boughrood. Powy 2E 47
Boughspring. Glos 2A 34
Boughton. Norf 5F 77
Boughton. Nptn 4E 63
Boughton. Notts 4D 86
Boughton Aluph. Kent 1E 29
Boughton Green. Kent 5B 40
Boughton Lees. Kent 1E 28
Boughton Malherbe. Kent 1C 28
Boughton Monchelsea
Kent 5B 40
Boughton under Blean
Kent 5E 41
Boulby. Red C 3E 107
Bouldon. IOW 4B 16
Bouldon. Shrp 2H 59
Boulmer. Nmbd 3G 121
Boulston. Pemb 3D 42
Boultham. Linc 4G 87
Boulton. Derb 2A 74
Boundary. Staf 1D 73
Bounds. Here 2B 48
Bourn. Cambs 5C 64
Bournbrook. W Mid 2E 61
Bourne. Linc 3H 75
The Bourne. Norf 2G 25
Bourne End. Bed 4H 63
Bourne End. Buck 3G 37
Bourne End. C Beds 1H 51
Bourne End. Herts 5A 52
Bournemouth. Bour 3F 15
Bournemouth Airport
Dors 3G 15
Bournes Green. Glos 5E 49
Bournes Green. S'end 2D 40
Bournheath. Worc 3D 60
Bournmoor. Dur 4G 115
Bournville. W Mid 2E 61
Bourton. Dors 3C 22
Bourton. N Som 5G 33
Bourton. Oxon 3H 35
Bourton. Shrp 1H 59
Bourton. Wilts 5F 35
Bourton on Dunsmore
Warw 3B 62
Bourton-on-the-Hill. Glos 2G 49
Bourton-on-the-Water
Glos 3G 49
Bousd. Arg 2D 138
Bousta. Shet 6D 173
Boustead Hill. Cumb 4D 112
Bouth. Cumb 1C 96
Bouthwaite. N Yor 2D 98
Boveney. Buck 3A 38
Boveridge. Dors 1F 15
Boverton. V Glam 5C 32
Bovey Tracey. Devn 5B 12
Bovingdon. Herts 5A 52
Bovingdon Green. Buck 3G 37
Bovinger. Essx 5F 53
Bovington Camp. Dors 4D 14
Bow. Devn 2H 11
Bow. Orkn 8C 172
Bowbank. Dur 2C 104
Bow Brickhill. Mil 2H 51
Bowbridge. Glos 5D 48
Bowburn. Dur 1A 106
Bowcombe. IOW 4C 16
Bowd. Devn 4E 12
Bowden. Devn 4E 9
Bowden. Bord 1H 119
Bowden Hill. Wilts 5E 35
Bowdens. Som 4H 21
Bowderdale. Cumb 4H 103
Bowdon. G Man 2B 84
Bower. Nmbd 1A 114
Bowerchalke. Wilts 4F 23
Bowerhill. Wilts 5E 35
Bower Hinton. Som 1H 13

Bowermadden. High 2E 169
Bowers. Staf 2C 72
Bowers Gifford. Essx 2B 40
Bowershall. Fife 4C 136
Bowertower. High 2E 169
Bowes. Dur 3C 104
Bowgreave. Lanc 5D 97
Bowhousebog. N Lan 4B 128
Bowithick. Corn 4B 10
Bowland Bridge. Cumb 1D 96
Bowlees. Dur 2C 104
Bowley. Here 5H 59
Bowlhead Green. Surr 2A 26
Bowling. W Dun 2F 127
Bowling. W Yor 1B 92
Bowling Bank. Wrex 1F 71
Bowling Green. Worc 5C 60
Bowlish. Som 2B 22
Bowmanstead. Cumb 5E 102
Bowmore. Arg 4B 124
Bowness-on-Solway
Cumb 3D 112
Bowness-on-Windermere
Cumb 5F 103
Bow of Fife. Fife 2F 137
Bowriefauld. Ang 4E 145
Bowscale. Cumb 1E 103
Bowsden. Nmbd 5F 131
Bowside Lodge. High 2A 168
Bowston. Cumb 5F 103
Bow Street. Cdgn 2F 57
Bowthorpe. Norf 5D 78
Box. Glos 5D 48
Box. Wilts 5D 34
Boxbush. Glos 3B 48
Box End. Bed 1A 52
Boxford. Suff 1C 54
Boxford. W Ber 4C 36
Boxgrove. W Sus 5A 26
Box Hill. Wilts 5D 34
Boxley. Kent 5B 40
Boxmoor. Herts 5A 52
Box's Shop. Corn 2C 10
Boxted. Essx 2C 54
Boxted. Suff 5H 65
Boxted Cross. Essx 2D 54
Boxworth. Cambs 4C 64
Boxworth End. Cambs 4C 64
Boyden Gate. Kent 4G 41
Boylestone. Derbs 2F 73
Boylestonfield. Derbs 2F 73
Boyndie. Abers 2D 160
Boynton. E Yor 3F 101
Boys Hill. Dors 1B 14
Boythorpe. Derbs 4A 86
Boyton. Corn 3D 10
Boyton. Suff 1G 55
Boyton. Wilts 3E 23
Boyton Cross. Essx 5G 53
Boyton End. Essx 2G 53
Boyton End. Suff 1H 53
Bozeat. Nptn 5G 63
Braaid. IOM 4C 108
Braal Castle. High 3D 168
Brabling Green. Suff 4E 67
Brabourne. Kent 1F 29
Brabourne Lees. Kent 1E 29
Brabster. High 2F 169
Bracadale. High 5C 154
Bracara. High 4F 147
Braceborough. Linc 4H 75
Bracebridge. Linc 4G 87
Bracebridge Heath. Linc 4G 87
Braceby. Linc 2H 75
Bracewell. Lanc 5A 98
Brackenber. Cumb 3A 104
Brackenfield. Derbs 5A 86
Brackenlands. Cumb 5D 112
Brackenthwaite. Cumb 5D 112
Brackenthwaite. N Yor 4E 99
Brackla. B'end 4C 32
Brackla. High 3C 158
Bracklesham. W Sus 3G 17

Brackletter. High 5D 148
Brackley. Nptn 2D 50
Brackley Hatch. Nptn 1E 51
Brackloch. High 1F 163
Bracknell. Brac 5G 37
Braco. Per 3H 135
Bracobrae. Mor 3C 160
Bracon. N Lin 4A 94
Bracon Ash. Norf 1D 66
Bradbourne. Derbs 5G 85
Bradbury. Dur 2A 106
Bradda. IOM 4A 108
Bradden. Nptn 1E 51
Bradenham. Buck 2G 37
Bradenham. Norf 5B 78
Bradenstoke. Wilts 4F 35
Bradfield. Essx 2E 55
Bradfield. Norf 2E 79
Bradfield. W Ber 4E 36
Bradfield Combust. Suff 5A 66
Bradfield Green. Ches E 5A 84
Bradfield Heath. Essx 3E 55
Bradfield St Clare. Suff 5B 66
Bradfield St George. Suff 4B 66
Bradford. Derbs 4G 85
Bradford. Devn 2E 11
Bradford. W Yor 1B 92
Bradford Abbas. Dors 1A 14
Bradford Barton. Devn 1B 12
Bradford Leigh. Wilts 5D 34
Bradford-on-Avon. Wilts 5D 34
Bradford-on-Tone. Som 4E 21
Bradiford. Devn 3F 19
Brading. IOW 4E 16
Bradley. Ches W 3H 83
Bradley. Derbs 1G 73
Bradley. Glos 2C 34
Bradley. Hants 2E 25
Bradley. NE Lin 4F 95
Bradley. N Yor 1C 98
Bradley. Staf 4C 72
Bradley. W Mid 1D 60
Bradley. W Yor 2B 92
Bradley. Wrex 5F 83
Bradley Cross. Som 1H 21
Bradley Green. Ches W 1H 71
Bradley Green. Som 3F 21
Bradley Green. Warw 5G 73
Bradley Green. Worc 4D 61
Bradley in the Moors. Staf 1E 73
Bradley Stoke. S Glo 3B 34
Bradlow. Here 2C 48
Bradmore. Notts 2C 74
Bradmore. W Mid 1C 60
Bradninch. Devn 2D 12
Bradnop. Staf 5E 85
Bradpole. Dors 3H 13
Bradshaw. G Man 3F 91
Bradstone. Devn 4D 11
Bradwall Green. Ches E 4B 84
Bradway. S Yor 2H 85
Bradwell. Derbs 2F 85
Bradwell. Essx 3B 54
Bradwell. Mil 2G 51
Bradwell. Norf 5H 79
Bradwell-on-Sea. Essx 5D 54
Bradwell Waterside. Essx 5C 54
Bradworthy. Devn 1D 10
Brae. High 5C 162
Brae. Shet 5E 173
Braeantra. High 1G 157
Braefield. High 5G 157
Braefindon. High 3A 158
Braegrum. Per 1C 136
Braehead. Ang 3F 145
Braehead. Dum 4B 110
Braehead. Mor 4G 159
Braehead. Orkn 3D 172
Braehead. S Lan
nr. Coalburn 1H 117
nr. Forth 4C 128

Braehoulland – Broadfield

Braehoulland. *Shet* 4D **173**
Braemar. *Abers* 4F **151**
Braemore. *High*
nr. Dunbeath 5C **168**
nr. Ullapool 1D **156**
Brae of Achnahaird. *High* 2E **163**
Brae Roy Lodge. *High* 4F **149**
Braeside. *Abers* 5G **161**
Braeside. *Inv* 2D **126**
Braes of Coul. *Ang* 3B **144**
Braeswick. *Orkn* 4F **172**
Braetongue. *High* 3F **167**
Braeval. *Stir* 3E **135**
Braevallich. *Arg* 3G **133**
Braewick. *Shet* 6E **173**
Brafferton. *Darl* 2F **105**
Brafferton. *N Yor* 2G **99**
Brafield-on-the-Green
Nptn 5F **63**
Bragar. *W Isl* 3E **171**
Bragbury End. *Herts* 3C **52**
Bragleenbeg. *Arg* 1G **133**
Braichmelyn. *Gwyn* 4F **81**
Braides. *Lanc* 4D **96**
Braidwood. *S Lan* 5B **128**
Braigo. *Arg* 3A **124**
Brailsford. *Derbs* 1G **73**
Braintree. *Essx* 3A **54**
Braiseworth. *Suff* 3D **66**
Braishfield. *Hants* 4B **24**
Braithwaite. *Cumb* 2D **102**
Braithwaite. *S Yor* 3G **93**
Braithwaite. *W Yor* 5C **98**
Braithwell. *S Yor* 1C **86**
Brakefield Green. *Norf* 5C **78**
Bramber. *W Sus* 4C **26**
Brambridge. *Hants* 4C **24**
Bramcote. *Notts* 2C **74**
Bramcote. *Warw* 2B **62**
Bramdean. *Hants* 4E **24**
Bramerton. *Norf* 5E **79**
Bramfield. *Herts* 4C **52**
Bramfield. *Suff* 3F **67**
Bramford. *Suff* 1E **54**
Bramhall. *G Man* 2C **84**
Bramham. *W Yor* 5G **99**
Bramhope. *W Yor* 5E **99**
Bramley. *Hants* 1E **25**
Bramley. *S Yor* 1B **86**
Bramley. *Surr* 1B **26**
Bramley. *W Yor* 1C **92**
Bramley Green. *Hants* 1E **25**
Bramley Head. *N Yor* 4D **98**
Bramley Vale. *Derbs* 4B **86**
Bramling. *Kent* 5G **41**
Brampford Speke. *Devn* 3C **12**
Brampton. *Cambs* 3B **64**
Brampton. *Cumb*
nr. Appleby-in-Westmorland
2H **103**
nr. Carlisle 3G **113**
Brampton. *Linc* 3F **87**
Brampton. *Norf* 3E **78**
Brampton. *S Yor* 4E **93**
Brampton. *Suff* 2G **67**
Brampton Abbotts. *Here* 3B **48**
Brampton Ash. *Nptn* 2E **63**
Brampton Bryan. *Here* 3F **59**
Brampton en le Morthen
S Yor 2B **86**
Bramshall. *Staf* 2E **73**
Bramshaw. *Hants* 1A **16**
Bramshill. *Hants* 5F **37**
Bramshott. *Hants* 3G **25**
Branault. *High* 2G **139**
Brancaster. *Norf* 1G **77**
Brancaster Staithe. *Norf* 1G **77**
Brancepeth. *Dur* 1F **105**
Branch End. *Nmbd* 3D **114**
Branchill. *Mor* 3E **159**
Brand End. *Linc* 1C **76**
Branderburgh. *Mor* 1G **159**
Brandesburton. *E Yor* 5F **101**
Brandeston. *Suff* 4E **67**
Brand Green. *Glos* 3C **48**
Brandhill. *Shrp* 3G **59**
Brandis Corner. *Devn* 2E **11**
Brandish Street. *Som* 2C **20**
Brandiston. *Norf* 3D **78**
Brandon. *Dur* 1F **105**
Brandon. *Linc* 1G **75**
Brandon. *Nmbd* 3E **121**
Brandon. *Suff* 2G **65**
Brandon. *Warw* 3B **62**
Brandon Bank. *Cambs* 2F **65**
Brandon Creek. *Norf* 1F **65**
Brandon Parva. *Norf* 5C **78**
Brandsby. *N Yor* 2H **99**
Brandy Wharf. *Linc* 1H **87**
Brane. *Corn* 4B **4**
Bran End. *Essx* 3G **53**
Branksome. *Pool* 3F **15**
Bransbury. *Hants* 2C **24**
Bransby. *Linc* 3F **87**
Branscombe. *Devn* 4E **13**
Bransford. *Worc* 5B **60**
Bransgore. *Hants* 3G **15**
Bransholme. *Hull* 1E **94**
Bransley. *Shrp* 3A **60**
Branston. *Leics* 3F **75**
Branston. *Linc* 4H **87**
Branston. *Staf* 3G **73**
Branston Booths. *Linc* 4H **87**
Branstone. *IOW* 4D **16**
Bransty. *Cumb* 3A **102**
Brant Broughton. *Linc* 5G **87**
Brantham. *Suff* 2E **54**
Branthwaite. *Cumb*
nr. Caldbeck 1D **102**
nr. Workington 2B **102**
Brantingham. *E Yor* 2C **94**
Branton. *Nmbd* 3E **121**
Branton. *S Yor* 4G **93**
Branton Green. *N Yor* 3G **99**
Branxholme. *Bord* 3G **119**
Branxton. *Nmbd* 1C **120**
Brassington. *Derbs* 5G **85**
Brasted. *Kent* 5F **39**
Brasted Chart. *Kent* 5F **39**
The Bratch. *Staf* 1C **60**
Brathens. *Abers* 4D **152**
Bratoft. *Linc* 4D **88**
Brattleby. *Linc* 2G **87**
Bratton. *Som* 2C **20**
Bratton. *Telf* 4A **72**
Bratton. *Wilts* 1E **23**
Bratton Clovelly. *Devn* 3E **11**
Bratton Fleming. *Devn* 3G **19**
Bratton Seymour. *Som* 4B **22**
Braughing. *Herts* 3D **53**
Braulen Lodge. *High* 5E **157**
Braunston. *Nptn* 4C **62**
Braunstone Town. *Leics* 5C **74**
Braunston-in-Rutland. *Rut* 5F **75**
Braunton. *Devn* 3E **19**
Brawby. *N Yor* 2B **100**
Brawl. *High* 2A **168**
Brawlbin. *High* 3C **168**
Bray. *Wind* 3A **38**
Braybrooke. *Nptn* 2E **63**
Brayford. *Devn* 3G **19**
Bray Shop. *Corn* 5D **10**
Braystones. *Cumb* 4B **102**
Brayton. *N Yor* 1G **93**
Bray Wick. *Wind* 4G **37**
Brazacott. *Corn* 3C **10**
Brea. *Corn* 4A **6**
Breach. *W Sus* 2F **17**
Breachwood Green. *Herts* 3B **52**
Breacleit. *W Isl* 4D **171**
Breaden Heath. *Shrp* 2G **71**
Breadsall. *Derbs* 1A **74**
Breadstone. *Glos* 5C **48**
Breage. *Corn* 4D **4**
Breakachy. *High* 4G **157**
Breakish. *High* 1E **147**
Bream. *Glos* 5B **48**
Breamore. *Hants* 1G **15**
Bream's Meend. *Glos* 5B **48**
Brean. *Som* 1F **21**
Breanais. *W Isl* 5B **171**
Brearton. *N Yor* 3F **99**
Breascleit. *W Isl* 4E **171**
Breaston. *Derbs* 2B **74**
Brecais Àrd. *High* 1E **147**
Brecais Iosal. *High* 1E **147**
Brechfa. *Carm* 2F **45**
Brechin. *Ang* 3F **145**
Breckles. *Norf* 1B **66**
Brecon. *Powy* 3D **46**
Bredbury. *G Man* 1D **84**
Brede. *E Sus* 4C **28**
Bredenbury. *Here* 5A **60**
Bredfield. *Suff* 5E **67**
Bredgar. *Kent* 4C **40**
Bredhurst. *Kent* 4B **40**
Bredicot. *Worc* 5D **60**
Bredon. *Worc* 2E **49**
Bredon's Norton. *Worc* 2E **49**
Bredwardine. *Here* 1G **47**
Breedon on the Hill. *Leics* 3B **74**
Breibhig. *W Isl*
on Barra 9B **170**
on Isle of Lewis 4G **171**
Breich. *W Lot* 3C **128**
Breightmet. *G Man* 4F **91**
Breighton. *E Yor* 1H **93**
Breinton. *Here* 2H **47**
Breinton Common. *Here* 2H **47**
Breiwick. *Shet* 7F **173**
Brelston Green. *Here* 3A **48**
Bremhill. *Wilts* 4E **35**
Brenachie. *High* 1B **158**
Brenchley. *Kent* 1A **28**
Brendon. *Devn* 2A **20**
Brent Cross. *G Lon* 2D **38**
Brent Eleigh. *Suff* 1C **54**
Brentford. *G Lon* 3C **38**
Brentingby. *Leics* 4E **75**
Brent Knoll. *Som* 1G **21**
Brent Pelham. *Herts* 2E **53**
Brentwood. *Essx* 1G **39**
Brenzett. *Kent* 3E **28**
Brereton. *Staf* 4E **73**
Brereton Cross. *Staf* 4E **73**
Brereton Green. *Ches E* 4B **84**
Brereton Heath. *Ches E* 4C **84**
Bressingham. *Norf* 2C **66**
Bretby. *Derbs* 3G **73**
Bretford. *Warw* 3B **62**
Bretforton. *Worc* 1F **49**
Bretherdale Head. *Cumb* 4G **103**
Bretherton. *Lanc* 2C **90**
Brettabister. *Shet* 6F **173**
Brettenham. *Norf* 2B **66**
Brettenham. *Suff* 5B **66**
Bretton. *Flin* 4F **83**
Bretton. *Pet* 5A **76**
Brewlands Bridge. *Ang* 2A **144**
Brewood. *Staf* 5C **72**
Briantspuddle. *Dors* 3D **14**
Bricket Wood. *Herts* 5B **52**
Bricklehampton. *Worc* 1E **49**
Bride. *IOM* 1D **108**
Bridekirk. *Cumb* 1C **102**
Bridell. *Pemb* 1B **44**
Bridestowe. *Devn* 4F **11**
Brideswell. *Abers* 5C **160**
Bridford. *Devn* 4B **12**
Bridge. *Corn* 4A **6**
Bridge. *Kent* 5F **41**
Bridge. *Som* 2G **13**
Bridge End. *Bed* 5H **63**
Bridge End. *Cumb*
nr. Broughton in Furness
5D **102**
nr. Dalston 5E **113**
Bridge End. *Linc* 2A **76**
Bridge End. *Shet* 8E **173**
Bridgefoot. *Ang* 5C **144**
Bridgefoot. *Cumb* 2B **102**
Bridge Green. *Essx* 2E **53**
Bridgehampton. *Som* 4A **22**
Bridge Hewick. *N Yor* 2F **99**
Bridgehill. *Dur* 4D **115**
Bridgemary. *Hants* 2D **16**
Bridgemere. *Ches E* 1B **72**
Bridgemont. *Derbs* 2E **85**
Bridgend. *Abers*
nr. Huntly 5C **160**
nr. Peterhead 5H **161**
Bridgend. *Ang*
nr. Brechin 2E **145**
nr. Kirriemuir 4C **144**
Bridgend. *Arg*
nr. Lochgilphead 4F **133**
on Islay 3B **124**
Bridgend. *B'end* 3C **32**
Bridgend. *Cumb* 3E **103**
Bridgend. *Devn* 4B **8**
Bridgend. *Fife* 2F **137**
Bridgend. *High* 3F **157**
Bridgend. *Mor* 5A **160**
Bridgend. *Per* 1D **136**
Bridgend. *W Lot* 2D **128**
Bridgend of Lintrathen
Ang 3B **144**
Bridgeness. *Falk* 1D **128**
Bridge of Alford. *Abers* 2C **152**
Bridge of Allan. *Stir* 4G **135**
Bridge of Avon. *Mor* 5F **159**
Bridge of Awe. *Arg* 1H **133**
Bridge of Balgie. *Per* 4C **142**
Bridge of Brown. *High* 1F **151**
Bridge of Cally. *Per* 3A **144**
Bridge of Canny. *Abers* 4D **152**
Bridge of Dee. *Dum* 3E **111**
Bridge of Don. *Aber* 2G **153**
Bridge of Dun. *Ang* 3F **145**
Bridge of Dye. *Abers* 5D **152**
Bridge of Earn. *Per* 2D **136**
Bridge of Ericht. *Per* 3C **142**
Bridge of Feugh. *Abers* 4E **152**
Bridge of Gairn. *Abers* 4A **152**
Bridge of Gaur. *Per* 3C **142**
Bridge of Muchalls
Abers 4F **153**
Bridge of Oich. *High* 3F **149**
Bridge of Orchy. *Arg* 5H **141**
Bridge of Walls. *Shet* 6D **173**
Bridge of Weir. *Ren* 3E **127**
Bridge Reeve. *Devn* 1G **11**
Bridgerule. *Devn* 2C **10**
Bridge Sollers. *Here* 1H **47**
Bridge Street. *Suff* 1B **54**
Bridge Town. *Warw* 5G **61**
Bridgetown. *Devn* 2E **9**
Bridgetown. *Som* 3C **20**
Bridge Trafford. *Ches W* 3G **83**
Bridgeyate. *S Glo* 4B **34**
Bridgham. *Norf* 2B **66**
Bridgnorth. *Shrp* 1B **60**
Bridgtown. *Staf* 5D **73**
Bridgwater. *Som* 3G **21**
Bridlington. *E Yor* 3F **101**
Bridport. *Dors* 3H **13**
Bridstow. *Here* 3A **48**
Brierfield. *Lanc* 1G **91**
Brierley. *Glos* 4B **48**
Brierley. *Here* 5G **59**
Brierley. *S Yor* 3E **93**
Brierley Hill. *W Mid* 2D **60**
Brierton. *Hart* 1B **106**
Briestfield. *W Yor* 3C **92**
Brigg. *N Lin* 4D **94**
Briggate. *Norf* 3F **79**
Briggswath. *N Yor* 4F **107**
Brigham. *Cumb* 1B **102**
Brigham. *E Yor* 4E **101**
Brighouse. *W Yor* 2B **92**
Brighstone. *IOW* 4C **16**
Brightgate. *Derbs* 5G **85**
Brighthampton. *Oxon* 5B **50**
Brightholmlee. *S Yor* 1G **85**
Brightley. *Devn* 3G **11**
Brightling. *E Sus* 3A **28**
Brightlingsea. *Essx* 4D **54**
Brighton. *Brig* 5E **27**
Brighton. *Corn* 3D **6**
Brighton Hill. *Hants* 2E **24**
Brightons. *Falk* 2C **128**
Brightwalton. *W Ber* 4C **36**
Brightwalton Green
W Ber 4C **36**
Brightwell. *Suff* 1F **55**
Brightwell Baldwin. *Oxon* 2E **37**
Brightwell-cum-Sotwell
Oxon 2D **36**
Brigmerston. *Wilts* 2G **23**
Brignall. *Dur* 3D **104**
Brig o' Turk. *Stir* 3E **135**
Brigsley. *NE Lin* 4F **95**
Brigsteer. *Cumb* 1D **97**
Brigstock. *Nptn* 2G **63**
Brill. *Buck* 4E **51**
Brill. *Corn* 4E **5**
Brilley. *Here* 1F **47**
Brimaston. *Pemb* 2D **42**
Brimfield. *Here* 4H **59**
Brimington. *Derbs* 3B **86**
Brimley. *Devn* 5B **12**
Brimpsfield. *Glos* 4E **49**
Brimpton. *W Ber* 5D **36**
Brims. *Orkn* 9B **172**
Brimscombe. *Glos* 5D **48**
Brimstage. *Mers* 2F **83**
Brincliffe. *S Yor* 2H **85**
Brind. *E Yor* 1H **93**
Brindister. *Shet*
nr. West Burrafirth 6D **173**
nr. West Lerwick 8F **173**
Brindle. *Lanc* 2D **90**
Brindley. *Ches E* 5H **83**
Brindley Ford. *Stoke* 5C **84**
Brineton. *Staf* 4C **72**
Bringhurst. *Leics* 1F **63**
Bringsty Common. *Here* 5A **60**
Brington. *Cambs* 3H **63**
Brinian. *Orkn* 5D **172**
Briningham. *Norf* 2C **78**
Brinkhill. *Linc* 3C **88**
Brinkley. *Cambs* 5F **65**
Brinklow. *Warw* 3B **62**
Brinkworth. *Wilts* 3F **35**
Brinscall. *Lanc* 2E **91**
Brinscombe. *Som* 1H **21**
Brinsley. *Notts* 1B **74**
Brinsworth. *S Yor* 2B **86**
Brinton. *Norf* 2C **78**
Brisco. *Cumb* 4F **113**
Brisley. *Norf* 3B **78**
Brislington. *Bris* 4B **34**
Brissenden Green. *Kent* 2D **28**
Bristol. *Bris* 4A **34**
Bristol Airport. *N Som* 5A **34**
Briston. *Norf* 2C **78**
Britannia. *Lanc* 2G **91**
Britford. *Wilts* 4G **23**
Brithdir. *Cphy* 5E **47**
Brithdir. *Cdgn* 1D **44**
Brithdir. *Gwyn* 4G **69**
Briton Ferry. *Neat* 3G **31**
Britwell Salome. *Oxon* 2E **37**
Brixham. *Torb* 3F **9**
Brixton. *Devn* 3B **8**
Brixton. *G Lon* 3E **39**
Brixton Deverill. *Wilts* 3D **22**
Brixworth. *Nptn* 3E **63**
Brize Norton. *Oxon* 5B **50**
The Broad. *Here* 4G **59**
Broad Alley. *Worc* 4C **60**
Broad Blunsdon. *Swin* 2G **35**
Broadbottom. *G Man* 1D **85**
Broadbridge. *W Sus* 2G **17**
Broadbridge Heath
W Sus 2C **26**
Broad Campden. *Glos* 2G **49**
Broad Chalke. *Wilts* 4F **23**
Broadclyst. *Devn* 3C **12**
Broadfield. *Inv* 2E **127**

Bwlch – Carlton

Bwlch. Powy 3E 47
Bwlchderwin. Gwyn 1D 68
Bwlchgwyn. Wrex 5E 83
Bwlch-Llan. Cdgn 5E 57
Bwlchnewydd. Carm 3D 44
Bwlchtocyn. Gwyn 3C 68
Bwlch-y-cibau. Powy 4D 70
Bwlchyddar. Powy 3D 70
Bwlch-y-fadfa. Cdgn 1E 45
Bwlch-y-ffridd. Powy 1C 58
Bwlch y Garreg. Powy 1C 58
Bwlch-y-groes. Pemb 1G 43
Bwlch-y-sarnau. Powy 3C 58
Bybrook. Kent 1E 28
Byermoor. Tyne 4E 115
Byers Garth. Dur 5G 115
Byers Green. Dur 1F 105
Byfield. Nptn 5C 62
Byfleet. Surr 4B 38
Byford. Here 1G 47
Bygrave. Herts 2C 52
Byker. Tyne 3F 115
Byland Abbey. N Yor 2H 99
Bylchau. Cnwy 4B 82
Byley. Ches W 4B 84
Bynea. Carm 3E 31
Byram. N Yor 2E 93
Byrness. Nmbd 4B 120
Bystock. Devn 4D 12
Bythorn. Cambs 3H 63
Byton. Here 4F 59
Bywell. Nmbd 3D 114
Byworth. W Sus 3A 26

C

Cabharstadh. W Isl 6F 171
Cabourne. Linc 4E 95
Cabrach. Arg 3C 124
Cabrach. Mor 1A 152
Cabus. Lanc 5D 97
Cadbury. Devn 2C 12
Cadder. E Dun 2H 127
Caddington. C Beds 4A 52
Caddonfoot. Bord 1G 119
Cadeby. Leics 5B 74
Cadeby. S Yor 4F 93
Cadeleigh. Devn 2C 12
Cade Street. E Sus 3H 27
Cadgwith. Corn 5E 5
Cadham. Fife 3E 137
Cadishead. G Man 1B 84
Cadle. Swan 3F 31
Cadley. Lanc 1D 90
Cadley. Wilts
nr. Ludgershall 1H 23
nr. Marlborough 5H 35
Cadmore End. Buck 2F 37
Cadnam. Hants 1A 16
Cadney. N Lin 4D 94
Cadole. Flin 4E 82
Cadoxton-juxta-Neath
Neat 2A 32
Cadwell. Herts 2B 52
Cadwst. Den 2C 70
Caeathro. Gwyn 4E 81
Caehopkin. Powy 4B 46
Caenby. Linc 2H 87
Caerau. B'end 2B 32
Caerau. Card 4E 33
Cae'r-bont. Powy 4B 46
Cae'r-bryn. Carm 4F 45
Caerdeon. Gwyn 4F 69
Caerdydd. Card 4E 33
Caerfarchell. Pemb 2B 42
Caerffili. Cphy 3E 33
Caerfyrddin. Carm 4E 45
Caergeiliog. IOA 3C 80
Caergwrle. Flin 5F 83
Caergybi. IOA 2B 80
Caerlaverock. Per 2A 136
Caerleon. Newp 2G 33
Caerlleon. Carm 2G 43
Caerllion. Newp 2G 33
Caernarfon. Gwyn 4D 81
Caerphilly. Cphy 3E 33
Caersws. Powy 1C 58
Caerwedros. Cdgn 5C 56
Caerwent. Mon 2H 33
Caerwys. Flin 3D 82
Caim. IOA 2F 81
Caio. Carm 2G 45
Cairinis. W Isl 2D 170
Cairisiadar. W Isl 4C 171
Cairminis. W Isl 9C 171
Cairnbaan. Arg 4F 133
Cairnbulg. Abers 2H 161
Cairncross. Ang 1D 145
Cairndow. Arg 2A 134
Cairness. Abers 2H 161
Cairneyhill. Fife 1D 128
Cairngarroch. Dum 5F 109
Cairnhill. Abers 5D 160
Cairnie. Abers 4B 160
Cairnorrie. Abers 4F 161
Cairnryan. Dum 3F 109
Cairston. Orkn 6B 172
Caister-on-Sea. Norf 4H 79
Caistor. Linc 4E 94
Caistor St Edmund. Norf 5E 79
Caistron. Nmbd 4D 121
Cakebole. Worc 3C 60
Calais Street. Suff 1C 54
Calanais. W Isl 4E 171
Calbost. W Isl 6G 171
Calbourne. IOW 4C 16
Calceby. Linc 3C 88
Calcot. Glos 4F 49
Calcot Row. W Ber 4E 37
Calcott. Kent 4F 41
Calcott. Shrp 4G 71
Caldback. Shet 1H 173
Caldbeck. Cumb 1E 102
Caldbergh. N Yor 1C 98
Caldecote. Cambs
nr. Cambridge 5C 64
nr. Peterborough 2A 64
Caldecote. Herts 2C 52
Caldecote. Nptn 5D 62
Caldecote. Warw 1A 62
Caldecott. Nptn 4G 63
Caldecott. Oxon 2C 36
Caldecott. Rut 1F 63
Calderbank. N Lan 3A 128
Calder Bridge. Cumb 4B 102
Calderbrook. G Man 3H 91
Caldercruix. N Lan 3B 128
Calder Grove. W Yor 3D 92
Calder Mains. High 3C 168
Caldermill. S Lan 5H 127
Calder Vale. Lanc 5E 97
Calderwood. S Lan 4H 127
Caldicot. Mon 3H 33
Caldwell. Derbs 4G 73
Caldwell. N Yor 3E 105
Caldy. Mers 2E 83
Calebrack. Cumb 1E 103
Calf Heath. Staf 5D 72
Calford Green. Suff 1G 53
Calfsound. Orkn 4E 172
Calgary. Arg 3E 139
Califer. Mor 3E 159
California. Cambs 2E 65
California. Falk 2C 128
California. Norf 4H 79
California. Suff 1E 55
Calke. Derbs 3A 74
Callakille. High 3F 155
Callaly. Nmbd 4E 121
Callander. Stir 3F 135
Callaughton. Shrp 1A 60
Callendoun. Arg 1E 127
Callestick. Corn 3B 6
Calligarry. High 3E 147
Callington. Corn 2H 7
Callingwood. Staf 3F 73
Callow. Here 2H 47
Callowell. Glos 5D 48
Callow End. Worc 1D 48
Callow Hill. Wilts 3F 35
Callow Hill. Worc
nr. Bewdley 3B 60
nr. Redditch 4E 61
Calmore. Hants 1B 16
Calmsden. Glos 5F 49
Calne. Wilts 4E 35
Calow. Derbs 3B 86
Calshot. Hants 2C 16
Calstock. Corn 2A 8
Calstone Wellington
Wilts 5F 35
Calthorpe. Norf 2D 78
Calthorpe Street. Norf 3G 79
Calthwaite. Cumb 5F 113
Calton. N Yor 4B 98
Calton. Staf 5F 85
Calveley. Ches E 5H 83
Calver. Derbs 3G 85
Calverhall. Shrp 2A 72
Calverleigh. Devn 1C 12
Calverley. W Yor 1C 92
Calvert. Buck 3E 51
Calverton. Mil 2F 51
Calverton. Notts 1D 74
Calvine. Per 2F 143
Calvo. Cumb 4C 112
Cam. Glos 2C 34
Camaghael. High 1F 141
Camas-luinie. High 1B 148
Camasnacroise. High 3C 140
Camastianavaig. High 5E 155
Camasunary. High 2D 146
Camault Muir. High 4H 157
Camb. Shet 2G 173
Camber. E Sus 4D 28
Camberley. Surr 5G 37
Camberwell. G Lon 3E 39
Camblesforth. N Yor 2G 93
Cambo. Nmbd 1D 114
Cambois. Nmbd 1G 115
Camborne. Corn 5A 6
Cambourne. Cambs 5C 64
Cambridge. Cambs 5D 64
Cambridge. Glos 5C 48
Cambrose. Corn 4A 6
Cambus. Clac 4A 136
Cambusbarron. Stir 4G 135
Cambuskenneth. Stir 4H 135
Cambuslang. S Lan 3H 127
Cambusnethan. N Lan 4B 128
Cambus o' May. Abers 4B 152
Camden Town. G Lon 2D 39
Cameley. Bath 1B 22
Camelford. Corn 4B 10
Camelon. Falk 1B 128
Camelsdale. W Sus 3G 25
Camer's Green. Worc 2C 48
Camerton. Bath 1B 22
Camerton. Cumb 1B 102
Camerton. E Yor 2F 95
Camghouran. Per 3C 142
Camlough. New M 6F 175
Cammachmore. Abers 4G 153
Cammeringham. Linc 2G 87
Camore. High 4E 165
The Camp. Glos 5E 49
Campbelton. N Ayr 4C 126
Campbeltown. Arg 3B 122
Campbeltown Airport
Arg 3A 122
Cample. Dum 5A 118
Campmuir. Per 5B 144
Campsall. S Yor 3F 93
Campsea Ashe. Suff 5F 67
Camps End. Cambs 1G 53
Campton. C Beds 2B 52
Camptoun. E Lot 2B 130
Camptown. Bord 3A 120
Camrose. Pemb 2D 42
Camserney. Per 4F 143
Camster. High 4E 169
Camus Croise. High 2E 147
Camuscross. High 2E 147
Camusdarach. High 4E 147
Camusnagaul. High
nr. Fort William 1E 141
nr. Little Loch Broom
5E 163
Camusteel. High 4G 155
Camusterrach. High 4G 155
Camusvrachan. Per 4D 142
Canada. Hants 1A 16
Canadia. E Sus 4B 28
Canaston Bridge. Pemb 3E 43
Candlesby. Linc 4D 88
Candle Street. Suff 3C 66
Candy Mill. S Lan 5D 128
Cane End. Oxon 4E 37
Canewdon. Essx 1D 40
Canford Cliffs. Pool 4F 15
Canford Heath. Pool 3F 15
Canford Magna. Pool 3F 15
Cangate. Norf 4F 79
Canham's Green. Suff 4C 66
Canholes. Derbs 3E 85
Canisbay. High 1F 169
Canley. W Mid 3H 61
Cann. Dors 4D 22
Cann Common. Dors 4D 23
Cannich. High 5F 157
Cannington. Som 3F 21
Cannock. Staf 4D 73
Cannock Wood. Staf 4E 73
Canonbie. Dum 2E 113
Canon Bridge. Here 1H 47
Canon Frome. Here 1B 48
Canon Pyon. Here 1H 47
Canons Ashby. Nptn 5C 62
Canonstown. Corn 3C 4
Canterbury. Kent 5F 41
Cantley. Norf 5F 79
Cantley. S Yor 4G 93
Cantlop. Shrp 5H 71
Canton. Card 4E 33
Cantray. High 4B 158
Cantraybruich. High 4B 158
Cantraywood. High 4B 158
Cantsdam. Fife 4D 136
Cantsfield. Lanc 2F 97
Canvey Island. Essx 2B 40
Canwick. Linc 4G 87
Canworthy Water. Corn 3C 10
Caol. High 1F 141
Caolas. Arg 4B 138
Caolas. W Isl 9B 170
Caolas Liubharsaigh
W Isl 4D 170
Caolas Scalpaigh. W Isl 8E 171
Caolas Stocinis. W Isl 8D 171
Caol Ila. Arg 2C 124
Caol Loch Ailse. High 1F 147
Caol Reatha. High 1F 147
Capel. Kent 1H 27
Capel. Surr 1C 26
Capel Bangor. Cdgn 2F 57
Capel Betws Lleucu. Cdgn 5F 57
Capel Coch. IOA 2D 80
Capel Curig. Cnwy 5G 81
Capel Cynon. Cdgn 1D 45
Capel Dewi. Carm 3E 45
Capel Dewi. Cdgn
nr. Aberystwyth 2F 57
nr. Llandysul 1E 45
Capel Garmon. Cnwy 5H 81
Capel Green. Suff 1G 55
Capel Gwyn. IOA 3C 80
Capel Gwynfe. Carm 3H 45
Capel Hendre. Carm 4F 45
Capel Isaac. Carm 3F 45
Capel Iwan. Carm 1G 43
Capel-le-Ferne. Kent 2G 29
Capel Llanilltern. Card 4D 32
Capel Mawr. IOA 3D 80
Capel Newydd. Pemb 1G 43
Capel St Andrew. Suff 1G 55
Capel St Mary. Suff 2D 54
Capel Seion. Carm 4F 45
Capel Seion. Cdgn 3F 57
Capel Uchaf. Gwyn 1D 68
Capel-y-ffin. Powy 2F 47
Capenhurst. Ches W 3F 83
Capernwray. Lanc 2E 97
Capheaton. Nmbd 1D 114
Cappercleuch. Bord 2E 119
Capplegill. Dum 4D 118
Capton. Devn 3E 9
Capton. Som 3D 20
Caputh. Per 5H 143
Caradon Town. Corn 5C 10
Carbis Bay. Corn 3C 4
Carbost. High
nr. Loch Harport 5C 154
nr. Portree 4D 154
Carbrook. S Yor 2A 86
Carbrooke. Norf 5B 78
Carburton. Notts 3D 86
Carcluie. S Ayr 3C 116
Car Colston. Notts 1E 74
Carcroft. S Yor 4F 93
Cardenden. Fife 4E 136
Cardeston. Shrp 4F 71
Cardewlees. Cumb 4E 113
Cardiff. Card 4E 33
Cardiff Airport. V Glam 5D 32
Cardigan. Cdgn 1B 44
Cardinal's Green. Cambs 1G 53
Cardington. Bed 1A 52
Cardington. Shrp 1H 59
Cardinham. Corn 2F 7
Cardno. Abers 2G 161
Cardow. Mor 4F 159
Cardross. Arg 2E 127
Cardurnock. Cumb 4C 112
Careby. Linc 4H 75
Careston. Ang 2E 145
Carew. Pemb 4E 43
Carew Cheriton. Pemb 4E 43
Carew Newton. Pemb 4E 43
Carey. Here 2A 48
Carfin. N Lan 4A 128
Carfrae. Bord 4B 130
Cargate Green. Norf 4F 79
Cargenbridge. Dum 2G 111
Cargill. Per 5A 144
Cargo. Cumb 4E 113
Cargreen. Corn 2A 8
Carham. Nmbd 1C 120
Carhampton. Som 2D 20
Carharrack. Corn 4B 6
Carie. Per
nr. Loch Rannah 3D 142
nr. Loch Tay 5D 142
Carisbrooke. IOW 4C 16
Cark. Cumb 2C 96
Carkeel. Corn 2A 8
Carlabhagh. W Isl 3E 171
Carland Cross. Corn 3C 6
Carlbury. Darl 3F 105
Carlby. Linc 4H 75
Carlecotes. S Yor 4B 92
Carleen. Corn 4D 4
Carlesmoor. N Yor 2D 98
Carleton. Cumb
nr. Carlisle 4F 113
nr. Egremont 4B 102
nr. Penrith 2G 103
Carleton. Lanc 5C 96
Carleton. N Yor 5B 98
Carleton. W Yor 2E 93
Carleton Forehoe. Norf 5C 78
Carleton Rode. Norf 1D 66
Carleton St Peter. Norf 5F 79
Carlidnack. Corn 4E 5
Carlingcott. Bath 1B 22
Carlin How. Red C 3E 107
Carlisle. Cumb 4F 113
Carloonan. Arg 2H 133
Carlops. Bord 4E 129
Carlton. Bed 5G 63

Carlton – Chapel

Carlton. Cambs 5F 65
Carlton. Leics 5A 74
Carlton. N Yor
nr. Helmsley 1A 100
nr. Middleham 1C 98
nr. Selby 2G 93
Carlton. Notts 1D 74
Carlton. S Yor 3D 92
Carlton. Stoc T 2A 106
Carlton. Suff 4F 67
Carlton. W Yor 2D 92
Carlton Colville. Suff 1H 67
Carlton Curlieu. Leics 1D 62
Carlton Husthwaite. N Yor 2G 99
Carlton in Cleveland N Yor 4C 106
Carlton in Lindrick. Notts 2C 86
Carlton-le-Moorland. Linc 5G 87
Carlton Miniott. N Yor 1F 99
Carlton-on-Trent. Notts 4F 87
Carlton Scroop. Linc 1G 75
Carluke. S Lan 4B 128
Carlyon Bay. Corn 3E 7
Carmarthen. Carm 4E 45
Carmel. Carm 4F 45
Carmel. Flin 3D 82
Carmel. Gwyn 5D 81
Carmel. IOA 2C 80
Carmichael. S Lan 1B 118
Carmunnock. Glas 4H 127
Carmyle. Glas 3H 127
Carmyllie. Ang 4E 145
Carnaby. E Yor 3F 101
Carnach. High
nr. Lochcarron 1C 148
nr. Ullapool 4E 163
Carnach. Mor 4E 159
Carnach. W Isl 8E 171
Carnachy. High 3H 167
Carnain. Arg 3B 124
Carnais. W Isl 4C 171
Carnan. Arg 4B 138
Carnan. W Isl 4C 170
Carnbee. Fife 3H 137
Carnbo. Per 3C 136
Carn Brea Village. Corn 4A 6
Carndu. High 1A 148
Carne. Corn 5D 6
Carnell. S Ayr 1D 116
Carnforth. Lanc 2E 97
Carn-gorm. High 1B 148
Carnhedryn. Pemb 2C 42
Carnhell Green. Corn 3D 4
Carnie. Abers 3F 153
Carnkie. Corn
nr. Falmouth 5B 6
nr. Redruth 5A 6
Carnkief. Corn 3B 6
Carno. Powy 1B 58
Carnock. Fife 1D 128
Carnon Downs. Corn 4B 6
Carnoustie. Ang 5E 145
Carntyne. Glas 3H 127
Carnwath. S Lan 5C 128
Carnyorth. Corn 3A 4
Carol Green. W Mid 3G 61
Carpalla. Corn 3D 6
Carperby. N Yor 1C 98
Carradale. Arg 2C 122
Carragraich. W Isl 8D 171
Carrbridge. High 1D 150
Carr Cross. Lanc 3B 90
Carreglefn. IOA 2C 80
Carrhouse. N Lin 4A 94
Carrick Castle. Arg 4A 134
Carrickfergus. ME Ant 3H 175
Carrick Ho. Orkn 4E 172
Carriden. Falk 1D 128
Carrington. G Man 1B 84
Carrington. Linc 5C 88
Carrington. Midl 3G 129
Carrog. Cnwy 1G 69
Carrog. Den 1D 70
Carron. Falk 1B 128
Carron. Mor 4G 159
Carronbridge. Dum 5A 118
Carronshore. Falk 1B 128
Carrow Hill. Mon 2H 33
Carr Shield. Nmbd 5B 114
Carrutherstown. Dum 2C 112
Carr Vale. Derbs 4B 86
Carrville. Dur 5G 115
Carryduff. Lis 4H 175
Carsaig. Arg 1C 132
Carscreugh. Dum 3H 109
Carsegowan. Dum 4B 110
Carse House. Arg 3F 125
Carseriggan. Dum 3A 110
Carsethorn. Dum 4A 112
Carshalton. G Lon 4D 39
Carsington. Derbs 5G 85
Carskiey. Arg 5A 122
Carsluith. Dum 4B 110
Carsphairn. Dum 5E 117
Carstairs. S Lan 5C 128
Carstairs Junction. S Lan 5C 128
Cartbridge. Surr 5B 38
Carterhaugh. Ang 4D 144
Carter's Clay. Hants 4B 24
Carterton. Oxon 5A 50
Carterway Heads. Nmbd 4D 114
Carthew. Corn 3E 6
Carthorpe. N Yor 1F 99
Cartington. Nmbd 4E 121
Cartland. S Lan 5B 128
Cartmel. Cumb 2C 96
Cartmel Fell. Cumb 1D 96
Cartworth. W Yor 4B 92
Carwath. Cumb 5E 112
Carway. Carm 5E 45
Carwinley. Cumb 2F 113
Cascob. Powy 4E 59
Cas-gwent. Mon 2A 34
Cash Feus. Fife 3E 136
Cashlie. Per 4B 142
Cashmoor. Dors 1E 15
Cas-Mael. Pemb 2E 43
Casnewydd. Newp 3G 33
Cassington. Oxon 4C 50
Cassop. Dur 1A 106
Castell. Cnwy 4G 81
Castell. Den 4D 82
Castell Hendre. Pemb 2E 43
Castell-Nedd. Neat 2A 32
Castell Newydd Emlyn Carm 1D 44
Castell-y-bwch. Torf 2F 33
Casterton. Cumb 2F 97
Castle. Som 2A 22
Castle Acre. Norf 4H 77
Castle Ashby. Nptn 5F 63
Castlebay. W Isl 9B 170
Castle Bolton. N Yor 5D 104
Castle Bromwich. W Mid 2F 61
Castle Bytham. Linc 4G 75
Castlebythe. Pemb 2E 43
Castle Caereinion. Powy 5D 70
Castle Camps. Cambs 1G 53
Castle Carrock. Cumb 4G 113
Castle Cary. Som 3B 22
Castlecary. N Lan 2A 128
Castle Combe. Wilts 4D 34
Castlecraig. High 2C 158
Castledawson. M Ulst 3F 175
Castlederg. Derr 3B 174
Castle Donington. Leics 3B 74
Castle Douglas. Dum 3E 111
Castle Eaton. Swin 2G 35
Castle Eden. Dur 1B 106
Castleford. W Yor 2E 93
Castle Frome. Here 1B 48
Castle Green. Surr 4A 38
Castle Green. Warw 3G 61
Castle Gresley. Derbs 4G 73
Castle Heaton. Nmbd 5F 131
Castle Hedingham. Essx 2A 54
Castle Hill. Kent 1A 28
Castle Hill. Suff 1E 55
Castlehill. Per 5B 144
Castlehill. S Lan 4B 128
Castlehill. W Dun 2E 127
Castle Kennedy. Dum 4G 109
Castle Lachlan. Arg 4H 133
Castlemartin. Pemb 5D 42
Castlemilk. Glas 4H 127
Castlemorris. Pemb 1D 42
Castlemorton. Worc 2C 48
Castle O'er. Dum 5E 119
Castle Park. N Yor 3F 107
Castlerigg. Cumb 2D 102
Castle Rising. Norf 3F 77
Castlerock. Caus 1E 174
Castleside. Dur 5D 115
Castlethorpe. Mil 1F 51
Castleton. Abers 4F 151
Castleton. Arg 1G 125
Castleton. Derbs 2F 85
Castleton. G Man 3G 91
Castleton. Mor 1F 151
Castleton. Newp 3F 33
Castleton. N Yor 4D 107
Castleton. Per 2B 136
Castletown. Cumb 1G 103
Castletown. Dors 5B 14
Castletown. High 2D 169
Castletown. IOM 5B 108
Castletown. Tyne 4G 115
Castlewellan. New M 6H 175
Castley. N Yor 5E 99
Caston. Norf 1B 66
Castor. Pet 1A 64
Caswell. Swan 4E 31
Catacol. N Ayr 5H 125
Catbrook. Mon 5A 48
Catchems End. Worc 3B 60
Catchgate. Dur 4E 115
Catcleugh. Nmbd 4B 120
Catcliffe. S Yor 2B 86
Catcott. Som 3G 21
Caterham. Surr 5E 39
Catfield. Norf 3F 79
Catfield Common. Norf 3F 79
Catfirth. Shet 6F 173
Catford. G Lon 3E 39
Catforth. Lanc 1C 90
Cathcart. Glas 3G 127
Cathedine. Powy 3E 47
Catherine-de-Barnes W Mid 2F 61
Catherington. Hants 1E 17
Catherston Leweston Dors 3G 13
Catherton. Shrp 3A 60
Catisfield. Hants 2D 16
Catlodge. High 4A 150
Catlowdy. Cumb 2F 113
Catmore. W Ber 3C 36
Caton. Devn 5A 12
Caton. Lanc 3E 97
Catrine. E Ayr 2E 117
Cat's Ash. Newp 2G 33
Catsfield. E Sus 4B 28
Catsgore. Som 4A 22
Catshill. Worc 3D 60
Cattal. N Yor 4G 99
Cattawade. Suff 2E 54
Catterall. Lanc 5E 97
Catterick. N Yor 5F 105
Catterick Bridge. N Yor 5F 105
Catterick Garrison N Yor 5E 105
Catterlen. Cumb 1F 103
Catterline. Abers 1H 145
Catterton. N Yor 5H 99
Catteshall. Surr 1A 26
Catthorpe. Leics 3C 62
Cattistock. Dors 3A 14
Catton. Nmbd 4B 114
Catton. N Yor 2F 99
Catwick. E Yor 5F 101
Catworth. Cambs 3H 63
Caudle Green. Glos 4E 49
Caulcott. Oxon 3D 50
Cauldhame. Stir 4F 135
Cauldmill. Bord 3H 119
Cauldon. Staf 1E 73
Cauldon Lowe. Staf 1E 73
Cauldwells. Abers 3E 161
Caulkerbush. Dum 4G 111
Caulside. Dum 1F 113
Caunsall. Worc 2C 60
Caunton. Notts 4E 87
Causewayend. S Lan 1C 118
Causewayhead. Stir 4H 135
Causey Park. Nmbd 5F 121
Caute. Devn 1E 11
Cautley. Cumb 5H 103
Cavendish. Suff 1B 54
Cavendish Bridge. Leics 3B 74
Cavenham. Suff 3G 65
Caversfield. Oxon 3D 50
Caversham. Read 4F 37
Caversham Heights Read 4F 37
Caverswall. Staf 1D 72
Cawdor. High 3C 158
Cawkwell. Linc 2B 88
Cawood. N Yor 1F 93
Cawsand. Corn 3A 8
Cawston. Norf 3D 78
Cawston. Warw 3B 62
Cawthorne. N Yor 1B 100
Cawthorne. S Yor 4C 92
Cawthorpe. Linc 3H 75
Cawton. N Yor 2A 100
Caxton. Cambs 5C 64
Caynham. Shrp 3H 59
Caythorpe. Linc 1G 75
Caythorpe. Notts 1D 74
Cayton. N Yor 1E 101
Ceallan. W Isl 3D 170
Ceann a Bhaigh. W Isl
on North Uist 2C 170
on Scalpay 8E 171
on South Harris 8D 171
Ceann a Bhàigh. W Isl 9C 171
Ceannacroc Lodge. High 2E 149
Ceann a Deas Loch Baghasdail W Isl 7C 170
Ceann an Leothaid. High 5E 147
Ceann a Tuath Loch Baghasdail. W Isl 6C 170
Ceann Loch Ailleart. High 5F 147
Ceann Loch Muideirt High 1B 140
Ceann-na-Cleithe. W Isl 8D 171
Ceann Shiphoirt. W Isl 6E 171
Ceann Tarabhaigh. W Isl 6E 171
Cearsiadar. W Isl 5F 171
Ceathramh Meadhanach W Isl 1D 170
Cefn Berain. Cnwy 4B 82
Cefn-brith. Cnwy 5B 82
Cefn-bryn-brain. Carm 4H 45
Cefn Bychan. Cphy 2F 33
Cefn-bychan. Flin 4D 82
Cefncaeau. Carm 3E 31
Cefn Canol. Powy 2E 71
Cefn Coch. Powy 5C 70
Cefn-coch. Powy 3D 70
Cefn-coed-y-cymmer Mer T 5D 46
Cefn Cribwr. B'end 3B 32
Cefn-ddwysarn. Gwyn 2B 70
Cefn Einion. Shrp 2E 59
Cefneithin. Carm 4F 45
Cefn Glas. B'end 3B 32
Cefngorwydd. Powy 1C 46
Cefn Llwyd. Cdgn 2F 57
Cefn-mawr. Wrex 1E 71
Cefn-y-bedd. Flin 5F 83
Cefn-y-coed. Powy 1D 58
Cefn-y-pant. Carm 2F 43
Cegidfa. Powy 4E 70
Ceinewydd. Cdgn 5C 56
Cellan. Cdgn 1G 45
Cellardyke. Fife 3H 137
Cellarhead. Staf 1D 72
Cemaes. IOA 1C 80
Cemmaes. Powy 5H 69
Cemmaes Road. Powy 5H 69
Cenarth. Cdgn 1C 44
Cenin. Gwyn 1D 68
Ceos. W Isl 5F 171
Ceres. Fife 2G 137
Ceri. Powy 2D 58
Cerist. Powy 2B 58
Cerne Abbas. Dors 2B 14
Cerney Wick. Glos 2F 35
Cerrigceinwen. IOA 3D 80
Cerrigydrudion. Cnwy 1B 70
Cess. Norf 4G 79
Cessford. Bord 2B 120
Ceunant. Gwyn 4E 81
Chaceley. Glos 2D 48
Chacewater. Corn 4B 6
Chackmore. Buck 2E 51
Chacombe. Nptn 1C 50
Chadderton. G Man 4H 91
Chaddesden. Derb 2A 74
Chaddesden Common Derb 2A 74
Chaddesley Corbett. Worc 3C 60
Chaddlehanger. Devn 5E 11
Chaddleworth. W Ber 4C 36
Chadlington. Oxon 3B 50
Chadshunt. Warw 5H 61
Chadstone. Nptn 5F 63
Chad Valley. W Mid 2E 61
Chadwell. Leics 3E 75
Chadwell. Shrp 4B 72
Chadwell Heath. G Lon 2F 39
Chadwell St Mary. Thur 3H 39
Chadwick End. W Mid 3G 61
Chadwick Green. Mers 1H 83
Chaffcombe. Som 1G 13
Chafford Hundred. Thur 3H 39
Chagford. Devn 4H 11
Chailey. E Sus 4E 27
Chain Bridge. Linc 1C 76
Chainbridge. Cambs 5D 76
Chainhurst. Kent 1B 28
Chalbury. Dors 2F 15
Chalbury Common. Dors 2F 15
Chaldon. Surr 5E 39
Chaldon Herring. Dors 4C 14
Chale. IOW 5C 16
Chale Green. IOW 5C 16
Chalfont Common. Buck 1B 38
Chalfont St Giles. Buck 1A 38
Chalfont St Peter. Buck 2B 38
Chalford. Glos 5D 49
Chalgrove. Oxon 2E 37
Chalk. Kent 3A 40
Chalk End. Essx 4G 53
Chalk Hill. Glos 3G 49
Challaborough. Devn 4C 8
Challacombe. Devn 2G 19
Challister. Shet 5G 173
Challoch. Dum 3A 110
Challock. Kent 5E 40
Chalton. C Beds
nr. Bedford 5A 64
nr. Luton 3A 52
Chalton. Hants 1F 17
Chalvington. E Sus 5G 27
Champany. Falk 2D 128
Chance Inn. Fife 2F 137
Chancery. Cdgn 3E 57
Chandler's Cross. Herts 1B 38
Chandler's Cross. Worc 2C 48
Chandler's Ford. Hants 4C 24
Chanlockfoot. Dum 4G 117
Channel's End. Bed 5A 64
Channel Tunnel. Kent 2F 29
Channerwick. Shet 9F 173
Chantry. Som 2C 22
Chantry. Suff 1E 55
Chapel. Cumb 1D 102
Chapel. Fife 4E 137

Chapel Allerton – Christleton

Chapel Allerton. *Som* 1H **21**
Chapel Allerton. *W Yor* 1C **92**
Chapel Amble. *Corn* 1D **6**
Chapel Brampton. *Nptn* 4E **63**
Chapelbridge. *Cambs* 1B **64**
Chapel Chorlton. *Staf* 2C **72**
Chapel Cleeve. *Som* 2D **20**
Chapel End. *C Beds* 1A **52**
Chapel-en-le-Frith. *Derbs* 2E **85**
Chapelfield. *Abers* 2G **145**
Chapelgate. *Linc* 3D **76**
Chapel Green. *Warw*
nr. Coventry 2G **61**
nr. Southam 4B **62**
Chapel Haddlesey. *N Yor* 2F **93**
Chapelhall. *N Lan* 3A **128**
Chapel Hill. *Abers* 5H **161**
Chapel Hill. *Linc* 5B **88**
Chapel Hill. *Mon* 5A **48**
Chapelhill. *Per*
nr. Glencarse 1E **136**
nr. Harrietfield 5H **143**
Chapelknowe. *Dum* 2E **112**
Chapel Lawn. *Shrp* 3F **59**
Chapel le Dale. *N Yor* 2G **97**
Chapel Milton. *Derbs* 2E **85**
Chapel of Garioch. *Abers* 1E **152**
Chapel Row. *W Ber* 5D **36**
Chapels. *Cumb* 1B **96**
Chapel St Leonards. *Linc* 3E **89**
Chapel Stile. *Cumb* 4E **102**
Chapelthorpe. *W Yor* 3D **92**
Chapelton. *Ang* 4F **145**
Chapelton. *Devn* 4F **19**
Chapelton. *High*
nr. Grantown-on-Spey 2D **150**
nr. Inverness 3H **157**
Chapelton. *S Lan* 5H **127**
Chapel Town. *Corn* 3C **6**
Chapeltown. *Bkbn* 3F **91**
Chapeltown. *Mor* 1G **151**
Chapeltown. *S Yor* 1A **86**
Chapmanslade. *Wilts* 2D **22**
Chapmans Well. *Devn* 3D **10**
Chapmore End. *Herts* 4D **52**
Chappel. *Essx* 3B **54**
Chard. *Som* 2G **13**
Chard Junction. *Dors* 2G **13**
Chardstock. *Devn* 2G **13**
Charfield. *S Glo* 2C **34**
Charing. *Kent* 1D **28**
Charing Heath. *Kent* 1D **28**
Charing Hill. *Kent* 5D **40**
Charingworth. *Glos* 2H **49**
Charlbury. *Oxon* 4B **50**
Charlcombe. *Bath* 5C **34**
Charlcutt. *Wilts* 4E **35**
Charlecote. *Warw* 5G **61**
Charles. *Devn* 3G **19**
Charlesfield. *Dum* 3C **112**
Charleshill. *Surr* 2G **25**
Charleston. *Ang* 4C **144**
Charleston. *Ren* 3F **127**
Charlestown. *Aber* 3G **153**
Charlestown. *Abers* 2H **161**
Charlestown. *Corn* 3E **7**
Charlestown. *Dors* 5B **14**
Charlestown. *Fife* 1D **128**
Charlestown. *G Man* 4G **91**
Charlestown. *High*
nr. Gairloch 1H **155**
nr. Inverness 4A **158**
Charlestown. *W Yor* 2H **91**
Charlestown of Aberlour
Mor 4G **159**
Charles Tye. *Suff* 5C **66**
Charlesworth. *Derbs* 1E **85**
Charlton. *G Lon* 3F **39**
Charlton. *Hants* 2B **24**
Charlton. *Herts* 3B **52**
Charlton. *Nptn* 2D **50**
Charlton. *Nmbd* 1B **114**
Charlton. *Oxon* 3C **36**
Charlton. *Som*
nr. Radstock 1B **22**
nr. Shepton Mallet 2B **22**
nr. Taunton 4F **21**
Charlton. *Telf* 4H **71**
Charlton. *W Sus* 1G **17**
Charlton. *Wilts*
nr. Malmesbury 3E **35**
nr. Pewsey 1G **23**
nr. Shaftesbury 4E **23**
Charlton. *Worc*
nr. Evesham 1F **49**
nr. Stourport-on-Severn
3C **60**
Charlton Abbots. *Glos* 3F **49**
Charlton Adam. *Som* 4A **22**
Charlton All Saints. *Wilts* 4G **23**
Charlton Down. *Dors* 3B **14**
Charlton Horethorne. *Som* 4B **22**
Charlton Kings. *Glos* 3E **49**
Charlton Mackrell. *Som* 4A **22**
Charlton Marshall. *Dors* 2E **15**
Charlton Musgrove. *Som* 4C **22**
Charlton-on-Otmoor. *Oxon* 4D **50**
Charlton on the Hill. *Dors* 2D **15**
Charlwood. *Hants* 3E **25**
Charlwood. *Surr* 1D **26**
Charlynch. *Som* 3F **21**
Charminster. *Dors* 3B **14**
Charmouth. *Dors* 3G **13**
Charndon. *Buck* 3E **51**
Charney Bassett. *Oxon* 2B **36**
Charnock Green. *Lanc* 3D **90**
Charnock Richard. *Lanc* 3D **90**
Charsfield. *Suff* 5E **67**
The Chart. *Kent* 5F **39**
Chart Corner. *Kent* 5B **40**
Charter Alley. *Hants* 1D **24**
Charterhouse. *Som* 1H **21**
Charterville Allotments
Oxon 4B **50**
Chartham. *Kent* 5F **41**
Chartham Hatch. *Kent* 5F **41**
Chartridge. *Buck* 5H **51**
Chart Sutton. *Kent* 5B **40**
Charvil. *Wok* 4F **37**
Charwelton. *Nptn* 5C **62**
Chase Terrace. *Staf* 5E **73**
Chasetown. *Staf* 5E **73**
Chastleton. *Oxon* 3H **49**
Chasty. *Devn* 2D **10**
Chatburn. *Lanc* 5G **97**
Chatcull. *Staf* 2B **72**
Chatham. *Medw* 4B **40**
Chatham Green. *Essx* 4H **53**
Chathill. *Nmbd* 2F **121**
Chatley. *Worc* 4C **60**
Chattenden. *Medw* 3B **40**
Chatteris. *Cambs* 2C **64**
Chattisham. *Suff* 1D **54**
Chatton. *Nmbd* 2E **121**
Chatwall. *Shrp* 1H **59**
Chaulden. *Herts* 5A **52**
Chaul End. *C Beds* 3A **52**
Chawleigh. *Devn* 1H **11**
Chawley. *Oxon* 5C **50**
Chawston. *Bed* 5A **64**
Chawton. *Hants* 3F **25**
Chaxhill. *Glos* 4C **48**
Cheadle. *G Man* 2C **84**
Cheadle. *Staf* 1E **73**
Cheadle Hulme. *G Man* 2C **84**
Cheam. *G Lon* 4D **38**
Cheapside. *Wind* 4A **38**
Chearsley. *Buck* 4F **51**
Chebsey. *Staf* 3C **72**
Checkendon. *Oxon* 3E **37**
Checkley. *Ches E* 1B **72**
Checkley. *Here* 2A **48**
Checkley. *Staf* 2E **73**
Chedburgh. *Suff* 5G **65**
Cheddar. *Som* 1H **21**
Cheddington. *Buck* 4H **51**
Cheddleton. *Staf* 5D **84**
Cheddon Fitzpaine. *Som* 4F **21**
Chedglow. *Wilts* 2E **35**
Chedgrave. *Norf* 1F **67**
Chedington. *Dors* 2H **13**
Chediston. *Suff* 3F **67**
Chediston Green. *Suff* 3F **67**
Chedworth. *Glos* 4F **49**
Chedzoy. *Som* 3G **21**
Cheeseman's Green. *Kent* 2E **29**
Cheetham Hill. *G Man* 4G **91**
Cheglinch. *Devn* 2F **19**
Cheldon. *Devn* 1H **11**
Chelford. *Ches E* 3C **84**
Chellaston. *Derb* 2A **74**
Chellington. *Bed* 5G **63**
Chelmarsh. *Shrp* 2B **60**
Chelmick. *Shrp* 1G **59**
Chelmondiston. *Suff* 2F **55**
Chelmorton. *Derbs* 4F **85**
Chelmsford. *Essx* 5H **53**
Chelsea. *G Lon* 3D **38**
Chelsfield. *G Lon* 4F **39**
Chelsham. *Surr* 5E **39**
Chelston. *Som* 4E **21**
Chelsworth. *Suff* 1C **54**
Cheltenham. *Glos* 3E **49**
Chelveston. *Nptn* 4G **63**
Chelvey. *N Som* 5H **33**
Chelwood. *Bath* 5B **34**
Chelwood Common. *E Sus* 3F **27**
Chelwood Gate. *E Sus* 3F **27**
Chelworth. *Wilts* 2E **35**
Chelworth Lower Green
Wilts 2F **35**
Chelworth Upper Green
Wilts 2F **35**
Chelynch. *Som* 2B **22**
Cheney Longville. *Shrp* 2G **59**
Chenies. *Buck* 1B **38**
Chepstow. *Mon* 2A **34**
Chequerfield. *W Yor* 2E **93**
Chequers Corner. *Norf* 5D **77**
Cherhill. *Wilts* 4F **35**
Cherington. *Glos* 2E **35**
Cherington. *Warw* 2A **50**
Cheriton. *Devn* 2H **19**
Cheriton. *Hants* 4D **24**
Cheriton. *Kent* 2G **29**
Cheriton. *Pemb* 5D **43**
Cheriton. *Swan* 3D **30**
Cheriton Bishop. *Devn* 3A **12**
Cheriton Cross. *Devn* 3A **12**
Cheriton Fitzpaine. *Devn* 2B **12**
Cherrington. *Telf* 3A **72**
Cherrybank. *Per* 1D **136**
Cherry Burton. *E Yor* 5D **101**
Cherry Green. *Herts* 3D **52**
Cherry Hinton. *Cambs* 5D **65**
Cherry Willingham. *Linc* 3H **87**
Chertsey. *Surr* 4B **38**
Cheselbourne. *Dors* 3C **14**
Chesham. *Buck* 5H **51**
Chesham. *G Man* 3G **91**
Chesham Bois. *Buck* 1A **38**
Cheshunt. *Herts* 5D **52**
Cheslyn Hay. *Staf* 5D **73**
Chessetts Wood. *Warw* 3F **61**
Chessington. *G Lon* 4C **38**
Chester. *Ches W* 4G **83**
Chesterblade. *Som* 2B **22**
Chesterfield. *Derbs* 3A **86**
Chesterfield. *Staf* 5F **73**
Chesterhope. *Nmbd* 1B **114**
Chester-le-Street. *Dur* 4F **115**
Chester Moor. *Dur* 5F **115**
Chesters. *Bord* 3A **120**
Chesterton. *Cambs*
nr. Cambridge 4D **64**
nr. Peterborough 1A **64**
Chesterton. *Glos* 5F **49**
Chesterton. *Oxon* 3D **50**
Chesterton. *Shrp* 1B **60**
Chesterton. *Staf* 1C **72**
Chesterton Green. *Warw* 5H **61**
Chesterwood. *Nmbd* 3B **114**
Chestfield. *Kent* 4F **41**
Cheston. *Devn* 3C **8**
Cheswardine. *Shrp* 2B **72**
Cheswell. *Telf* 4B **72**
Cheswick. *Nmbd* 5G **131**
Cheswick Green. *W Mid* 3F **61**
Chetnole. *Dors* 2B **14**
Chettiscombe. *Devn* 1C **12**
Chettisham. *Cambs* 2E **65**
Chettle. *Dors* 1E **15**
Chetton. *Shrp* 1A **60**
Chetwode. *Buck* 3E **51**
Chetwynd Aston. *Telf* 4B **72**
Cheveley. *Cambs* 4F **65**
Chevening. *Kent* 5F **39**
Chevington. *Suff* 5G **65**
Chevithorne. *Devn* 1C **12**
Chew Magna. *Bath* 5A **34**
Chew Moor. *G Man* 4E **91**
Chew Stoke. *Bath* 5A **34**
Chewton Keynsham. *Bath* 5B **34**
Chewton Mendip. *Som* 1A **22**
Chichacott. *Devn* 3G **11**
Chicheley. *Mil* 1H **51**
Chichester. *W Sus* 2G **17**
Chickerell. *Dors* 4B **14**
Chickering. *Suff* 3E **66**
Chicklade. *Wilts* 3E **23**
Chicksands. *C Beds* 2B **52**
Chickward. *Here* 5E **59**
Chidden. *Hants* 1E **17**
Chiddingfold. *Surr* 2A **26**
Chiddingly. *E Sus* 4G **27**
Chiddingstone. *Kent* 1G **27**
Chiddingstone Causeway
Kent 1G **27**
Chiddingstone Hoath. *Kent* 1F **27**
Chideock. *Dors* 3H **13**
Chidgley. *Som* 3D **20**
Chidham. *W Sus* 2F **17**
Chieveley. *W Ber* 4C **36**
Chignal St James. *Essx* 5G **53**
Chignal Smealy. *Essx* 4G **53**
Chigwell. *Essx* 1F **39**
Chigwell Row. *Essx* 1F **39**
Chilbolton. *Hants* 2B **24**
Chilcomb. *Hants* 4D **24**
Chilcombe. *Dors* 3A **14**
Chilcompton. *Som* 1B **22**
Chilcote. *Leics* 4G **73**
Childer Thornton. *Ches W* 3F **83**
Child Okeford. *Dors* 1D **14**
Childrey. *Oxon* 3B **36**
Child's Ercall. *Shrp* 3A **72**
Childswickham. *Worc* 2F **49**
Childwall. *Mers* 2G **83**
Childwick Green. *Herts* 4B **52**
Chilfrome. *Dors* 3A **14**
Chilgrove. *W Sus* 1G **17**
Chilham. *Kent* 5E **41**
Chilhampton. *Wilts* 3F **23**
Chilla. *Devn* 2E **11**
Chilland. *Hants* 3D **24**
Chillaton. *Devn* 4E **11**
Chillenden. *Kent* 5G **41**
Chillerton. *IOW* 4C **16**
Chillesford. *Suff* 5F **67**
Chillingham. *Nmbd* 2E **121**
Chillington. *Devn* 4D **9**
Chillington. *Som* 1G **13**
Chilmark. *Wilts* 3E **23**
Chilmington Green. *Kent* 1D **28**
Chilson. *Oxon* 4B **50**
Chilsworthy. *Corn* 5E **11**
Chilsworthy. *Devn* 2D **10**
Chiltern Green. *C Beds* 4B **52**
Chilthorne Domer. *Som* 1A **14**
Chilton. *Buck* 4E **51**
Chilton. *Devn* 2B **12**
Chilton. *Dur* 2F **105**
Chilton. *Oxon* 3C **36**
Chilton Candover. *Hants* 2D **24**
Chilton Cantelo. *Som* 4A **22**
Chilton Foliat. *Wilts* 4B **36**
Chilton Lane. *Dur* 1A **106**
Chilton Polden. *Som* 3G **21**
Chilton Street. *Suff* 1A **54**
Chilton Trinity. *Som* 3F **21**
Chilwell. *Notts* 2C **74**
Chilworth. *Hants* 1C **16**
Chilworth. *Surr* 1B **26**
Chimney. *Oxon* 5B **50**
Chimney Street. *Suff* 1H **53**
Chineham. *Hants* 1E **25**
Chingford. *G Lon* 1E **39**
Chinley. *Derbs* 2E **85**
Chinnor. *Oxon* 5F **51**
Chipley. *Som* 4E **20**
Chipnall. *Shrp* 2B **72**
Chippenham. *Cambs* 4F **65**
Chippenham. *Wilts* 4E **35**
Chipperfield. *Herts* 5A **52**
Chipping. *Herts* 2D **52**
Chipping. *Lanc* 5F **97**
Chipping Campden. *Glos* 2G **49**
Chipping Hill. *Essx* 4B **54**
Chipping Norton. *Oxon* 3B **50**
Chipping Ongar. *Essx* 5F **53**
Chipping Sodbury. *S Glo* 3C **34**
Chipping Warden. *Nptn* 1C **50**
Chipstable. *Som* 4D **20**
Chipstead. *Kent* 5G **39**
Chipstead. *Surr* 5D **38**
Chirbury. *Shrp* 1E **59**
Chirk. *Wrex* 2E **71**
Chirmorie. *S Ayr* 2H **109**
Chirnside. *Bord* 4E **131**
Chirnsidebridge. *Bord* 4E **131**
Chirton. *Wilts* 1F **23**
Chisbridge Cross. *Buck* 3G **37**
Chisbury. *Wilts* 5A **36**
Chiselborough. *Som* 1H **13**
Chiseldon. *Swin* 4G **35**
Chiselhampton. *Oxon* 2D **36**
Chiserley. *W Yor* 2A **92**
Chislehurst. *G Lon* 3F **39**
Chislet. *Kent* 4G **41**
Chiswell. *Dors* 5B **14**
Chiswell Green. *Herts* 5B **52**
Chiswick. *G Lon* 3D **38**
Chisworth. *Derbs* 1D **85**
Chitcombe. *E Sus* 3C **28**
Chithurst. *W Sus* 4G **25**
Chittering. *Cambs* 4D **65**
Chitterley. *Devn* 2C **12**
Chitterne. *Wilts* 2E **23**
Chittlehamholt. *Devn* 4G **19**
Chittlehampton. *Devn* 4G **19**
Chittoe. *Wilts* 5E **35**
Chivelstone. *Devn* 5D **9**
Chivenor. *Devn* 3F **19**
Chobham. *Surr* 4A **38**
Cholderton. *Wilts* 2H **23**
Cholesbury. *Buck* 5H **51**
Chollerford. *Nmbd* 2C **114**
Chollerton. *Nmbd* 2C **114**
Cholsey. *Oxon* 3D **36**
Cholstrey. *Here* 5G **59**
Chop Gate. *N Yor* 5C **106**
Choppington. *Nmbd* 1F **115**
Chopwell. *Tyne* 4E **115**
Chorley. *Ches E* 5H **83**
Chorley. *Lanc* 3D **90**
Chorley. *Shrp* 2A **60**
Chorley. *Staf* 4E **73**
Chorleywood. *Herts* 1B **38**
Chorlton. *Ches E* 5B **84**
Chorlton-cum-Hardy
G Man 1C **84**
Chorlton Lane. *Ches W* 1G **71**
Choulton. *Shrp* 2F **59**
Chrishall. *Essx* 2E **53**
Christchurch. *Cambs* 1D **65**
Christchurch. *Dors* 3G **15**
Christchurch. *Glos* 4A **48**
Christian Malford. *Wilts* 4E **35**
Christleton. *Ches W* 4G **83**

Cloughton Newlands – Coniston Cold

Cloughton Newlands N Yor 5H 107
Clousta. Shet 6E 173
Clouston. Orkn 6B 172
Clova. Abers 1B 152
Clova. Ang 1C 144
Clovelly. Devn 4D 18
Clovenfords. Bord 1G 119
Clovenstone. Abers 2E 153
Clovullin. High 2E 141
Clowne. Derbs 3B 86
Clows Top. Worc 3B 60
Cloy. Wrex 1F 71
Cluanie Inn. High 2C 148
Cluanie Lodge. High 2C 148
Cluddley. Telf 4A 72
Clun. Shrp 2F 59
Y Clun. Neat 5B 46
Clunas. High 4C 158
Clunbury. Shrp 2F 59
Clunderwen. Pemb 3F 43
Clune. High 1B 150
Clunes. High 5E 148
Clungunford. Shrp 3F 59
Clunie. Per 4A 144
Clunton. Shrp 2F 59
Cluny. Fife 4E 137
Clutton. Bath 1B 22
Clutton. Ches W 5G 83
Clwt-y-bont. Gwyn 4E 81
Clwydfagwyr. Mer T 5D 46
Clydach. Mon 4F 47
Clydach. Swan 5G 45
Clydach Vale. Rhon 2C 32
Clydebank. W Dun 3G 127
Clydey. Pemb 1G 43
Clyffe Pypard. Wilts 4F 35
Clynder. Arg 1D 126
Clyne. Neat 5B 46
Clynelish. High 3F 165
Clynnog-fawr. Gwyn 1D 68
Clyro. Powy 1F 47
Clyst Honiton. Devn 3C 12
Clyst Hydon. Devn 2D 12
Clyst St George. Devn 4C 12
Clyst St Lawrence. Devn 2D 12
Clyst St Mary. Devn 3C 12
Clyth. High 5E 169
Cnip. W Isl 4C 171
Cnoc Amhlaigh. W Isl 4H 171
Cnwcau. Pemb 1C 44
Cnwch Coch. Cdgn 3F 57
Coad's Green. Corn 5C 10
Coal Aston. Derbs 3A 86
Coalbrookdale. Telf 5A 72
Coalbrookvale. Blae 5E 47
Coalburn. S Lan 1H 117
Coalburns. Tyne 3E 115
Coalcleugh. Nmbd 5B 114
Coaley. Glos 5C 48
Coalford. Abers 4F 153
Coalhall. E Ayr 3D 116
Coalhill. Essx 1B 40
Coalisland. M Ulst 4E 175
Coalpit Heath. S Glo 3B 34
Coal Pool. W Mid 5E 73
Coalport. Telf 5B 72
Coalsnaughton. Clac 4B 136
Coaltown of Balgonie. Fife 4F 137
Coaltown of Wemyss. Fife 4F 137
Coalville. Leics 4B 74
Coalway. Glos 4A 48
Coanwood. Nmbd 4H 113
Coat. Som 4H 21
Coatbridge. N Lan 3A 128
Coatdyke. N Lan 3A 128
Coate. Swin 3G 35
Coate. Wilts 5F 35
Coates. Cambs 1C 64
Coates. Glos 5E 49
Coates. Linc 2G 87
Coates. W Sus 4A 26
Coatham. Red C 2C 106
Coatham Mundeville. Darl 2F 105
Cobbaton. Devn 4G 19
Coberley. Glos 4E 49
Cobhall Common. Here 2H 47
Cobham. Kent 4A 40
Cobham. Surr 5C 38
Cobnash. Here 4G 59
Coburg. Devn 5B 12
Cockayne. N Yor 5D 106
Cockayne Hatley. C Beds 1C 52
Cock Bank. Wrex 1F 71
Cock Bridge. Abers 3G 151
Cockburnspath. Bord 2D 130
Cock Clarks. Essx 5B 54
Cockenzie and Port Seton E Lot 2H 129
Cockerham. Lanc 4D 96
Cockermouth. Cumb 1C 102
Cockernhoe. Herts 3B 52
Cockfield. Dur 2E 105
Cockfield. Suff 5B 66
Cockfosters. G Lon 1D 39
Cock Gate. Here 4G 59
Cock Green. Essx 4G 53
Cocking. W Sus 1G 17
Cocking Causeway. W Sus 1G 17
Cockington. Torb 2E 9
Cocklake. Som 2H 21
Cocklaw. Abers 4H 161
Cocklaw. Nmbd 2C 114
Cockley Beck. Cumb 4D 102
Cockley Cley. Norf 5G 77
Cockmuir. Abers 3G 161
Cockpole Green. Wok 3F 37
Cockshutford. Shrp 2H 59
Cockshutt. Shrp 3G 71
Cockthorpe. Norf 1B 78
Cockwood. Devn 4C 12
Cockyard. Derbs 3E 85
Cockyard. Here 2H 47
Codda. Corn 5B 10
Coddenham. Suff 5D 66
Coddenham Green. Suff 5D 66
Coddington. Ches W 5G 83
Coddington. Here 1C 48
Coddington. Notts 5F 87
Codford. Wilts 3E 23
Codicote. Herts 4C 52
Codmore Hill. W Sus 3B 26
Codnor. Derbs 1B 74
Codrington. S Glo 4C 34
Codsall. Staf 5C 72
Codsall Wood. Staf 5C 72
Coed Duon. Cphy 2E 33
Coedely. Rhon 3D 32
Coedglasson. Powy 4C 58
Coedkernew. Newp 3F 33
Coed Morgan. Mon 4G 47
Coedpoeth. Wrex 5E 83
Coedway. Powy 4F 71
Coed-y-bryn. Cdgn 1D 44
Coed-y-paen. Mon 2G 33
Coed Ystumgwern. Gwyn 3E 69
Coelbren. Powy 4B 46
Coffinswell. Devn 2E 9
Cofton Hackett. Worc 3E 61
Cogan. V Glam 4E 33
Cogenhoe. Nptn 4F 63
Cogges. Oxon 5B 50
Coggeshall. Essx 3B 54
Coggeshall Hamlet. Essx 3B 54
Coggins Mill. E Sus 3G 27
Coignafearn Lodge. High 2A 150
Coig Peighinnean. W Isl 1H 171
Coig Peighinnean Bhuirgh W Isl 2G 171
Coilleag. W Isl 7C 170
Coillemore. High 1A 158
Coillore. High 5C 154
Coire an Fhuarain. W Isl 4E 171
Coity. B'end 3C 32
Cokhay Green. Derbs 3G 73
Col. W Isl 3G 171
Colaboll. High 2C 164
Colan. Corn 2C 6
Colaton Raleigh. Devn 4D 12
Colbost. High 4B 154
Colburn. N Yor 5E 105
Colby. Cumb 2H 103
Colby. IOM 4B 108
Colby. Norf 2E 78
Colchester. Essx 3D 54
Cold Ash. W Ber 5D 36
Cold Ashby. Nptn 3D 62
Cold Ashton. S Glo 4C 34
Cold Aston. Glos 4G 49
Coldbackie. High 3G 167
Cold Blow. Pemb 3F 43
Cold Brayfield. Mil 5G 63
Cold Cotes. N Yor 2G 97
Coldean. Brig 5E 27
Coldeast. Devn 5B 12
Colden. W Yor 2H 91
Colden Common. Hants 4C 24
Coldfair Green. Suff 4G 67
Coldham. Cambs 5D 76
Coldham. Staf 5C 72
Cold Hanworth. Linc 2H 87
Cold Harbour. Dors 3E 15
Coldharbour. Corn 4B 6
Coldharbour. Glos 5A 48
Coldharbour. Kent 5G 39
Coldharbour. Surr 1C 26
Cold Hatton. Telf 3A 72
Cold Hatton Heath. Telf 3A 72
Cold Hesledon. Dur 5H 115
Cold Hiendley. W Yor 3D 92
Cold Higham. Nptn 5D 62
Coldingham. Bord 3F 131
Cold Kirby. N Yor 1H 99
Coldmeece. Staf 2C 72
Cold Northcott. Corn 4C 10
Cold Norton. Essx 5B 54
Cold Overton. Leics 4F 75
Coldrain. Per 3C 136
Coldred. Kent 1G 29
Coldridge. Devn 2G 11
Cold Row. Lanc 5C 96
Coldstream. Bord 5E 131
Coldwaltham. W Sus 4B 26
Coldwell. Here 2H 47
Coldwells. Abers 5H 161
Coldwells Croft. Abers 1C 152
Cole. Shet 5E 173
Cole. Som 3B 22
Colebatch. Shrp 2F 59
Colebrook. Devn 2D 12
Colebrooke. Devn 3A 12
Coleburn. Mor 3G 159
Coleby. Linc 4G 87
Coleby. N Lin 3B 94
Cole End. Warw 2G 61
Coleford. Devn 2A 12
Coleford. Glos 4A 48
Coleford. Som 2B 22
Colegate End. Norf 2D 66
Cole Green. Herts 4C 52
Cole Henley. Hants 1C 24
Colehill. Dors 2F 15
Coleman Green. Herts 4B 52
Coleman's Hatch. E Sus 2F 27
Colemere. Shrp 2G 71
Colemore. Hants 3F 25
Colemore Green. Shrp 1B 60
Coleorton. Leics 4B 74
Coleraine. Caus 1E 175
Colerne. Wilts 4D 34
Colesbourne. Glos 4F 49
Colesden. Bed 5A 64
Coles Green. Worc 5B 60
Coleshill. Buck 1A 38
Coleshill. Oxon 2H 35
Coleshill. Warw 2G 61
Colestocks. Devn 2D 12
Colethrop. Glos 4D 48
Coley. Bath 1A 22
Colgate. W Sus 2D 26
Colinsburgh. Fife 3G 137
Colinton. Edin 3F 129
Colintraive. Arg 2B 126
Colkirk. Norf 3B 78
Collace. Per 5B 144
Collam. W Isl 8D 171
Collaton. Devn 5D 8
Collaton St Mary. Torb 2E 9
College of Roseisle. Mor 2F 159
Collessie. Fife 2E 137
Collier Row. G Lon 1F 39
Colliers End. Herts 3D 52
Collier Street. Kent 1B 28
Colliery Row. Tyne 5G 115
Collieston. Abers 1H 153
Collin. Dum 2B 112
Collingbourne Ducis. Wilts 1H 23
Collingbourne Kingston Wilts 1H 23
Collingham. Notts 4F 87
Collingham. W Yor 5F 99
Collingtree. Nptn 5E 63
Collins Green. Warr 1H 83
Collins Green. Worc 5B 60
Colliston. Ang 4F 145
Colliton. Devn 2D 12
Collydean. Fife 3E 137
Collyweston. Nptn 5G 75
Colmonell. S Ayr 1G 109
Colmworth. Bed 5A 64
Colnbrook. Slo 3B 38
Colne. Cambs 3C 64
Colne. Lanc 5A 98
Colne Engaine. Essx 2B 54
Colney. Norf 5D 78
Colney Heath. Herts 5C 52
Colney Street. Herts 5B 52
Coln Rogers. Glos 5F 49
Coln St Aldwyns. Glos 5G 49
Coln St Dennis. Glos 4F 49
Colpitts Grange. Nmbd 4C 114
Colpy. Abers 5D 160
Colscott. Devn 1D 10
Colsterdale. N Yor 1D 98
Colsterworth. Linc 3G 75
Colston Bassett. Notts 2E 74
Colstoun House. E Lot 2B 130
Coltfield. Mor 2F 159
Colthouse. Cumb 5E 103
Coltishall. Norf 4E 79
Coltness. N Lan 4B 128
Colton. Cumb 1C 96
Colton. Norf 5D 78
Colton. N Yor 5H 99
Colton. Staf 3E 73
Colton. W Yor 1D 92
Colt's Hill. Kent 1H 27
Col Uarach. W Isl 4G 171
Colvend. Dum 4F 111
Colvister. Shet 2G 173
Colwall. Here 1C 48
Colwall Green. Here 1C 48
Colwell. Nmbd 2C 114
Colwich. Staf 3E 73
Colwick. Notts 1D 74
Colwinston. V Glam 4C 32
Colworth. W Sus 5A 26
Colwyn Bay. Cnwy 3A 82
Colyford. Devn 3F 13
Colyton. Devn 3F 13
Combe. Devn 2D 8
Combe. Here 4F 59
Combe. Oxon 4C 50
Combe. W Ber 5B 36
Combe Almer. Dors 3E 15
Combebow. Devn 4E 11
Combe Down. Bath 5C 34
Combe Fishacre. Devn 2E 9
Combe Florey. Som 3E 21
Combe Hay. Bath 5C 34
Combeinteignhead. Devn 5C 12
Combe Martin. Devn 2F 19
Combe Moor. Here 4F 59
Comber. Ards 4H 175
Combe Raleigh. Devn 2E 13
Comberbach. Ches W 3A 84
Comberford. Staf 5F 73
Comberton. Cambs 5C 64
Comberton. Here 4G 59
Combe St Nicholas. Som 1G 13
Combpyne. Devn 3F 13
Combridge. Staf 2E 73
Combrook. Warw 5H 61
Combs. Derbs 3E 85
Combs. Suff 5C 66
Combs Ford. Suff 5C 66
Combwich. Som 2F 21
Comers. Abers 3D 152
Comhampton. Worc 4C 60
Comins Coch. Cdgn 2F 57
Comley. Shrp 1G 59
Commercial End. Cambs 4E 65
Commins. Powy 3D 70
Commins Coch. Powy 5H 69
The Common. Wilts
nr. Salisbury 3H 23
nr. Swindon 3F 35
Commondale. N Yor 3D 106
Common End. Cumb 2B 102
Common Hill. Here 2A 48
Common Moor. Corn 2G 7
Common Side. Derbs 3H 85
Commonside. Ches W 3H 83
Commonside. Derbs 1G 73
Compstall. G Man 1D 84
Compton. Devn 2E 9
Compton. Hants 4C 24
Compton. Staf 2C 60
Compton. Surr 1A 26
Compton. W Ber 4D 36
Compton. W Sus 1F 17
Compton. Wilts 1G 23
Compton Abbas. Dors 1D 15
Compton Abdale. Glos 4F 49
Compton Bassett. Wilts 4F 35
Compton Beauchamp Oxon 3A 36
Compton Bishop. Som 1G 21
Compton Chamberlayne Wilts 4F 23
Compton Dando. Bath 5B 34
Compton Dundon. Som 3H 21
Compton Greenfield. S Glo 3A 34
Compton Martin. Bath 1A 22
Compton Pauncefoot. Som 4B 22
Compton Valence. Dors 3A 14
Comrie. Fife 1D 128
Comrie. Per 1G 135
Conaglen. High 2E 141
Conchra. Arg 1B 126
Conchra. High 1A 148
Conder Green. Lanc 4D 96
Conderton. Worc 2E 49
Condicote. Glos 3G 49
Condorrat. N Lan 2A 128
Condover. Shrp 5G 71
Coneyhurst. W Sus 3C 26
Coneysthorpe. N Yor 2B 100
Coneythorpe. N Yor 4F 99
Coney Weston. Suff 3B 66
Conford. Hants 3G 25
Congdon's Shop. Corn 5C 10
Congerstone. Leics 5A 74
Congham. Norf 3G 77
Congleton. Ches E 4C 84
Congl-y-wal. Gwyn 1G 69
Congresbury. N Som 5H 33
Congreve. Staf 4D 72
Conham. S Glo 4B 34
Conicavel. Mor 3D 159
Coningsby. Linc 5B 88
Conington. Cambs
nr. Fenstanton 4C 64
nr. Sawtry 2A 64
Conisbrough. S Yor 1C 86
Conisby. Arg 3A 124
Conisholme. Linc 1D 88
Coniston. Cumb 5E 102
Coniston. E Yor 1E 95
Coniston Cold. N Yor 4B 98

Craigellachie – Crows-an-wra

Craigellachie. Mor 4G 159
Craigend. Per 1D 136
Craigendoran. Arg 1E 126
Craigends. Ren 3F 127
Craigenputtock. Dum 1E 111
Craigens. E Ayr 3E 117
Craighall. Edin 2E 129
Craighead. Fife 2H 137
Craighouse. Arg 3D 124
Craigie. Abers 2G 153
Craigie. D'dee 5D 144
Craigie. Per
nr. Blairgowrie 4A 144
nr. Perth 1D 136
Craigie. S Ayr 1D 116
Craigielaw. E Lot 2A 130
Craiglemine. Dum 5B 110
Craig-llwyn. Shrp 3E 71
Craiglockhart. Edin 2F 129
Craig Lodge. Arg 2B 126
Craigmalloch. E Ayr 5D 117
Craigmaud. Abers 3F 161
Craigmill. Stir 4H 135
Craigmillar. Edin 2F 129
Craigmore. Arg 3C 126
Craigmuie. Dum 1E 111
Craignair. Dum 3F 111
Craignant. Shrp 2E 71
Craigneuk. N Lan
nr. Airdrie 3A 128
nr. Motherwell 4A 128
Craignure. Arg 5B 140
Craigo. Ang 2F 145
Craigrory. High 4A 158
Craigrothie. Fife 2F 137
Craigs. Dum 2D 112
The Craigs. High 4B 164
Craigshill. W Lot 3D 128
Craigton. Aber 3F 153
Craigton. Abers 3E 152
Craigton. Ang
nr. Carnoustie 5E 145
nr. Kirriemuir 3C 144
Craigton. High 4A 158
Craigtown. High 3A 168
Craig-y-Duke. Neat 5H 45
Craig-y-nos. Powy 4B 46
Craik. Bord 4F 119
Crail. Fife 3H 137
Crailing. Bord 2A 120
Crailinghall. Bord 2A 120
Crakehill. N Yor 2G 99
Crakemarsh. Staf 2E 73
Crambe. N Yor 3B 100
Crambeck. N Yor 3B 100
Cramlington. Nmbd 2F 115
Cramond. Edin 2E 129
Cramond Bridge. Edin 2E 129
Cranage. Ches E 4B 84
Cranberry. Staf 2C 72
Cranborne. Dors 1F 15
Cranbourne. Brac 3A 38
Cranbrook. Devn 3D 12
Cranbrook. Kent 2B 28
Cranbrook Common. Kent 2B 28
Crane Moor. S Yor 4D 92
Crane's Corner. Norf 4B 78
Cranfield. C Beds 1H 51
Cranford. G Lon 3C 38
Cranford St Andrew. Nptn 3G 63
Cranford St John. Nptn 3G 63
Cranham. Glos 4D 49
Cranham. G Lon 2G 39
Crank. Mers 1H 83
Cranleigh. Surr 2B 26
Cranley. Suff 3D 66
Cranloch. Mor 3G 159
Cranmer Green. Suff 3C 66
Cranmore. IOW 3C 16
Cranmore. Linc 5A 76
Crannich. Arg 4G 139
Crannoch. Mor 3B 160
Cranoe. Leics 1E 63
Cransford. Suff 4F 67
Cranshaws. Bord 3C 130
Cranstal. IOM 1D 108
Crantock. Corn 2B 6
Cranwell. Linc 1H 75
Cranwich. Norf 1G 65
Cranworth. Norf 5B 78
Craobh Haven. Arg 3E 133
Craobhnaclag. High 4G 157
Crapstone. Devn 2B 8
Crarae. Arg 4G 133
Crask. High
nr. Bettyhill 2H 167
nr. Lairg 1C 164
Crask of Aigas. High 4G 157
Craster. Nmbd 2G 121
Craswall. Here 2F 47
Cratfield. Suff 3F 67
Crathes. Abers 4E 153
Crathie. Abers 4G 151
Crathie. High 4H 149
Crathorne. N Yor 4B 106
Craven Arms. Shrp 2G 59
Crawcrook. Tyne 3E 115
Crawford. Lanc 4C 90
Crawford. S Lan 2B 118
Crawforddyke. S Lan 4B 128
Crawfordjohn. S Lan 2A 118
Crawick. Dum 3G 117
Crawley. Devn 2F 13
Crawley. Hants 3C 24
Crawley. Oxon 4B 50
Crawley. W Sus 2D 26
Crawley Down. W Sus 2E 27
Crawley End. Essx 1E 53
Crawley Side. Dur 5C 114
Crawshawbooth. Lanc 2G 91
Crawton. Abers 5F 153
Cray. N Yor 2B 98
Cray. Per 2A 144
Crayford. G Lon 3G 39
Crayke. N Yor 2H 99
Craymere Beck. Norf 2C 78
Crays Hill. Essx 1B 40
Cray's Pond. Oxon 3E 37
Crazies Hill. Wok 3F 37
Creacombe. Devn 1B 12
Creagan. Arg 4D 140
Creag Aoil. High 1F 141
Creag Ghoraidh. W Isl 4C 170
Creaguaineach Lodge
High 2H 141
Creamore Bank. Shrp 2H 71
Creaton. Nptn 3E 62
Creca. Dum 2D 112
Credenhill. Here 1H 47
Crediton. Devn 2B 12
Creebridge. Dum 3B 110
Creech. Dors 4E 15
Creech Heathfield. Som 4F 21
Creech St Michael. Som 4F 21
Creed. Corn 4D 6
Creekmoor. Pool 3E 15
Creekmouth. G Lon 2F 39
Creeting St Mary. Suff 5C 66
Creeting St Peter. Suff 5C 66
Creeton. Linc 3H 75
Creetown. Dum 4B 110
Creggans. Arg 3H 133
Cregneash. IOM 5A 108
Cregrina. Powy 5D 58
Creich. Arg 2B 132
Creich. Fife 1F 137
Creighton. Staf 2E 73
Creigiau. Card 3D 32
Cremyll. Corn 3A 8
Crendell. Dors 1F 15
Crepkill. High 4D 154
Cressage. Shrp 5H 71
Cressbrook. Derbs 3F 85
Cresselly. Pemb 4E 43
Cressing. Essx 3A 54
Cresswell. Nmbd 5G 121
Cresswell. Staf 2D 73
Cresswell Quay. Pemb 4E 43
Creswell. Derbs 3C 86
Creswell Green. Staf 4E 73
Cretingham. Suff 4E 67
Crewe. Ches E 5B 84
Crewe-by-Farndon. Ches W 5G 83
Crewgreen. Powy 4F 71
Crewkerne. Som 2H 13
Crews Hill. G Lon 5D 52
Crewton. Derb 2A 74
Crianlarich. Stir 1C 134
Cribbs Causeway. S Glo 3A 34
Cribyn. Cdgn 5E 57
Criccieth. Gwyn 2D 69
Crich. Derbs 5A 86
Crichton. Midl 3G 129
Crick. Mon 2H 33
Crick. Nptn 3C 62
Crickadarn. Powy 1D 46
Cricket Hill. Hants 5G 37
Cricket Malherbie. Som 1G 13
Cricket St Thomas. Som 2G 13
Crickham. Som 2H 21
Crickheath. Shrp 3E 71
Crickhowell. Powy 4F 47
Cricklade. Wilts 2G 35
Cricklewood. G Lon 2D 38
Cridling Stubbs. N Yor 2F 93
Crieff. Per 1A 136
Criftins. Shrp 2F 71
Criggion. Powy 4E 71
Crigglestone. W Yor 3D 92
Crimchard. Som 2G 13
Crimdon Park. Dur 1B 106
Crimond. Abers 3H 161
Crimonmogate. Abers 3H 161
Crimplesham. Norf 5F 77
Crimscote. Warw 1H 49
Crinan. Arg 4E 133
Cringleford. Norf 5D 78
Crinow. Pemb 3F 43
Cripplesease. Corn 3C 4
Cripplestyle. Dors 1F 15
Cripp's Corner. E Sus 3B 28
Croanford. Corn 5A 10
Crockenhill. Kent 4G 39
Crocker End. Oxon 3F 37
Crockerhill. Hants 2D 16
Crockernwell. Devn 3A 12
Crocker's Ash. Here 4A 48
Crockerton. Wilts 2D 22
Crocketford. Dum 2F 111
Crockey Hill. York 5A 100
Crockham Hill. Kent 5F 39
Crockhurst Street. Kent 1H 27
Crockleford Heath. Essx 3D 54
Croeserw. Neat 2B 32
Croes-Goch. Pemb 1C 42
Croes Hywel. Mon 4G 47
Croes-lan. Cdgn 1D 45
Croesor. Gwyn 1F 69
Croesoswallt. Shrp 3E 71
Croesyceiliog. Carm 4E 45
Croesyceiliog. Torf 2G 33
Croes-y-mwyalch. Torf 2G 33
Croesywaun. Gwyn 5E 81
Croford. Som 4E 20
Croft. Leics 1C 62
Croft. Linc 4E 89
Croft. Warr 1A 84
Croftamie. Stir 1F 127
Croftfoot. Glas 3G 127
Croftmill. Per 5F 143
Crofton. Cumb 4E 112
Crofton. W Yor 3D 93
Crofton. Wilts 5A 36
Croft-on-Tees. N Yor 4F 105
Crofts. Dum 2E 111
Crofts of Benachielt. High 5D 169
Crofts of Dipple. Mor 3H 159
Crofty. Swan 3E 31
Croggan. Arg 1E 132
Croglin. Cumb 5G 113
Croich. High 4B 164
Croick. High 3A 168
Croig. Arg 3E 139
Cromarty. High 2B 158
Crombie. Fife 1D 128
Cromdale. High 1E 151
Cromer. Herts 3C 52
Cromer. Norf 1E 78
Cromford. Derbs 5G 85
Cromhall. S Glo 2B 34
Cromor. W Isl 5G 171
Cromra. High 5H 149
Cromwell. Notts 4E 87
Cronberry. E Ayr 2F 117
Crondall. Hants 2F 25
The Cronk. IOM 2C 108
Cronk-y-Voddy. IOM 3C 108
Cronton. Mers 2G 83
Crook. Cumb 5F 103
Crook. Dur 1E 105
Crookdake. Cumb 5C 112
Crooke. G Man 4D 90
Crookedholm. E Ayr 1D 116
Crooked Soley. Wilts 4B 36
Crookes. S Yor 2H 85
Crookgate Bank. Dur 4E 115
Crookhall. Dur 4E 115
Crookham. Nmbd 1D 120
Crookham. W Ber 5D 36
Crookham Village. Hants 1F 25
Crooklands. Cumb 1E 97
Crook of Devon. Per 3C 136
Crookston. Glas 3G 127
Cropredy. Oxon 1C 50
Cropston. Leics 4C 74
Cropthorne. Worc 1E 49
Cropton. N Yor 1B 100
Cropwell Bishop. Notts 2D 74
Cropwell Butler. Notts 2D 74
Cros. W Isl 1H 171
Crosbie. N Ayr 4D 126
Crosbost. W Isl 5F 171
Crosby. Cumb 1B 102
Crosby. IOM 4C 108
Crosby. Mers 1F 83
Crosby. N Lin 3B 94
Crosby Court. N Yor 5A 106
Crosby Garrett. Cumb 4A 104
Crosby Ravensworth
Cumb 3H 103
Crosby Villa. Cumb 1B 102
Croscombe. Som 2A 22
Crosland Moor. W Yor 3B 92
Cross. Som 1H 21
Crossaig. Arg 4G 125
Crossapol. Arg 4A 138
Cross Ash. Mon 4H 47
Cross-at-Hand. Kent 1B 28
Crossbush. W Sus 5B 26
Crosscanonby. Cumb 1B 102
Crossdale Street. Norf 2E 79
Cross End. Essx 2B 54
Crossens. Mers 2B 90
Crossford. Fife 1D 128
Crossford. S Lan 5B 128
Cross Foxes. Gwyn 4G 69
Crossgar. New M 5H 175
Crossgate. Orkn 6D 172
Crossgate. Staf 2D 72
Crossgatehall. E Lot 3G 129
Cross Gates. W Yor 1D 92
Crossgates. Fife 1E 129
Crossgates. N Yor 1E 101
Crossgates. Powy 4C 58
Crossgill. Lanc 3E 97
Cross Green. Devn 4D 11
Cross Green. Staf 5D 72
Cross Green. Suff
nr. Cockfield 5A 66
nr. Hitcham 5B 66
Cross Hands. Carm 4F 45
Crosshands. Carm 2F 43
Crosshands. E Ayr 1D 117
Cross Hill. Derbs 1B 74
Cross Hill. Glos 2A 34
Crosshill. E Ayr 2D 117
Crosshill. Fife 4D 136
Crosshill. S Ayr 4C 116
Cross Hills. N Yor 5C 98
Crosshills. High 1A 158
Cross Holme. N Yor 5C 106
Crosshouse. E Ayr 1C 116
Cross Houses. Shrp 5H 71
Crossings. Cumb 2G 113
Cross in Hand. E Sus 3G 27
Cross Inn. Cdgn
nr. Aberaeron 4E 57
nr. New Quay 5C 56
Cross Inn. Rhon 3D 32
Crosskeys. Cphy 2F 33
Crosskirk. High 2C 168
Crosslands. Cumb 1C 96
Cross Lane Head. Shrp 1B 60
Cross Lanes. Corn 4D 5
Cross Lanes. Dur 3D 104
Cross Lanes. N Yor 3H 99
Cross Lanes. Wrex 1F 71
Crosslanes. Shrp 4F 71
Crosslee. Ren 3F 127
Crossmaglen. New M 6F 175
Crossmichael. Dum 3E 111
Crossmoor. Lanc 1C 90
Cross Oak. Powy 3E 46
Cross of Jackston. Abers 5E 161
Cross o' th' Hands. Derbs 1G 73
Crossroads. Abers
nr. Aberdeen 3G 153
nr. Banchory 4E 153
Crossroads. E Ayr 1D 116
Cross Side. Devn 4B 20
Cross Street. Suff 3D 66
Crosston. Ang 3E 145
Cross Town. Ches E 3B 84
Crossway. Mon 4H 47
Crossway. Powy 5C 58
Crossway Green. Mon 2A 34
Crossway Green. Worc 4C 60
Crossways. Dors 4C 14
Crosswell. Pemb 1F 43
Crosswood. Cdgn 3F 57
Crosthwaite. Cumb 5F 103
Croston. Lanc 3C 90
Crostwick. Norf 4E 79
Crostwight. Norf 3F 79
Crothair. W Isl 4D 171
Crouch. Kent 5H 39
Croucheston. Wilts 4F 23
Crouch Hill. Dors 1C 14
Croughton. Nptn 2D 50
Crovie. Abers 2F 161
Crow. Hants 2G 15
Crowan. Corn 3D 4
Crowborough. E Sus 2G 27
Crowcombe. Som 3E 21
Crowcroft. Worc 5B 60
Crowdecote. Derbs 4F 85
Crowden. Derbs 1E 85
Crowden. Devn 3E 11
Crowdhill. Hants 1C 16
Crowdon. N Yor 5G 107
Crow Edge. S Yor 4B 92
Crow End. Cambs 5C 64
Crowfield. Nptn 1E 50
Crowfield. Suff 5D 66
Crow Green. Essx 1G 39
Crow Hill. Here 3B 48
Crowhurst. E Sus 4B 28
Crowhurst. Surr 1E 27
Crowhurst Lane End. Surr 1E 27
Crowland. Linc 4B 76
Crowland. Suff 3C 66
Crowlas. Corn 3C 4
Crowle. N Lin 3A 94
Crowle. Worc 5D 60
Crowle Green. Worc 5D 60
Crowmarsh Gifford. Oxon 3E 36
Crown Corner. Suff 3E 67
Crownthorpe. Norf 5C 78
Crowntown. Corn 3D 4
Crows-an-wra. Corn 4A 4

Darnhall – Dormans Park

Darnhall. *Ches W* 4A 84
Darnick. *Bord* 1H 119
Darowen. *Powy* 5H 69
Darra. *Abers* 4E 161
Darracott. *Devn* 3E 19
Darras Hall. *Nmbd* 2E 115
Darrington. *W Yor* 2E 93
Darrow Green. *Norf* 2E 67
Darsham. *Suff* 4G 67
Dartfield. *Abers* 3H 161
Dartford. *Kent* 3G 39
Dartford-Thurrock River Crossing. *Kent* 3G 39
Dartington. *Devn* 2D 9
Dartmeet. *Devn* 5G 11
Dartmouth. *Devn* 3E 9
Darton. *S Yor* 3D 92
Darvel. *E Ayr* 1E 117
Darwen. *Bkbn* 2E 91
Dassels. *Herts* 3D 53
Datchet. *Wind* 3A 38
Datchworth. *Herts* 4C 52
Datchworth Green. *Herts* 4C 52
Daubhill. *G Man* 4F 91
Dauntsey. *Wilts* 3E 35
Dauntsey Green. *Wilts* 3E 35
Dauntsey Lock. *Wilts* 3E 35
Dava. *Mor* 5E 159
Davenham. *Ches W* 3A 84
Daventry. *Nptn* 4C 62
Davidson's Mains. *Edin* 2F 129
Davidston. *High* 2B 158
Davidstow. *Corn* 4B 10
David's Well. *Powy* 3C 58
Davington. *Dum* 4E 119
Daviot. *Abers* 1E 153
Daviot. *High* 5B 158
Davyhulme. *G Man* 1B 84
Daw Cross. *N Yor* 4E 99
Dawdon. *Dur* 5H 115
Dawesgreen. *Surr* 1D 26
Dawley. *Telf* 5A 72
Dawlish. *Devn* 5C 12
Dawlish Warren. *Devn* 5C 12
Dawn. *Cnwy* 3A 82
Daws Heath. *Essx* 2C 40
Dawshill. *Worc* 5C 60
Daw's House. *Corn* 4D 10
Dawsmere. *Linc* 2D 76
Dayhills. *Staf* 2D 72
Dayhouse Bank. *Worc* 3D 60
Daylesford. *Glos* 3H 49
Daywall. *Shrp* 2E 71
Ddol. *Flin* 3D 82
Ddol Cownwy. *Powy* 4C 70
Deadman's Cross. *C Beds* 1B 52
Deadwater. *Nmbd* 5A 120
Deaf Hill. *Dur* 1A 106
Deal. *Kent* 5H 41
Dean. *Cumb* 2B 102
Dean. *Devn*
nr. Combe Martin 2G 19
nr. Lynton 2H 19
Dean. *Dors* 1E 15
Dean. *Hants*
nr. Bishop's Waltham 1D 16
nr. Winchester 3C 24
Dean. *Oxon* 3B 50
Dean. *Som* 2B 22
Dean Bank. *Dur* 1F 105
Deanburnhaugh. *Bord* 3F 119
Dean Cross. *Devn* 2F 19
Deane. *Hants* 1D 24
Deanich Lodge. *High* 5A 164
Deanland. *Dors* 1E 15
Deanlane End. *W Sus* 1F 17
Dean Park. *Shrp* 4A 60
Dean Prior. *Devn* 2D 8
Dean Row. *Ches E* 2C 84
Deans. *W Lot* 3D 128
Deanscales. *Cumb* 2B 102
Deanshanger. *Nptn* 1F 51
Deanston. *Stir* 3G 135
Dearham. *Cumb* 1B 102
Dearne Valley. *S Yor* 4D 93
Debach. *Suff* 5E 67
Debden. *Essx* 2F 53
Debden Green. *Essx*
nr. Loughton 1F 39
nr. Saffron Walden 2F 53
Debenham. *Suff* 4D 66
Dechmont. *W Lot* 2D 128
Deddington. *Oxon* 2C 50
Dedham. *Essx* 2D 54
Dedham Heath. *Essx* 2D 54
Deebank. *Abers* 4D 152
Deene. *Nptn* 1G 63
Deenethorpe. *Nptn* 1G 63
Deepcar. *S Yor* 1G 85
Deepcut. *Surr* 5A 38
Deepdale. *Cumb* 1G 97
Deepdale. *N Lin* 3D 94
Deepdale. *N Yor* 2A 98
Deeping Gate. *Pet* 5A 76
Deeping St James. *Linc* 4A 76
Deeping St Nicholas. *Linc* 4B 76
Deerhill. *Mor* 3B 160
Deerhurst. *Glos* 3D 48
Deerhurst Walton. *Glos* 3D 49
Deerness. *Orkn* 7E 172
Defford. *Worc* 1E 49
Defynnog. *Powy* 3C 46
Deganwy. *Cnwy* 3G 81
Deighton. *N Yor* 4A 106
Deighton. *W Yor* 3B 92
Deighton. *York* 5A 100
Deiniolen. *Gwyn* 4E 81
Delabole. *Corn* 4A 10
Delamere. *Ches W* 4H 83
Delfour. *High* 3C 150
The Dell. *Suff* 1G 67
Delliefure. *High* 5E 159
Delly End. *Oxon* 4B 50
Delny. *High* 1B 158
Delph. *G Man* 4H 91
Delves. *Dur* 5E 115
The Delves. *W Mid* 1E 61
Delvin End. *Essx* 2A 54
Dembleby. *Linc* 2H 75
Demelza. *Corn* 2D 6
The Den. *N Ayr* 4E 127
Denaby Main. *S Yor* 1B 86
Denbeath. *Fife* 4F 137
Denbigh. *Den* 4C 82
Denbury. *Devn* 2E 9
Denby. *Derbs* 1A 74
Denby Common. *Derbs* 1B 74
Denby Dale. *W Yor* 4C 92
Denchworth. *Oxon* 2B 36
Dendron. *Cumb* 2B 96
Deneside. *Dur* 5H 115
Denford. *Nptn* 3G 63
Dengie. *Essx* 5C 54
Denham. *Buck* 2B 38
Denham. *Suff*
nr. Bury St Edmunds 4G 65
nr. Eye 3D 66
Denham Green. *Buck* 2B 38
Denham Street. *Suff* 3D 66
Denhead. *Abers*
nr. Ellon 5G 161
nr. Strichen 3G 161
Denhead. *Fife* 2G 137
Denholm. *Bord* 3H 119
Denholme. *W Yor* 1A 92
Denholme Clough. *W Yor* 1A 92
Denholme Gate. *W Yor* 1A 92
Denio. *Gwyn* 2C 68
Denmead. *Hants* 1E 17
Dennington. *Suff* 4E 67
Denny. *Falk* 1B 128
Denny End. *Cambs* 4D 65
Dennyloanhead. *Falk* 1B 128
Den of Lindores. *Fife* 2E 137
Denshaw. *G Man* 3H 91
Denside. *Abers* 4F 153
Densole. *Kent* 1G 29
Denston. *Suff* 5G 65
Denstone. *Staf* 1F 73
Denstroude. *Kent* 4F 41
Dent. *Cumb* 1G 97
Denton. *Cambs* 2A 64
Denton. *Darl* 3F 105
Denton. *E Sus* 5F 27
Denton. *G Man* 1D 84
Denton. *Kent* 1G 29
Denton. *Linc* 2F 75
Denton. *Norf* 2E 67
Denton. *Nptn* 5F 63
Denton. *N Yor* 5D 98
Denton. *Oxon* 5D 50
Denver. *Norf* 5F 77
Denwick. *Nmbd* 3G 121
Deopham. *Norf* 5C 78
Deopham Green. *Norf* 1C 66
Depden. *Suff* 5G 65
Depden Green. *Suff* 5G 65
Deptford. *G Lon* 3E 39
Deptford. *Wilts* 3F 23
Derby. *Derb* 2A 74
Derbyhaven. *IOM* 5B 108
Derculich. *Per* 3F 143
Dereham. *Norf* 4B 78
Deri. *Cphy* 5E 47
Derril. *Devn* 2D 10
Derringstone. *Kent* 1G 29
Derrington. *Shrp* 1A 60
Derrington. *Staf* 3C 72
Derriton. *Devn* 2D 10
Derry. *Derr* 2C 174
Derryguaig. *Arg* 5F 139
Derry Hill. *Wilts* 4E 35
Derrythorpe. *N Lin* 4B 94
Dersingham. *Norf* 2F 77
Dervaig. *Arg* 3F 139
Derwen. *Den* 5C 82
Derwen Gam. *Cdgn* 5D 56
Derwenlas. *Powy* 1G 57
Desborough. *Nptn* 2F 63
Desford. *Leics* 5B 74
Detchant. *Nmbd* 1E 121
Dethick. *Derbs* 5H 85
Detling. *Kent* 5B 40
Deuchar. *Ang* 2D 144
Deuddwr. *Powy* 4E 71
Devauden. *Mon* 2H 33
Devil's Bridge. *Cdgn* 3G 57
Devitts Green. *Warw* 1G 61
Devizes. *Wilts* 5F 35
Devonport. *Plym* 3A 8
Devonside. *Clac* 4B 136
Devoran. *Corn* 5B 6
Dewartown. *Midl* 3G 129
Dewlish. *Dors* 3C 14
Dewsall Court. *Here* 2H 47
Dewsbury. *W Yor* 2C 92
Dexbeer. *Devn* 2C 10
Dhoon. *IOM* 3D 108
Dhoor. *IOM* 2D 108
Dhowin. *IOM* 1D 108
Dial Green. *W Sus* 3A 26
Dial Post. *W Sus* 4C 26
Dibberford. *Dors* 2H 13
Dibden. *Hants* 2C 16
Dibden Purlieu. *Hants* 2C 16
Dickleburgh. *Norf* 2D 66
Didbrook. *Glos* 2F 49
Didcot. *Oxon* 2D 36
Diddington. *Cambs* 4A 64
Diddlebury. *Shrp* 2H 59
Didley. *Here* 2H 47
Didling. *W Sus* 1G 17
Didmarton. *Glos* 3D 34
Didsbury. *G Man* 1C 84
Didworthy. *Devn* 2C 8
Digby. *Linc* 5H 87
Digg. *High* 2D 154
Diggle. *G Man* 4A 92
Digmoor. *Lanc* 4C 90
Digswell. *Herts* 4C 52
Dihewyd. *Cdgn* 5D 57
Dilham. *Norf* 3F 79
Dilhorne. *Staf* 1D 72
Dillarburn. *S Lan* 5B 128
Dillington. *Cambs* 4A 64
Dilston. *Nmbd* 3C 114
Dilton Marsh. *Wilts* 2D 22
Dilwyn. *Here* 5G 59
Dimmer. *Som* 3B 22
Dimple. *G Man* 3F 91
Dinas. *Carm* 1G 43
Dinas. *Gwyn*
nr. Caernarfon 5D 81
nr. Tudweiliog 2B 68
Dinas Cross. *Pemb* 1E 43
Dinas Dinlle. *Gwyn* 5D 80
Dinas Mawddwy. *Gwyn* 4A 70
Dinas Powys. *V Glam* 4E 33
Dinbych. *Den* 4C 82
Dinbych-y-Pysgod. *Pemb* 4F 43
Dinckley. *Lanc* 1E 91
Dinder. *Som* 2A 22
Dinedor. *Here* 2A 48
Dinedor Cross. *Here* 2A 48
Dingestow. *Mon* 4H 47
Dingle. *Mers* 2F 83
Dingleden. *Kent* 2C 28
Dingleton. *Bord* 1H 119
Dingley. *Nptn* 2E 63
Dingwall. *High* 3H 157
Dinmael. *Cnwy* 1C 70
Dinnet. *Abers* 4B 152
Dinnington. *Som* 1H 13
Dinnington. *S Yor* 2C 86
Dinnington. *Tyne* 2F 115
Dinorwig. *Gwyn* 4E 81
Dinton. *Buck* 4F 51
Dinton. *Wilts* 3F 23
Dinworthy. *Devn* 1D 10
Dipley. *Hants* 1F 25
Dippen. *Arg* 2B 122
Dippenhall. *Surr* 2G 25
Dippertown. *Devn* 4E 11
Dippin. *N Ayr* 3E 123
Dipple. *S Ayr* 4B 116
Diptford. *Devn* 3D 8
Dipton. *Dur* 4E 115
Dirleton. *E Lot* 1B 130
Dirt Pot. *Nmbd* 5B 114
Discoed. *Powy* 4E 59
Diseworth. *Leics* 3B 74
Dishes. *Orkn* 5F 172
Dishforth. *N Yor* 2F 99
Disley. *Ches E* 2D 85
Diss. *Norf* 3D 66
Disserth. *Powy* 5C 58
Distington. *Cumb* 2B 102
Ditchampton. *Wilts* 3F 23
Ditcheat. *Som* 3B 22
Ditchingham. *Norf* 1F 67
Ditchling. *E Sus* 4E 27
Ditteridge. *Wilts* 5D 34
Dittisham. *Devn* 3E 9
Ditton. *Hal* 2G 83
Ditton. *Kent* 5B 40
Ditton Green. *Cambs* 5F 65
Ditton Priors. *Shrp* 2A 60
Divach. *High* 1G 149
Dixonfield. *High* 2D 168
Dixton. *Glos* 2E 49
Dixton. *Mon* 4A 48
Dizzard. *Corn* 3B 10
Doagh. *Ant* 3G 175
Dobcross. *G Man* 4H 91
Dobs Hill. *Flin* 4F 83
Dobson's Bridge. *Shrp* 2G 71
Dobwalls. *Corn* 2G 7
Doccombe. *Devn* 4A 12
Dochgarroch. *High* 4A 158
Docking. *Norf* 2G 77
Docklow. *Here* 5H 59
Dockray. *Cumb* 2E 103
Doc Penfro. *Pemb* 4D 42
Dodbrooke. *Devn* 4D 8
Doddenham. *Worc* 5B 60
Doddinghurst. *Essx* 1G 39
Doddington. *Cambs* 1C 64
Doddington. *Kent* 5D 40
Doddington. *Linc* 3G 87
Doddington. *Nmbd* 1D 121
Doddington. *Shrp* 3A 60
Doddiscombsleigh. *Devn* 4B 12
Doddshill. *Norf* 2G 77
Dodford. *Nptn* 4D 62
Dodford. *Worc* 3D 60
Dodington. *Som* 2E 21
Dodington. *S Glo* 3C 34
Dodleston. *Ches W* 4F 83
Dods Leigh. *Staf* 2E 73
Dodworth. *S Yor* 4D 92
Doe Lea. *Derbs* 4B 86
Dogdyke. *Linc* 5B 88
Dogmersfield. *Hants* 1F 25
Dogsthorpe. *Pet* 5B 76
Dog Village. *Devn* 3C 12
Dolanog. *Powy* 4C 70
Dolau. *Powy* 4D 58
Dolau. *Rhon* 3D 32
Dolbenmaen. *Gwyn* 1E 69
Doley. *Staf* 3B 72
Dol-fâch. *Powy* 5B 70
Dolfach. *Powy* 3B 58
Dolfor. *Powy* 2D 58
Dolgarrog. *Cnwy* 4G 81
Dolgellau. *Gwyn* 4G 69
Dolgoch. *Gwyn* 5F 69
Dol-gran. *Carm* 2E 45
Dolhelfa. *Powy* 3B 58
Doll. *High* 3F 165
Dollar. *Clac* 4B 136
Dolley Green. *Powy* 4E 59
Dollingstown. *Arm* 5G 175
Dollwen. *Cdgn* 2F 57
Dolphin. *Flin* 3D 82
Dolphinholme. *Lanc* 4E 97
Dolphinton. *S Lan* 5E 129
Dolton. *Devn* 1F 11
Dolwen. *Cnwy* 3A 82
Dolwyddelan. *Cnwy* 5G 81
Dol-y-Bont. *Cdgn* 2F 57
Dolyhir. *Powy* 5E 59
Domgay. *Powy* 4E 71
Donaghadee. *Ards* 4J 175
Doncaster. *S Yor* 4F 93
Doncaster Sheffield Airport *S Yor* 1D 86
Donhead St Andrew. *Wilts* 4E 23
Donhead St Mary. *Wilts* 4E 23
Doniford. *Som* 2D 20
Donington. *Linc* 2B 76
Donington. *Shrp* 5C 72
Donington Eaudike. *Linc* 2B 76
Donington le Heath. *Leics* 4B 74
Donington on Bain. *Linc* 2B 88
Donington South Ing. *Linc* 2B 76
Donisthorpe. *Leics* 4H 73
Donkey Street. *Kent* 2F 29
Donkey Town. *Surr* 4A 38
Donna Nook. *Linc* 1D 88
Donnington. *Glos* 3G 49
Donnington. *Here* 2C 48
Donnington. *Shrp* 5H 71
Donnington. *Telf* 4B 72
Donnington. *W Ber* 5C 36
Donnington. *W Sus* 2G 17
Donyatt. *Som* 1G 13
Doomsday Green. *W Sus* 3C 26
Doonfoot. *S Ayr* 3C 116
Doonholm. *S Ayr* 3C 116
Dorback Lodge. *High* 2E 151
Dorchester. *Dors* 3B 14
Dorchester on Thames *Oxon* 2D 36
Dordon. *Warw* 5G 73
Dore. *S Yor* 2H 85
Dores. *High* 5H 157
Dorking. *Surr* 1C 26
Dorking Tye. *Suff* 2C 54
Dormansland. *Surr* 1F 27
Dormans Park. *Surr* 1E 27

Dunster – East Markham

Dunster. *Som* 2C **20**
Duns Tew. *Oxon* 3C **50**
Dunston. *Linc* 4H **87**
Dunston. *Norf* 5E **79**
Dunston. *Staf* 4D **72**
Dunston. *Tyne* 3F **115**
Dunstone. *Devn* 3B **8**
Dunston Heath. *Staf* 4D **72**
Dunsville. *S Yor* 4G **93**
Dunswell. *E Yor* 1D **94**
Dunsyre. *S Lan* 5D **128**
Dunterton. *Devn* 5D **11**
Duntisbourne Abbots
Glos 5E **49**
Duntisbourne Leer. *Glos* 5E **49**
Duntisbourne Rouse. *Glos* 5E **49**
Duntish. *Dors* 2B **14**
Duntocher. *W Dun* 2F **127**
Dunton. *Buck* 3G **51**
Dunton. *C Beds* 1C **52**
Dunton. *Norf* 2A **78**
Dunton Bassett. *Leics* 1C **62**
Dunton Green. *Kent* 5G **39**
Dunton Patch. *Norf* 2A **78**
Duntulm. *High* 1D **154**
Dunure. *S Ayr* 3B **116**
Dunvant. *Swan* 3E **31**
Dunvegan. *High* 4B **154**
Dunwich. *Suff* 3G **67**
Dunwood. *Staf* 5D **84**
Durdar. *Cumb* 4F **113**
Durgates. *E Sus* 2H **27**
Durham. *Dur* 5F **115**
Durham Tees Valley Airport
Darl 3A **106**
Durisdeer. *Dum* 4A **118**
Durisdeermill. *Dum* 4A **118**
Durkar. *W Yor* 3D **92**
Durleigh. *Som* 3F **21**
Durley. *Hants* 1D **16**
Durley. *Wilts* 5H **35**
Durley Street. *Hants* 1D **16**
Durlow Common. *Here* 2B **48**
Durnamuck. *High* 4E **163**
Durness. *High* 2E **166**
Durno. *Abers* 1E **152**
Durns Town. *Hants* 3A **16**
Duror. *High* 3D **141**
Durran. *Arg* 3G **133**
Durran. *High* 2D **169**
Durrant Green. *Kent* 2C **28**
Durrants. *Hants* 1F **17**
Durrington. *W Sus* 5C **26**
Durrington. *Wilts* 2G **23**
Dursley. *Glos* 2C **34**
Dursley Cross. *Glos* 4B **48**
Durston. *Som* 4F **21**
Durweston. *Dors* 2D **14**
Dury. *Shet* 6F **173**
Duston. *Nptn* 4E **63**
Duthil. *High* 1D **150**
Dutlas. *Powy* 3E **58**
Duton Hill. *Essx* 3G **53**
Dutson. *Corn* 4D **10**
Dutton. *Ches W* 3H **83**
Duxford. *Cambs* 1E **53**
Duxford. *Oxon* 2B **36**
Dwygyfylchi. *Cnwy* 3G **81**
Dwyran. *IOA* 4D **80**
Dyce. *Aber* 2F **153**
Dyffryn. *B'end* 2B **32**
Dyffryn. *Carm* 2H **43**
Dyffryn. *Pemb* 1D **42**
Dyffryn. *V Glam* 4D **32**
Dyffryn Ardudwy. *Gwyn* 3E **69**
Dyffryn Castell. *Cdgn* 2G **57**
Dyffryn Ceidrych. *Carm* 3H **45**
Dyffryn Cellwen. *Neat* 5B **46**
Dyke. *Linc* 3A **76**
Dyke. *Mor* 3D **159**
Dykehead. *Ang* 2C **144**
Dykehead. *N Lan* 3B **128**
Dykehead. *Stir* 4E **135**
Dykend. *Ang* 3B **144**
Dykesfield. *Cumb* 4E **112**
Dylife. *Powy* 1A **58**
Dymchurch. *Kent* 3F **29**
Dymock. *Glos* 2C **48**
Dyrham. *S Glo* 4C **34**
Dysart. *Fife* 4F **137**
Dyserth. *Den* 3C **82**

E

Eachwick. *Nmbd* 2E **115**
Eadar Dha Fhadhail. *W Isl* 4C **171**
Eagland Hill. *Lanc* 5D **96**
Eagle. *Linc* 4F **87**
Eagle Barnsdale. *Linc* 4F **87**
Eagle Moor. *Linc* 4F **87**
Eaglescliffe. *Stoc T* 3B **106**
Eaglesfield. *Cumb* 2B **102**
Eaglesfield. *Dum* 2D **112**
Eaglesham. *E Ren* 4G **127**
Eaglethorpe. *Nptn* 1H **63**
Eagley. *G Man* 3F **91**
Eairy. *IOM* 4B **108**
Eakley Lanes. *Mil* 5F **63**
Eakring. *Notts* 4D **86**
Ealand. *N Lin* 3A **94**
Ealing. *G Lon* 2C **38**
Eallabus. *Arg* 3B **124**
Eals. *Nmbd* 4H **113**
Eamont Bridge. *Cumb* 2G **103**
Earby. *Lanc* 5B **98**
Earcroft. *Bkbn* 2E **91**
Eardington. *Shrp* 1B **60**
Eardisland. *Here* 5G **59**
Eardisley. *Here* 1G **47**
Eardiston. *Shrp* 3F **71**
Eardiston. *Worc* 4A **60**
Earith. *Cambs* 3C **64**
Earlais. *High* 2C **154**
Earle. *Nmbd* 2D **121**
Earlesfield. *Linc* 2G **75**
Earlestown. *Mers* 1H **83**
Earley. *Wok* 4F **37**
Earlham. *Norf* 5D **78**
Earlish. *High* 2C **154**
Earls Barton. *Nptn* 4F **63**
Earls Colne. *Essx* 3B **54**
Earls Common. *Worc* 5D **60**
Earl's Croome. *Worc* 1D **48**
Earlsdon. *W Mid* 3H **61**
Earlsferry. *Fife* 3G **137**
Earlsford. *Abers* 5F **161**
Earl's Green. *Suff* 4C **66**
Earlsheaton. *W Yor* 2C **92**
Earl Shilton. *Leics* 1B **62**
Earl Soham. *Suff* 4E **67**
Earl Sterndale. *Derbs* 4E **85**
Earlston. *E Ayr* 1D **116**
Earlston. *Bord* 1H **119**
Earl Stonham. *Suff* 5D **66**
Earlstoun. *Dum* 1D **110**
Earlswood. *Mon* 2H **33**
Earlswood. *Warw* 3F **61**
Earlyvale. *Bord* 4F **129**
Earnley. *W Sus* 3G **17**
Earsairidh. *W Isl* 9C **170**
Earsdon. *Tyne* 2G **115**
Earsham. *Norf* 2F **67**
Earsham Street. *Suff* 3E **67**
Earswick. *York* 4A **100**
Eartham. *W Sus* 5A **26**
Earthcott Green. *S Glo* 3B **34**
Easby. *N Yor*
nr. Great Ayton 4C **106**
nr. Richmond 4E **105**
Easdale. *Arg* 2E **133**
Easebourne. *W Sus* 4G **25**
Easenhall. *Warw* 3B **62**
Eashing. *Surr* 1A **26**
Easington. *Buck* 4E **51**
Easington. *Dur* 5H **115**
Easington. *E Yor* 3G **95**
Easington. *Nmbd* 1F **121**
Easington. *Oxon*
nr. Banbury 2C **50**
nr. Watlington 2E **37**
Easington. *Red C* 3E **107**
Easington Colliery. *Dur* 5H **115**
Easington Lane. *Tyne* 5G **115**
Easingwold. *N Yor* 2H **99**
Eassie. *Ang* 4C **144**
Eassie and Nevay. *Ang* 4C **144**
East Aberthaw. *V Glam* 5D **32**
Eastacombe. *Devn* 4F **19**
Eastacott. *Devn* 4G **19**
East Allington. *Devn* 4D **8**
East Anstey. *Devn* 4B **20**
East Anton. *Hants* 2B **24**
East Appleton. *N Yor* 5F **105**
East Ardsley. *W Yor* 2D **92**
East Ashley. *Devn* 1G **11**
East Ashling. *W Sus* 2G **17**
East Aston. *Hants* 2C **24**
East Ayton. *N Yor* 1D **101**
East Barkwith. *Linc* 2A **88**
East Barnby. *N Yor* 3F **107**
East Barnet. *G Lon* 1D **39**
East Barns. *E Lot* 2D **130**
East Barsham. *Norf* 2B **78**
East Beach. *W Sus* 3G **17**
East Beckham. *Norf* 2D **78**
East Bedfont. *G Lon* 3B **38**
East Bennan. *N Ayr* 3D **123**
East Bergholt. *Suff* 2D **54**
East Bierley. *W Yor* 2C **92**
East Bilney. *Norf* 4B **78**
East Blatchington. *E Sus* 5F **27**
East Bloxworth. *Dors* 3D **15**
East Boldre. *Hants* 2B **16**
East Bolton. *Nmbd* 3F **121**
Eastbourne. *Darl* 3F **105**
Eastbourne. *E Sus* 5H **27**
East Brent. *Som* 1G **21**
East Bridge. *Suff* 4G **67**
East Bridgford. *Notts* 1D **74**
East Briscoe. *Dur* 3C **104**
East Buckland. *Devn*
nr. Barnstaple 3G **19**
nr. Thurlestone 4C **8**
East Budleigh. *Devn* 4D **12**
Eastburn. *W Yor* 5C **98**
East Burnham. *Buck* 2A **38**
East Burrafirth. *Shet* 6E **173**
East Burton. *Dors* 4D **14**
Eastbury. *Herts* 1B **38**
Eastbury. *W Ber* 4B **36**
East Butsfield. *Dur* 5E **115**
East Butterleigh. *Devn* 2C **12**
East Butterwick. *N Lin* 4B **94**
Eastby. *N Yor* 4C **98**
East Calder. *W Lot* 3D **129**
East Carleton. *Norf* 5D **78**
East Carlton. *Nptn* 2F **63**
East Carlton. *W Yor* 5E **98**
East Chaldon. *Dors* 4C **14**
East Challow. *Oxon* 3B **36**
East Charleton. *Devn* 4D **8**
East Chelborough. *Dors* 2A **14**
East Chiltington. *E Sus* 4E **27**
East Chinnock. *Som* 1H **13**
East Chisenbury. *Wilts* 1G **23**
Eastchurch. *Kent* 3D **40**
East Clandon. *Surr* 5B **38**
East Claydon. *Buck* 3F **51**
East Clevedon. *N Som* 4H **33**
East Clyne. *High* 3F **165**
East Clyth. *High* 5E **169**
East Coker. *Som* 1A **14**
East Combe. *Som* 3E **21**
Eastcombe. *Glos* 5D **49**
East Common. *N Yor* 1G **93**
East Compton. *Som* 2B **22**
East Cornworthy. *Devn* 3E **9**
Eastcote. *G Lon* 2C **38**
Eastcote. *Nptn* 5D **62**
Eastcote. *W Mid* 3F **61**
Eastcott. *Corn* 1C **10**
Eastcott. *Wilts* 1F **23**
East Cottingwith. *E Yor* 5B **100**
Eastcourt. *Wilts*
nr. Pewsey 5H **35**
nr. Tetbury 2E **35**
East Cowes. *IOW* 3D **16**
East Cowick. *E Yor* 2G **93**
East Cowton. *N Yor* 4A **106**
East Cramlington. *Nmbd* 2F **115**
East Cranmore. *Som* 2B **22**
East Creech. *Dors* 4E **15**
East Croachy. *High* 1A **150**
East Dean. *E Sus* 5G **27**
East Dean. *Glos* 3B **48**
East Dean. *Hants* 4A **24**
East Dean. *W Sus* 4A **26**
East Down. *Devn* 2G **19**
East Drayton. *Notts* 3E **87**
East Dundry. *N Som* 5A **34**
East Ella. *Hull* 2D **94**
East End. *Cambs* 3C **64**
East End. *Dors* 3E **15**
East End. *E Yor*
nr. Ulrome 4F **101**
nr. Withernsea 2F **95**
East End. *Hants*
nr. Lymington 3B **16**
nr. Newbury 5C **36**
East End. *Herts* 3E **53**
East End. *Kent*
nr. Minster 3D **40**
nr. Tenterden 2C **28**
East End. *N Som* 4H **33**
East End. *Oxon* 4B **50**
East End. *Som* 1A **22**
East End. *Suff* 2E **54**
Easter Ardross. *High* 1A **158**
Easter Balgedie. *Per* 3D **136**
Easter Balmoral. *Abers* 4G **151**
Easter Brae. *High* 2A **158**
Easter Buckieburn. *Stir* 1A **128**
Easter Compton. *S Glo* 3A **34**
Easter Fearn. *High* 5D **164**
Easter Galcantray. *High* 4C **158**
Eastergate. *W Sus* 5A **26**
Easterhouse. *Glas* 3H **127**
Easter Howgate. *Midl* 3F **129**
Easter Kinkell. *High* 3H **157**
Easter Lednathie. *Ang* 2C **144**
Easter Ogil. *Ang* 2D **144**
Easter Ord. *Abers* 3F **153**
Easter Quarff. *Shet* 8F **173**
Easter Rhynd. *Per* 2D **136**
Easter Skeld. *Shet* 7E **173**
Easter Suddie. *High* 3A **158**
Easterton. *Wilts* 1F **23**
Eastertown. *Som* 1G **21**
Easter Tulloch. *Abers* 1G **145**
East Everleigh. *Wilts* 1H **23**
East Farleigh. *Kent* 5B **40**
East Farndon. *Nptn* 2E **62**
East Ferry. *Linc* 1F **87**
Eastfield. *N Lan*
nr. Caldercruix 3B **128**
nr. Harthill 3B **128**
Eastfield. *N Yor* 1E **101**
Eastfield. *S Lan* 3H **127**
Eastfield Hall. *Nmbd* 4G **121**
East Fortune. *E Lot* 2B **130**
East Garforth. *W Yor* 1E **93**
East Garston. *W Ber* 4B **36**
Eastgate. *Dur* 1C **104**
Eastgate. *Norf* 3D **78**
East Ginge. *Oxon* 3C **36**
East Gores. *Essx* 3B **54**
East Goscote. *Leics* 4D **74**
East Grafton. *Wilts* 5A **36**
East Green. *Suff* 5F **65**
East Grimstead. *Wilts* 4H **23**
East Grinstead. *W Sus* 2E **27**
East Guldeford. *E Sus* 3D **28**
East Haddon. *Nptn* 4D **62**
East Hagbourne. *Oxon* 3D **36**
East Halton. *N Lin* 2E **95**
East Ham. *G Lon* 2F **39**
Eastham. *Mers* 2F **83**
Eastham. *Worc* 4A **60**
Eastham Ferry. *Mers* 2F **83**
Easthampstead. *Brac* 5G **37**
Easthampton. *Here* 4G **59**
East Hanney. *Oxon* 2C **36**
East Hanningfield. *Essx* 5A **54**
East Hardwick. *W Yor* 3E **93**
East Harling. *Norf* 2B **66**
East Harlsey. *N Yor* 5B **106**
East Harptree. *Bath* 1A **22**
East Hartford. *Nmbd* 2F **115**
East Harting. *W Sus* 1G **17**
East Hatch. *Wilts* 4E **23**
East Hatley. *Cambs* 5B **64**
Easthaugh. *Norf* 4C **78**
East Hauxwell. *N Yor* 5E **105**
East Haven. *Ang* 5E **145**
Eastheath. *Wok* 5G **37**
East Heckington. *Linc* 1A **76**
East Hedleyhope. *Dur* 5E **115**
East Helmsdale. *High* 2H **165**
East Hendred. *Oxon* 3C **36**
East Heslerton. *N Yor* 2D **100**
East Hoathly. *E Sus* 4G **27**
East Holme. *Dors* 4D **15**
Easthope. *Shrp* 1H **59**
Easthorpe. *Essx* 3C **54**
Easthorpe. *Leics* 2F **75**
East Horrington. *Som* 2A **22**
East Horsley. *Surr* 5B **38**
East Horton. *Nmbd* 1E **121**
Easthouses. *Midl* 3G **129**
East Howe. *Bour* 3F **15**
East Huntspill. *Som* 2G **21**
East Hyde. *C Beds* 4B **52**
East Ilsley. *W Ber* 3C **36**
Eastington. *Devn* 2H **11**
Eastington. *Glos*
nr. Northleach 4G **49**
nr. Stonehouse 5C **48**
East Keal. *Linc* 4C **88**
East Kennett. *Wilts* 5G **35**
East Keswick. *W Yor* 5F **99**
East Kilbride. *S Lan* 4H **127**
East Kirkby. *Linc* 4C **88**
East Knapton. *N Yor* 2C **100**
East Knighton. *Dors* 4D **14**
East Knowstone. *Devn* 4B **20**
East Knoyle. *Wilts* 3D **23**
East Kyloe. *Nmbd* 1E **121**
East Lambrook. *Som* 1H **13**
East Langdon. *Kent* 1H **29**
East Langton. *Leics* 1E **63**
East Langwell. *High* 3E **164**
East Lavant. *W Sus* 2G **17**
East Lavington. *W Sus* 4A **26**
East Layton. *N Yor* 4E **105**
Eastleach Martin. *Glos* 5H **49**
Eastleach Turville. *Glos* 5G **49**
East Leake. *Notts* 3C **74**
East Learmouth. *Nmbd* 1C **120**
East Leigh. *Devn*
nr. Crediton 2G **11**
nr. Modbury 3C **8**
Eastleigh. *Devn* 4E **19**
Eastleigh. *Hants* 1C **16**
East Lexham. *Norf* 4A **78**
East Lilburn. *Nmbd* 2E **121**
Eastling. *Kent* 5D **40**
East Linton. *E Lot* 2B **130**
East Liss. *Hants* 4F **25**
East Lockinge. *Oxon* 3C **36**
East Looe. *Corn* 3G **7**
East Lound. *N Lin* 1E **87**
East Lulworth. *Dors* 4D **14**
East Lutton. *N Yor* 3D **100**
East Lydford. *Som* 3A **22**
East Lyng. *Som* 4G **21**
East Mains. *Abers* 4D **152**
East Malling. *Kent* 5B **40**
East Marden. *W Sus* 1G **17**
East Markham. *Notts* 3E **87**

East Marton. *N Yor*....4B 98
East Meon. *Hants*....4E 25
East Mersea. *Essx*....4D 54
East Mey. *High*....1F 169
East Midlands Airport. *Leics*....3B 74
East Molesey. *Surr*....4C 38
Eastmoor. *Norf*....5G 77
East Morden. *Dors*....3E 15
East Morton. *W Yor*....5D 98
East Ness. *N Yor*....2A 100
East Newton. *E Yor*....1F 95
East Newton. *N Yor*....2A 100
Eastney. *Port*....3E 17
Eastnor. *Here*....2C 48
East Norton. *Leics*....5E 75
East Nynehead. *Som*....4E 21
East Oakley. *Hants*....1D 24
Eastoft. *N Lin*....3B 94
East Ogwell. *Devn*....5B 12
Easton. *Cambs*....3A 64
Easton. *Cumb*
  nr. Burgh by Sands....4D 112
  nr. Longtown....2F 113
Easton. *Devn*....4H 11
Easton. *Dors*....5B 14
Easton. *Hants*....3D 24
Easton. *Linc*....3G 75
Easton. *Norf*....4D 78
Easton. *Som*....2A 22
Easton. *Suff*....5E 67
Easton. *Wilts*....4D 35
Easton-in-Gordano. *N Som*....4A 34
Easton Maudit. *Nptn*....5F 63
Easton on the Hill. *Nptn*....5H 75
Easton Royal. *Wilts*....5H 35
East Orchard. *Dors*....1D 14
East Ord. *Nmbd*....4F 131
East Panson. *Devn*....3D 10
East Peckham. *Kent*....1A 28
East Pennard. *Som*....3A 22
East Perry. *Cambs*....4A 64
East Pitcorthie. *Fife*....3H 137
East Portlemouth. *Devn*....5D 8
East Prawle. *Devn*....5D 9
East Preston. *W Sus*....5B 26
East Putford. *Devn*....1D 10
East Quantoxhead. *Som*....2E 21
East Rainton. *Tyne*....5G 115
East Ravendale. *NE Lin*....1B 88
East Raynham. *Norf*....3A 78
Eastrea. *Cambs*....1B 64
East Rhidorroch Lodge
  High....4G 163
Eastriggs. *Dum*....3D 112
East Rigton. *W Yor*....5F 99
Eastrington. *E Yor*....2A 94
East Rounton. *N Yor*....4B 106
East Row. *N Yor*....3F 107
East Rudham. *Norf*....3H 77
East Runton. *Norf*....1D 78
East Ruston. *Norf*....3F 79
Eastry. *Kent*....5H 41
East Saltoun. *E Lot*....3A 130
East Shaws. *Dur*....3D 105
East Shefford. *W Ber*....4B 36
Eastshore. *Shet*....10E 173
East Sleekburn. *Nmbd*....1F 115
East Somerton. *Norf*....4G 79
East Stockwith. *Linc*....1E 87
East Stoke. *Dors*....4D 14
East Stoke. *Notts*....1E 75
East Stoke. *Som*....1H 13
East Stour. *Dors*....4D 22
East Stourmouth. *Kent*....4G 41
East Stowford. *Devn*....4G 19
East Stratton. *Hants*....2D 24
East Studdal. *Kent*....1H 29
East Taphouse. *Corn*....2F 7
East-the-Water. *Devn*....4E 19
East Thirston. *Nmbd*....5F 121
East Tilbury. *Thur*....3A 40
East Tisted. *Hants*....3F 25
East Torrington. *Linc*....2A 88

East Tuddenham. *Norf*....4C 78
East Tytherley. *Hants*....4A 24
East Tytherton. *Wilts*....4E 35
East Village. *Devn*....2B 12
Eastville. *Linc*....5D 88
East Wall. *Shrp*....1H 59
East Walton. *Norf*....4G 77
East Week. *Devn*....3G 11
Eastwell. *Leics*....3E 75
East Wellow. *Hants*....4B 24
East Wemyss. *Fife*....4F 137
East Whitburn. *W Lot*....3C 128
Eastwick. *Herts*....4E 53
Eastwick. *Shet*....4E 173
East Williamston. *Pemb*....4E 43
East Winch. *Norf*....4F 77
East Winterslow. *Wilts*....3H 23
East Wittering. *W Sus*....3F 17
East Witton. *N Yor*....1D 98
Eastwood. *Notts*....1B 74
Eastwood. *S'end*....2C 40
East Woodburn. *Nmbd*....1C 114
Eastwood End. *Cambs*....1D 64
East Woodhay. *Hants*....5C 36
East Woodlands. *Som*....2C 22
East Worldham. *Hants*....3F 25
East Worlington. *Devn*....1A 12
East Wretham. *Norf*....1B 66
East Youlstone. *Devn*....1C 10
Eathorpe. *Warw*....4A 62
Eaton. *Ches E*....4C 84
Eaton. *Ches W*....4H 83
Eaton. *Leics*....3E 75
Eaton. *Norf*
  nr. Heacham....2F 77
  nr. Norwich....5E 78
Eaton. *Notts*....3E 86
Eaton. *Oxon*....5C 50
Eaton. *Shrp*
  nr. Bishop's Castle....2F 59
  nr. Church Stretton....2H 59
Eaton Bishop. *Here*....2H 47
Eaton Bray. *C Beds*....3H 51
Eaton Constantine. *Shrp*....5H 71
Eaton Hastings. *Oxon*....2A 36
Eaton Socon. *Cambs*....5A 64
Eaton upon Tern. *Shrp*....3A 72
Eau Brink. *Norf*....4E 77
Eaves Green. *W Mid*....2G 61
Ebberston. *N Yor*....1C 100
Ebberley Hill. *Devn*....1F 11
Ebbesbourne Wake. *Wilts*....4E 23
Ebblake. *Dors*....2G 15
Ebbsfleet. *Kent*....3H 39
Ebbw Vale. *Blae*....5E 47
Ebchester. *Dur*....4E 115
Ebernoe. *W Sus*....3A 26
Ebford. *Devn*....4C 12
Ebley. *Glos*....5D 48
Ebnal. *Ches W*....1G 71
Ebrington. *Glos*....1G 49
Ecchinswell. *Hants*....1D 24
Ecclefechan. *Dum*....2C 112
Eccles. *G Man*....1B 84
Eccles. *Kent*....4B 40
Eccles. *Bord*....5D 130
Ecclesall. *S Yor*....2H 85
Ecclesfield. *S Yor*....1A 86
Eccles Green. *Here*....1G 47
Eccleshall. *Staf*....3C 72
Eccleshill. *W Yor*....1B 92
Ecclesmachan. *W Lot*....2D 128
Eccles on Sea. *Norf*....3G 79
Eccles Road. *Norf*....1C 66
Eccleston. *Ches W*....4G 83
Eccleston. *Lanc*....3D 90
Eccleston. *Mers*....1G 83
Eccup. *W Yor*....5E 99
Echt. *Abers*....3E 153
Eckford. *Bord*....2B 120
Eckington. *Derbs*....3B 86
Eckington. *Worc*....1E 49
Ecton. *Nptn*....4F 63
Edale. *Derbs*....2F 85

Eday Airport. *Orkn*....4E 172
Edburton. *W Sus*....4D 26
Edderside. *Cumb*....5C 112
Edderton. *High*....5E 164
Eddington. *Kent*....4F 41
Eddington. *W Ber*....5B 36
Eddleston. *Bord*....5F 129
Eddlewood. *S Lan*....4A 128
Edenbridge. *Kent*....1F 27
Edendonich. *Arg*....1A 134
Edenfield. *Lanc*....3F 91
Edenhall. *Cumb*....1G 103
Edenham. *Linc*....3H 75
Edensor. *Derbs*....3G 85
Edentaggart. *Arg*....4C 134
Edenthorpe. *S Yor*....4G 93
Eden Vale. *Dur*....1B 106
Edern. *Gwyn*....2B 68
Edgarley. *Som*....3A 22
Edgbaston. *W Mid*....2E 61
Edgcott. *Buck*....3E 51
Edgcott. *Som*....3B 20
Edge. *Glos*....5D 48
Edge. *Shrp*....5F 71
Edgebolton. *Shrp*....3H 71
Edge End. *Glos*....4A 48
Edgefield. *Norf*....2C 78
Edgefield Street. *Norf*....2C 78
Edge Green. *Ches W*....5G 83
Edgehead. *Midl*....3G 129
Edgeley. *Shrp*....1H 71
Edgeside. *Lanc*....2G 91
Edgeworth. *Glos*....5E 49
Edgiock. *Worc*....4E 61
Edgmond. *Telf*....4B 72
Edgmond Marsh. *Telf*....3B 72
Edgton. *Shrp*....2F 59
Edgware. *G Lon*....1C 38
Edgworth. *Bkbn*....3F 91
Edinbane. *High*....3C 154
Edinburgh. *Edin*....2F 129
Edinburgh Airport. *Edin*....2E 129
Edingale. *Staf*....4G 73
Edingley. *Notts*....5D 86
Edingthorpe. *Norf*....2F 79
Edington. *Som*....3G 21
Edington. *Wilts*....1E 23
Edingworth. *Som*....1G 21
Edistone. *Devn*....4C 18
Edithmead. *Som*....2G 21
Edith Weston. *Rut*....5G 75
Edlaston. *Derbs*....1F 73
Edlesborough. *Buck*....4H 51
Edlingham. *Nmbd*....4F 121
Edlington. *Linc*....3B 88
Edmondsham. *Dors*....1F 15
Edmondsley. *Dur*....5F 115
Edmondthorpe. *Leics*....4F 75
Edmonstone. *Orkn*....5E 172
Edmonton. *Corn*....1D 6
Edmonton. *G Lon*....1E 39
Edmundbyers. *Dur*....4D 114
Ednam. *Bord*....1B 120
Ednaston. *Derbs*....1G 73
Edney Common. *Essx*....5G 53
Edstaston. *Shrp*....2H 71
Edstone. *Warw*....4F 61
Edwalton. *Notts*....2C 74
Edwardstone. *Suff*....1C 54
Edwardsville. *Mer T*....2D 32
Edwinsford. *Carm*....2G 45
Edwinstowe. *Notts*....4D 86
Edworth. *C Beds*....1C 52
Edwyn Ralph. *Here*....5A 60
Edzell. *Ang*....2F 145
Efail-fach. *Neat*....2A 32
Efail Isaf. *Rhon*....3D 32
Efailnewydd. *Gwyn*....2C 68
Efail-rhyd. *Powy*....3D 70
Efailwen. *Carm*....2F 43
Efenechtyd. *Den*....5D 82
Effingham. *Surr*....5C 38
Effingham Common. *Surr*....5C 38

Effirth. *Shet*....6E 173
Efflinch. *Staf*....4F 73
Efford. *Devn*....2B 12
Efstigarth. *Shet*....2F 173
Egbury. *Hants*....1C 24
Egdon. *Worc*....5D 60
Egerton. *G Man*....3F 91
Egerton. *Kent*....1D 28
Egerton Forstal. *Kent*....1C 28
Eggborough. *N Yor*....2F 93
Eggbuckland. *Plym*....3A 8
Eggesford. *Devn*....1G 11
Eggington. *C Beds*....3H 51
Eggington. *Derbs*....3G 73
Egglescliffe. *Stoc T*....3B 106
Eggleston. *Dur*....2C 104
Egham. *Surr*....3B 38
Egham Hythe. *Surr*....3B 38
Egleton. *Rut*....5F 75
Eglingham. *Nmbd*....3F 121
Eglinton. *Derr*....1D 174
Egloshayle. *Corn*....5A 10
Egloskerry. *Corn*....4C 10
Eglwysbach. *Cnwy*....3H 81
Eglwys-Brewis. *V Glam*....5D 32
Eglwys Fach. *Cdgn*....1F 57
Eglwyswrw. *Pemb*....1F 43
Egmanton. *Notts*....4E 87
Egmere. *Norf*....2B 78
Egremont. *Cumb*....3B 102
Egremont. *Mers*....1F 83
Egton. *N Yor*....4F 107
Egton Bridge. *N Yor*....4F 107
Egypt. *Buck*....2A 38
Egypt. *Hants*....2C 24
Eight Ash Green. *Essx*....3C 54
Eight Mile Burn. *Midl*....4E 129
Eignaig. *High*....4B 140
Eilanreach. *High*....2G 147
Eildon. *Bord*....1H 119
Eileanach Lodge. *High*....2H 157
Eilean Fhlodaigh. *W Isl*....3D 170
Eilean Iarmain. *High*....2F 147
Einacleit. *W Isl*....5D 171
Eisgein. *W Isl*....6F 171
Eisingrug. *Gwyn*....2F 69
Elan Village. *Powy*....4B 58
Elberton. *S Glo*....3B 34
Elbridge. *W Sus*....5A 26
Elburton. *Plym*....3B 8
Elcho. *Per*....1D 136
Elcombe. *Swin*....3G 35
Elcot. *W Ber*....5B 36
Eldernell. *Cambs*....1C 64
Eldersfield. *Worc*....2D 48
Elderslie. *Ren*....3F 127
Elder Street. *Essx*....2F 53
Eldon. *Dur*....2F 105
Eldroth. *N Yor*....3G 97
Eldwick. *W Yor*....5D 98
Elfhowe. *Cumb*....5F 103
Elford. *Nmbd*....1F 121
Elford. *Staf*....4F 73
Elford Closes. *Cambs*....3D 65
Elgin. *Mor*....2G 159
Elgol. *High*....2D 146
Elham. *Kent*....1F 29
Elie. *Fife*....3G 137
Eling. *Hants*....1B 16
Eling. *W Ber*....4D 36
Elishaw. *Nmbd*....5C 120
Elizafield. *Dum*....2B 112
Elkesley. *Notts*....3D 86
Elkington. *Nptn*....3D 62
Elkins Green. *Essx*....5G 53
Elkstone. *Glos*....4E 49
Ellan. *High*....1C 150
Elland. *W Yor*....2B 92
Ellary. *Arg*....2F 125
Ellastone. *Staf*....1F 73
Ellbridge. *Corn*....2A 8
Ellel. *Lanc*....4D 97

Ellenborough. *Cumb*....1B 102
Ellenbrook. *Herts*....5C 52
Ellenhall. *Staf*....3C 72
Ellen's Green. *Surr*....2B 26
Ellerbeck. *N Yor*....5B 106
Ellerburn. *N Yor*....1C 100
Ellerby. *N Yor*....3E 107
Ellerdine. *Telf*....3A 72
Ellerdine Heath. *Telf*....3A 72
Ellerhayes. *Devn*....2C 12
Elleric. *Arg*....4E 141
Ellerker. *E Yor*....2C 94
Ellerton. *E Yor*....1H 93
Ellerton. *Shrp*....3B 72
Ellerton-on-Swale. *N Yor*....5F 105
Ellesborough. *Buck*....5G 51
Ellesmere. *Shrp*....2G 71
Ellesmere Port. *Ches W*....3G 83
Ellingham. *Hants*....2G 15
Ellingham. *Norf*....1F 67
Ellingham. *Nmbd*....2F 121
Ellingstring. *N Yor*....1D 98
Ellington. *Cambs*....3A 64
Ellington. *Nmbd*....5G 121
Ellington Thorpe. *Cambs*....3A 64
Elliot. *Ang*....5F 145
Ellisfield. *Hants*....2E 25
Ellishadder. *High*....2E 155
Ellistown. *Leics*....4B 74
Ellon. *Abers*....5G 161
Ellonby. *Cumb*....1F 103
Ellough. *Suff*....2G 67
Elloughton. *E Yor*....2C 94
Ellwood. *Glos*....5A 48
Elm. *Cambs*....5D 76
Elmbridge. *Glos*....4D 48
Elmbridge. *Worc*....4D 60
Elmdon. *Essx*....2E 53
Elmdon. *W Mid*....2F 61
Elmdon Heath. *W Mid*....2F 61
Elmesthorpe. *Leics*....1B 62
Elmfield. *IOW*....3E 16
Elm Hill. *Dors*....4D 22
Elmhurst. *Staf*....4F 73
Elmley Castle. *Worc*....1E 49
Elmley Lovett. *Worc*....4C 60
Elmore. *Glos*....4C 48
Elmore Back. *Glos*....4C 48
Elm Park. *G Lon*....2G 39
Elmscott. *Devn*....4C 18
Elmsett. *Suff*....1D 54
Elmstead. *Essx*....3D 54
Elmstead Heath. *Essx*....3D 54
Elmstead Market. *Essx*....3D 54
Elmsted. *Kent*....1F 29
Elmstone. *Kent*....4G 41
Elmstone Hardwicke
  Glos....3E 49
Elmswell. *E Yor*....4D 101
Elmswell. *Suff*....4B 66
Elmton. *Derbs*....3C 86
Elphin. *High*....2G 163
Elphinstone. *E Lot*....2G 129
Elrick. *Abers*....3F 153
Elrick. *Mor*....1B 152
Elrig. *Dum*....5A 110
Elsdon. *Nmbd*....5D 120
Elsecar. *S Yor*....1A 86
Elsenham. *Essx*....3F 53
Elsfield. *Oxon*....4D 50
Elsham. *N Lin*....3D 94
Elslack. *N Yor*....5B 98
Elsrickle. *S Lan*....5D 128
Elsted. *W Sus*....1G 17
Elsted Marsh. *W Sus*....4G 25
Elsthorpe. *Linc*....3H 75
Elstob. *Dur*....2A 106
Elston. *Devn*....2A 12
Elston. *Lanc*....1E 90
Elston. *Notts*....1E 75
Elston. *Wilts*....2F 23
Elstone. *Devn*....1G 11

H

Hamstead. *IOW* 3C **16**
Hamstead. *W Mid* 1E **61**
Hamstead Marshall *W Ber* 5C **36**
Hamsterley. *Dur*
nr. Consett 4E **115**
nr. Wolsingham 1E **105**
Hamsterley Mill. *Dur* 4E **115**
Ham Street. *Som* 3A **22**
Hamstreet. *Kent* 2E **28**
Hamworthy. *Pool* 3E **15**
Hanbury. *Staf* 3F **73**
Hanbury. *Worc* 4D **60**
Hanbury Woodend. *Staf* 3F **73**
Hanby. *Linc* 2H **75**
Hanchurch. *Staf* 1C **72**
Hand and Pen. *Devn* 3D **12**
Handbridge. *Ches W* 4G **83**
Handcross. *W Sus* 2D **26**
Handforth. *Ches E* 2C **84**
Handley. *Ches W* 5G **83**
Handley. *Derbs* 4A **86**
Handsacre. *Staf* 4E **73**
Handsworth. *S Yor* 2B **86**
Handsworth. *W Mid* 1E **61**
Handy Cross. *Buck* 2G **37**
Hanford. *Dors* 1D **14**
Hanford. *Stoke* 1C **72**
Hangersley. *Hants* 2G **15**
Hanging Houghton. *Nptn* 3E **63**
Hanging Langford. *Wilts* 3F **23**
Hangleton. *Brig* 5D **26**
Hangleton. *W Sus* 5B **26**
Hanham. *S Glo* 4B **34**
Hanham Green. *S Glo* 4B **34**
Hankelow. *Ches E* 1A **72**
Hankerton. *Wilts* 2E **35**
Hankham. *E Sus* 5H **27**
Hanley. *Stoke* 1C **72**
Hanley Castle. *Worc* 1D **48**
Hanley Childe. *Worc* 4A **60**
Hanley Swan. *Worc* 1D **48**
Hanley William. *Worc* 4A **60**
Hanlith. *N Yor* 3B **98**
Hanmer. *Wrex* 2G **71**
Hannaborough. *Devn* 2F **11**
Hannaford. *Devn* 4G **19**
Hannah. *Linc* 3E **89**
Hannington. *Hants* 1D **24**
Hannington. *Nptn* 3F **63**
Hannington. *Swin* 2G **35**
Hannington Wick. *Swin* 2G **35**
Hanscombe End. *C Beds* 2B **52**
Hanslope. *Mil* 1G **51**
Hanthorpe. *Linc* 3H **75**
Hanwell. *G Lon* 2C **38**
Hanwell. *Oxon* 1C **50**
Hanwood. *Shrp* 5G **71**
Hanworth. *G Lon* 3C **38**
Hanworth. *Norf* 2D **78**
Happas. *Ang* 4D **144**
Happendon. *S Lan* 1A **118**
Happisburgh. *Norf* 2F **79**
Happisburgh Common *Norf* 3F **79**
Hapsford. *Ches W* 3G **83**
Hapton. *Lanc* 1F **91**
Hapton. *Norf* 1D **66**
Harberton. *Devn* 3D **9**
Harbertonford. *Devn* 3D **9**
Harbledown. *Kent* 5F **41**
Harborne. *W Mid* 2E **61**
Harborough Magna. *Warw* 3B **62**
Harbottle. *Nmbd* 4D **120**
Harbourneford. *Devn* 2D **8**
Harbours Hill. *Worc* 4D **60**
Harbridge. *Hants* 1G **15**
Harbury. *Warw* 4A **62**
Harby. *Leics* 2E **75**
Harby. *Notts* 3F **87**
Harcombe. *Devn* 3E **13**
Harcombe Bottom. *Devn* 3G **13**
Harcourt. *Corn* 5C **6**
Harden. *W Yor* 1A **92**
Hardenhuish. *Wilts* 4E **35**
Hardgate. *Abers* 3E **153**
Hardgate. *Dum* 3F **111**
Hardham. *W Sus* 4B **26**
Hardingham. *Norf* 5C **78**
Hardingstone. *Nptn* 5E **63**
Hardings Wood. *Staf* 5C **84**
Hardington. *Som* 1C **22**
Hardington Mandeville. *Som* 1A **14**
Hardington Marsh. *Som* 2A **14**
Hardington Moor. *Som* 1A **14**
Hardley. *Hants* 2C **16**
Hardley Street. *Norf* 5F **79**
Hardmead. *Mil* 1H **51**
Hardraw. *N Yor* 5B **104**
Hardstoft. *Derbs* 4B **86**
Hardway. *Hants* 2E **16**
Hardway. *Som* 3C **22**
Hardwick. *Buck* 4G **51**
Hardwick. *Cambs* 5C **64**
Hardwick. *Norf* 2E **66**
Hardwick. *Nptn* 4F **63**
Hardwick. *Oxon*
nr. Bicester 3D **50**
nr. Witney 5B **50**
Hardwick. *Shrp* 1F **59**
Hardwick. *S Yor* 2B **86**
Hardwick. *Stoc T* 2B **106**
Hardwick. *W Mid* 1E **61**
Hardwicke. *Glos*
nr. Cheltenham 3E **49**
nr. Gloucester 4C **48**
Hardwicke. *Here* 1F **47**
Hardwick Village. *Notts* 3D **86**
Hardy's Green. *Essx* 3C **54**
Hare. *Som* 1F **13**
Hareby. *Linc* 4C **88**
Hareden. *Lanc* 4F **97**
Harefield. *G Lon* 1B **38**
Hare Green. *Essx* 3D **54**
Hare Hatch. *Wok* 4G **37**
Harehill. *Derbs* 2F **73**
Harehills. *W Yor* 1D **92**
Harehope. *Nmbd* 2E **121**
Harelaw. *Dum* 2F **113**
Harelaw. *Dur* 4E **115**
Hareplain. *Kent* 2C **28**
Haresceugh. *Cumb* 5H **113**
Harescombe. *Glos* 4D **48**
Haresfield. *Glos* 4D **48**
Haresfinch. *Mers* 1H **83**
Hareshaw. *N Lan* 3B **128**
Hare Street. *Essx* 5E **53**
Hare Street. *Herts* 3D **53**
Harewood. *W Yor* 5F **99**
Harewood End. *Here* 3A **48**
Harford. *Devn* 3C **8**
Hargate. *Norf* 1D **66**
Hargatewall. *Derbs* 3F **85**
Hargrave. *Ches W* 4G **83**
Hargrave. *Nptn* 3H **63**
Hargrave. *Suff* 5G **65**
Harker. *Cumb* 3E **113**
Harkland. *Shet* 3F **173**
Harkstead. *Suff* 2E **55**
Harlaston. *Staf* 4G **73**
Harlaxton. *Linc* 2F **75**
Harlech. *Gwyn* 2E **69**
Harlequin. *Notts* 2D **74**
Harlescott. *Shrp* 4H **71**
Harleston. *Devn* 4D **9**
Harleston. *Norf* 2E **67**
Harleston. *Suff* 4C **66**
Harlestone. *Nptn* 4E **62**
Harley. *Shrp* 5H **71**
Harley. *S Yor* 1A **86**
Harling Road. *Norf* 2B **66**
Harlington. *C Beds* 2A **52**
Harlington. *G Lon* 3B **38**
Harlington. *S Yor* 4E **93**
Harlosh. *High* 4B **154**
Harlow. *Essx* 4E **53**
Harlow Hill. *Nmbd* 3D **115**
Harlsey Castle. *N Yor* 5B **106**
Harlthorpe. *E Yor* 1H **93**
Harlton. *Cambs* 5C **64**
Harlyn Bay. *Corn* 1C **6**
Harman's Cross. *Dors* 4E **15**
Harmby. *N Yor* 1D **98**
Harmer Green. *Herts* 4C **52**
Harmer Hill. *Shrp* 3G **71**
Harmondsworth. *G Lon* 3B **38**
Harmston. *Linc* 4G **87**
Harnage. *Shrp* 5H **71**
Harnham. *Nmbd* 1D **115**
Harnham. *Wilts* 4G **23**
Harnhill. *Glos* 5F **49**
Harold Hill. *G Lon* 1G **39**
Haroldston West. *Pemb* 3C **42**
Haroldswick. *Shet* 1H **173**
Harold Wood. *G Lon* 1G **39**
Harome. *N Yor* 1A **100**
Harpenden. *Herts* 4B **52**
Harpford. *Devn* 3D **12**
Harpham. *E Yor* 3E **101**
Harpley. *Norf* 3G **77**
Harpley. *Worc* 4A **60**
Harpole. *Nptn* 4D **62**
Harpsdale. *High* 3D **168**
Harpsden. *Oxon* 3F **37**
Harpswell. *Linc* 2G **87**
Harpurhey. *G Man* 4G **91**
Harpur Hill. *Derbs* 3E **85**
Harraby. *Cumb* 4F **113**
Harracott. *Devn* 4F **19**
Harrapool. *High* 1E **147**
Harrapul. *High* 1E **147**
Harrietfield. *Per* 1B **136**
Harrietsham. *Kent* 5C **40**
Harrington. *Cumb* 2A **102**
Harrington. *Linc* 3C **88**
Harrington. *Nptn* 2E **63**
Harringworth. *Nptn* 1G **63**
Harriseahead. *Staf* 5C **84**
Harriston. *Cumb* 5C **112**
Harrogate. *N Yor* 4F **99**
Harrold. *Bed* 5G **63**
Harrop Dale. *G Man* 4A **92**
Harrow. *G Lon* 2C **38**
Harrowbarrow. *Corn* 2H **7**
Harrowden. *Bed* 1A **52**
Harrowgate Hill. *Darl* 3F **105**
Harrow on the Hill *G Lon* 2C **38**
Harrow Weald. *G Lon* 1C **38**
Harry Stoke. *S Glo* 4B **34**
Harston. *Cambs* 5D **64**
Harston. *Leics* 2F **75**
Harswell. *E Yor* 5C **100**
Hart. *Hart* 1B **106**
Hartburn. *Nmbd* 1D **115**
Hartburn. *Stoc T* 3B **106**
Hartest. *Suff* 5H **65**
Hartfield. *E Sus* 2F **27**
Hartford. *Cambs* 3B **64**
Hartford. *Ches W* 3A **84**
Hartford. *Som* 4C **20**
Hartford Bridge. *Hants* 1F **25**
Hartford End. *Essx* 4G **53**
Harthill. *Ches W* 5H **83**
Harthill. *N Lan* 3C **128**
Harthill. *S Yor* 2B **86**
Hartington. *Derbs* 4F **85**
Hartland. *Devn* 4C **18**
Hartland Quay. *Devn* 4C **18**
Hartle. *Worc* 3D **60**
Hartlebury. *Worc* 3C **60**
Hartlepool. *Hart* 1C **106**
Hartley. *Cumb* 4A **104**
Hartley. *Kent*
nr. Cranbrook 2B **28**
nr. Dartford 4H **39**
Hartley. *Nmbd* 2G **115**
Hartley Green. *Staf* 3D **73**
Hartley Mauditt. *Hants* 3F **25**
Hartley Wespall. *Hants* 1E **25**
Hartley Wintney. *Hants* 1F **25**
Hartlip. *Kent* 4C **40**
Hartmount Holdings *High* 1B **158**
Hartoft End. *N Yor* 5E **107**
Harton. *N Yor* 3B **100**
Harton. *Shrp* 2G **59**
Harton. *Tyne* 3G **115**
Hartpury. *Glos* 3D **48**
Hartshead. *W Yor* 2B **92**
Hartshill. *Warw* 1H **61**
Hartshorne. *Derbs* 3H **73**
Hartsop. *Cumb* 3F **103**
Hart Station. *Hart* 1B **106**
Hartswell. *Som* 4D **20**
Hartwell. *Nptn* 5E **63**
Hartwood. *Lanc* 3D **90**
Hartwood. *N Lan* 4B **128**
Harvel. *Kent* 4A **40**
Harvington. *Worc*
nr. Evesham 1F **49**
nr. Kidderminster 3C **60**
Harwell. *Oxon* 3C **36**
Harwich. *Essx* 2F **55**
Harwood. *Dur* 1B **104**
Harwood. *G Man* 3F **91**
Harwood Dale. *N Yor* 5G **107**
Harworth. *Notts* 1D **86**
Hascombe. *Surr* 2A **26**
Haselbech. *Nptn* 3E **62**
Haselbury Plucknett *Som* 1H **13**
Haseley. *Warw* 4G **61**
Hasfield. *Glos* 3D **48**
Hasguard. *Pemb* 4C **42**
Haskayne. *Lanc* 4B **90**
Hasketon. *Suff* 5E **67**
Hasland. *Derbs* 4A **86**
Haslemere. *Surr* 2A **26**
Haslingden. *Lanc* 2F **91**
Haslingfield. *Cambs* 5D **64**
Haslington. *Ches E* 5B **84**
Hassall. *Ches E* 5B **84**
Hassall Green. *Ches E* 5B **84**
Hassell Street. *Kent* 1E **29**
Hassendean. *Bord* 2H **119**
Hassingham. *Norf* 5F **79**
Hassness. *Cumb* 3C **102**
Hassocks. *W Sus* 4E **27**
Hassop. *Derbs* 3G **85**
Haster. *High* 3F **169**
Hasthorpe. *Linc* 4D **89**
Hastigrow. *High* 2E **169**
Hastingleigh. *Kent* 1E **29**
Hastings. *E Sus* 5C **28**
Hastingwood. *Essx* 5E **53**
Hastoe. *Herts* 5H **51**
Haston. *Shrp* 3H **71**
Haswell. *Dur* 5G **115**
Haswell Plough. *Dur* 5G **115**
Hatch. *C Beds* 1B **52**
Hatch Beauchamp. *Som* 4G **21**
Hatch End. *G Lon* 1C **38**
Hatch Green. *Som* 1G **13**
Hatching Green. *Herts* 4B **52**
Hatchmere. *Ches W* 3H **83**
Hatch Warren. *Hants* 2E **24**
Hatcliffe. *NE Lin* 4F **95**
Hatfield. *Here* 5H **59**
Hatfield. *Herts* 5C **52**
Hatfield. *S Yor* 4G **93**
Hatfield. *Worc* 5C **60**
Hatfield Broad Oak. *Essx* 4F **53**
Hatfield Garden Village *Herts* 5C **52**
Hatfield Heath. *Essx* 4F **53**
Hatfield Hyde. *Herts* 4C **52**
Hatfield Peverel. *Essx* 4A **54**
Hatfield Woodhouse. *S Yor* 4G **93**
Hatford. *Oxon* 2B **36**
Hatherden. *Hants* 1B **24**
Hatherleigh. *Devn* 2F **11**
Hathern. *Leics* 3B **74**
Hatherop. *Glos* 5G **49**
Hathersage. *Derbs* 2G **85**
Hathersage Booths. *Derbs* 2G **85**
Hatherton. *Ches E* 1A **72**
Hatherton. *Staf* 4D **72**
Hatley St George. *Cambs* 5B **64**
Hatt. *Corn* 2H **7**
Hattersley. *G Man* 1D **85**
Hattingley. *Hants* 3E **25**
Hatton. *Abers* 5H **161**
Hatton. *Derbs* 2G **73**
Hatton. *G Lon* 3B **38**
Hatton. *Linc* 3A **88**
Hatton. *Shrp* 1G **59**
Hatton. *Warr* 2A **84**
Hatton. *Warw* 4G **61**
Hattoncrook. *Abers* 1F **153**
Hatton Heath. *Ches W* 4G **83**
Hatton of Fintray. *Abers* 2F **153**
Haugh. *E Ayr* 2D **117**
Haugh. *Linc* 3D **88**
Haugham. *Linc* 2C **88**
Haugh Head. *Nmbd* 2E **121**
Haughley. *Suff* 4C **66**
Haughley Green. *Suff* 4C **66**
Haugh of Ballechin. *Per* 3G **143**
Haugh of Glass. *Mor* 5B **160**
Haugh of Urr. *Dum* 3F **111**
Haughton. *Ches E* 5H **83**
Haughton. *Notts* 3D **86**
Haughton. *Shrp*
nr. Bridgnorth 1A **60**
nr. Oswestry 3F **71**
nr. Shifnal 5B **72**
nr. Shrewsbury 4H **71**
Haughton. *Staf* 3C **72**
Haughton Green. *G Man* 1D **84**
Haughton le Skerne. *Darl* 3A **106**
Haultwick. *Herts* 3D **52**
Haunn. *Arg* 4E **139**
Haunn. *W Isl* 7C **170**
Haunton. *Staf* 4G **73**
Hauxton. *Cambs* 5D **64**
Havannah. *Ches E* 4C **84**
Havant. *Hants* 2F **17**
Haven. *Here* 5G **59**
The Haven. *W Sus* 2B **26**
Haven Bank. *Linc* 5B **88**
Havenstreet. *IOW* 3D **16**
Havercroft. *W Yor* 3D **93**
Haverfordwest. *Pemb* 3D **42**
Haverhill. *Suff* 1G **53**
Haverigg. *Cumb* 2A **96**
Havering-Atte-Bower *G Lon* 1G **39**
Havering's Grove. *Essx* 1A **40**
Haversham. *Mil* 1G **51**
Haverthwaite. *Cumb* 1C **96**
Haverton Hill. *Stoc T* 2B **106**
Havyatt. *Som* 3A **22**
Hawarden. *Flin* 4F **83**
Hawbridge. *Worc* 1E **49**
Hawcoat. *Cumb* 2B **96**
Hawcross. *Glos* 2C **48**
Hawen. *Cdgn* 1D **44**
Hawes. *N Yor* 1A **98**
Hawes Green. *Norf* 1E **67**
Hawick. *Bord* 3H **119**
Hawkchurch. *Devn* 2G **13**
Hawkedon. *Suff* 5G **65**
Hawkenbury. *Kent* 1C **28**
Hawkeridge. *Wilts* 1D **22**
Hawkerland. *Devn* 4D **12**
Hawkesbury. *S Glo* 3C **34**
Hawkesbury. *Warw* 2A **62**
Hawkesbury Upton. *S Glo* 3C **34**
Hawkes End. *W Mid* 2G **61**
Hawk Green. *G Man* 2D **84**
Hawkhurst. *Kent* 2B **28**
Hawkhurst Common *E Sus* 4G **27**
Hawkinge. *Kent* 1G **29**
Hawkley. *Hants* 4F **25**
Hawkridge. *Som* 3B **20**
Hawksdale. *Cumb* 5E **113**
Hawkshaw. *G Man* 3F **91**
Hawkshead. *Cumb* 5E **103**

Laggan – Leek Wootton

Laggan. *Arg* 4A 124
Laggan. *High*
nr. Fort Augustus 4E 149
nr. Newtonmore 4A 150
Laggan. *Mor* 5H 159
Lagganlia. *High* 3C 150
Lagganulva. *Arg* 4F 139
Laglingarten. *Arg* 3A 134
Lagness. *W Sus* 2G 17
Laid. *High* 3E 166
Laide. *High* 4C 162
Laigh Fenwick. *E Ayr* 5F 127
Laindon. *Essx* 2A 40
Lairg. *High* 3C 164
Lairg Muir. *High* 3C 164
Laithes. *Cumb* 1F 103
Laithkirk. *Dur* 2C 104
Lake. *Devn* 3F 19
Lake. *IOW* 4D 16
Lake. *Wilts* 3G 23
Lakenham. *Norf* 5E 79
Lakenheath. *Suff* 2G 65
Lakesend. *Norf* 1E 65
Lakeside. *Cumb* 1C 96
Laleham. *Surr* 4B 38
Laleston. *B'end* 3B 32
Lamancha. *Bord* 4F 129
Lamarsh. *Essx* 2B 54
Lamas. *Norf* 3E 79
Lamb Corner. *Essx* 2D 54
Lambden. *Bord* 5D 130
Lamberhead Green. *G Man* 4D 90
Lamberhurst. *Kent* 2A 28
Lamberhurst Quarter. *Kent* 2A 28
Lamberton. *Bord* 4F 131
Lambeth. *G Lon* 3E 39
Lambfell Moar. *IOM* 3B 108
Lambhill. *Glas* 3G 127
Lambley. *Nmbd* 4H 113
Lambley. *Notts* 1D 74
Lambourn. *W Ber* 4B 36
Lambourne End. *Essx* 1F 39
Lambourn Woodlands
W Ber 4B 36
Lambs Green. *Dors* 3E 15
Lambs Green. *W Sus* 2D 26
Lambston. *Pemb* 3D 42
Lamellion. *Corn* 2G 7
Lamerton. *Devn* 5E 11
Lamesley. *Tyne* 4F 115
Laminess. *Orkn* 4F 172
Lamington. *High* 1B 158
Lamington. *S Lan* 1B 118
Lamlash. *N Ayr* 2E 123
Lamonby. *Cumb* 1F 103
Lamorick. *Corn* 2E 7
Lamorna. *Corn* 4B 4
Lamorran. *Corn* 4C 6
Lampeter. *Cdgn* 1F 45
Lampeter Velfrey. *Pemb* 3F 43
Lamphey. *Pemb* 4E 43
Lamplugh. *Cumb* 2B 102
Lamport. *Nptn* 3E 63
Lamyatt. *Som* 3B 22
Lana. *Devn*
nr. Ashwater 3D 10
nr. Holsworthy 2D 10
Lanark. *S Lan* 5B 128
Lanarth. *Corn* 4E 5
Lancaster. *Lanc* 3D 97
Lanchester. *Dur* 5E 115
Lancing. *W Sus* 5C 26
Landbeach. *Cambs* 4D 65
Landcross. *Devn* 4E 19
Landerberry. *Abers* 3E 153
Landford. *Wilts* 1A 16
Land Gate. *G Man* 4D 90
Landhallow. *High* 5D 169
Landimore. *Swan* 3D 30
Landkey. *Devn* 3F 19
Landkey Newland. *Devn* 3F 19
Landore. *Swan* 3F 31
Landport. *Port* 2E 17
Landrake. *Corn* 2H 7
Landscove. *Devn* 2D 9
Land's End Airport. *Corn* 4A 4
Landshipping. *Pemb* 3E 43
Landulph. *Corn* 2A 8
Landywood. *Staf* 5D 73
Lane. *Corn* 2C 6
Laneast. *Corn* 4C 10
Lane Bottom. *Lanc* 1G 91
Lane End. *Buck* 2G 37
Lane End. *Hants* 4D 24
Lane End. *IOW* 4E 17
Lane End. *Wilts* 2D 22
Lane Ends. *Derbs* 2G 73
Lane Ends. *Dur* 1E 105
Lane Ends. *Lanc* 4G 97
Laneham. *Notts* 3F 87
Lane Head. *Dur*
nr. Hutton Magna 3E 105
nr. Woodland 2D 105
Lane Head. *G Man* 1A 84
Lane Head. *W Yor* 4B 92
Lanehead. *Dur* 5B 114
Lanehead. *Nmbd* 1A 114
Lane Heads. *Lanc* 1C 90
Lanercost. *Cumb* 3G 113
Laneshaw Bridge. *Lanc* 5B 98
Laney Green. *Staf* 5D 72
Langais. *W Isl* 2D 170
Langal. *High* 2B 140
Langar. *Notts* 2E 74
Langbank. *Ren* 2E 127
Langbar. *N Yor* 4C 98
Langburnshiels. *Bord* 4H 119
Langcliffe. *N Yor* 3H 97
Langdale End. *N Yor* 5G 107
Langdon. *Corn* 3C 10
Langdon Beck. *Dur* 1B 104
Langdon Cross. *Corn* 4D 10
Langdon Hills. *Essx* 2A 40
Langdown. *Hants* 2C 16
Langdyke. *Fife* 3F 137
Langenhoe. *Essx* 4D 54
Langford. *C Beds* 1B 52
Langford. *Devn* 2D 12
Langford. *Essx* 5B 54
Langford. *Notts* 5F 87
Langford. *Oxon* 5H 49
Langford. *Som* 4F 21
Langford Budville. *Som* 4E 20
Langham. *Dors* 4C 22
Langham. *Essx* 2D 54
Langham. *Norf* 1C 78
Langham. *Rut* 4F 75
Langham. *Suff* 4B 66
Langho. *Lanc* 1F 91
Langholm. *Dum* 1E 113
Langland. *Swan* 4F 31
Langleeford. *Nmbd* 2D 120
Langley. *Ches E* 3D 84
Langley. *Derbs* 1B 74
Langley. *Essx* 2E 53
Langley. *Glos* 3F 49
Langley. *Hants* 2C 16
Langley. *Herts* 3C 52
Langley. *Kent* 5C 40
Langley. *Nmbd* 3B 114
Langley. *Slo* 3B 38
Langley. *Som* 4D 20
Langley. *Warw* 4F 61
Langley. *W Sus* 4G 25
Langley Burrell. *Wilts* 4E 35
Langleybury. *Herts* 5A 52
Langley Common. *Derbs* 2G 73
Langley Green. *Derbs* 2G 73
Langley Green. *Norf* 5F 79
Langley Green. *Warw* 4F 61
Langley Green. *W Sus* 2D 26
Langley Heath. *Kent* 5C 40
Langley Marsh. *Som* 4D 20
Langley Moor. *Dur* 5F 115
Langley Park. *Dur* 5F 115
Langley Street. *Norf* 5F 79
Langney. *E Sus* 5H 27
Langold. *Notts* 2C 86
Langore. *Corn* 4C 10
Langport. *Som* 4H 21
Langrick. *Linc* 1B 76
Langridge. *Bath* 5C 34
Langridgeford. *Devn* 4F 19
Langrigg. *Cumb* 5C 112
Langrish. *Hants* 4F 25
Langsett. *S Yor* 4C 92
Langshaw. *Bord* 1H 119
Langstone. *Hants* 2F 17
Langthorne. *N Yor* 5F 105
Langthorpe. *N Yor* 3F 99
Langthwaite. *N Yor* 4D 104
Langtoft. *E Yor* 3E 101
Langtoft. *Linc* 4A 76
Langton. *Dur* 3E 105
Langton. *Linc*
nr. Horncastle 4B 88
nr. Spilsby 3C 88
Langton. *N Yor* 3B 100
Langton by Wragby. *Linc* 3A 88
Langton Green. *Kent* 2G 27
Langton Herring. *Dors* 4B 14
Langton Long Blandford
Dors 2D 15
Langton Matravers. *Dors* 5E 15
Langtree. *Devn* 1E 11
Langwathby. *Cumb* 1G 103
Langwith. *Derbs* 3C 86
Langworth. *Linc* 3H 87
Lanivet. *Corn* 2E 7
Lanjeth. *Corn* 3D 6
Lank. *Corn* 5A 10
Lanlivery. *Corn* 3E 7
Lanner. *Corn* 5B 6
Lanreath. *Corn* 3F 7
Lansallos. *Corn* 3F 7
Lansdown. *Bath* 5C 34
Lansdown. *Glos* 3E 49
Lanteglos Highway. *Corn* 3F 7
Lanton. *Nmbd* 1D 120
Lanton. *Bord* 2A 120
Lapford. *Devn* 2H 11
Lapford Cross. *Devn* 2H 11
Laphroaig. *Arg* 5B 124
Lapley. *Staf* 4C 72
Lapworth. *Warw* 3F 61
Larachbeg. *High* 4A 140
Larbert. *Falk* 1B 128
Larden Green. *Ches E* 5H 83
Larel. *High* 3D 169
Largie. *Abers* 5D 160
Largiemore. *Arg* 1H 125
Largoward. *Fife* 3G 137
Largs. *N Ayr* 4D 126
Largue. *Abers* 4D 160
Largybeg. *N Ayr* 3E 123
Largymeanoch. *N Ayr* 3E 123
Largymore. *N Ayr* 3E 123
Larkfield. *Inv* 2D 126
Larkfield. *Kent* 5B 40
Larkhall. *Bath* 5C 34
Larkhall. *S Lan* 4A 128
Larkhill. *Wilts* 2G 23
Larling. *Norf* 2B 66
Larne. *ME Ant* 2H 175
Larport. *Here* 2A 48
Lartington. *Dur* 3D 104
Lary. *Abers* 3H 151
Lasham. *Hants* 2E 25
Lashenden. *Kent* 1C 28
Lasswade. *Midl* 3G 129
Lastingham. *N Yor* 5E 107
Latchford. *Herts* 3D 53
Latchford. *Oxon* 5E 51
Latchingdon. *Essx* 5B 54
Latchley. *Corn* 5E 11
Latchmere Green. *Hants* 1E 25
Lathbury. *Mil* 1G 51
Latheron. *High* 5D 169
Latheronwheel. *High* 5D 169
Lathom. *Lanc* 4C 90
Lathones. *Fife* 3G 137
Latimer. *Buck* 1B 38
Latteridge. *S Glo* 3B 34
Lattiford. *Som* 4B 22
Latton. *Wilts* 2F 35
Laudale House. *High* 3B 140
Lauder. *Bord* 5B 130
Laugharne. *Carm* 3H 43
Laughterton. *Linc* 3F 87
Laughton. *E Sus* 4G 27
Laughton. *Leics* 2D 62
Laughton. *Linc*
nr. Gainsborough 1F 87
nr. Grantham 2H 75
Laughton Common. *S Yor* 2C 86
Laughton en le Morthen
S Yor 2C 86
Launcells. *Corn* 2C 10
Launceston. *Corn* 4D 10
Launcherley. *Som* 2A 22
Launton. *Oxon* 3E 50
Laurencekirk. *Abers* 1G 145
Laurieston. *Dum* 3D 111
Laurieston. *Falk* 2C 128
Lavendon. *Mil* 5G 63
Lavenham. *Suff* 1C 54
Laverhay. *Dum* 5D 118
Laversdale. *Cumb* 3F 113
Laverstock. *Wilts* 3G 23
Laverstoke. *Hants* 2C 24
Laverton. *Glos* 2F 49
Laverton. *N Yor* 2E 99
Laverton. *Som* 1C 22
Lavister. *Wrex* 5F 83
Law. *S Lan* 4B 128
Lawers. *Per* 5D 142
Lawford. *Essx* 2D 54
Lawhitton. *Corn* 4D 10
Lawkland. *N Yor* 3G 97
Lawley. *Telf* 5A 72
Lawnhead. *Staf* 3C 72
Lawrenny. *Pemb* 4E 43
Lawshall. *Suff* 5A 66
Lawton. *Here* 5G 59
Laxey. *IOM* 3D 108
Laxfield. *Suff* 3E 67
Laxfirth. *Shet* 6F 173
Laxo. *Shet* 5F 173
Laxton. *E Yor* 2A 94
Laxton. *Nptn* 1G 63
Laxton. *Notts* 4E 86
Laycock. *W Yor* 5C 98
Layer Breton. *Essx* 4C 54
Layer-de-la-Haye. *Essx* 3C 54
Layer Marney. *Essx* 4C 54
Laymore. *Dors* 2G 13
Laysters Pole. *Here* 4H 59
Layter's Green. *Buck* 1A 38
Laytham. *E Yor* 1H 93
Lazenby. *Red C* 3C 106
Lazonby. *Cumb* 1G 103
Lea. *Derbs* 5H 85
Lea. *Here* 3B 48
Lea. *Linc* 2F 87
Lea. *Shrp*
nr. Bishop's Castle 2F 59
nr. Shrewsbury 5G 71
Lea. *Wilts* 3E 35
Leabrooks. *Derbs* 5B 86
Leac a Li. *W Isl* 8D 171
Leachd. *Arg* 4H 133
Leachkin. *High* 4A 158
Leachpool. *Pemb* 3D 42
Leadburn. *Midl* 4F 129
Leadenham. *Linc* 5G 87
Leaden Roding. *Essx* 4F 53
Leaderfoot. *Bord* 1H 119
Leadgate. *Cumb* 5A 114
Leadgate. *Dur* 4E 115
Leadgate. *Nmbd* 4E 115
Leadhills. *S Lan* 3A 118
Leadingcross Green. *Kent* 5C 40
Lea End. *Worc* 3E 61
Leafield. *Oxon* 4B 50
Leagrave. *Lutn* 3A 52
Lea Hall. *W Mid* 2F 61
Lea Heath. *Staf* 3E 73
Leake. *N Yor* 5B 106
Leake Common Side. *Linc* 5C 88
Leake Fold Hill. *Linc* 5D 88
Leake Hurn's End. *Linc* 1D 76
Lealholm. *N Yor* 4E 107
Lealt. *Arg* 4D 132
Lealt. *High* 2E 155
Leam. *Derbs* 3G 85
Lea Marston. *Warw* 1G 61
Leamington Hastings. *Warw* 4B 62
Leamington Spa, Royal
Warw 4H 61
Leamonsley. *Staf* 5F 73
Leamside. *Dur* 5G 115
Leargybreck. *Arg* 2D 124
Lease Rigg. *N Yor* 4F 107
Leasgill. *Cumb* 1D 97
Leasingham. *Linc* 1H 75
Leasingthorne. *Dur* 1F 105
Leasowe. *Mers* 1E 83
Leatherhead. *Surr* 5C 38
Leathley. *N Yor* 5E 99
Leaths. *Dum* 3E 111
Leaton. *Shrp* 4G 71
Leaton. *Telf* 4A 72
Lea Town. *Lanc* 1C 90
Leaveland. *Kent* 5E 40
Leavenheath. *Suff* 2C 54
Leavening. *N Yor* 3B 100
Leaves Green. *G Lon* 4F 39
Lea Yeat. *Cumb* 1G 97
Leazes. *Dur* 4E 115
Lebberston. *N Yor* 1E 101
Lechlade on Thames. *Glos* 2H 35
Leck. *Lanc* 2F 97
Leckford. *Hants* 3B 24
Leckfurin. *High* 3H 167
Leckgruinart. *Arg* 3A 124
Leckhampstead. *Buck* 2F 51
Leckhampstead. *W Ber* 4C 36
Leckhampton. *Glos* 4E 49
Leckmelm. *High* 4F 163
Leckwith. *V Glam* 4E 33
Leconfield. *E Yor* 5E 101
Ledaig. *Arg* 5D 140
Ledburn. *Buck* 3H 51
Ledbury. *Here* 2C 48
Ledgemoor. *Here* 5G 59
Ledgowan. *High* 3D 156
Ledicot. *Here* 4G 59
Ledmore. *High* 2G 163
Lednabirichen. *High* 4E 165
Lednagullin. *High* 2A 168
Ledsham. *Ches W* 3F 83
Ledsham. *W Yor* 2E 93
Ledston. *W Yor* 2E 93
Ledstone. *Devn* 4D 8
Ledwell. *Oxon* 3C 50
Lee. *Devn*
nr. Ilfracombe 2E 19
nr. South Molton 4B 20
Lee. *G Lon* 3E 39
Lee. *Hants* 1B 16
Lee. *Lanc* 4E 97
Lee. *Shrp* 2G 71
The Lee. *Buck* 5H 51
Leeans. *Shet* 7E 173
Leebotten. *Shet* 9F 173
Leebotwood. *Shrp* 1G 59
Lee Brockhurst. *Shrp* 3H 71
Leece. *Cumb* 3B 96
Leechpool. *Mon* 3A 34
Lee Clump. *Buck* 5H 51
Leeds. *Kent* 5C 40
Leeds. *W Yor* 1C 92
Leeds Bradford Airport
W Yor 5E 99
Leedstown. *Corn* 3D 4
Leegomery. *Telf* 4A 72
Lee Head. *Derbs* 1E 85
Leek. *Staf* 5D 85
Leekbrook. *Staf* 5D 85
Leek Wootton. *Warw* 4G 61

Lee Mill – Little Cubley

Lee Mill. *Devn* 3B 8
Leeming. *N Yor* 1E 99
Leeming Bar. *N Yor* 5F 105
Lee Moor. *Devn* 2B 8
Lee Moor. *W Yor* 2D 92
Lee-on-the-Solent. *Hants* 2D 16
Lees. *Derbs* 2G 73
Lees. *G Man* 4H 91
Lees. *W Yor* 1A 92
The Lees. *Kent* 5E 40
Leeswood. *Flin* 4E 83
Leetown. *Per* 1E 136
Leftwich. *Ches W* 3A 84
Legbourne. *Linc* 2C 88
Legburthwaite. *Cumb* 3E 102
Legerwood. *Bord* 5B 130
Legsby. *Linc* 2A 88
Leicester. *Leic* 5C 74
Leicester Forest East. *Leics* 5C 74
Leigh. *Dors* 2B 14
Leigh. *G Man* 4E 91
Leigh. *Kent* 1G 27
Leigh. *Shrp* 5F 71
Leigh. *Surr* 1D 26
Leigh. *Wilts* 2F 35
Leigh. *Worc* 5B 60
The Leigh. *Glos* 3D 48
Leigham. *Plym* 3B 8
Leigh Beck. *Essx* 2C 40
Leigh Common. *Som* 4C 22
Leigh Delamere. *Wilts* 4D 35
Leigh Green. *Kent* 2D 28
Leighland Chapel. *Som* 3D 20
Leigh-on-Sea. *S'end* 2C 40
Leigh Park. *Hants* 2F 17
Leigh Sinton. *Worc* 5B 60
Leighterton. *Glos* 2D 34
Leighton. *N Yor* 2D 98
Leighton. *Powy* 5E 71
Leighton. *Shrp* 5A 72
Leighton. *Som* 2C 22
Leighton Bromswold. *Cambs* 3A 64
Leighton Buzzard. *C Beds* 3H 51
Leigh-upon-Mendip. *Som* 2B 22
Leinthall Earls. *Here* 4G 59
Leinthall Starkes. *Here* 4G 59
Leintwardine. *Here* 3G 59
Leire. *Leics* 1C 62
Leirinmore. *High* 2E 166
Leishmore. *High* 4G 157
Leiston. *Suff* 4G 67
Leitfie. *Per* 4B 144
Leith. *Edin* 2F 129
Leitholm. *Bord* 5D 130
Lelant. *Corn* 3C 4
Lelant Downs. *Corn* 3C 4
Lelley. *E Yor* 1F 95
Lem Hill. *Shrp* 3B 60
Lemington. *Tyne* 3E 115
Lempitlaw. *Bord* 1B 120
Lemsford. *Herts* 4C 52
Lenacre. *Cumb* 1F 97
Lenchie. *Abers* 5C 160
Lenchwick. *Worc* 1F 49
Lendalfoot. *S Ayr* 1G 109
Lendrick. *Stir* 3E 135
Lenham. *Kent* 5C 40
Lenham Heath. *Kent* 1D 28
Lenimore. *N Ayr* 5G 125
Lennel. *Bord* 5E 131
Lennoxtown. *E Dun* 2H 127
Lenton. *Linc* 2H 75
Lentran. *High* 4H 157
Lenwade. *Norf* 4C 78
Lenzie. *E Dun* 2H 127
Leochel Cushnie. *Abers* 2C 152
Leogh. *Shet* 1B 172
Leominster. *Here* 5G 59
Leonard Stanley. *Glos* 5D 48
Lepe. *Hants* 3C 16
Lephenstrath. *Arg* 5A 122
Lephin. *High* 4A 154
Lephinchapel. *Arg* 4G 133
Lephinmore. *Arg* 4G 133
Leppington. *N Yor* 3B 100
Lepton. *W Yor* 3C 92
Lerryn. *Corn* 3F 7
Lerwick. *Shet* 7F 173
Lerwick (Tingwall) Airport
  Shet 7F 173
Lesbury. *Nmbd* 3G 121
Leslie. *Abers* 1C 152
Leslie. *Fife* 3E 137
Lesmahagow. *S Lan* 1H 117
Lesnewth. *Corn* 3B 10
Lessingham. *Norf* 3F 79
Lessonhall. *Cumb* 4D 112
Leswalt. *Dum* 3F 109
Letchmore Heath. *Herts* 1C 38
Letchworth Garden City
  Herts 2C 52
Letcombe Bassett. *Oxon* 3B 36
Letcombe Regis. *Oxon* 3B 36
Letham. *Ang* 4E 145
Letham. *Falk* 1B 128
Letham. *Fife* 2F 137
Lethanhill. *E Ayr* 3D 116
Lethenty. *Abers* 4F 161
Letheringham. *Suff* 5E 67
Letheringsett. *Norf* 2C 78
Lettaford. *Devn* 4H 11
Lettan. *Orkn* 3G 172
Letter. *Abers* 2E 153
Letterewe. *High* 1B 156
Letterfearn. *High* 1A 148
Lettermore. *Arg* 4F 139
Letters. *High* 5F 163
Letterston. *Pemb* 2D 42
Letton. *Here*
  nr. Kington 1G 47
  nr. Leintwardine 3F 59
Letty Green. *Herts* 4C 52
Letwell. *S Yor* 2C 86
Leuchars. *Fife* 1G 137
Leumrabhagh. *W Isl* 6F 171
Leusdon. *Devn* 5H 11
Levaneap. *Shet* 5F 173
Levedale. *Staf* 4C 72
Leven. *E Yor* 5F 101
Leven. *Fife* 3F 137
Levencorroch. *N Ayr* 3E 123
Levenhall. *E Lot* 2G 129
Levens. *Cumb* 1D 97
Levens Green. *Herts* 3D 52
Levenshulme. *G Man* 1C 84
Levenwick. *Shet* 9F 173
Leverburgh. *W Isl* 9C 171
Leverington. *Cambs* 4D 76
Leverton. *Linc* 1C 76
Leverton. *W Ber* 4B 36
Leverton Lucasgate. *Linc* 1D 76
Leverton Outgate. *Linc* 1D 76
Levington. *Suff* 2F 55
Levisham. *N Yor* 5F 107
Levishie. *High* 2G 149
Lew. *Oxon* 5B 50
Lewaigue. *IOM* 2D 108
Lewannick. *Corn* 4C 10
Lewdown. *Devn* 4E 11
Lewes. *E Sus* 4F 27
Leweston. *Pemb* 2D 42
Lewisham. *G Lon* 3E 39
Lewiston. *High* 1H 149
Lewistown. *B'end* 3C 32
Lewknor. *Oxon* 2F 37
Leworthy. *Devn*
  nr. Barnstaple 3G 19
  nr. Holsworthy 2D 10
Lewson Street. *Kent* 4D 40
Lewthorn Cross. *Devn* 5A 12
Lewtrenchard. *Devn* 4E 11
Ley. *Corn* 2F 7
Leybourne. *Kent* 5A 40
Leyburn. *N Yor* 5E 105
Leycett. *Staf* 1B 72
Leyfields. *Staf* 5G 73
Ley Green. *Herts* 3B 52
Ley Hill. *Buck* 5H 51
Leyland. *Lanc* 2D 90
Leylodge. *Abers* 2E 153
Leymoor. *W Yor* 3B 92
Leys. *Per* 5B 144
Leysdown-on-Sea. *Kent* 3E 41
Leysmill. *Ang* 4F 145
Leyton. *G Lon* 2E 39
Leytonstone. *G Lon* 2F 39
Lezant. *Corn* 5D 10
Leziate. *Norf* 4F 77
Lhanbryde. *Mor* 2G 159
The Lhen. *IOM* 1C 108
Liatrie. *High* 5E 157
Libanus. *Powy* 3C 46
Libberton. *S Lan* 5C 128
Libbery. *Worc* 5D 60
Liberton. *Edin* 3F 129
Liceasto. *W Isl* 8D 171
Lichfield. *Staf* 5F 73
Lickey. *Worc* 3D 61
Lickey End. *Worc* 3D 60
Lickfold. *W Sus* 3A 26
Liddaton. *Devn* 4E 11
Liddington. *Swin* 3H 35
Liddle. *Orkn* 9D 172
Lidgate. *Suff* 5G 65
Lidgett. *Notts* 4D 86
Lidham Hill. *E Sus* 4C 28
Lidlington. *C Beds* 2H 51
Lidsey. *W Sus* 5A 26
Lidstone. *Oxon* 3B 50
Lienassie. *High* 1B 148
Liff. *Ang* 5C 144
Lifford. *W Mid* 2E 61
Lifton. *Devn* 4D 11
Liftondown. *Devn* 4D 10
Lighthorne. *Warw* 5H 61
Light Oaks. *Stoke* 5D 84
Lightwater. *Surr* 4A 38
Lightwood. *Staf* 1E 73
Lightwood. *Stoke* 1D 72
Lightwood Green. *Ches E* 1A 72
Lightwood Green. *Wrex* 1F 71
Lilbourne. *Nptn* 3C 62
Lilburn Tower. *Nmbd* 2E 121
Lillesdon. *Som* 4G 21
Lilleshall. *Telf* 4B 72
Lilley. *Herts* 3B 52
Lilliesleaf. *Bord* 2H 119
Lillingstone Dayrell. *Buck* 2F 51
Lillingstone Lovell. *Buck* 1F 51
Lillington. *Dors* 1B 14
Lilstock. *Som* 2E 21
Lilybank. *Inv* 2E 126
Lilyhurst. *Shrp* 4B 72
Limavady. *Caus* 1D 174
Limbrick. *Lanc* 3E 90
Limbury. *Lutn* 3A 52
Limekilnburn. *S Lan* 4A 128
Limekilns. *Fife* 1D 129
Limerigg. *Falk* 2B 128
Limestone Brae. *Nmbd* 5A 114
Lime Street. *Worc* 2D 48
Limington. *Som* 4A 22
Limpenhoe. *Norf* 5F 79
Limpley Stoke. *Wilts* 5C 34
Limpsfield. *Surr* 5F 39
Limpsfield Chart. *Surr* 5F 39
Linburn. *W Lot* 3E 129
Linby. *Notts* 5C 86
Linchmere. *W Sus* 3G 25
Lincluden. *Dum* 2A 112
Lincoln. *Linc* 3G 87
Lincomb. *Worc* 4C 60
Lindale. *Cumb* 1D 96
Lindal in Furness. *Cumb* 2B 96
Lindean. *Bord* 1G 119
Linden. *Glos* 4D 48
Lindfield. *W Sus* 3E 27
Lindford. *Hants* 3G 25
Lindores. *Fife* 2E 137
Lindridge. *Worc* 4A 60
Lindsell. *Essx* 3G 53
Lindsey. *Suff* 1C 54
Lindsey Tye. *Suff* 1C 54
Linford. *Hants* 2G 15
Linford. *Thur* 3A 40
Lingague. *IOM* 4B 108
Lingdale. *Red C* 3D 106
Lingen. *Here* 4F 59
Lingfield. *Surr* 1E 27
Lingreabhagh. *W Isl* 9C 171
Lingwood. *Norf* 5F 79
Lingy Close. *Cumb* 4E 113
Linicro. *High* 2C 154
Linkend. *Worc* 2D 48
Linkenholt. *Hants* 1B 24
Linkinhorne. *Corn* 5D 10
Linklater. *Orkn* 9D 172
Linksness. *Orkn* 6E 172
Linktown. *Fife* 4E 137
Linkwood. *Mor* 2G 159
Linley. *Shrp*
  nr. Bishop's Castle 1F 59
  nr. Bridgnorth 1A 60
Linley Green. *Here* 5A 60
Linlithgow. *W Lot* 2C 128
Linlithgow Bridge. *Falk* 2C 128
Linneraineach. *High* 3F 163
Linshiels. *Nmbd* 4C 120
Linsiadar. *W Isl* 4E 171
Linsidemore. *High* 4C 164
Linslade. *C Beds* 3H 51
Linstead Parva. *Suff* 3F 67
Linstock. *Cumb* 4F 113
Linthwaite. *W Yor* 3B 92
Lintlaw. *Bord* 4E 131
Lintmill. *Mor* 2C 160
Linton. *Cambs* 1F 53
Linton. *Derbs* 4G 73
Linton. *Here* 3B 48
Linton. *Kent* 1B 28
Linton. *N Yor* 3B 98
Linton. *Bord* 2B 120
Linton. *W Yor* 5F 99
Linton Colliery. *Nmbd* 5G 121
Linton Hill. *Here* 3B 48
Linton-on-Ouse. *N Yor* 3G 99
Lintzford. *Dur* 4E 115
Lintzgarth. *Dur* 5C 114
Linwood. *Hants* 2G 15
Linwood. *Linc* 2A 88
Linwood. *Ren* 3F 127
Lionacleit. *W Isl* 4C 170
Lionacro. *High* 2C 154
Lionacuidhe. *W Isl* 4C 170
Lional. *W Isl* 1H 171
Liphook. *Hants* 3G 25
Lipley. *Shrp* 2B 72
Lipyeate. *Som* 1B 22
Liquo. *N Lan* 4B 128
Lisbellaw. *Ferm* 5C 174
Lisburn. *Lis* 4G 175
Liscard. *Mers* 1F 83
Liscombe. *Som* 3B 20
Liskeard. *Corn* 2G 7
Lisle Court. *Hants* 3B 16
Lisnaskea. *Ferm* 6C 174
Liss. *Hants* 4F 25
Lissett. *E Yor* 4F 101
Liss Forest. *Hants* 4F 25
Lissington. *Linc* 2A 88
Liston. *Essx* 1B 54
Lisvane. *Card* 3E 33
Liswerry. *Newp* 3G 33
Litcham. *Norf* 4A 78
Litchard. *B'end* 3C 32
Litchborough. *Nptn* 5D 62
Litchfield. *Hants* 1C 24
Litherland. *Mers* 1F 83
Litlington. *Cambs* 1D 52
Litlington. *E Sus* 5G 27
Littemill. *Nmbd* 3G 121
Litterty. *Abers* 3E 161
Little Abington. *Cambs* 1F 53
Little Addington. *Nptn* 3G 63
Little Airmyn. *N Yor* 2H 93
Little Alne. *Warw* 4F 61
Little Ardo. *Abers* 5F 161
Little Asby. *Cumb* 4H 103
Little Aston. *Staf* 5E 73
Little Atherfield. *IOW* 4C 16
Little Ayton. *N Yor* 3C 106
Little Baddow. *Essx* 5A 54
Little Badminton. *S Glo* 3D 34
Little Ballinluig. *Per* 3G 143
Little Bampton. *Cumb* 4D 112
Little Bardfield. *Essx* 2G 53
Little Barford. *Bed* 5A 64
Little Barningham. *Norf* 2D 78
Little Barrington. *Glos* 4H 49
Little Barrow. *Ches W* 4G 83
Little Barugh. *N Yor* 2B 100
Little Bavington. *Nmbd* 2C 114
Little Bealings. *Suff* 1F 55
Littlebeck. *Cumb* 3H 103
Little Bedwyn. *Wilts* 5A 36
Little Bentley. *Essx* 3E 54
Little Berkhamsted. *Herts* 5C 52
Little Billing. *Nptn* 4F 63
Little Billington. *C Beds* 3H 51
Little Birch. *Here* 2A 48
Little Bispham. *Bkpl* 5C 96
Little Blakenham. *Suff* 1E 54
Little Blencow. *Cumb* 1F 103
Little Bognor. *W Sus* 3B 26
Little Bolas. *Shrp* 3A 72
Little Bollington. *Ches E* 2B 84
Little Bookham. *Surr* 5C 38
Littleborough. *Devn* 1B 12
Littleborough. *G Man* 3H 91
Littleborough. *Notts* 2F 87
Littlebourne. *Kent* 5G 41
Little Bourton. *Oxon* 1C 50
Little Bowden. *Leics* 2E 63
Little Bradley. *Suff* 5F 65
Little Brampton. *Shrp* 2F 59
Little Brechin. *Ang* 2E 145
Littlebredy. *Dors* 4A 14
Little Brickhill. *Mil* 2H 51
Little Bridgeford. *Staf* 3C 72
Little Brington. *Nptn* 4D 62
Little Bromley. *Essx* 3D 54
Little Broughton. *Cumb* 1B 102
Little Budworth. *Ches W* 4H 83
Little Burstead. *Essx* 1A 40
Little Burton. *E Yor* 5F 101
Littlebury. *Essx* 2F 53
Littlebury Green. *Essx* 2E 53
Little Bytham. *Linc* 4H 75
Little Canfield. *Essx* 3F 53
Little Canford. *Dors* 3F 15
Little Carlton. *Linc* 2C 88
Little Carlton. *Notts* 5E 87
Little Casterton. *Rut* 5H 75
Little Catwick. *E Yor* 5F 101
Little Catworth. *Cambs* 3A 64
Little Cawthorpe. *Linc* 2C 88
Little Chalfont. *Buck* 1A 38
Little Chart. *Kent* 1D 28
Little Chesterford. *Essx* 1F 53
Little Cheverell. *Wilts* 1E 23
Little Chishill. *Cambs* 2E 53
Little Clacton. *Essx* 4E 55
Little Clanfield. *Oxon* 5A 50
Little Clifton. *Cumb* 2B 102
Little Coates. *NE Lin* 4F 95
Little Comberton. *Worc* 1E 49
Little Common. *E Sus* 5B 28
Little Compton. *Warw* 2A 50
Little Cornard. *Suff* 2B 54
Littlecote. *Buck* 3G 51
Littlecott. *Wilts* 1G 23
Little Cowarne. *Here* 5A 60
Little Coxwell. *Oxon* 2A 36
Little Crakehall. *N Yor* 5F 105
Little Crawley. *Mil* 1H 51
Little Creich. *High* 5D 164
Little Cressingham. *Norf* 5A 78
Little Crosby. *Mers* 4B 90
Little Crosthwaite. *Cumb* 2D 102
Little Cubley. *Derbs* 2F 73

Llanfair Clydogau – Lonemore

Llanfair Clydogau. *Cdgn* 5F 57
Llanfair Dyffryn Clwyd. *Den* 5D 82
Llanfairfechan. *Cnwy* 3F 81
Llanfair-Nant-Gwyn. *Pemb* 1F 43
Llanfair Pwllgwyngyll. *IOA* 3E 81
Llanfair Talhaiarn. *Cnwy* 3B 82
Llanfair Waterdine. *Shrp* 3E 59
Llanfair-ym-Muallt. *Powy* 5C 58
Llanfairyneubwll. *IOA* 3C 80
Llanfairynghornwy. *IOA* 1C 80
Llanfallteg. *Carm* 3F 43
Llanfallteg West. *Carm* 3F 43
Llanfaredd. *Powy* 5C 58
Llanfarian. *Cdgn* 3E 57
Llanfechain. *Powy* 3D 70
Llanfechell. *IOA* 1C 80
Llanfendigaid. *Gwyn* 5E 69
Llanferres. *Den* 4D 82
Llan Ffestiniog. *Gwyn* 1G 69
Llanfflewyn. *IOA* 2C 80
Llanfihangel-ar-Arth. *Carm* 2E 45
Llanfihangel Glyn Myfyr
Cnwy 1B 70
Llanfihangel Nant Bran
Powy 2C 46
Llanfihangel-Nant-Melan
Powy 5D 58
Llanfihangel near Rogiet
Mon 3H 33
Llanfihangel Rhydithon
Powy 4D 58
Llanfihangel Tal-y-llyn. *Powy* 3E 46
Llanfihangel-uwch-Gwili
Carm 3E 45
Llanfihangel-y-Creuddyn
Cdgn 3F 57
Llanfihangel-yng-Ngwynfa
Powy 4C 70
Llanfihangel yn Nhowyn. *IOA* 3C 80
Llanfihangel-y-pennant. *Gwyn*
nr. Golan 1E 69
nr. Tywyn 5F 69
Llanfihangel-y-traethau. *Gwyn* 2E 69
Llanfilo. *Powy* 2E 46
Llanfleiddan. *V Glam* 4C 32
Llanfoist. *Mon* 4F 47
Llanfor. *Gwyn* 2B 70
Llanfrechfa. *Torf* 2G 33
Llanfrothen. *Gwyn* 1F 69
Llanfrynach. *Powy* 3D 46
Llanfwrog. *Den* 5D 82
Llanfwrog. *IOA* 2C 80
Llanfyllin. *Powy* 4D 70
Llanfynydd. *Carm* 3F 45
Llanfynydd. *Flin* 5E 83
Llanfyrnach. *Pemb* 1G 43
Llangadfan. *Powy* 4C 70
Llangadog. *Carm*
nr. Llandovery 3H 45
nr. Llanelli 5E 45
Llangadwaladr. *IOA* 4C 80
Llangadwaladr. *Powy* 2D 70
Llangaffo. *IOA* 4D 80
Llangain. *Carm* 4D 45
Llangammarch Wells. *Powy* 1C 46
Llangan. *V Glam* 4C 32
Llangarron. *Here* 3A 48
Llangasty-Talyllyn. *Powy* 3E 47
Llangathen. *Carm* 3F 45
Llangattock. *Powy* 4F 47
Llangattock Lingoed. *Mon* 3G 47
Llangattock-Vibon-Avel. *Mon* 4H 47
Llangedwyn. *Powy* 3D 70
Llangefni. *IOA* 3D 80
Llangeinor. *B'end* 3C 32
Llangeitho. *Cdgn* 5F 57
Llangeler. *Carm* 2D 44
Llangelynin. *Gwyn* 5E 69
Llangendeirne. *Carm* 4E 45
Llangennech. *Carm* 5F 45
Llangennith. *Swan* 3D 30
Llangenny. *Powy* 4F 47
Llangernyw. *Cnwy* 4A 82
Llangian. *Gwyn* 3B 68
Llangiwg. *Neat* 5H 45
Llangloffan. *Pemb* 1D 42
Llanglydwen. *Carm* 2F 43
Llangoed. *IOA* 3F 81
Llangoedmor. *Cdgn* 1B 44
Llangollen. *Den* 1E 70
Llangolman. *Pemb* 2F 43
Llangorse. *Powy* 3E 47
Llangorwen. *Cdgn* 2F 57
Llangovan. *Mon* 5H 47
Llangower. *Gwyn* 2B 70
Llangranog. *Cdgn* 5C 56
Llangristiolus. *IOA* 3D 80
Llangrove. *Here* 4A 48
Llangua. *Mon* 3G 47
Llangunllo. *Powy* 3E 58
Llangunnor. *Carm* 3E 45
Llangurig. *Powy* 3B 58
Llangwm. *Cnwy* 1B 70
Llangwm. *Mon* 5H 47
Llangwm. *Pemb* 4D 43
Llangwm-isaf. *Mon* 5H 47
Llangwnnadl. *Gwyn* 2B 68
Llangwyfan. *Den* 4D 82
Llangwyfan-isaf. *IOA* 4C 80
Llangwyllog. *IOA* 3D 80
Llangwyryfon. *Cdgn* 3F 57
Llangybi. *Cdgn* 5F 57
Llangybi. *Gwyn* 1D 68
Llangybi. *Mon* 2G 33
Llangyfelach. *Swan* 3F 31
Llangynhafal. *Den* 4D 82
Llangynidr. *Powy* 4E 47
Llangynin. *Carm* 3G 43
Llangynog. *Carm* 3H 43
Llangynog. *Powy* 3C 70
Llangynwyd. *B'end* 3B 32
Llanhamlach. *Powy* 3D 46
Llanharan. *Rhon* 3D 32
Llanharry. *Rhon* 3D 32
Llanhennock. *Mon* 2G 33
Llanhilleth. *Blae* 5F 47
Llanidloes. *Powy* 2B 58
Llaniestyn. *Gwyn* 2B 68
Llanigon. *Powy* 1F 47
Llanilar. *Cdgn* 3F 57
Llanilid. *Rhon* 3C 32
Llanilltud Fawr. *V Glam* 5C 32
Llanishen. *Card* 3E 33
Llanishen. *Mon* 5H 47
Llanllawddog. *Carm* 3E 45
Llanllechid. *Gwyn* 4F 81
Llanllowell. *Mon* 2G 33
Llanllugan. *Powy* 5C 70
Llanllwch. *Carm* 4D 45
Llanllwchaiarn. *Powy* 1D 58
Llanllwni. *Carm* 2E 45
Llanllyfni. *Gwyn* 5D 80
Llanmadoc. *Swan* 3D 30
Llanmaes. *V Glam* 5C 32
Llanmartin. *Newp* 3G 33
Llanmerwig. *Powy* 1D 58
Llanmihangel. *V Glam* 4C 32
Llan-mill. *Pemb* 3F 43
Llanmiloe. *Carm* 4G 43
Llanmorlais. *Swan* 3E 31
Llannefydd. *Cnwy* 3B 82
Llan-non. *Cdgn* 4E 57
Llannon. *Carm* 5F 45
Llannor. *Gwyn* 2C 68
Llanover. *Mon* 5G 47
Llanpumsaint. *Carm* 3E 45
Llanrhaeadr. *Den* 4C 82
Llanrhaeadr-ym-Mochnant
Powy 3D 70
Llanrhian. *Pemb* 1C 42
Llanrhidian. *Swan* 3D 31
Llanrhos. *Cnwy* 2G 81
Llanrhyddlad. *IOA* 2C 80
Llanrhystud. *Cdgn* 4E 57
Llanrothal. *Here* 4H 47
Llanrug. *Gwyn* 4E 81
Llanrumney. *Card* 3F 33
Llanrwst. *Cnwy* 4G 81
Llansadurnen. *Carm* 3G 43
Llansadwrn. *Carm* 2G 45
Llansadwrn. *IOA* 3E 81
Llansaint. *Carm* 5D 45
Llansamlet. *Swan* 3F 31
Llansanffraid Glan Conwy
Cnwy 3H 81
Llansannan. *Cnwy* 4B 82
Llansannor. *V Glam* 4C 32
Llansantffraed. *Cdgn* 4E 57
Llansantffraed. *Powy* 3E 46
Llansantffraed
Cwmdeuddwr. *Powy* 4B 58
Llansantffraed-in-Elwel
Powy 5C 58
Llansantffraid-ym-Mechain
Powy 3E 70
Llansawel. *Carm* 2G 45
Llansawel. *Neat* 3G 31
Llansilin. *Powy* 3E 70
Llansoy. *Mon* 5H 47
Llanspyddid. *Powy* 3D 46
Llanstadwell. *Pemb* 4D 42
Llansteffan. *Carm* 4D 44
Llanstephan. *Powy* 1E 46
Llantarnam. *Torf* 2G 33
Llanteg. *Pemb* 3F 43
Llanthony. *Mon* 3F 47
Llantilio Crossenny. *Mon* 4G 47
Llantilio Pertholey. *Mon* 4G 47
Llantood. *Pemb* 1B 44
Llantrisant. *Mon* 2G 33
Llantrisant. *Rhon* 3D 32
Llantrithyd. *V Glam* 4D 32
Llantwit Fardre. *Rhon* 3D 32
Llantwit Major. *V Glam* 5C 32
Llanuwchllyn. *Gwyn* 2A 70
Llanvaches. *Newp* 2H 33
Llanvair Discoed. *Mon* 2H 33
Llanvapley. *Mon* 4G 47
Llanvetherine. *Mon* 4G 47
Llanveynoe. *Here* 2G 47
Llanvihangel Crucorney
Mon 3G 47
Llanvihangel Gobion. *Mon* 5G 47
Llanvihangel Ystern-
Llewern. *Mon* 4H 47
Llanwarne. *Here* 3A 48
Llanwddyn. *Powy* 4C 70
Llanwenarth. *Mon* 4F 47
Llanwenog. *Cdgn* 1E 45
Llanwern. *Newp* 3G 33
Llanwinio. *Carm* 2G 43
Llanwnda. *Gwyn* 5D 80
Llanwnda. *Pemb* 1D 42
Llanwnnen. *Cdgn* 1F 45
Llanwnog. *Powy* 1C 58
Llanwrda. *Carm* 2H 45
Llanwrin. *Powy* 5G 69
Llanwrthwl. *Powy* 4B 58
Llanwrtud. *Powy* 1B 46
Llanwrtyd. *Powy* 1B 46
Llanwrtyd Wells. *Powy* 1B 46
Llanwyddelan. *Powy* 5C 70
Llanyblodwel. *Shrp* 3E 71
Llanybri. *Carm* 3H 43
Llanybydder. *Carm* 1F 45
Llanycefn. *Pemb* 2E 43
Llanychaer. *Pemb* 1D 43
Llanycil. *Gwyn* 2B 70
Llanymawddwy. *Gwyn* 4B 70
Llanymddyfri. *Carm* 2A 46
Llanymynech. *Powy* 3E 71
Llanynghenedl. *IOA* 2C 80
Llanynys. *Den* 4D 82
Llan-y-pwll. *Wrex* 5F 83
Llanyrafon. *Torf* 2G 33
Llanyre. *Powy* 4C 58
Llanystumdwy. *Gwyn* 2D 68
Llanywern. *Powy* 3E 46
Llawhaden. *Pemb* 3E 43
Llawndy. *Flin* 2D 82
Llawnt. *Shrp* 2E 71
Llawr Dref. *Gwyn* 3B 68
Llawryglyn. *Powy* 1B 58
Llay. *Wrex* 5F 83
Llechfaen. *Powy* 3D 46
Llechryd. *Cphy* 5E 46
Llechryd. *Cdgn* 1C 44
Llechrydau. *Wrex* 2E 71
Lledrod. *Cdgn* 3F 57
Llethrid. *Swan* 3E 31
Llidiad-Nenog. *Carm* 2F 45
Llidiardau. *Gwyn* 2A 70
Llidiart y Parc. *Den* 1D 70
Llithfaen. *Gwyn* 1C 68
Lloc. *Flin* 3D 82
Llong. *Flin* 4E 83
Llowes. *Powy* 1E 47
Lloyney. *Powy* 3E 59
Llundain-fach. *Cdgn* 5E 57
Llwydcoed. *Rhon* 5C 46
Llwyncelyn. *Cdgn* 5D 56
Llwyncelyn. *Swan* 5G 45
Llwyndafydd. *Cdgn* 5C 56
Llwynderw. *Powy* 5E 70
Llwyn-du. *Mon* 4F 47
Llwyngwril. *Gwyn* 5E 69
Llwynhendy. *Carm* 3E 31
Llwynmawr. *Wrex* 2E 71
Llwyn-on Village. *Mer T* 4D 46
Llwyn-têg. *Carm* 5F 45
Llwyn-y-brain. *Carm* 3F 43
Llwynygog. *Powy* 1A 58
Llwyn-y-groes. *Cdgn* 5E 57
Llwynypia. *Rhon* 2C 32
Llynclys. *Shrp* 3E 71
Llynfaes. *IOA* 3D 80
Llysfaen. *Cnwy* 3A 82
Llyswen. *Powy* 2E 47
Llysworney. *V Glam* 4C 32
Llys-y-fran. *Pemb* 2E 43
Llywel. *Powy* 2B 46
Llywernog. *Cdgn* 2G 57
Loan. *Falk* 2C 128
Loanend. *Nmbd* 4F 131
Loanhead. *Midl* 3F 129
Loaningfoot. *Dum* 4A 112
Loanreoch. *High* 1A 158
Loans. *S Ayr* 1C 116
Loansdean. *Nmbd* 1E 115
Lobb. *Devn* 3E 19
Lobhillcross. *Devn* 4E 11
Lochaber. *Mor* 3E 159
Loch a Charnain. *W Isl* 4D 170
Loch a Ghainmhich. *W Isl* 5E 171
Lochailort. *High* 5F 147
Lochaline. *High* 4A 140
Lochans. *Dum* 4F 109
Locharbriggs. *Dum* 1A 112
Lochardil. *High* 4A 158
Lochassynt Lodge. *High* 1F 163
Lochavich. *Arg* 2G 133
Lochawe. *Arg* 1A 134
Loch Baghasdail. *W Isl* 7C 170
Lochboisdale. *W Isl* 7C 170
Lochbuie. *Arg* 1D 132
Lochcarron. *High* 5A 156
Loch Choire Lodge. *High* 5G 167
Lochdochart House. *Stir* 1D 134
Lochdon. *Arg* 5B 140
Lochearnhead. *Stir* 1E 135
Lochee. *D'dee* 5C 144
Lochend. *High*
nr. Inverness 5H 157
nr. Thurso 2E 169
Locherben. *Dum* 5B 118
Loch Euphort. *W Isl* 2D 170
Lochfoot. *Dum* 2F 111
Lochgair. *Arg* 4G 133
Lochgarthside. *High* 2H 149
Lochgelly. *Fife* 4D 136
Lochgilphead. *Arg* 1G 125
Lochgoilhead. *Arg* 3A 134
Loch Head. *Dum* 5A 110
Lochhill. *Mor* 2G 159
Lochindorb Lodge. *High* 5D 158
Lochinver. *High* 1E 163
Lochlane. *Per* 1H 135
Loch Lomond. *Arg* 3C 134
Loch Loyal Lodge. *High* 4G 167
Lochluichart. *High* 2F 157
Lochmaben. *Dum* 1B 112
Lochmaddy. *W Isl* 2E 170
Loch nam Madadh. *W Isl* 2E 170
Lochore. *Fife* 4D 136
Lochportain. *W Isl* 1E 170
Lochranza. *N Ayr* 4H 125
Loch Sgioport. *W Isl* 5D 170
Lochside. *Abers* 2G 145
Lochside. *High*
nr. Achentoul 5A 168
nr. Nairn 3C 158
Lochslin. *High* 5F 165
Lochstack Lodge. *High* 4C 166
Lochton. *Abers* 4E 153
Lochty. *Fife* 3H 137
Lochuisge. *High* 3B 140
Lochussie. *High* 3G 157
Lochwinnoch. *Ren* 4E 127
Lochyside. *High* 1F 141
Lockengate. *Corn* 2E 7
Lockerbie. *Dum* 1C 112
Lockeridge. *Wilts* 5G 35
Lockerley. *Hants* 4A 24
Lockhills. *Cumb* 5G 113
Locking. *N Som* 1G 21
Lockington. *E Yor* 5D 101
Lockington. *Leics* 3B 74
Lockleywood. *Shrp* 3A 72
Locksgreen. *IOW* 3C 16
Locks Heath. *Hants* 2D 16
Lockton. *N Yor* 5F 107
Loddington. *Leics* 5E 75
Loddington. *Nptn* 3F 63
Loddiswell. *Devn* 4D 8
Loddon. *Norf* 1F 67
Lode. *Cambs* 4E 65
Loders. *Dors* 3H 13
Lodsworth. *W Sus* 3A 26
Lofthouse. *N Yor* 2D 98
Lofthouse. *W Yor* 2D 92
Lofthouse Gate. *W Yor* 2D 92
Loftus. *Red C* 3E 107
Logan. *E Ayr* 2E 117
Loganlea. *W Lot* 3C 128
Logaston. *Here* 5F 59
Loggerheads. *Den* 4D 82
Loggerheads. *Staf* 2B 72
Loggie. *High* 4F 163
Logie. *Ang* 2F 145
Logie. *Fife* 1G 137
Logie. *Mor* 3E 159
Logie Coldstone. *Abers* 3B 152
Logie Pert. *Ang* 2F 145
Logierait. *Per* 3G 143
Login. *Carm* 2F 43
Lolworth. *Cambs* 4C 64
Lonbain. *High* 3F 155
Londesborough. *E Yor* 5C 100
London. *G Lon* 2E 39
London Apprentice. *Corn* 3E 6
London Ashford Airport. *Kent* 3E 29
London City Airport. *G Lon* 2F 39
London Colney. *Herts* 5B 52
Londonderry. *Derr* 2C 174
Londonderry. *N Yor* 1F 99
London Gatwick Airport
W Sus 1D 26
London Heathrow Airport
G Lon 3B 38
London Luton Airport. *Lutn* 3B 52
London Southend Airport
Essx 2C 40
London Stansted Airport
Essx 3F 53
Londonthorpe. *Linc* 2G 75
Londubh. *High* 5C 162
Lone. *High* 4D 166
Lonemore. *High*
nr. Dornoch 5E 165
nr. Gairloch 1G 155

Long Ashton – Low Worsall

Long Ashton. *N Som* 4A 34
Long Bank. *Worc* 3B 60
Longbar. *N Ayr* 4E 127
Long Bennington. *Linc* 1F 75
Longbenton. *Tyne* 3F 115
Longborough. *Glos* 3G 49
Long Bredy. *Dors* 3A 14
Longbridge. *Warw* 4G 61
Longbridge. *W Mid* 3E 61
Longbridge Deverill. *Wilts* 2D 22
Long Buckby. *Nptn* 4D 62
Long Buckby Wharf. *Nptn* 4D 62
Longburgh. *Cumb* 4E 112
Longburton. *Dors* 1B 14
Long Clawson. *Leics* 3E 74
Longcliffe. *Derbs* 5G 85
Long Common. *Hants* 1D 16
Long Compton. *Staf* 3C 72
Long Compton. *Warw* 2A 50
Longcot. *Oxon* 2A 36
Long Crendon. *Buck* 5E 51
Long Crichel. *Dors* 1E 15
Longcroft. *Cumb* 4D 112
Longcroft. *Falk* 2A 128
Longcross. *Surr* 4A 38
Longdale. *Cumb* 4H 103
Longdales. *Cumb* 5G 113
Longden. *Shrp* 5G 71
Longden Common. *Shrp* 5G 71
Long Ditton. *Surr* 4C 38
Longdon. *Staf* 4E 73
Longdon. *Worc* 2D 48
Longdon Green. *Staf* 4E 73
Longdon on Tern. *Telf* 4A 72
Longdown. *Devn* 3B 12
Longdowns. *Corn* 5B 6
Long Drax. *N Yor* 2G 93
Long Duckmanton. *Derbs* 3B 86
Long Eaton. *Derbs* 2B 74
Longfield. *Kent* 4H 39
Longfield. *Shet* 10E 173
Longfield Hill. *Kent* 4H 39
Longford. *Derbs* 2G 73
Longford. *Glos* 3D 48
Longford. *G Lon* 3B 38
Longford. *Shrp* 2A 72
Longford. *Telf* 4B 72
Longford. *W Mid* 2A 62
Longforgan. *Per* 5C 144
Longformacus. *Bord* 4C 130
Longframlington. *Nmbd* 4F 121
Long Gardens. *Essx* 2B 54
Long Green. *Ches W* 3G 83
Long Green. *Worc* 2D 48
Longham. *Dors* 3F 15
Longham. *Norf* 4B 78
Long Hanborough. *Oxon* 4C 50
Longhedge. *Wilts* 2D 22
Longhill. *Abers* 3H 161
Longhirst. *Nmbd* 1F 115
Longhope. *Glos* 4B 48
Longhope. *Orkn* 8C 172
Longhorsley. *Nmbd* 5F 121
Longhoughton. *Nmbd* 3G 121
Long Itchington. *Warw* 4B 62
Longlands. *Cumb* 1D 102
Long Lane. *Telf* 4A 72
Longlane. *Derbs* 2G 73
Longlane. *W Ber* 4C 36
Long Lawford. *Warw* 3B 62
Long Lease. *N Yor* 4G 107
Longley Green. *Worc* 5B 60
Long Load. *Som* 4H 21
Longmanhill. *Abers* 2E 161
Long Marston. *Herts* 4G 51
Long Marston. *N Yor* 4H 99
Long Marston. *Warw* 1G 49
Long Marton. *Cumb* 2H 103
Long Meadow. *Cambs* 4E 65
Long Meadowend. *Shrp* 2G 59
Long Melford. *Suff* 1B 54
Longmoor Camp. *Hants* 3F 25
Longmorn. *Mor* 3G 159
Longmoss. *Ches E* 3C 84
Long Newnton. *Glos* 2E 35
Long Newton. *Stoc T* 3A 106
Longnewton. *Bord* 2H 119
Longney. *Glos* 4C 48
Longniddry. *E Lot* 2H 129
Longnor. *Shrp* 5G 71
Longnor. *Staf*
  nr. Leek 4E 85
  nr. Stafford 4C 72
Longparish. *Hants* 2C 24
Longpark. *Cumb* 3F 113
Long Preston. *N Yor* 4H 97
Longridge. *Lanc* 1E 90
Longridge. *Staf* 4D 72
Longridge. *W Lot* 3C 128
Longriggend. *N Lan* 2B 128
Long Riston. *E Yor* 5F 101
Longrock. *Corn* 3C 4
Longsdon. *Staf* 5D 84
Longshaw. *G Man* 4D 90
Longshaw. *Staf* 1E 73
Longside. *Abers* 4H 161
Longslow. *Shrp* 2A 72
Longstanton. *Cambs* 4C 64
Longstock. *Hants* 3B 24
Longstowe. *Cambs* 5C 64
Long Stratton. *Norf* 1D 66
Long Street. *Mil* 1F 51
Longstreet. *Wilts* 1G 23
Long Sutton. *Hants* 2F 25
Long Sutton. *Linc* 3D 76
Long Sutton. *Som* 4H 21
Longthorpe. *Pet* 1A 64
Long Thurlow. *Suff* 4C 66
Longthwaite. *Cumb* 2F 103
Longton. *Lanc* 2C 90
Longton. *Stoke* 1D 72
Longtown. *Cumb* 3E 113
Longtown. *Here* 3G 47
Longville in the Dale. *Shrp* 1H 59
Long Whatton. *Leics* 3B 74
Longwick. *Buck* 5F 51
Long Wittenham. *Oxon* 2D 36
Longwitton. *Nmbd* 1D 115
Longworth. *Oxon* 2B 36
Longyester. *E Lot* 3B 130
Lonmore. *High* 4B 154
Looe. *Corn* 3G 7
Loose. *Kent* 5B 40
Loosegate. *Linc* 3C 76
Loosley Row. *Buck* 5G 51
Lopcombe Corner. *Wilts* 3A 24
Lopen. *Som* 1H 13
Loppington. *Shrp* 3G 71
Lorbottle. *Nmbd* 4E 121
Lordington. *W Sus* 2F 17
Loscoe. *Derbs* 1B 74
Loscombe. *Dors* 3A 14
Losgaintir. *W Isl* 8C 171
Lossiemouth. *Mor* 2G 159
Lossit. *Arg* 4A 124
Lostock Gralam. *Ches W* 3A 84
Lostock Green. *Ches W* 3A 84
Lostock Hall. *Lanc* 2D 90
Lostock Junction. *G Man* 4E 91
Lostwithiel. *Corn* 3F 7
Lothbeg. *High* 2G 165
Lothersdale. *N Yor* 5B 98
Lothianbridge. *Midl* 3G 129
Lothianburn. *Midl* 3F 129
Lothmore. *High* 2G 165
Lottisham. *Som* 3A 22
Loudwater. *Buck* 1A 38
Loughborough. *Leics* 4C 74
Loughor. *Swan* 3E 31
Loughton. *Essx* 1F 39
Loughton. *Mil* 2G 51
Loughton. *Shrp* 2A 60
Lound. *Linc* 4H 75
Lound. *Notts* 2D 86
Lound. *Suff* 1H 67
Lount. *Leics* 4A 74
Louth. *Linc* 2C 88
Love Clough. *Lanc* 2G 91
Lovedean. *Hants* 1E 17
Lover. *Wilts* 4H 23
Loversall. *S Yor* 1C 86
Loves Green. *Essx* 5G 53
Loveston. *Pemb* 4E 43
Lovington. *Som* 3A 22
Low Ackworth. *W Yor* 3E 93
Low Angerton. *Nmbd* 1D 115
Low Ardwell. *Dum* 5F 109
Low Ballochdowan. *S Ayr* 2F 109
Lowbands. *Glos* 2C 48
Low Barlings. *Linc* 3H 87
Low Bell End. *N Yor* 5E 107
Low Bentham. *N Yor* 3F 97
Low Borrowbridge. *Cumb* 4H 103
Low Bradfield. *S Yor* 1G 85
Low Bradley. *N Yor* 5C 98
Low Braithwaite. *Cumb* 5F 113
Low Brunton. *Nmbd* 2C 114
Low Burnham. *N Lin* 4A 94
Lowca. *Cumb* 2A 102
Low Catton. *E Yor* 4B 100
Low Coniscliffe. *Darl* 3F 105
Low Coylton. *S Ayr* 3D 116
Low Crosby. *Cumb* 4F 113
Low Dalby. *N Yor* 1C 100
Lowdham. *Notts* 1D 74
Low Dinsdale. *Darl* 3A 106
Lowe. *Shrp* 2H 71
Low Ellington. *N Yor* 1E 98
Lower Amble. *Corn* 1D 6
Lower Ansty. *Dors* 2C 14
Lower Arboll. *High* 5F 165
Lower Arncott. *Oxon* 4E 50
Lower Ashton. *Devn* 4B 12
Lower Assendon. *Oxon* 3F 37
Lower Auchenreath. *Mor* 2A 160
Lower Badcall. *High* 4B 166
Lower Ballam. *Lanc* 1B 90
Lower Basildon. *W Ber* 4E 36
Lower Beeding. *W Sus* 3D 26
Lower Benefield. *Nptn* 2G 63
Lower Bentley. *Worc* 4D 61
Lower Beobridge. *Shrp* 1B 60
Lower Bockhampton. *Dors* 3C 14
Lower Boddington. *Nptn* 5B 62
Lower Bordean. *Hants* 4E 25
Lower Brailes. *Warw* 2B 50
Lower Breakish. *High* 1E 147
Lower Broadheath. *Worc* 5C 60
Lower Brynamman. *Neat* 4H 45
Lower Bullingham. *Here* 2A 48
Lower Bullington. *Hants* 2C 24
Lower Burgate. *Hants* 1G 15
Lower Cam. *Glos* 5C 48
Lower Catesby. *Nptn* 5C 62
Lower Chapel. *Powy* 2D 46
Lower Cheriton. *Devn* 2E 12
Lower Chicksgrove. *Wilts* 3E 23
Lower Chute. *Wilts* 1B 24
Lower Clopton. *Warw* 5F 61
Lower Common. *Hants* 2E 25
Lower Crossings. *Derbs* 2E 85
Lower Cumberworth. *W Yor* 4C 92
Lower Darwen. *Bkbn* 2E 91
Lower Dean. *Bed* 4H 63
Lower Dean. *Devn* 2D 8
Lower Diabaig. *High* 2G 155
Lower Dicker. *E Sus* 4G 27
Lower Dounreay. *High* 2B 168
Lower Down. *Shrp* 2F 59
Lower Dunsforth. *N Yor* 3G 99
Lower East Carleton. *Norf* 5D 78
Lower Egleton. *Here* 1B 48
Lower Ellastone. *Staf* 1F 73
Lower End. *Nptn* 4F 63
Lower Everleigh. *Wilts* 1G 23
Lower Eype. *Dors* 3H 13
Lower Failand. *N Som* 4A 34
Lower Faintree. *Shrp* 2A 60
Lower Farringdon. *Hants* 3F 25
Lower Foxdale. *IOM* 4B 108
Lower Frankton. *Shrp* 2F 71
Lower Froyle. *Hants* 2F 25
Lower Gabwell. *Devn* 2F 9
Lower Gledfield. *High* 4C 164
Lower Godney. *Som* 2H 21
Lower Gravenhurst. *C Beds* 2B 52
Lower Green. *Essx* 2E 53
Lower Green. *Norf* 2B 78
Lower Green. *W Ber* 5B 36
Lower Halstow. *Kent* 4C 40
Lower Hardres. *Kent* 5F 41
Lower Hardwick. *Here* 5G 59
Lower Hartshay. *Derbs* 5A 86
Lower Hawthwaite. *Cumb* 1B 96
Lower Haysden. *Kent* 1G 27
Lower Hayton. *Shrp* 2H 59
Lower Hergest. *Here* 5E 59
Lower Heyford. *Oxon* 3C 50
Lower Heysham. *Lanc* 3D 96
Lower Higham. *Kent* 3B 40
Lower Holbrook. *Suff* 2E 55
Lower Holditch. *Dors* 2G 13
Lower Hordley. *Shrp* 3F 71
Lower Horncroft. *W Sus* 4B 26
Lower Horsebridge. *E Sus* 4G 27
Lower Kilcott. *Glos* 3C 34
Lower Killeyan. *Arg* 5A 124
Lower Kingcombe. *Dors* 3A 14
Lower Kingswood. *Surr* 5D 38
Lower Kinnerton. *Ches W* 4F 83
Lower Langford. *N Som* 5H 33
Lower Largo. *Fife* 3G 137
Lower Layham. *Suff* 1D 54
Lower Ledwyche. *Shrp* 3H 59
Lower Leigh. *Staf* 2E 73
Lower Lemington. *Glos* 2H 49
Lower Lenie. *High* 1H 149
Lower Ley. *Glos* 4C 48
Lower Llanfadog. *Powy* 4B 58
Lower Lode. *Glos* 2D 49
Lower Lovacott. *Devn* 4F 19
Lower Loxhore. *Devn* 3G 19
Lower Loxley. *Staf* 2E 73
Lower Lydbrook. *Glos* 4A 48
Lower Lye. *Here* 4G 59
Lower Machen. *Newp* 3F 33
Lower Maes-coed. *Here* 2G 47
Lower Meend. *Glos* 5A 48
Lower Midway. *Derbs* 3H 73
Lower Milovaig. *High* 3A 154
Lower Moor. *Worc* 1E 49
Lower Morton. *S Glo* 2B 34
Lower Mountain. *Flin* 5F 83
Lower Nazeing. *Essx* 5D 53
Lower Netchwood. *Shrp* 1A 60
Lower Nyland. *Dors* 4C 22
Lower Oakfield. *Fife* 4D 136
Lower Oddington. *Glos* 3H 49
Lower Ollach. *High* 5E 155
Lower Penarth. *V Glam* 5E 33
Lower Penn. *Staf* 1C 60
Lower Pennington. *Hants* 3B 16
Lower Peover. *Ches W* 3B 84
Lower Pilsley. *Derbs* 4B 86
Lower Pitkerrie. *High* 1C 158
Lower Place. *G Man* 3H 91
Lower Quinton. *Warw* 1G 49
Lower Rainham. *Medw* 4C 40
Lower Raydon. *Suff* 2D 54
Lower Seagry. *Wilts* 3E 35
Lower Shelton. *C Beds* 1H 51
Lower Shiplake. *Oxon* 4F 37
Lower Shuckburgh. *Warw* 4B 62
Lower Sketty. *Swan* 3F 31
Lower Slade. *Devn* 2F 19
Lower Slaughter. *Glos* 3G 49
Lower Soudley. *Glos* 4B 48
Lower Stanton St Quintin
  Wilts 3E 35
Lower Stoke. *Medw* 3C 40
Lower Stondon. *C Beds* 2B 52
Lower Stonnall. *Staf* 5E 73
Lower Stow Bedon. *Norf* 1B 66
Lower Street. *Norf* 2E 79
Lower Strensham. *Worc* 1E 49
Lower Sundon. *C Beds* 3A 52
Lower Swanwick. *Hants* 2C 16
Lower Swell. *Glos* 3G 49
Lower Tale. *Devn* 2D 12
Lower Tean. *Staf* 2E 73
Lower Thurlton. *Norf* 1G 67
Lower Thurnham. *Lanc* 4D 96
Lower Thurvaston. *Derbs* 2G 73
Lower Town. *Here* 1B 48
Lower Town. *IOS* 1B 4
Lower Town. *Pemb* 1D 42
Lowertown. *Corn* 4D 4
Lowertown. *Orkn* 8D 172
Lower Tysoe. *Warw* 1B 50
Lower Upham. *Hants* 1D 16
Lower Upnor. *Medw* 3B 40
Lower Vexford. *Som* 3E 20
Lower Walton. *Warr* 2A 84
Lower Wear. *Devn* 4C 12
Lower Weare. *Som* 1H 21
Lower Welson. *Here* 5E 59
Lower Whatcombe. *Dors* 2D 14
Lower Whitley. *Ches W* 3A 84
Lower Wield. *Hants* 2E 25
Lower Withington. *Ches E* 4C 84
Lower Woodend. *Buck* 3G 37
Lower Woodford. *Wilts* 3G 23
Lower Wraxall. *Dors* 2A 14
Lower Wych. *Ches W* 1G 71
Lower Wyche. *Worc* 1C 48
Lowesby. *Leics* 5E 74
Lowestoft. *Suff* 1H 67
Loweswater. *Cumb* 2C 102
Low Etherley. *Dur* 2E 105
Lowfield Heath. *W Sus* 1D 26
Lowford. *Hants* 1C 16
Low Fulney. *Linc* 3B 76
Low Gate. *Nmbd* 3C 114
Lowgill. *Cumb* 5H 103
Lowgill. *Lanc* 3F 97
Low Grantley. *N Yor* 2E 99
Low Green. *N Yor* 4E 98
Low Habberley. *Worc* 3C 60
Low Ham. *Som* 4H 21
Low Hameringham. *Linc* 4C 88
Low Hawsker. *N Yor* 4G 107
Low Hesket. *Cumb* 5F 113
Low Hesleyhurst. *Nmbd* 5E 121
Lowick. *Cumb* 1B 96
Lowick. *Nptn* 2G 63
Lowick. *Nmbd* 1E 121
Lowick Bridge. *Cumb* 1B 96
Lowick Green. *Cumb* 1B 96
Low Knipe. *Cumb* 2G 103
Low Leighton. *Derbs* 2E 85
Low Lorton. *Cumb* 2C 102
Low Marishes. *N Yor* 2C 100
Low Marnham. *Notts* 4F 87
Low Mill. *N Yor* 5D 106
Low Moor. *Lanc* 5G 97
Low Moor. *W Yor* 2B 92
Low Moorsley. *Tyne* 5G 115
Low Newton-by-the-Sea
  Nmbd 2G 121
Lownie Moor. *Ang* 4D 145
Lowood. *Bord* 1H 119
Low Row. *Cumb*
  nr. Brampton 3G 113
  nr. Wigton 5C 112
Low Row. *N Yor* 5C 104
Lowsonford. *Warw* 4F 61
Low Street. *Norf* 5C 78
Lowther. *Cumb* 2G 103
Lowthorpe. *E Yor* 3E 101
Lowton. *Devn* 2G 11
Lowton. *G Man* 1A 84
Lowton. *Som* 1E 13
Lowton Common. *G Man* 1A 84
Low Torry. *Fife* 1D 128
Low Toynton. *Linc* 3B 88
Low Valleyfield. *Fife* 1C 128
Low Westwood. *Dur* 4E 115
Low Whinnow. *Cumb* 4E 112
Low Wood. *Cumb* 1C 96
Low Worsall. *N Yor* 4A 106

Mardy – Mepal

Mardy. Mon 4G 47
Marefield. Leics 5E 75
Mareham le Fen. Linc 4B 88
Mareham on the Hill. Linc 4B 88
Marehay. Derbs 1B 74
Marehill. W Sus 4B 26
Maresfield. E Sus 3F 27
Marfleet. Hull 2E 95
Marford. Wrex 5F 83
Margam. Neat 3A 32
Margaret Marsh. Dors 1D 14
Margaret Roding. Essx 4F 53
Margaretting. Essx 5G 53
Margaretting Tye. Essx 5G 53
Margate. Kent 3H 41
Margery. Surr 5D 38
Margnaheglish. N Ayr 2E 123
Marham. Norf 5G 77
Marhamchurch. Corn 2C 10
Marholm. Pet 5A 76
Marian Cwm. Den 3C 82
Mariandyrys. IOA 2F 81
Marian-glas. IOA 2E 81
Mariansleigh. Devn 4H 19
Marian-y-de. Gwyn 2C 68
Marian-y-mor. Gwyn 2C 68
Marine Town. Kent 3D 40
Marishader. High 2D 155
Marjoriebanks. Dum 1B 112
Mark. Dum 4G 109
Mark. Som 2G 21
Markbeech. Kent 1F 27
Markby. Linc 3D 89
Mark Causeway. Som 2G 21
Mark Cross. E Sus 2G 27
Markeaton. Derb 2H 73
Market Bosworth. Leics 5B 74
Market Deeping. Linc 4A 76
Market Drayton. Shrp 2A 72
Market End. Warw 2H 61
Market Harborough. Leics 2E 63
Markethill. Arm 6F 175
Markethill. Per 5B 144
Market Lavington. Wilts 1F 23
Market Overton. Rut 4F 75
Market Rasen. Linc 2A 88
Market Stainton. Linc 2B 88
Market Weighton. E Yor 5C 100
Market Weston. Suff 3B 66
Markfield. Leics 4B 74
Markham. Cphy 5E 47
Markinch. Fife 3E 137
Markington. N Yor 3E 99
Marksbury. Bath 5B 34
Mark's Corner. IOW 3C 16
Marks Tey. Essx 3C 54
Markwell. Corn 3H 7
Markyate. Herts 4A 52
Marlborough. Wilts 5G 35
Marlcliff. Warw 5E 61
Marldon. Devn 2E 9
Marle Green. E Sus 4G 27
Marlesford. Suff 5F 67
Marley Green. Ches E 1H 71
Marley Hill. Tyne 4F 115
Marlingford. Norf 5D 78
Mar Lodge. Abers 5E 151
Marloes. Pemb 4B 42
Marlow. Buck 3G 37
Marlow. Here 3F 59
Marlow Bottom. Buck 3G 37
Marlow Common. Buck 3G 37
Marlpit Hill. Kent 1F 27
Marlpits. E Sus 3F 27
Marlpool. Derbs 1B 74
Marnhull. Dors 1C 14
Marnoch. Abers 3C 160
Marnock. N Lan 3A 128
Marple. G Man 2D 84
Marr. S Yor 4F 93
Marrel. High 2H 165
Marrick. N Yor 5D 105
Marrister. Shet 5G 173
Marros. Carm 4G 43
Marsden. Tyne 3G 115
Marsden. W Yor 3A 92
Marsett. N Yor 1B 98
Marsh. Buck 5G 51
Marsh. Devn 1F 13
The Marsh. Powy 1F 59
The Marsh. Shrp 3A 72
Marshall Meadows. Nmbd 4F 131
Marshalsea. Dors 2G 13
Marshalswick. Herts 5B 52
Marsham. Norf 3D 78
Marshaw. Lanc 4E 97
Marsh Baldon. Oxon 2D 36
Marsh Benham. W Ber 5C 36
Marshborough. Kent 5H 41
Marshbrook. Shrp 2G 59
Marshchapel. Linc 1C 88
Marshfield. Newp 3F 33
Marshfield. S Glo 4C 34
Marshgate. Corn 3B 10
Marsh Gibbon. Buck 3E 51
Marsh Green. Devn 3D 12
Marsh Green. Kent 1F 27
Marsh Green. Staf 5C 84
Marsh Green. Telf 4A 72
Marsh Lane. Derbs 3B 86
Marsh Side. Norf 1G 77
Marshside. Kent 4G 41
Marshside. Mers 3B 90
Marsh Street. Som 2C 20
Marshwood. Dors 3G 13
Marske. N Yor 4E 105
Marske-by-the-Sea
Red C 2D 106
Marston. Ches W 3A 84
Marston. Here 5F 59
Marston. Linc 1F 75
Marston. Oxon 5D 50
Marston. Staf
nr. Stafford 3D 72
nr. Wheaton Aston 4C 72
Marston. Warw 1G 61
Marston. Wilts 1E 23
Marston Doles. Warw 5B 62
Marston Green. W Mid 2F 61
Marston Hill. Glos 2G 35
Marston Jabbett. Warw 2A 62
Marston Magna. Som 4A 22
Marston Meysey. Wilts 2G 35
Marston Montgomery
Derbs 2F 73
Marston Moretaine. C Beds 1H 51
Marston on Dove. Derbs 3G 73
Marston St Lawrence. Nptn 1D 50
Marston Stannett. Here 5H 59
Marston Trussell. Nptn 2D 62
Marstow. Here 4A 48
Marsworth. Buck 4H 51
Marten. Wilts 1A 24
Marthall. Ches E 3C 84
Martham. Norf 4G 79
Marthwaite. Cumb 5H 103
Martin. Hants 1F 15
Martin. Kent 1H 29
Martin. Linc
nr. Horncastle 4B 88
nr. Metheringham 5A 88
Martindale. Cumb 3F 103
Martin Dales. Linc 4A 88
Martin Drove End. Hants 4F 23
Martinhoe. Devn 2G 19
Martinhoe Cross. Devn 2G 19
Martin Hussingtree. Worc 4C 60
Martin Mill. Kent 1H 29
Martinscroft. Warr 2A 84
Martin's Moss. Ches E 4C 84
Martinstown. Dors 4B 14
Martlesham. Suff 1F 55
Martlesham Heath. Suff 1F 55
Martletwy. Pemb 3E 43
Martley. Worc 4B 60
Martock. Som 1H 13
Marton. Ches E 4C 84
Marton. Cumb 2B 96
Marton. E Yor
nr. Bridlington 3G 101
nr. Hull 1E 95
Marton. Linc 2F 87
Marton. Midd 3C 106
Marton. N Yor
nr. Boroughbridge 3G 99
nr. Pickering 1B 100
Marton. Shrp
nr. Myddle 3G 71
nr. Worthen 5E 71
Marton. Warw 4B 62
Marton Abbey. N Yor 3H 99
Marton-le-Moor. N Yor 2F 99
Martyr's Green. Surr 5B 38
Martyr Worthy. Hants 3D 24
Marwick. Orkn 5B 172
Marwood. Devn 3F 19
Marybank. High
nr. Dingwall 3G 157
nr. Invergordon 1B 158
Maryburgh. High 3H 157
Maryfield. Corn 3A 8
Maryhill. Glas 3G 127
Marykirk. Abers 2F 145
Marylebone. G Lon 2D 39
Marylebone. G Man 4D 90
Marypark. Mor 5F 159
Maryport. Cumb 1B 102
Maryport. Dum 5E 109
Marystow. Devn 4E 11
Mary Tavy. Devn 5F 11
Maryton. Ang
nr. Kirriemuir 3C 144
nr. Montrose 3F 145
Marywell. Abers 4C 152
Marywell. Ang 4F 145
Masham. N Yor 1E 98
Mashbury. Essx 4G 53
Masongill. N Yor 2F 97
Masons Lodge. Abers 3F 153
Mastin Moor. Derbs 3B 86
Mastrick. Aber 3G 153
Matching. Essx 4F 53
Matching Green. Essx 4F 53
Matching Tye. Essx 4F 53
Matfen. Nmbd 2D 114
Matfield. Kent 1A 28
Mathern. Mon 2A 34
Mathon. Here 1C 48
Mathry. Pemb 1C 42
Matlaske. Norf 2D 78
Matlock. Derbs 5G 85
Matlock Bath. Derbs 5G 85
Matterdale End. Cumb 2E 103
Mattersey. Notts 2D 86
Mattersey Thorpe. Notts 2D 86
Mattingley. Hants 1F 25
Mattishall. Norf 4C 78
Mattishall Burgh. Norf 4C 78
Mauchline. E Ayr 2D 117
Maud. Abers 4G 161
Maudlin. Corn 2E 7
Maugersbury. Glos 3G 49
Maughold. IOM 2D 108
Maulden. C Beds 2A 52
Maulds Meaburn. Cumb 3H 103
Maunby. N Yor 1F 99
Maund Bryan. Here 5H 59
Mautby. Norf 4G 79
Mavesyn Ridware. Staf 4E 73
Mavis Enderby. Linc 4C 88
Mawbray. Cumb 5B 112
Mawdesley. Lanc 3C 90
Mawdlam. B'end 3B 32
Mawgan. Corn 4E 5
Mawgan Porth. Corn 2C 6
Maw Green. Ches E 5B 84
Mawla. Corn 4B 6
Mawnan. Corn 4E 5
Mawnan Smith. Corn 4E 5
Mawsley Village. Nptn 3E 63
Mawthorpe. Linc 3D 88
Maxey. Pet 5A 76
Maxstoke. Warw 2G 61
Maxted Street. Kent 1F 29
Maxton. Kent 1G 29
Maxton. Bord 1A 120
Maxwellheugh. Bord 1B 120
Maxwelltown. Dum 2A 112
Maxworthy. Corn 3C 10
Mayals. Swan 4F 31
Maybole. S Ayr 3C 116
Maybush. Sotn 1B 16
Mayes Green. Surr 2C 26
Mayfield. E Sus 3G 27
Mayfield. Midl 3G 129
Mayfield. Per 1C 136
Mayfield. Staf 1F 73
Mayford. Surr 5A 38
Mayhill. Swan 3F 31
Mayland. Essx 5C 54
Maylandsea. Essx 5C 54
Maynard's Green. E Sus 4G 27
Maypole. IOS 1B 4
Maypole. Kent 4G 41
Maypole. Mon 4H 47
Maypole Green. Norf 1G 67
Maypole Green. Suff 5B 66
Maywick. Shet 9E 173
Mead. Devn 1C 10
Meadgate. Bath 1B 22
Meadle. Buck 5G 51
Meadowbank. Ches W 4A 84
Meadowfield. Dur 1F 105
Meadow Green. Here 5B 60
Meadowmill. E Lot 2H 129
Meadows. Nott 2C 74
Meadowtown. Shrp 5F 71
Meadwell. Devn 4E 11
Meaford. Staf 2C 72
Mealabost. W Isl nr. Borgh 2G 171
nr. Stornoway 4G 171
Mealasta. W Isl 5B 171
Meal Bank. Cumb 5G 103
Mealrigg. Cumb 5C 112
Mealsgate. Cumb 5D 112
Meanwood. W Yor 1C 92
Mearbeck. N Yor 3H 97
Meare. Som 2H 21
Meare Green. Som
nr. Curry Mallet 4F 21
nr. Stoke St Gregory 4G 21
Mears Ashby. Nptn 4F 63
Measham. Leics 4H 73
Meath Green. Surr 1D 27
Meathop. Cumb 1D 96
Meaux. E Yor 1D 94
Meavy. Devn 2B 8
Medbourne. Leics 1E 63
Medburn. Nmbd 2E 115
Meddon. Devn 1C 10
Meden Vale. Notts 4C 86
Medlam. Linc 5C 88
Medlicott. Shrp 1G 59
Medmenham. Buck 3G 37
Medomsley. Dur 4E 115
Medstead. Hants 3E 25
Medway Towns. Medw 4B 40
Meerbrook. Staf 4D 85
Meer End. W Mid 3G 61
Meers Bridge. Linc 2D 89
Meesden. Herts 2E 53
Meeson. Telf 3A 72
Meeth. Devn 2F 11
Meeting Green. Suff 5G 65
Meeting House Hill. Norf 3F 79
Meidrim. Carm 2G 43
Meifod. Powy 4D 70
Meigle. Per 4B 144
Meikle Earnock. S Lan 4A 128
Meikle Kilchattan Butts. Arg 4B 126
Meikleour. Per 5A 144
Meikle Tarty. Abers 1G 153
Meikle Wartle. Abers 5E 160
Meinciau. Carm 4E 45
Meir. Stoke 1D 72
Meir Heath. Staf 1D 72
Melbourn. Cambs 1D 53
Melbourne. Derbs 3A 74
Melbourne. E Yor 5B 100
Melbury Abbas. Dors 4D 23
Melbury Bubb. Dors 2A 14
Melbury Osmond. Dors 2A 14
Melbury Sampford. Dors 2A 14
Melby. Shet 6C 173
Melchbourne. Bed 4H 63
Melcombe Bingham. Dors 2C 14
Melcombe Regis. Dors 4B 14
Meldon. Devn 3F 11
Meldon. Nmbd 1E 115
Meldreth. Cambs 1D 53
Melfort. Arg 2F 133
Melgarve. High 4G 149
Meliden. Den 2C 82
Melinbyrhedyn. Powy 1H 57
Melincourt. Neat 5B 46
Melin-y-coed. Cnwy 4H 81
Melin-y-ddol. Powy 5C 70
Melin-y-wig. Den 1C 70
Melkington. Nmbd 5E 131
Melkinthorpe. Cumb 2G 103
Melkridge. Nmbd 3A 114
Melksham. Wilts 5E 35
Mellangaun. High 5C 162
Melldalloch. Arg 2H 125
Mellguards. Cumb 5F 113
Melling. Lanc 2E 97
Melling. Mers 4B 90
Melling Mount. Mers 4C 90
Mellis. Suff 3C 66
Mellon Charles. High 4C 162
Mellon Udrigle. High 4C 162
Mellor. G Man 2D 85
Mellor. Lanc 1E 91
Mellor Brook. Lanc 1E 91
Mells. Som 2C 22
Melmerby. Cumb 1H 103
Melmerby. N Yor
nr. Middleham 1C 98
nr. Ripon 2F 99
Melplash. Dors 3H 13
Melrose. Bord 1H 119
Melsetter. Orkn 9B 172
Melsonby. N Yor 4E 105
Meltham. W Yor 3B 92
Meltham Mills. W Yor 3B 92
Melton. E Yor 2C 94
Melton. Suff 5E 67
Meltonby. E Yor 4B 100
Melton Constable. Norf 2C 78
Melton Mowbray. Leics 4E 75
Melton Ross. N Lin 3D 94
Melvaig. High 5B 162
Melverley. Shrp 4F 71
Melverley Green. Shrp 4F 71
Melvich. High 2A 168
Membury. Devn 2F 13
Memsie. Abers 2G 161
Memus. Ang 3D 144
Menabilly. Corn 3E 7
Menai Bridge. IOA 3E 81
Mendham. Suff 2E 67
Mendlesham. Suff 4D 66
Mendlesham Green. Suff 4C 66
Menethorpe. N Yor 3B 100
Menheniot. Corn 2G 7
Menithwood. Worc 4B 60
Menna. Corn 3D 6
Mennock. Dum 4H 117
Menston. W Yor 5D 98
Menstrie. Clac 4H 135
Menthorpe. N Yor 1H 93
Mentmore. Buck 4H 51
Meole Brace. Shrp 4G 71
Meols. Mers 1E 83
Meon. Hants 2D 16
Meonstoke. Hants 1E 16
Meopham. Kent 4H 39
Meopham Green. Kent 4H 39
Meopham Station. Kent 4H 39
Mepal. Cambs 2D 64

Milton of Finavon – Mount Pleasant

Milton of Finavon. Ang 3D 145
Milton of Gollanfield. High 3B 158
Milton of Lesmore. Abers 1B 152
Milton of Leys. High 4A 158
Milton of Tullich. Abers 4A 152
Milton on Stour. Dors 4C 22
Milton Regis. Kent 4C 40
Milton Street. E Sus 5G 27
Milton-under-Wychwood
Oxon 4A 50
Milverton. Som 4E 20
Milverton. Warw 4H 61
Milwich. Staf 2D 72
Mimbridge. Surr 4A 38
Minard. Arg 4G 133
Minchington. Dors 1E 15
Minchinhampton. Glos 5D 48
Mindrum. Nmbd 1C 120
Minehead. Som 2C 20
Minera. Wrex 5E 83
Minety. Wilts 2F 35
Minffordd. Gwyn 2E 69
Mingarrypark. High 2A 140
Mingary. High 2G 139
Mingearraidh. W Isl 6C 170
Miningsby. Linc 4C 88
Minions. Corn 5C 10
Minishant. S Ayr 3C 116
Minllyn. Gwyn 4A 70
Minnigaff. Dum 3B 110
Minorca. IOM 3D 108
Minskip. N Yor 3F 99
Minstead. Hants 1A 16
Minsted. W Sus 4G 25
Minster. Kent
nr. Ramsgate 4H 41
Minster. Kent
nr. Sheerness 3D 40
Minsteracres. Nmbd 4D 114
Minsterley. Shrp 5F 71
Minster Lovell. Oxon 4B 50
Minsterworth. Glos 4C 48
Minterne Magna. Dors 2B 14
Minterne Parva. Dors 2B 14
Minting. Linc 3A 88
Mintlaw. Abers 4H 161
Minto. Bord 2H 119
Minton. Shrp 1G 59
Minwear. Pemb 3E 43
Minworth. W Mid 1F 61
Miodar. Arg 4B 138
Mirbister. Orkn 5C 172
Mirehouse. Cumb 3A 102
Mireland. High 2F 169
Mirfield. W Yor 3C 92
Miserden. Glos 5E 49
Miskin. Rhon 3D 32
Misson. Notts 1D 86
Misterton. Leics 2C 62
Misterton. Notts 1E 87
Misterton. Som 2H 13
Mistley. Essx 2E 54
Mistley Heath. Essx 2E 55
Mitcham. G Lon 4D 39
Mitcheldean. Glos 4B 48
Mitchell. Corn 3C 6
Mitchel Troy. Mon 4H 47
Mitcheltroy Common. Mon 5H 47
Mitford. Nmbd 1E 115
Mithian. Corn 3B 6
Mitton. Staf 4C 72
Mixbury. Oxon 2E 50
Mixenden. W Yor 2A 92
Mixon. Staf 5E 85
Moaness. Orkn 7B 172
Moarfield. Shet 1G 173
Moat. Cumb 2F 113
Moats Tye. Suff 5C 66
Mobberley. Ches E 3B 84
Mobberley. Staf 1E 73
Moccas. Here 1G 47
Mochdre. Cnwy 3H 81
Mochdre. Powy 2C 58
Mochrum. Dum 5A 110
Mockbeggar. Hants 2G 15
Mockerkin. Cumb 2B 102
Modbury. Devn 3C 8
Moddershall. Staf 2D 72
Modsarie. High 2G 167
Moelfre. Cnwy 3B 82
Moelfre. IOA 2E 81
Moelfre. Powy 3D 70
Moffat. Dum 4C 118
Moggerhanger. C Beds 1B 52
Mogworthy. Devn 1B 12
Moira. Leics 4H 73
Moira. Lis 4G 175
Molash. Kent 5E 41
Mol-chlach. High 2C 146
Mold. Flin 4E 83
Molehill Green. Essx 3F 53
Molescroft. E Yor 5E 101
Molesden. Nmbd 1E 115
Molesworth. Cambs 3H 63
Moll. High 1D 146
Molland. Devn 4B 20
Mollington. Ches W 3F 83
Mollington. Oxon 1C 50
Mollinsburn. N Lan 2A 128
Monachty. Cdgn 4E 57
Monachyle. Stir 2D 135
Monar Lodge. High 4E 156
Monaughty. Powy 4E 59
Monewden. Suff 5E 67
Moneydie. Per 1C 136
Moneymore. M Ulst 3E 175
Moneyrow Green. Wind 4G 37
Moniaive. Dum 5G 117
Monifieth. Ang 5E 145
Monikie. Ang 5E 145
Monimail. Fife 2E 137
Monington. Pemb 1B 44
Monk Bretton. S Yor 4D 92
Monken Hadley. G Lon 1D 38
Monk Fryston. N Yor 2F 93
Monk Hesleden. Dur 1B 106
Monkhide. Here 1B 48
Monkhill. Cumb 4E 113
Monkhopton. Shrp 1A 60
Monkland. Here 5G 59
Monkleigh. Devn 4E 19
Monknash. V Glam 4C 32
Monkokehampton. Devn 2F 11
Monkseaton. Tyne 2G 115
Monks Eleigh. Suff 1C 54
Monk's Gate. W Sus 3D 26
Monk's Heath. Ches E 3C 84
Monk Sherborne. Hants 1E 24
Monkshill. Abers 4E 161
Monksilver. Som 3D 20
Monks Kirby. Warw 2B 62
Monk Soham. Suff 4E 66
Monk Soham Green. Suff 4E 66
Monkspath. W Mid 3F 61
Monks Risborough. Buck 5G 51
Monksthorpe. Linc 4D 88
Monk Street. Essx 3G 53
Monkswood. Mon 5G 47
Monkton. Devn 2E 13
Monkton. Kent 4G 41
Monkton. Pemb 4D 42
Monkton. S Ayr 2C 116
Monkton Combe. Bath 5C 34
Monkton Deverill. Wilts 3D 22
Monkton Farleigh. Wilts 5D 34
Monkton Heathfield. Som 4F 21
Monktonhill. S Ayr 2C 116
Monkton Up Wimborne
Dors 1F 15
Monkton Wyld. Dors 3G 13
Monkwearmouth. Tyne 4G 115
Monkwood. Dors 3H 13
Monkwood. Hants 3E 25
Monmarsh. Here 1A 48
Monmouth. Mon 4A 48
Monnington on Wye. Here 1G 47
Monreith. Dum 5A 110
Montacute. Som 1H 13
Montford. Arg 3C 126
Montford. Shrp 4G 71
Montford Bridge. Shrp 4G 71
Montgarrie. Abers 2C 152
Montgarswood. E Ayr 2E 117
Montgomery. Powy 1E 58
Montgreenan. N Ayr 5E 127
Montrave. Fife 3F 137
Montrose. Ang 3G 145
Monxton. Hants 2B 24
Monyash. Derbs 4F 85
Monymusk. Abers 2D 152
Monzie. Per 1A 136
Moodiesburn. N Lan 2H 127
Moon's Green. Kent 3C 28
Moonzie. Fife 2F 137
Moor. Som 1H 13
The Moor. Kent 3B 28
Moor Allerton. W Yor 1C 92
Moorbath. Dors 3H 13
Moorbrae. Shet 3F 173
Moorby. Linc 4B 88
Moorcot. Here 5F 59
Moor Crichel. Dors 2E 15
Moor Cross. Devn 3C 8
Moordown. Bour 3F 15
Moore. Hal 2H 83
Moor End. E Yor 1B 94
Moorend. Dum 2D 112
Moorend. Glos
nr. Dursley 5C 48
nr. Gloucester 4D 48
Moorends. S Yor 3G 93
Moorgate. S Yor 1B 86
Moor Green. Wilts 5D 34
Moorgreen. Hants 1C 16
Moorgreen. Notts 1B 74
Moorhaigh. Notts 4C 86
Moorhall. Derbs 3H 85
Moorhampton. Here 1G 47
Moorhouse. Cumb
nr. Carlisle 4E 113
nr. Wigton 4D 112
Moorhouse. Notts 4E 87
Moorhouse. Surr 5F 39
Moorhouses. Linc 5B 88
Moorland. Som 3G 21
Moorlinch. Som 3H 21
Moor Monkton. N Yor 4H 99
Moor of Granary. Mor 3E 159
Moor Row. Cumb
nr. Whitehaven 3B 102
nr. Wigton 5D 112
Moorsholm. Red C 3D 107
Moorside. Dors 1C 14
Moorside. G Man 4H 91
Moortown. Devn 3D 10
Moortown. Hants 2G 15
Moortown. IOW 4C 16
Moortown. Linc 1H 87
Moortown. Telf 4A 72
Moortown. W Yor 1D 92
Morangie. High 5E 165
Morar. High 4E 147
Morborne. Cambs 1A 64
Morchard Bishop. Devn 2A 12
Morcombelake. Dors 3H 13
Morcott. Rut 5G 75
Morda. Shrp 3E 71
Morden. G Lon 4D 38
Mordiford. Here 2A 48
Mordon. Dur 2A 106
More. Shrp 1F 59
Morebath. Devn 4C 20
Morebattle. Bord 2B 120
Morecambe. Lanc 3D 96
Morefield. High 4F 163
Moreleigh. Devn 3D 8
Morenish. Per 5C 142
Moresby Parks. Cumb 3A 102
Morestead. Hants 4D 24
Moreton. Dors 4D 14
Moreton. Essx 5F 53
Moreton. Here 4H 59
Moreton. Mers 1E 83
Moreton. Oxon 5E 51
Moreton. Staf 4B 72
Moreton Corbet. Shrp 3H 71
Moretonhampstead. Devn 4A 12
Moreton-in-Marsh. Glos 2H 49
Moreton Jeffries. Here 1B 48
Moreton Morrell. Warw 5H 61
Moreton on Lugg. Here 1A 48
Moreton Pinkney. Nptn 1D 50
Moreton Say. Shrp 2A 72
Moreton Valence. Glos 5C 48
Morfa. Cdgn 5C 56
Morfa Bach. Carm 4D 44
Morfa Bychan. Gwyn 2E 69
Morfa Glas. Neat 5B 46
Morfa Nefyn. Gwyn 1B 68
Morganstown. Card 3E 33
Morgan's Vale. Wilts 4G 23
Morham. E Lot 2B 130
Moriah. Cdgn 3F 57
Morland. Cumb 2G 103
Morley. Ches E 2C 84
Morley. Derbs 1A 74
Morley. Dur 2E 105
Morley. W Yor 2C 92
Morley St Botolph. Norf 1C 66
Morningside. Edin 2F 129
Morningside. N Lan 4B 128
Morningthorpe. Norf 1E 66
Morpeth. Nmbd 1F 115
Morrey. Staf 4F 73
Morridge Side. Staf 5E 85
Morridge Top. Staf 4E 85
Morrington. Dum 1F 111
Morris Green. Essx 2H 53
Morriston. Swan 3F 31
Morston. Norf 1C 78
Mortehoe. Devn 2E 19
Morthen. S Yor 2B 86
Mortimer. W Ber 5E 37
Mortimer's Cross. Here 4G 59
Mortimer West End. Hants 5E 37
Mortomley. S Yor 1H 85
Morton. Cumb
nr. Calthwaite 1F 103
nr. Carlisle 4E 113
Morton. Derbs 4B 86
Morton. Linc
nr. Bourne 3H 75
nr. Gainsborough 1F 87
nr. Lincoln 4F 87
Morton. Norf 4D 78
Morton. Notts 5E 87
Morton. Shrp 3E 71
Morton. S Glo 2B 34
Morton Bagot. Warw 4F 61
Morton Mill. Shrp 3H 71
Morton-on-Swale. N Yor 5A 106
Morton Tinmouth. Dur 2E 105
Morvah. Corn 3B 4
Morval. Corn 3G 7
Morvich. High
nr. Golspie 3E 165
nr. Shiel Bridge 1B 148
Morvil. Pemb 1E 43
Morville. Shrp 1A 60
Morwenstow. Corn 1C 10
Morwick. Nmbd 4G 121
Mosborough. S Yor 2B 86
Moscow. E Ayr 5F 127
Mose. Shrp 1B 60
Mosedale. Cumb 1E 103
Moseley. W Mid
nr. Birmingham 2E 61
nr. Wolverhampton 5D 72
Moseley. Worc 5C 60
Moss. Arg 4A 138
Moss. High 2A 140
Moss. S Yor 3F 93
Moss. Wrex 5F 83
Mossatt. Abers 2B 152
Moss Bank. Mers 1H 83
Mossbank. Shet 4F 173
Mossblown. S Ayr 2D 116
Mossbrow. G Man 2B 84
Mossburnford. Bord 3A 120
Mossdale. Dum 2D 110
Mossedge. Cumb 3F 113
Mossend. N Lan 3A 128
Mossgate. Staf 2D 72
Moss Lane. Ches E 3D 84
Mossley. Ches E 4C 84
Mossley. G Man 4H 91
Mossley Hill. Mers 2F 83
Moss of Barmuckity. Mor 2G 159
Mosspark. Glas 3G 127
Mosspaul. Bord 5G 119
Moss Side. Cumb 4C 112
Moss Side. G Man 1C 84
Moss Side. Lanc
nr. Blackpool 1B 90
nr. Preston 2D 90
Moss Side. Mers 4B 90
Moss-side. High 3C 158
Moss-side of Cairness
Abers 2H 161
Mosstodloch. Mor 2H 159
Mosswood. Nmbd 4D 114
Mossy Lea. Lanc 3D 90
Mosterton. Dors 2H 13
Moston. Shrp 3H 71
Moston Green. Ches E 4B 84
Mostyn. Flin 2D 82
Mostyn Quay. Flin 2D 82
Motcombe. Dors 4D 22
Mothecombe. Devn 4C 8
Motherby. Cumb 2F 103
Motherwell. N Lan 4A 128
Mottingham. G Lon 3F 39
Mottisfont. Hants 4B 24
Mottistone. IOW 4C 16
Mottram in Longdendale
G Man 1D 85
Mottram St Andrew. Ches E 3C 84
Mott's Mill. E Sus 2G 27
Mouldsworth. Ches W 3H 83
Moulin. Per 3G 143
Moulsecoomb. Brig 5E 27
Moulsford. Oxon 3D 36
Moulsoe. Mil 1H 51
Moulton. Ches W 4A 84
Moulton. Linc 3C 76
Moulton. Nptn 4E 63
Moulton. N Yor 4F 105
Moulton. Suff 4F 65
Moulton. V Glam 4D 32
Moulton Chapel. Linc 4B 76
Moulton Eaugate. Linc 4C 76
Moulton St Mary. Norf 5F 79
Moulton Seas End. Linc 3C 76
Mount. Corn
nr. Bodmin 2F 7
nr. Newquay 3B 6
Mountain Ash. Rhon 2D 32
Mountain Cross. Bord 5E 129
Mountain Street. Kent 5E 41
Mountain Water. Pemb 2D 42
Mount Ambrose. Corn 4B 6
Mountbenger. Bord 2F 119
Mountblow. W Dun 2F 127
Mount Bures. Essx 2C 54
Mountfield. E Sus 3B 28
Mountgerald. High 2H 157
Mount Hawke. Corn 4B 6
Mount High. High 2A 158
Mountjoy. Corn 2C 6
Mount Lothian. Midl 4F 129
Mountnessing. Essx 1H 39
Mounton. Mon 2A 34
Mount Pleasant. Buck 2E 51
Mount Pleasant. Ches E 5C 84
Mount Pleasant. Derbs
nr. Derby 1H 73
nr. Swadlincote 4G 73
Mount Pleasant. E Sus 4F 27
Mount Pleasant. Hants 3A 16
Mount Pleasant. Norf 1B 66

Mount Skippett – Newbiggin

Mount Skippett. Oxon 4B 50
Mountsorrel. Leics 4C 74
Mount Stuart. Arg 4C 126
Mousehole. Corn 4B 4
Mouswald. Dum 2B 112
Mow Cop. Ches E 5C 84
Mowden. Darl 3F 105
Mowhaugh. Bord 2C 120
Mowmacre Hill. Leic 5C 74
Mowsley. Leics 2D 62
Moy. High 5B 158
Moy. M Ulst 5E 175
Moygashel. M Ulst 4E 175
Moylgrove. Pemb 1B 44
Moy Lodge. High 5G 149
Muasdale. Arg 5E 125
Muchalls. Abers 4G 153
Much Birch. Here 2A 48
Much Cowarne. Here 1B 48
Much Dewchurch. Here 2H 47
Muchelney. Som 4H 21
Muchelney Ham. Som 4H 21
Much Hadham. Herts 4E 53
Much Hoole. Lanc 2C 90
Muchlarnick. Corn 3G 7
Much Marcle. Here 2B 48
Muchrachd. High 5E 157
Much Wenlock. Shrp 5A 72
Mucking. Thur 2A 40
Muckle Breck. Shet 5G 173
Muckleford. Dors 3B 14
Mucklestone. Staf 2B 72
Muckleton. Norf 2H 77
Muckleton. Shrp 3H 71
Muckley. Shrp 1A 60
Muckley Corner. Staf 5E 73
Muckton. Linc 2C 88
Mudale. High 5F 167
Muddiford. Devn 3F 19
Mudeford. Dors 3G 15
Mudford. Som 1A 14
Mudgley. Som 2H 21
Mugdock. Stir 2G 127
Mugeary. High 5D 154
Muggington. Derbs 1G 73
Muggintonlane End. Derbs 1G 73
Muggleswick. Dur 4D 114
Mugswell. Surr 5D 38
Muie. High 3D 164
Muirden. Abers 3E 160
Muirdrum. Ang 5E 145
Muiredge. Per 1E 137
Muirend. Glas 3G 127
Muirhead. Ang 5C 144
Muirhead. Fife 3E 137
Muirhead. N Lan 3H 127
Muirhouses. Falk 1D 128
Muirkirk. E Ayr 2F 117
Muir of Alford. Abers 2C 152
Muir of Fairburn. High 3G 157
Muir of Fowlis. Abers 2C 152
Muir of Miltonduff. Mor 3F 159
Muir of Ord. High 3H 157
Muir of Tarradale. High 3H 157
Muirshearlich. High 5D 148
Muirtack. Abers 5G 161
Muirton. High 2B 158
Muirton. Per 1D 136
Muirton of Ardblair. Per 4A 144
Muirtown. Per 2B 136
Muiryfold. Abers 3E 161
Muker. N Yor 5C 104
Mulbarton. Norf 5D 78
Mulben. Mor 3A 160
Mulindry. Arg 4B 124
Mulla. Shet 5F 173
Mullach Charlabhaigh W Isl 3E 171
Mullacott. Devn 2F 19
Mullion. Corn 5D 5
Mullion Cove. Corn 5D 4
Mumbles. Swan 4F 31
Mumby. Linc 3E 89
Munderfield Row. Here 5A 60
Munderfield Stocks. Here 5A 60
Mundesley. Norf 2F 79
Mundford. Norf 1H 65
Mundham. Norf 1F 67
Mundon. Essx 5B 54
Munerigie. High 3E 149
Muness. Shet 1H 173
Mungasdale. High 4D 162
Mungrisdale. Cumb 1E 103
Munlochy. High 3A 158
Munsley. Here 1B 48
Munslow. Shrp 2H 59
Murchington. Devn 4G 11
Murcot. Worc 1F 49
Murcott. Oxon 4D 50
Murdishaw. Hal 2H 83
Murieston. W Lot 3D 128
Murkle. High 2D 168
Murlaggan. High 4C 148
Murra. Orkn 7B 172
The Murray. S Lan 4H 127
Murrayfield. Edin 2F 129
Murrell Green. Hants 1F 25
Murroes. Ang 5D 144
Murrow. Cambs 5C 76
Mursley. Buck 3G 51
Murthly. Per 5H 143
Murton. Cumb 2A 104
Murton. Dur 5G 115
Murton. Nmbd 5F 131
Murton. Swan 4E 31
Murton. York 4A 100
Musbury. Devn 3F 13
Muscoates. N Yor 1A 100
Muscott. Nptn 4D 62
Musselburgh. E Lot 2G 129
Muston. Leics 2F 75
Muston. N Yor 2E 101
Mustow Green. Worc 3C 60
Muswell Hill. G Lon 2D 39
Mutehill. Dum 5D 111
Mutford. Suff 2G 67
Muthill. Per 2A 136
Mutterton. Devn 2D 12
Muxton. Telf 4B 72
Mwmbwls. Swan 4F 31
Mybster. High 3D 168
Myddfai. Carm 2A 46
Myddle. Shrp 3G 71
Mydroilyn. Cdgn 5D 56
Myerscough. Lanc 1C 90
Mylor Bridge. Corn 5C 6
Mylor Churchtown. Corn 5C 6
Mynachlog-ddu. Pemb 1F 43
Mynydd-bach. Mon 2H 33
Mynydd Isa. Flin 4E 83
Mynyddislwyn. Cphy 2E 33
Mynydd Llandegai. Gwyn 4F 81
Mynydd Mechell. IOA 1C 80
Mynydd-y-briw. Powy 3D 70
Mynyddygarreg. Carm 5E 45
Mynytho. Gwyn 2C 68
Myrebird. Abers 4E 153
Myrelandhorn. High 3E 169
Mytchett. Surr 1G 25
The Mythe. Glos 2D 49
Mytholmroyd. W Yor 2A 92
Myton-on-Swale. N Yor 3G 99
Mytton. Shrp 4G 71

N

Naast. High 5C 162
Na Buirgh. W Isl 8C 171
Naburn. York 5H 99
Nab Wood. W Yor 1B 92
Nackington. Kent 5F 41
Nacton. Suff 1F 55
Nafferton. E Yor 4E 101
Na Gearrannan. W Isl 3D 171
Nailbridge. Glos 4B 48
Nailsbourne. Som 4F 21
Nailsea. N Som 4H 33
Nailstone. Leics 5B 74
Nailsworth. Glos 2D 34
Nairn. High 3C 158
Nalderswood. Surr 1D 26
Nancegollan. Corn 3D 4
Nancledra. Corn 3B 4
Nangreaves. G Man 3G 91
Nanhyfer. Pemb 1E 43
Nannerch. Flin 4D 82
Nanpantan. Leics 4C 74
Nanpean. Corn 3D 6
Nansledan C2 6
Nanstallon. Corn 2E 7
Nant-ddu. Powy 4D 46
Nanternis. Cdgn 5C 56
Nantgaredig. Carm 3E 45
Nantgarw. Rhon 3E 33
Nant Glas. Powy 4B 58
Nantglyn. Den 4C 82
Nantgwyn. Powy 3B 58
Nantlle. Gwyn 5E 81
Nantmawr. Shrp 3E 71
Nantmel. Powy 4C 58
Nantmor. Gwyn 1F 69
Nant Peris. Gwyn 5F 81
Nantwich. Ches E 5A 84
Nant-y-bai. Carm 1A 46
Nant-y-bwch. Blae 4E 47
Nant-y-Derry. Mon 5G 47
Nant-y-dugoed. Powy 4B 70
Nant-y-felin. Cnwy 3F 81
Nantyffyllon. B'end 2B 32
Nantyglo. Blae 4E 47
Nant-y-meichiaid. Powy 4D 70
Nant-y-moel. B'end 2C 32
Nant-y-pandy. Cnwy 3F 81
Naphill. Buck 2G 37
Nappa. N Yor 4A 98
Napton on the Hill. Warw 4B 62
Narberth. Pemb 3F 43
Narberth Bridge. Pemb 3F 43
Narborough. Leics 1C 62
Narborough. Norf 4G 77
Narkurs. Corn 3H 7
The Narth. Mon 5A 48
Narthwaite. Cumb 5A 104
Nasareth. Gwyn 5D 80
Naseby. Nptn 3D 62
Nash. Buck 2F 51
Nash. Here 4F 59
Nash. Kent 5G 41
Nash. Newp 3G 33
Nash. Shrp 3A 60
Nash Lee. Buck 5G 51
Nassington. Nptn 1H 63
Nasty. Herts 3D 52
Natcott. Devn 4C 18
Nateby. Cumb 4A 104
Nateby. Lanc 5D 96
Nately Scures. Hants 1F 25
Natland. Cumb 1E 97
Naughton. Suff 1D 54
Naunton. Glos 3G 49
Naunton. Worc 2D 49
Naunton Beauchamp. Worc 5D 60
Navenby. Linc 5G 87
Navestock. Essx 1G 39
Navestock Side. Essx 1G 39
Navidale. High 2H 165
Nawton. N Yor 1A 100
Nayland. Suff 2C 54
Nazeing. Essx 5E 53
Neacroft. Hants 3G 15
Nealhouse. Cumb 4E 113
Neal's Green. Warw 2H 61
Near Sawrey. Cumb 5E 103
Neasden. G Lon 2D 38
Neasham. Darl 3A 106
Neath. Neat 2A 32
Neath Abbey. Neat 3G 31
Neatishead. Norf 3F 79
Neaton. Norf 5B 78
Nebo. Cdgn 4E 57
Nebo. Cnwy 5H 81
Nebo. Gwyn 5D 81
Nebo. IOA 1D 80
Necton. Norf 5A 78
Nedd. High 5B 166
Nedderton. Nmbd 1F 115
Nedging. Suff 1D 54
Nedging Tye. Suff 1D 54
Needham. Norf 2E 67
Needham Market. Suff 5C 66
Needham Street. Suff 4G 65
Needingworth. Cambs 3C 64
Needwood. Staf 3F 73
Neen Savage. Shrp 3A 60
Neen Sollars. Shrp 3A 60
Neenton. Shrp 2A 60
Nefyn. Gwyn 1C 68
Neilston. E Ren 4F 127
Neithrop. Oxon 1C 50
Nelly Andrews Green. Powy 5E 71
Nelson. Cphy 2E 32
Nelson. Lanc 1G 91
Nelson Village. Nmbd 2F 115
Nemphlar. S Lan 5B 128
Nempnett Thrubwell. Bath 5A 34
Nene Terrace. Linc 5B 76
Nenthall. Cumb 5A 114
Nenthead. Cumb 5A 114
Nenthorn. Bord 1A 120
Nercwys. Flin 4E 83
Neribus. Arg 4A 124
Nerston. S Lan 4H 127
Nesbit. Nmbd 1D 121
Nesfield. N Yor 5C 98
Ness. Ches W 3F 83
Nesscliffe. Shrp 4F 71
Ness of Tenston. Orkn 6B 172
Neston. Ches W 3E 83
Neston. Wilts 5D 34
Nethanfoot. S Lan 5B 128
Nether Alderley. Ches E 3C 84
Netheravon. Wilts 2G 23
Nether Blainslie. Bord 5B 130
Netherbrae. Abers 3E 161
Netherbrough. Orkn 6C 172
Nether Broughton. Leics 3D 74
Netherburn. S Lan 5B 128
Nether Burrow. Lanc 2F 97
Netherbury. Dors 3H 13
Netherby. Cumb 2E 113
Nether Careston. Ang 3E 145
Nether Cerne. Dors 3B 14
Nether Compton. Dors 1A 14
Nethercote. Glos 3G 49
Nethercote. Warw 4C 62
Nethercott. Devn 3E 19
Nethercott. Oxon 3C 50
Nether Dallachy. Mor 2A 160
Nether Durdie. Per 1E 136
Nether End. Derbs 3G 85
Netherend. Glos 5A 48
Nether Exe. Devn 2C 12
Netherfield. E Sus 4B 28
Netherfield. Notts 1D 74
Nethergate. Norf 3C 78
Netherhampton. Wilts 4G 23
Nether Handley. Derbs 3B 86
Nether Haugh. S Yor 1B 86
Nether Heage. Derbs 5A 86
Nether Heyford. Nptn 5D 62
Netherhouses. Cumb 1B 96
Nether Howcleugh S Lan 3C 118
Nether Kellet. Lanc 3E 97
Nether Kinmundy. Abers 4H 161
Netherland Green. Staf 2F 73
Nether Langwith. Notts 3C 86
Netherlaw. Dum 5E 111
Netherley. Abers 4F 153
Nethermill. Dum 1B 112
Nethermills. Mor 3C 160
Nether Moor. Derbs 4A 86
Nether Padley. Derbs 3G 85
Netherplace. E Ren 4G 127
Nether Poppleton. York 4H 99
Netherseal. Derbs 4G 73
Nether Silton. N Yor 5B 106
Nether Stowey. Som 3E 21
Nether Street. Essx 4F 53
Netherstreet. Wilts 5E 35
Netherthird. E Ayr 3E 117
Netherthong. W Yor 4B 92
Netherton. Ang 3E 145
Netherton. Cumb 1B 102
Netherton. Devn 5B 12
Netherton. Hants 1B 24
Netherton. Here 3A 48
Netherton. Mers 1F 83
Netherton. N Lan 4A 128
Netherton. Nmbd 4D 121
Netherton. Per 3A 144
Netherton. Shrp 2B 60
Netherton. Stir 2G 127
Netherton. W Mid 2D 60
Netherton. W Yor
nr. Armitage Bridge 3B 92
nr. Horbury 3C 92
Netherton. Worc 1E 49
Nethertown. Cumb 4A 102
Nethertown. High 1F 169
Nethertown. Staf 4F 73
Nether Urquhart. Fife 3D 136
Nether Wallop. Hants 3B 24
Nether Wasdale. Cumb 4C 102
Nether Welton. Cumb 5E 113
Nether Westcote. Glos 3H 49
Nether Whitacre. Warw 1G 61
Nether Winchendon. Buck 4F 51
Netherwitton. Nmbd 5F 121
Nether Worton. Oxon 2C 50
Nethy Bridge. High 1E 151
Netley. Shrp 5G 71
Netley Abbey. Hants 2C 16
Netley Marsh. Hants 1B 16
Nettlebed. Oxon 3F 37
Nettlebridge. Som 2B 22
Nettlecombe. Dors 3A 14
Nettlecombe. IOW 5D 16
Nettleden. Herts 4A 52
Nettleham. Linc 3H 87
Nettlestead. Kent 5A 40
Nettlestead Green. Kent 5A 40
Nettlestone. IOW 3E 16
Nettlesworth. Dur 5F 115
Nettleton. Linc 4E 94
Nettleton. Wilts 4D 34
Netton. Devn 4B 8
Netton. Wilts 3G 23
Neuadd. Powy 5C 70
The Neuk. Abers 4E 153
Nevendon. Essx 1B 40
Nevern. Pemb 1E 43
New Abbey. Dum 3A 112
New Aberdour. Abers 2F 161
New Addington. G Lon 4E 39
Newall. W Yor 5E 98
New Alresford. Hants 3D 24
New Alyth. Per 4B 144
Newark. Orkn 3G 172
Newark. Pet 5B 76
Newark-on-Trent. Notts 5E 87
New Arley. Warw 2G 61
Newarthill. N Lan 4A 128
New Ash Green. Kent 4H 39
New Balderton. Notts 5F 87
New Barn. Kent 4H 39
New Barnetby. N Lin 3D 94
Newbattle. Midl 3G 129
New Bewick. Nmbd 2E 121
Newbie. Dum 3C 112
Newbiggin. Cumb
nr. Appleby 2H 103
nr. Barrow-in-Furness 3B 96
nr. Cumrew 5G 113
nr. Penrith 2F 103
nr. Seascale 5B 102
Newbiggin. Dur
nr. Consett 5E 115
nr. Holwick 2C 104
Newbiggin. Nmbd 5C 114

Newbiggin. N Yor
 nr. Askrigg 5C 104
 nr. Filey 1F 101
 nr. Thoralby 1B 98
Newbiggin-by-the-Sea
 Nmbd 1G 115
Newbigging. Ang
 nr. Monikie 5D 145
 nr. Newtyle 4B 144
 nr. Tealing 5D 144
Newbigging. Edin 2E 129
Newbigging. S Lan 5D 128
Newbiggin-on-Lune
 Cumb 4A 104
Newbold. Derbs 3A 86
Newbold. Leics 4B 74
Newbold on Avon. Warw 3B 62
Newbold on Stour. Warw 1H 49
Newbold Pacey. Warw 5G 61
Newbold Verdon. Leics 5B 74
New Bolingbroke. Linc 5C 88
Newborough. IOA 4D 80
Newborough. Pet 5B 76
Newborough. Staf 3F 73
Newbottle. Nptn 2D 50
Newbottle. Tyne 4G 115
New Boultham. Linc 3G 87
Newbourne. Suff 1F 55
New Brancepeth. Dur 5F 115
New Bridge. Dum 2G 111
Newbridge. Cphy 2F 33
Newbridge. Cdgn 5E 57
Newbridge. Corn 3B 4
Newbridge. Edin 2E 129
Newbridge. Hants 1A 16
Newbridge. IOW 4C 16
Newbridge. N Yor 1C 100
Newbridge. Pemb 1D 42
Newbridge. Wrex 1E 71
Newbridge Green. Worc 2D 48
Newbridge-on-Usk. Mon 2G 33
Newbridge on Wye. Powy 5C 58
New Brighton. Flin 4E 83
New Brighton. Hants 2F 17
New Brighton. Mers 1F 83
New Brinsley. Notts 5B 86
Newbrough. Nmbd 3B 114
New Broughton. Wrex 5F 83
New Buckenham. Norf 1C 66
New Buildings. Derr 2C 174
Newbuildings. Devn 2A 12
Newburgh. Abers 1G 153
Newburgh. Fife 2E 137
Newburgh. Lanc 3C 90
Newburn. Tyne 3E 115
Newbury. W Ber 5C 36
Newbury. Wilts 2D 22
Newby. Cumb 2G 103
Newby. N Yor
 nr. Ingleton 2G 97
 nr. Scarborough 1E 101
 nr. Stokesley 3C 106
Newby Bridge. Cumb 1C 96
Newby Cote. N Yor 2G 97
Newby East. Cumb 4F 113
Newby Head. Cumb 2G 103
New Byth. Abers 3F 161
Newby West. Cumb 4E 113
Newby Wiske. N Yor 1F 99
Newcastle. B'end 3B 32
Newcastle. Mon 4H 47
Newcastle. New M 6H 175
Newcastle. Shrp 2E 59
Newcastle Emlyn. Carm 1D 44
Newcastle International Airport
 Tyne 2E 115
Newcastleton. Bord 1F 113
Newcastle-under-Lyme
 Staf 1C 72
Newcastle upon Tyne. Tyne 3F 115
Newchapel. Pemb 1G 43
Newchapel. Powy 2B 58
Newchapel. Staf 5C 84
Newchapel. Surr 1E 27

New Cheriton. Hants 4D 24
Newchurch. Carm 3D 45
Newchurch. Here 5F 59
Newchurch. IOW 4D 16
Newchurch. Kent 2E 29
Newchurch. Lanc 2G 91
Newchurch. Mon 2H 33
Newchurch. Powy 5E 58
Newchurch. Staf 3F 73
Newchurch in Pendle. Lanc 1G 91
New Costessey. Norf 4D 78
Newcott. Devn 2F 13
New Cowper. Cumb 5C 112
Newcraighall. Edin 2G 129
New Crofton. W Yor 3D 93
New Cross. Cdgn 3F 57
New Cross. Som 1H 13
New Cumnock. E Ayr 3F 117
New Deer. Abers 4F 161
New Denham. Buck 2B 38
Newdigate. Surr 1C 26
New Duston. Nptn 4E 62
New Earswick. York 4A 100
New Edlington. S Yor 1C 86
New Elgin. Mor 2G 159
New Ellerby. E Yor 1E 95
Newell Green. Brac 4G 37
New Eltham. G Lon 3F 39
New End. Warw 4F 61
New End. Worc 5E 61
Newenden. Kent 3C 28
New England. Essx 1H 53
New England. Pet 5A 76
Newent. Glos 3C 48
New Ferry. Mers 2F 83
Newfield. Dur
 nr. Chester-le-Street 4F 115
 nr. Willington 1F 105
Newfound. Hants 1D 24
New Fryston. W Yor 2E 93
Newgale. Pemb 2C 42
New Galloway. Dum 2D 110
Newgate. Norf 1C 78
Newgate Street. Herts 5D 52
New Greens. Herts 5B 52
New Grimsby. IOS 1A 4
New Hainford. Norf 4E 78
Newhall. Ches E 1A 72
Newhall. Derbs 3G 73
Newham. Nmbd 2F 121
New Hartley. Nmbd 2G 115
Newhaven. Derbs 4F 85
Newhaven. E Sus 5F 27
Newhaven. Edin 2F 129
New Haw. Surr 4B 38
New Hedges. Pemb 4F 43
New Herrington. Tyne 4G 115
Newhey. G Man 3H 91
New Holkham. Norf 2A 78
New Holland. N Lin 2D 94
Newholm. N Yor 3F 107
New Houghton. Derbs 4C 86
New Houghton. Norf 3G 77
Newhouse. N Lan 3A 128
New Houses. N Yor 2G 97
New Hutton. Cumb 5G 103
New Hythe. Kent 5B 40
Newick. E Sus 3F 27
Newingreen. Kent 2F 29
Newington. Edin 2F 129
Newington. Kent
 nr. Folkestone 2F 29
 nr. Sittingbourne 4C 40
Newington. Notts 1D 86
Newington. Oxon 2E 36
Newington Bagpath. Glos 2D 34
New Inn. Carm 2E 45
New Inn. Mon 5H 47
New Inn. N Yor 2G 97
New Inn. Torf 2G 33
New Invention. Shrp 3E 59
New Kelso. High 4B 156
New Lanark. S Lan 5B 128
Newland. Glos 5A 48

Newland. Hull 1D 94
Newland. N Yor 2G 93
Newland. Som 3B 20
Newland. Worc 1C 48
Newlandrig. Midl 3G 129
Newlands. Cumb 1E 103
Newlands. High 4B 158
Newlands. Nmbd 4D 115
Newlands. Staf 3E 73
Newlands of Geise. High 2C 168
Newlands of Tynet. Mor 2A 160
Newlands Park. IOA 2B 80
New Lane. Lanc 3C 90
New Lane End. Warr 1A 84
New Langholm. Dum 1E 113
New Leake. Linc 5D 88
New Leeds. Abers 3G 161
New Lenton. Nott 2C 74
New Longton. Lanc 2D 90
Newlot. Orkn 6E 172
New Luce. Dum 3G 109
Newlyn. Corn 4B 4
Newmachar. Abers 2F 153
Newmains. N Lan 4B 128
New Mains of Ury. Abers 5F 153
New Malden. G Lon 4D 38
Newman's Green. Suff 1B 54
Newmarket. Suff 4F 65
Newmarket. W Isl 4G 171
New Marske. Red C 2D 106
New Marton. Shrp 2F 71
New Micklefield. W Yor 1E 93
New Mill. Abers 4E 160
New Mill. Corn 3B 4
New Mill. Herts 4H 51
New Mill. W Yor 4B 92
New Mill. Wilts 5G 35
Newmill. Mor 3B 160
Newmill. Bord 3G 119
New Mills. Corn 3C 6
New Mills. Derbs 2E 85
New Mills. Mon 5A 48
New Mills. Powy 1D 128
Newmills. High 2A 158
Newmills. Fife 5A 144
Newmiln. E Ayr 1E 117
New Milton. Hants 3H 15
New Mistley. Essx 2E 54
New Moat. Pemb 2E 43
Newmore. High
 nr. Dingwall 3H 157
 nr. Invergordon 1A 158
Newnham. Cambs 5D 64
Newnham. Glos 4B 48
Newnham. Hants 1F 25
Newnham. Herts 2C 52
Newnham. Kent 5D 40
Newnham. Nptn 5C 62
Newnham. Warw 4F 61
Newnham Bridge. Worc 4A 60
New Ollerton. Notts 4D 86
New Oscott. W Mid 1E 61
New Park. N Yor 4E 99
Newpark. Fife 2G 137
New Pitsligo. Abers 3F 161
New Polzeath. Corn 1D 6
Newport. Corn 4D 10
Newport. Devn 3F 19
Newport. E Yor 1B 94
Newport. Essx 2F 53
Newport. Glos 2B 34
Newport. High 1H 165
Newport. IOW 4D 16
Newport. Newp 3G 33
Newport. Norf 4H 79
Newport. Pemb 1E 43
Newport. Som 4G 21
Newport. Telf 4B 72
Newport-on-Tay. Fife 1G 137
Newport Pagnell. Mil 1G 51
Newpound Common
 W Sus 3B 26

New Prestwick. S Ayr 2C 116
New Quay. Cdgn 5C 56
Newquay. Corn 2C 6
Newquay Cornwall Airport
 Corn 2C 6
New Rackheath. Norf 4E 79
New Radnor. Powy 4E 58
New Rent. Cumb 1F 103
New Ridley. Nmbd 4D 114
New Romney. Kent 3E 29
New Rossington. S Yor 1D 86
New Row. Cdgn 3G 57
Newry. New M 6F 175
New Sauchie. Clac 4A 136
Newsbank. Ches E 4C 84
Newseat. Abers 5E 160
Newsham. Lanc 1D 90
Newsham. Nmbd 2G 115
Newsham. N Yor
 nr. Richmond 3E 105
 nr. Thirsk 1F 99
New Sharlston. W Yor 2D 93
Newsholme. E Yor 2H 93
Newsholme. Lanc 4H 97
New Shoreston. Nmbd 1F 121
New Springs. G Man 4D 90
Newstead. Notts 5C 86
Newstead. Bord 1H 119
New Stevenston. N Lan 4A 128
Newstreet Lane. Shrp 2A 72
New Swanage. Dors 4F 15
New Swannington. Leics 4B 74
Newthorpe. N Yor 1E 93
Newthorpe. Notts 1B 74
Newton. Arg 4H 133
Newton. B'end 4B 32
Newton. Cambs
 nr. Cambridge 1E 53
 nr. Wisbech 4D 76
Newton. Ches W
 nr. Chester 4G 83
 nr. Tattenhall 5H 83
Newton. Cumb 2B 96
Newton. Derbs 5B 86
Newton. Dors 1C 14
Newton. Dum
 nr. Annan 2D 112
 nr. Moffat 5D 118
Newton. G Man 1D 84
Newton. Here
 nr. Ewyas Harold 2G 47
 nr. Leominster 5H 59
Newton. High
 nr. Cromarty 2B 158
 nr. Inverness 4B 158
 nr. Kylestrome 5C 166
 nr. Wick 4F 169
Newton. Lanc
 nr. Blackpool 1B 90
 nr. Carnforth 2E 97
 nr. Clitheroe 4F 97
Newton. Linc 2H 75
Newton. Mers 2E 83
Newton. Mor 2F 159
Newton. Norf 4H 77
Newton. Nptn 2F 63
Newton. Nmbd 3D 114
Newton. Notts 1D 74
Newton. Bord 2H 119
Newton. Shet 8E 173
Newton. Shrp
 nr. Bridgnorth 1B 60
 nr. Wem 2H 71
Newton. Som 3E 20
Newton. S Lan
 nr. Glasgow 3H 127
 nr. Lanark 1B 118
Newton. Staf 3E 73
Newton. Suff 1C 54
Newton. Swan 4F 31
Newton. Warw 3C 62
Newton. W Lot 2D 129
Newton. Wilts 4H 23

Newton Abbot. Devn 5B 12
Newton Arlosh. Cumb 4D 112
Newton Aycliffe. Dur 2F 105
Newton Bewley. Hart 2B 106
Newton Blossomville. Mil 5G 63
Newton Bromswold. Nptn 4G 63
Newton Burgoland. Leics 5A 74
Newton by Toft. Linc 2H 87
Newton Ferrers. Devn 4B 8
Newton Flotman. Norf 1E 66
Newtongrange. Midl 3G 129
Newton Green. Mon 2A 34
Newton Hall. Dur 5F 115
Newton Hall. Nmbd 3D 114
Newton Harcourt. Leics 1D 62
Newton Heath. G Man 4G 91
Newtonhill. Abers 4G 153
Newtonhill. High 4H 157
Newton Ketton. Darl 2A 106
Newton Kyme. N Yor 5G 99
Newton-le-Willows. Mers 1H 83
Newton-le-Willows. N Yor 1E 98
Newton Longville. Buck 2G 51
Newton Mearns. E Ren 4G 127
Newtonmore. High 4B 150
Newton Morrell. N Yor 4F 105
Newton Mulgrave. N Yor 3E 107
Newton of Ardtoe. High 1A 140
Newton of Balcanquhal
 Per 2D 136
Newton of Beltrees. Ren 4E 127
Newton of Falkland. Fife 3E 137
Newton of Mountblairy
 Abers 3D 160
Newton of Pitcairns. Per 2C 136
Newton-on-Ouse. N Yor 4H 99
Newton-on-Rawcliffe
 N Yor 5F 107
Newton on the Hill. Shrp 3G 71
Newton-on-the-Moor
 Nmbd 4F 121
Newton on Trent. Linc 3F 87
Newton Poppleford. Devn 4D 12
Newton Purcell. Oxon 2E 51
Newton Regis. Warw 5G 73
Newton Reigny. Cumb 1F 103
Newton Rigg. Cumb 1F 103
Newton St Cyres. Devn 3 12
Newton St Faith. Norf 4E 78
Newton St Loe. Bath 5C 34
Newton St Petrock. Devn 1E 11
Newton Solney. Derbs 3G 73
Newton Stacey. Hants 2C 24
Newton Stewart. Dum 3B 110
Newton Toney. Wilts 2H 23
Newton Tony. Wilts 2H 23
Newton Tracey. Devn 4F 19
Newton under Roseberry
 Red C 3C 106
Newton upon Ayr. S Ayr 2C 116
Newton upon Derwent
 E Yor 5B 100
Newton Valence. Hants 3F 25
Newton-with-Scales. Lanc 1C 90
New Town. Dors 1E 15
New Town. E Lot 2H 129
New Town. Lutn 3A 52
Newtown. Abers 2E 160
Newtown. Cambs 4H 63
Newtown. Corn 5C 10
Newtown. Cumb
 nr. Aspatria 5B 112
 nr. Brampton 3G 113
 nr. Penrith 2G 103
Newtown. Derbs 2D 85
Newtown. Devn
 nr. Aveton 4A 20
 nr. Dawlish 2H 13
Newtown. Falk 1C 128
Newtown. Glos
 nr. Lydney 5B 48
 nr. Tewkesbury 2E 49

Norton – Ormsaigmore

Norton. *Shrp*
nr. Ludlow 2G 59
nr. Madeley 5B 72
nr. Shrewsbury 5H 71
Norton. *S Yor*
nr. Askern 3F 93
nr. Sheffield 2A 86
Norton. *Stoc T* 2B 106
Norton. *Suff* 4B 66
Norton. *Swan* 4F 31
Norton. *W Sus*
nr. Selsey 3G 17
nr. Westergate 5A 26
Norton. *Wilts* 3D 35
Norton. *Worc*
nr. Evesham 1F 49
nr. Worcester 5C 60
Norton Bavant. *Wilts* 2E 23
Norton Bridge. *Staf* 2C 72
Norton Canes. *Staf* 5E 73
Norton Canon. *Here* 1G 47
Norton Corner. *Norf* 3C 78
Norton Disney. *Linc* 5F 87
Norton East. *Staf* 5E 73
Norton Ferris. *Wilts* 3C 22
Norton Fitzwarren. *Som* 4F 21
Norton Green. *IOW* 4B 16
Norton Green. *Stoke* 5D 84
Norton Hawkfield. *Bath* 5A 34
Norton Heath. *Essx* 5F 53
Norton in Hales. *Shrp* 2B 72
Norton in the Moors. *Stoke* 5C 84
Norton-Juxta-Twycross
Leics 5H 73
Norton-le-Clay. *N Yor* 2G 99
Norton Lindsey. *Warw* 4G 61
Norton Little Green. *Suff* 4B 66
Norton Malreward. *Bath* 5B 34
Norton Mandeville. *Essx* 5F 53
Norton-on-Derwent. *N Yor* 2B 100
Norton St Philip. *Som* 1C 22
Norton Subcourse. *Norf* 1G 67
Norton sub Hamdon. *Som* 1H 13
Norton Woodseats. *S Yor* 2A 86
Norwell. *Notts* 4E 87
Norwell Woodhouse. *Notts* 4E 87
Norwich. *Norf* 5E 79
Norwich Airport. *Norf* 4E 79
Norwick. *Shet* 1H 173
Norwood. *Derbs* 2B 86
Norwood Green. *W Yor* 2B 92
Norwood Hill. *Surr* 1D 26
Norwood Park. *Som* 3A 22
Norwoodside. *Cambs* 1D 64
Noseley. *Leics* 1E 63
Noss. *Shet* 10E 173
Noss Mayo. *Devn* 4B 8
Nosterfield. *N Yor* 1E 99
Nostie. *High* 1A 148
Notgrove. *Glos* 3G 49
Nottage. *B'end* 4B 32
Nottingham. *Nott* 1C 74
Nottington. *Dors* 4B 14
Notton. *Dors* 3B 14
Notton. *W Yor* 3D 92
Notton. *Wilts* 5E 35
Nounsley. *Essx* 4A 54
Noutard's Green. *Worc* 4B 60
Nox. *Shrp* 4G 71
Noyadd Trefawr. *Cdgn* 1C 44
Nuffield. *Oxon* 3E 37
Nunburnholme. *E Yor* 5C 100
Nuncargate. *Notts* 5C 86
Nunclose. *Cumb* 5F 113
Nuneaton. *Warw* 1A 62
Nuneham Courtenay. *Oxon* 2D 36
Nun Monkton. *N Yor* 4H 99
Nunnerie. *S Lan* 3B 118
Nunney. *Som* 2C 22
Nunnington. *N Yor* 2A 100
Nunnykirk. *Nmbd* 5E 121
Nunsthorpe. *NE Lin* 4F 95
Nunthorpe. *Midd* 3C 106
Nunthorpe. *York* 4H 99
Nunton. *Wilts* 4G 23
Nunwick. *Nmbd* 2B 114
Nunwick. *N Yor* 2F 99
Nupend. *Glos* 5C 48
Nursling. *Hants* 1B 16
Nursted. *Hants* 4F 25
Nursteed. *Wilts* 5F 35
Nurston. *V Glam* 5D 32
Nutbourne. *W Sus*
nr. Chichester 2F 17
nr. Pulborough 4B 26
Nutfield. *Surr* 5E 39
Nuthall. *Notts* 1C 74
Nuthampstead. *Herts* 2E 53
Nuthurst. *Warw* 3F 61
Nuthurst. *W Sus* 3C 26
Nutley. *E Sus* 3F 27
Nuttall. *G Man* 3F 91
Nutwell. *S Yor* 4G 93
Nybster. *High* 2F 169
Nyetimber. *W Sus* 3G 17
Nyewood. *W Sus* 4G 25
Nymet Rowland. *Devn* 2H 11
Nymet Tracey. *Devn* 2H 11
Nympsfield. *Glos* 5D 48
Nynehead. *Som* 4E 21
Nyton. *W Sus* 5A 26

O

Oadby. *Leics* 5D 74
Oad Street. *Kent* 4C 40
Oakamoor. *Staf* 1E 73
Oakbank. *Arg* 5B 140
Oakbank. *W Lot* 3D 129
Oakdale. *Cphy* 2E 33
Oakdale. *Pool* 3F 15
Oake. *Som* 4E 21
Oaken. *Staf* 5C 72
Oakenclough. *Lanc* 5E 97
Oakengates. *Telf* 4A 72
Oakenholt. *Flin* 3E 83
Oakenshaw. *Dur* 1F 105
Oakenshaw. *W Yor* 2B 92
Oakerthorpe. *Derbs* 5A 86
Oakford. *Cdgn* 5D 56
Oakford. *Devn* 4C 20
Oakfordbridge. *Devn* 4C 20
Oakgrove. *Ches E* 4D 84
Oakham. *Rut* 5F 75
Oakhanger. *Ches E* 5B 84
Oakhanger. *Hants* 3F 25
Oakhill. *Som* 2B 22
Oakington. *Cambs* 4D 64
Oaklands. *Powy* 5C 58
Oakle Street. *Glos* 4C 48
Oakley. *Bed* 5H 63
Oakley. *Buck* 4E 51
Oakley. *Fife* 1D 128
Oakley. *Hants* 1D 24
Oakley. *Suff* 3D 66
Oakley Green. *Wind* 3A 38
Oakley Park. *Powy* 2B 58
Oakmere. *Ches W* 4H 83
Oakridge Lynch. *Glos* 5E 49
Oaks. *Shrp* 5G 71
Oaksey. *Wilts* 2E 35
Oaks Green. *Derbs* 2F 73
Oakshaw Ford. *Cumb* 2G 113
Oakshott. *Hants* 4F 25
Oakthorpe. *Leics* 4H 73
Oak Tree. *Darl* 3A 106
Oakwood. *Derb* 2A 74
Oakwood. *W Yor* 1D 92
Oakwoodhill. *Surr* 2C 26
Oakworth. *W Yor* 1A 92
Oape. *High* 3B 164
Oare. *Kent* 4E 40
Oare. *Som* 2B 20
Oare. *W Ber* 4D 36
Oare. *Wilts* 5G 35
Oareford. *Som* 2B 20
Oasby. *Linc* 2H 75
Oath. *Som* 4G 21
Oathlaw. *Ang* 3D 145
Oatlands. *N Yor* 4F 99
Oban. *Arg* 1F 133
Oban. *W Isl* 7D 171
Oborne. *Dors* 1B 14
Obsdale. *High* 2A 158
Obthorpe. *Linc* 4H 75
Occlestone Green. *Ches W* 4A 84
Occold. *Suff* 3D 66
Ochiltree. *E Ayr* 2E 117
Ochtermuthill. *Per* 2H 135
Ochtertyre. *Per* 1H 135
Ockbrook. *Derbs* 2B 74
Ockeridge. *Worc* 4B 60
Ockham. *Surr* 5B 38
Ockle. *High* 1G 139
Ockley. *Surr* 1C 26
Ocle Pychard. *Here* 1A 48
Octofad. *Arg* 4A 124
Octomore. *Arg* 4A 124
Octon. *E Yor* 3E 101
Odcombe. *Som* 1A 14
Odd Down. *Bath* 5C 34
Oddingley. *Worc* 5D 60
Oddington. *Oxon* 4D 50
Oddsta. *Shet* 2G 173
Odell. *Bed* 5G 63
Odie. *Orkn* 5F 172
Odiham. *Hants* 1F 25
Odsey. *Cambs* 2C 52
Odstock. *Wilts* 4G 23
Odstone. *Leics* 5A 74
Offchurch. *Warw* 4A 62
Offenham. *Worc* 1F 49
Offenham Cross. *Worc* 1F 49
Offerton. *G Man* 2D 84
Offerton. *Tyne* 4G 115
Offham. *E Sus* 4E 27
Offham. *Kent* 5A 40
Offham. *W Sus* 5B 26
Offleyhay. *Staf* 3C 72
Offley Hoo. *Herts* 3B 52
Offleymarsh. *Staf* 3B 72
Offord Cluny. *Cambs* 4B 64
Offord D'Arcy. *Cambs* 4B 64
Offton. *Suff* 1D 54
Offwell. *Devn* 3E 13
Ogbourne Maizey. *Wilts* 4G 35
Ogbourne St Andrew. *Wilts* 4G 35
Ogbourne St George. *Wilts* 4H 35
Ogden. *G Man* 3H 91
Ogle. *Nmbd* 2E 115
Ogmore. *V Glam* 4B 32
Ogmore-by-Sea. *V Glam* 4B 32
Ogmore Vale. *B'end* 2C 32
Okeford Fitzpaine. *Dors* 1D 14
Okehampton. *Devn* 3F 11
Okehampton Camp. *Devn* 3F 11
Okraquoy. *Shet* 8F 173
Okus. *Swin* 3G 35
Old. *Nptn* 3E 63
Old Aberdeen. *Aber* 3G 153
Old Alresford. *Hants* 3D 24
Oldany. *High* 5B 166
Old Arley. *Warw* 1G 61
Old Basford. *Nott* 1C 74
Old Basing. *Hants* 1E 25
Oldberrow. *Warw* 4F 61
Old Bewick. *Nmbd* 2E 121
Old Bexley. *G Lon* 3F 39
Old Blair. *Per* 2F 143
Old Bolingbroke. *Linc* 4C 88
Oldborough. *Devn* 2A 12
Old Brampton. *Derbs* 3H 85
Old Bridge of Tilt. *Per* 2F 143
Old Bridge of Urr. *Dum* 3E 111
Old Brumby. *N Lin* 4B 94
Old Buckenham. *Norf* 1C 66
Old Burghclere. *Hants* 1C 24
Oldbury. *Shrp* 1B 60
Oldbury. *Warw* 1H 61
Oldbury. *W Mid* 2D 61
Oldbury-on-Severn. *S Glo* 2B 34
Oldbury on the Hill. *Glos* 3D 34
Old Byland. *N Yor* 1H 99
Old Cassop. *Dur* 1A 106
Oldcastle. *Mon* 3G 47
Oldcastle Heath. *Ches W* 1G 71
Old Catton. *Norf* 4E 79
Old Clee. *NE Lin* 4F 95
Old Cleeve. *Som* 2D 20
Old Colwyn. *Cnwy* 3A 82
Oldcotes. *Notts* 2C 86
Old Coulsdon. *G Lon* 5E 39
Old Dailly. *S Ayr* 5B 116
Old Dalby. *Leics* 3D 74
Old Dam. *Derbs* 3F 85
Old Deer. *Abers* 4G 161
Old Dilton. *Wilts* 2D 22
Old Down. *S Glo* 3B 34
Oldeamere. *Cambs* 1C 64
Old Edlington. *S Yor* 1C 86
Old Eldon. *Dur* 2F 105
Old Ellerby. *E Yor* 1E 95
Old Fallings. *W Mid* 5D 72
Oldfallow. *Staf* 4D 73
Old Felixstowe. *Suff* 2G 55
Oldfield. *Shrp* 2A 60
Oldfield. *Worc* 4C 60
Old Fletton. *Pet* 1A 64
Oldford. *Som* 1C 22
Old Forge. *Here* 4A 48
Old Glossop. *Derbs* 1E 85
Old Goole. *E Yor* 2H 93
Old Gore. *Here* 3B 48
Old Graitney. *Dum* 3E 112
Old Grimsby. *IOS* 1A 4
Oldhall. *High* 3E 169
Old Hall Street. *Norf* 2F 79
Oldham. *G Man* 4H 91
Oldhamstocks. *E Lot* 2D 130
Old Heathfield. *E Sus* 3G 27
Old Hill. *W Mid* 2D 60
Old Hunstanton. *Norf* 1F 77
Oldhurst. *Cambs* 3B 64
Old Hutton. *Cumb* 1E 97
Old Kea. *Corn* 4C 6
Old Kilpatrick. *W Dun* 2F 127
Old Kinnernie. *Abers* 3E 152
Old Knebworth. *Herts* 3C 52
Oldland. *S Glo* 4B 34
Old Laxey. *IOM* 3D 108
Old Leake. *Linc* 5D 88
Old Lenton. *Nott* 2C 74
Old Llanberis. *Gwyn* 5F 81
Old Malton. *N Yor* 2B 100
Oldmeldrum. *Abers* 1F 153
Old Micklefield. *W Yor* 1E 93
Old Mill. *Corn* 5D 10
Oldmixon. *N Som* 1G 21
Old Monkland. *N Lan* 3A 128
Old Newton. *Suff* 4C 66
Old Park. *Telf* 5A 72
Old Pentland. *Midl* 3F 129
Old Philpstoun. *W Lot* 2D 128
Old Quarrington. *Dur* 1A 106
Old Radnor. *Powy* 5E 59
Old Rayne. *Abers* 1D 152
Oldridge. *Devn* 3B 12
Old Romney. *Kent* 3E 29
Old Scone. *Per* 1D 136
Oldshore Beg. *High* 3B 166
Oldshoremore. *High* 3C 166
Old Snydale. *W Yor* 2E 93
Old Sodbury. *S Glo* 3C 34
Old Somerby. *Linc* 2G 75
Old Spital. *Dur* 3C 104
Oldstead. *N Yor* 1H 99
Old Stratford. *Nptn* 1F 51
Old Swan. *Mers* 1F 83
Old Swarland. *Nmbd* 4F 121
Old Tebay. *Cumb* 4H 103
Old Town. *Cumb* 5F 113
Old Town. *E Sus* 5G 27
Old Town. *IOS* 1B 4
Old Town. *Nmbd* 5C 120
Oldtown. *High* 5C 164
Old Trafford. *G Man* 1C 84
Old Tupton. *Derbs* 4A 86
Oldwall. *Cumb* 3F 113
Oldwalls. *Swan* 3D 31
Old Warden. *C Beds* 1B 52
Oldways End. *Som* 4B 20
Old Westhall. *Abers* 1D 152
Old Weston. *Cambs* 3H 63
Oldwhat. *Abers* 3F 161
Old Windsor. *Wind* 3A 38
Old Wives Lees. *Kent* 5E 41
Old Woking. *Surr* 5B 38
Oldwood Common. *Worc* 4H 59
Old Woodstock. *Oxon* 4C 50
Olgrinmore. *High* 3C 168
Oliver's Battery. *Hants* 4C 24
Ollaberry. *Shet* 3E 173
Ollerton. *Ches E* 3B 84
Ollerton. *Notts* 4D 86
Ollerton. *Shrp* 3A 72
Olmarch. *Cdgn* 5F 57
Olmstead Green. *Cambs* 1G 53
Olney. *Mil* 5F 63
Olrig. *High* 2D 169
Olton. *W Mid* 2F 61
Olveston. *S Glo* 3B 34
Omagh. *Ferm* 4C 174
Ombersley. *Worc* 4C 60
Ompton. *Notts* 4D 86
Omunsgarth. *Shet* 7E 173
Onchan. *IOM* 4D 108
Onecote. *Staf* 5E 85
Onehouse. *Suff* 5C 66
Onen. *Mon* 4H 47
Ongar Hill. *Norf* 3E 77
Ongar Street. *Here* 4F 59
Onibury. *Shrp* 3G 59
Onich. *High* 2E 141
Onllwyn. *Neat* 4B 46
Onneley. *Staf* 1B 72
Onslow Green. *Essx* 4G 53
Onslow Village. *Surr* 1A 26
Onthank. *E Ayr* 1D 116
Openwoodgate. *Derbs* 1A 74
Opinan. *High*
nr. Gairloch 1G 155
nr. Laide 4C 162
Orasaigh. *W Isl* 6F 171
Orbost. *High* 4B 154
Orby. *Linc* 4D 89
Orchard Hill. *Devn* 4E 19
Orchard Portman. *Som* 4F 21
Orcheston. *Wilts* 2F 23
Orcop. *Here* 3H 47
Orcop Hill. *Here* 3H 47
Ord. *High* 2E 147
Ordale. *Shet* 1H 173
Ordhead. *Abers* 2D 152
Ordie. *Abers* 3B 152
Ordiquish. *Mor* 3H 159
Ordley. *Nmbd* 4C 114
Ordsall. *Notts* 3E 86
Ore. *E Sus* 4C 28
Oreton. *Shrp* 2A 60
Orford. *Suff* 1H 55
Orford. *Warr* 1A 84
Organford. *Dors* 3E 15
Orgil. *Orkn* 7B 172
Orgreave. *Staf* 4F 73
Oridge Street. *Glos* 3C 48
Orlestone. *Kent* 2D 28
Orleton. *Here* 4G 59
Orleton. *Worc* 4A 60
Orleton Common. *Here* 4G 59
Orlingbury. *Nptn* 3F 63
Ormacleit. *W Isl* 5C 170
Ormathwaite. *Cumb* 2D 102
Ormesby. *Red C* 3C 106
Ormesby St Margaret. *Norf* 4G 79
Ormesby St Michael. *Norf* 4G 79
Ormiscaig. *High* 4C 162
Ormiston. *E Lot* 3H 129
Ormsaigbeg. *High* 2F 139
Ormsaigmore. *High* 2F 139

Peterlee – Portadown

Peterlee. *Dur* 5H 115
Petersfield. *Hants* 4F 25
Petersfinger. *Wilts* 4G 23
Peters Green. *Herts* 4B 52
Peters Marland. *Devn* 1E 11
Peterstone Wentlooge
Newp 3F 33
Peterston-super-Ely
V Glam 4D 32
Peterstow. *Here* 3A 48
Peters Village. *Kent* 4B 40
Peter Tavy. *Devn* 5F 11
Petertown. *Orkn* 7C 172
Petham. *Kent* 5F 41
Petherwin Gate. *Corn* 4C 10
Petrockstowe. *Devn* 2F 11
Petsoe End. *Mil* 1G 51
Pett. *E Sus* 4C 28
Pettaugh. *Suff* 5D 66
Pett Bottom. *Kent* 5F 41
Petteridge. *Kent* 1A 28
Pettinain. *S Lan* 5C 128
Pettistree. *Suff* 5E 67
Petton. *Devn* 4D 20
Petton. *Shrp* 3G 71
Petts Wood. *G Lon* 4F 39
Pettycur. *Fife* 1F 129
Pettywell. *Norf* 3C 78
Petworth. *W Sus* 3A 26
Pevensey. *E Sus* 5H 27
Pevensey Bay. *E Sus* 5A 28
Pewsey. *Wilts* 5G 35
Pheasants Hill. *Buck* 3F 37
Philadelphia. *Tyne* 4G 115
Philham. *Devn* 4C 18
Philiphaugh. *Bord* 2G 119
Phillack. *Corn* 3C 4
Philleigh. *Corn* 5C 6
Philpstoun. *W Lot* 2D 128
Phocle Green. *Here* 3B 48
Phoenix Green. *Hants* 1F 25
Pibsbury. *Som* 4H 21
Pibwrlwyd. *Carm* 4E 45
Pica. *Cumb* 2B 102
Piccadilly. *Warw* 1G 61
Piccadilly Corner. *Norf* 2E 67
Piccotts End. *Herts* 5A 52
Pickering. *N Yor* 1B 100
Picket Piece. *Hants* 2B 24
Picket Post. *Hants* 2G 15
Pickford. *W Mid* 2G 61
Pickhill. *N Yor* 1F 99
Picklenash. *Glos* 3C 48
Picklescott. *Shrp* 1G 59
Pickletillem. *Fife* 1G 137
Pickmere. *Ches E* 3A 84
Pickstock. *Telf* 3B 72
Pickwell. *Devn* 2E 19
Pickwell. *Leics* 4E 75
Pickworth. *Linc* 2H 75
Pickworth. *Rut* 4G 75
Picton. *Ches W* 3G 83
Picton. *Flin* 2D 82
Picton. *N Yor* 4B 106
Pict's Hill. *Som* 4H 21
Piddinghoe. *E Sus* 5F 27
Piddington. *Buck* 2G 37
Piddington. *Nptn* 5F 63
Piddington. *Oxon* 4E 51
Piddlehinton. *Dors* 3C 14
Piddletrenthide. *Dors* 2C 14
Pidley. *Cambs* 3C 64
Pidney. *Dors* 2C 14
Pie Corner. *Here* 4A 60
Piercebridge. *Darl* 3F 105
Pierowall. *Orkn* 3D 172
Pigdon. *Nmbd* 1E 115
Pightley. *Som* 3F 21
Pikehall. *Derbs* 5F 85
Pikeshill. *Hants* 2A 16
Pilford. *Dors* 2F 15
Pilgrims Hatch. *Essx* 1G 39
Pilham. *Linc* 1F 87
Pill. *N Som* 4A 34
The Pill. *Mon* 3H 33
Pillaton. *Corn* 2H 7
Pillaton. *Staf* 4D 72
Pillerton Hersey. *Warw* 1B 50
Pillerton Priors. *Warw* 1A 50
Pilleth. *Powy* 4E 59
Pilley. *Hants* 3B 16
Pilley. *S Yor* 4D 92
Pillgwenlly. *Newp* 3G 33
Pilling. *Lanc* 5D 96
Pilling Lane. *Lanc* 5C 96
Pillowell. *Glos* 5B 48
Pillwell. *Dors* 1C 14
Pilning. *S Glo* 3A 34
Pilsbury. *Derbs* 4F 85
Pilsdon. *Dors* 3H 13
Pilsgate. *Pet* 5H 75
Pilsley. *Derbs*
nr. Bakewell 3G 85
nr. Clay Cross 4B 86
Pilson Green. *Norf* 4F 79
Piltdown. *E Sus* 3F 27
Pilton. *Edin* 2F 129
Pilton. *Nptn* 2H 63
Pilton. *Rut* 5G 75
Pilton. *Som* 2A 22
Pilton Green. *Swan* 4D 30
Pimperne. *Dors* 2E 15
Pinchbeck. *Linc* 3B 76
Pinchbeck Bars. *Linc* 3A 76
Pinchbeck West. *Linc* 3B 76
Pinfold. *Lanc* 3B 90
Pinford End. *Suff* 5H 65
Pinged. *Carm* 5E 45
Pinhoe. *Devn* 3C 12
Pinkerton. *E Lot* 2D 130
Pinkneys Green. *Wind* 3G 37
Pinley. *W Mid* 3A 62
Pinley Green. *Warw* 4G 61
Pinmill. *Suff* 2F 55
Pinmore. *S Ayr* 5B 116
Pinner. *G Lon* 2C 38
Pins Green. *Worc* 1C 48
Pinsley Green. *Ches E* 1H 71
Pinvin. *Worc* 1E 49
Pinwherry. *S Ayr* 1G 109
Pinxton. *Derbs* 5B 86
Pipe and Lyde. *Here* 1A 48
Pipe Aston. *Here* 3G 59
Pipe Gate. *Shrp* 1B 72
Pipehill. *Staf* 5E 73
Piperhill. *High* 3C 158
Pipe Ridware. *Staf* 4E 73
Pipers Pool. *Corn* 4C 10
Pipewell. *Nptn* 2F 63
Pippacott. *Devn* 3F 19
Pipton. *Powy* 2E 47
Pirbright. *Surr* 5A 38
Pirnmill. *N Ayr* 5G 125
Pirton. *Herts* 2B 52
Pirton. *Worc* 1D 49
Pisgah. *Stir* 3G 135
Pishill. *Oxon* 3F 37
Pistyll. *Gwyn* 1C 68
Pitagowan. *Per* 2F 143
Pitcairn. *Per* 3F 143
Pitcairngreen. *Per* 1C 136
Pitcalnie. *High* 1C 158
Pitcaple. *Abers* 1E 152
Pitchcombe. *Glos* 5D 48
Pitchcott. *Buck* 3F 51
Pitchford. *Shrp* 5H 71
Pitch Green. *Buck* 5F 51
Pitch Place. *Surr* 5A 38
Pitcombe. *Som* 3B 22
Pitcox. *E Lot* 2C 130
Pitcur. *Per* 5B 144
Pitfichie. *Abers* 2D 152
Pitgrudy. *High* 4E 165
Pitkennedy. *Ang* 3E 145
Pitlessie. *Fife* 3F 137
Pitlochry. *Per* 3G 143
Pitmachie. *Abers* 1D 152
Pitmaduthy. *High* 1B 158
Pitmedden. *Abers* 1F 153
Pitminster. *Som* 1F 13
Pitnacree. *Per* 3G 143
Pitney. *Som* 4H 21
Pitroddie. *Per* 1E 136
Pitscottie. *Fife* 2G 137
Pitsea. *Essx* 2B 40
Pitsford. *Nptn* 4E 63
Pitsford Hill. *Som* 3E 20
Pitsmoor. *S Yor* 2A 86
Pitstone. *Buck* 4H 51
Pitt. *Hants* 4C 24
Pitt Court. *Glos* 2C 34
Pittentrail. *High* 3E 164
Pittenweem. *Fife* 3H 137
Pittington. *Dur* 5G 115
Pitton. *Swan* 4D 30
Pitton. *Wilts* 3H 23
Pittswood. *Kent* 1H 27
Pittulie. *Abers* 2G 161
Pittville. *Glos* 3E 49
Pitversie. *Per* 2D 136
Pity Me. *Dur* 5F 115
Pityme. *Corn* 1D 6
Pixey Green. *Suff* 3E 67
Pixley. *Here* 2B 48
Place Newton. *N Yor* 2C 100
Plaidy. *Abers* 3E 161
Plaidy. *Corn* 3G 7
Plain Dealings. *Pemb* 3E 43
Plains. *N Lan* 3A 128
Plainsfield. *Som* 3E 21
Plaish. *Shrp* 1H 59
Plaistow. *Here* 2B 48
Plaistow. *W Sus* 2B 26
Plaitford. *Wilts* 1A 16
Plastow Green. *Hants* 5D 36
Plas yn Cefn. *Den* 3C 82
The Platt. *E Sus* 2G 27
Platt Bridge. *G Man* 4E 90
Platt Lane. *Shrp* 2H 71
Platts Common. *S Yor* 4D 92
Platt's Heath. *Kent* 5C 40
Plawsworth. *Dur* 5F 115
Plaxtol. *Kent* 5H 39
Playden. *E Sus* 3D 28
Playford. *Suff* 1F 55
Play Hatch. *Oxon* 4F 37
Playing Place. *Corn* 4C 6
Playley Green. *Glos* 2C 48
Plealey. *Shrp* 5G 71
Plean. *Stir* 1B 128
Pleasington. *Bkbn* 2E 91
Pleasley. *Derbs* 4C 86
Pledgdon Green. *Essx* 3F 53
Plenmeller. *Nmbd* 3A 114
Pleshey. *Essx* 4G 53
Plockton. *High* 5H 155
Plocrapol. *W Isl* 8D 171
Ploughfield. *Here* 1G 47
Plowden. *Shrp* 2F 59
Ploxgreen. *Shrp* 5F 71
Pluckley. *Kent* 1D 28
Plucks Gutter. *Kent* 4G 41
Plumbland. *Cumb* 1C 102
Plumgarths. *Cumb* 5F 103
Plumley. *Ches E* 3B 84
Plummers Plain. *W Sus* 3D 26
Plumpton. *Cumb* 1F 103
Plumpton. *E Sus* 4E 27
Plumpton. *Nptn* 1D 50
Plumpton Foot. *Cumb* 1F 103
Plumpton Green. *E Sus* 4E 27
Plumpton Head. *Cumb* 1G 103
Plumstead. *G Lon* 3F 39
Plumstead. *Norf* 2D 78
Plumtree. *Notts* 2D 74
Plumtree Park. *Notts* 2D 74
Plungar. *Leics* 2E 75
Plush. *Dors* 2C 14
Plushabridge. *Corn* 5D 10
Plwmp. *Cdgn* 5C 56
Plymouth. *Plym* 3A 8
Plympton. *Plym* 3B 8
Plymstock. *Plym* 3B 8
Plymtree. *Devn* 2D 12
Pockley. *N Yor* 1A 100
Pocklington. *E Yor* 5C 100
Pode Hole. *Linc* 3B 76
Podimore. *Som* 4A 22
Podington. *Bed* 4G 63
Podmore. *Staf* 2B 72
Poffley End. *Oxon* 4B 50
Point Clear. *Essx* 4D 54
Pointon. *Linc* 2A 76
Pokesdown. *Bour* 3G 15
Polbae. *Dum* 2H 109
Polbain. *High* 3E 163
Polbathic. *Corn* 3H 7
Polbeth. *W Lot* 3D 128
Polbrock. *Corn* 2E 6
Polchar. *High* 3C 150
Polebrook. *Nptn* 2H 63
Pole Elm. *Worc* 1D 48
Polegate. *E Sus* 5G 27
Pole Moor. *W Yor* 3A 92
Poles. *High* 4E 165
Polesworth. *Warw* 5G 73
Polglass. *High* 3E 163
Polgooth. *Corn* 3D 6
Poling. *W Sus* 5B 26
Poling Corner. *W Sus* 5B 26
Polio. *High* 1B 158
Polkerris. *Corn* 3E 7
Polla. *High* 3D 166
Pollard Street. *Norf* 2F 79
Pollicott. *Buck* 4F 51
Pollington. *E Yor* 3G 93
Polloch. *High* 2B 140
Pollok. *Glas* 3G 127
Pollokshaws. *Glas* 3G 127
Pollokshields. *Glas* 3G 127
Polmaily. *High* 5G 157
Polmassick. *Corn* 4D 6
Polmont. *Falk* 2C 128
Polnessan. *E Ayr* 3D 116
Polnish. *High* 5F 147
Polperro. *Corn* 3G 7
Polruan. *Corn* 3F 7
Polscoe. *Corn* 2F 7
Polsham. *Som* 2A 22
Polskeoch. *Dum* 4F 117
Polstead. *Suff* 2C 54
Polstead Heath. *Suff* 1C 54
Poltesco. *Corn* 5E 5
Poltimore. *Devn* 3C 12
Polton. *Midl* 3F 129
Polwarth. *Bord* 4D 130
Polyphant. *Corn* 4C 10
Polzeath. *Corn* 1D 6
Ponde. *Powy* 2E 46
Pondersbridge. *Cambs* 1B 64
Ponders End. *G Lon* 1E 39
Pond Street. *Essx* 2E 53
Pondtail. *Hants* 1G 25
Ponsanooth. *Corn* 5B 6
Ponsongath. *Corn* 5E 5
Ponsworthy. *Devn* 5H 11
Pontamman. *Carm* 4G 45
Pontantwn. *Carm* 4E 45
Pontardawe. *Neat* 5H 45
Pontarddulais. *Swan* 5F 45
Pontarfynach. *Cdgn* 3G 57
Pont-ar-gothi. *Carm* 3F 45
Pont ar Hydfer. *Powy* 3B 46
Pontarllechau. *Carm* 3H 45
Pontarsais. *Carm* 3E 45
Pontblyddyn. *Flin* 4E 83
Pontbren Llwyd. *Rhon* 5C 46
Pont-Cyfyng. *Cnwy* 5G 81
Pontdolgoch. *Powy* 1C 58
Pontefract. *W Yor* 2E 93
Ponteland. *Nmbd* 2E 115
Ponterwyd. *Cdgn* 2G 57
Pontesbury. *Shrp* 5G 71
Pontesford. *Shrp* 5G 71
Pontfadog. *Wrex* 2E 71
Pont-Faen. *Shrp* 2E 71
Pont-faen. *Powy* 2C 46
Pontfaen. *Pemb* 1E 43
Pontgarreg. *Cdgn* 5C 56
Pont-Henri. *Carm* 5E 45
Ponthir. *Torf* 2G 33
Ponthirwaun. *Cdgn* 1C 44
Pont-iets. *Carm* 5E 45
Pontllanfraith. *Cphy* 2E 33
Pontlliw. *Swan* 5G 45
Pont Llogel. *Powy* 4C 70
Pontllyfni. *Gwyn* 5D 80
Pontlottyn. *Cphy* 5E 46
Pontneddfechan. *Powy* 5C 46
Pont-newydd. *Carm* 5E 45
Pont-newydd. *Flin* 4D 82
Pontnewydd. *Torf* 2F 33
Ponton. *Shet* 6E 173
Pont Pen-y-benglog. *Gwyn* 4F 81
Pontrhydfendigaid. *Cdgn* 4G 57
Pont Rhyd-y-cyff. *B'end* 3B 32
Pontrhydyfen. *Neat* 2A 32
Pont-rhyd-y-groes. *Cdgn* 3G 57
Pontrhydyrun. *Torf* 2F 33
Pont-Rhythallt. *Gwyn* 4E 81
Pontrilas. *Here* 3G 47
Pontrilas Road. *Here* 3G 47
Pontrobert. *Powy* 4D 70
Pont-rug. *Gwyn* 4E 81
Ponts Green. *E Sus* 4A 28
Pontshill. *Here* 3B 48
Pont-Sian. *Cdgn* 1E 45
Pontsticill. *Mer T* 4D 46
Pont-Walby. *Neat* 5B 46
Pontwelly. *Carm* 2E 45
Pontwgan. *Cnwy* 3G 81
Pontyates. *Carm* 5E 45
Pontyberem. *Carm* 4F 45
Pontybodkin. *Flin* 5E 83
Pontyclun. *Rhon* 3D 32
Pontycymer. *B'end* 2C 32
Pontyglazier. *Pemb* 1F 43
Pontygwaith. *Rhon* 2D 32
Pont-y-pant. *Cnwy* 5G 81
Pontypool. *Torf* 2F 33
Pontypridd. *Rhon* 3D 32
Pontypwl. *Torf* 2F 33
Pontywaun. *Cphy* 2F 33
Pooksgreen. *Hants* 1B 16
Pool. *Corn* 4A 6
Pool. *W Yor* 5E 99
Poole. *N Yor* 2E 93
Poole. *Pool* 3F 15
Poole. *Som* 4E 21
Poole Keynes. *Glos* 2E 35
Poolend. *Staf* 5D 84
Poolewe. *High* 5C 162
Pooley Bridge. *Cumb* 2F 103
Poolfold. *Staf* 5C 84
Pool Head. *Here* 5H 59
Pool Hey. *Lanc* 3B 90
Poolhill. *Glos* 3C 48
Poolmill. *Here* 3A 48
Pool o' Muckhart. *Clac* 3C 136
Pool Quay. *Powy* 4E 71
Poolsbrook. *Derbs* 3B 86
Pool Street. *Essx* 2A 54
Pootings. *Kent* 1F 27
Pope Hill. *Pemb* 3D 42
Pope's Hill. *Glos* 4B 48
Popeswood. *Brac* 5G 37
Popham. *Hants* 2D 24
Poplar. *G Lon* 2E 39
Popley. *Hants* 1E 25
Porchfield. *IOW* 3C 16
Porin. *High* 3F 157
Poringland. *Norf* 5E 79
Porkellis. *Corn* 5A 6
Porlock. *Som* 2B 20
Porlock Weir. *Som* 2B 20
Portachoillan. *Arg* 4F 125
Port Adhair Bheinn na
Faoghla. *W Isl* 3C 170
Port Adhair Thirlodh. *Arg* 4B 138
Portadown. *Arm* 5F 175

Queenborough – Rhondda

Queenborough. Kent 3D 40
Queen Camel. Som 4A 22
Queen Charlton. Bath 5B 34
Queen Dart. Devn 1B 12
Queenhill. Worc 2D 48
Queen Oak. Dors 3C 22
Queensbury. W Yor 1B 92
Queensferry. Flin 4F 83
Queensferry Crossing
Edin 2E 129
Queenstown. Bkpl 1B 90
Queen Street. Kent 1A 28
Queenzieburn. N Lan 2H 127
Quemerford. Wilts 5F 35
Quendale. Shet 10E 173
Quendon. Essx 2F 53
Queniborough. Leics 4D 74
Quenington. Glos 5G 49
Quernmore. Lanc 3E 97
Quethiock. Corn 2H 7
Quholm. Orkn 6B 172
Quick's Green. W Ber 4D 36
Quidenham. Norf 2C 66
Quidhampton. Hants 1D 24
Quidhampton. Wilts 3G 23
Quilquox. Abers 5G 161
Quina Brook. Shrp 2H 71
Quindry. Orkn 8D 172
Quine's Hill. IOM 4C 108
Quinton. Nptn 5E 63
Quinton. W Mid 2D 61
Quintrell Downs. Corn 2C 6
Quixhill. Staf 1F 73
Quoditch. Devn 3E 11
Quorn. Leics 4C 74
Quorndon. Leics 4C 74
Quothquan. S Lan 1B 118
Quoyloo. Orkn 5B 172
Quoyness. Orkn 7B 172
Quoys. Shet
on Mainland 5F 173
on Unst 1H 173

R

Rableyheath. Herts 4C 52
Raby. Cumb 4C 112
Raby. Mers 3F 83
Rachan Mill. Bord 1D 118
Rachub. Gwyn 4F 81
Rack End. Oxon 5C 50
Rackenford. Devn 1B 12
Rackham. W Sus 4B 26
Rackheath. Norf 4E 79
Racks. Dum 2B 112
Rackwick. Orkn
on Hoy 8B 172
on Westray 3D 172
Radbourne. Derbs 2G 73
Radcliffe. G Man 4F 91
Radcliffe. Nmbd 4G 121
Radcliffe on Trent. Notts 2D 74
Radclive. Buck 2E 51
Radernie. Fife 3G 137
Radfall. Kent 4F 41
Radford. Bath 1B 22
Radford. Nott 1C 74
Radford. Oxon 3C 50
Radford. W Mid 2H 61
Radford. Worc 5E 61
Radford Semele. Warw 4H 61
Radipole. Dors 4B 14
Radlett. Herts 1C 38
Radley. Oxon 2D 36
Radnage. Buck 2F 37
Radstock. Bath 1B 22
Radstone. Nptn 1D 50
Radway. Warw 1B 50
Radway Green. Ches E 5B 84
Radwell. Bed 5H 63
Radwell. Herts 2C 52
Radwinter. Essx 2G 53
Radyr. Card 3E 33
RAF Coltishall. Norf 3E 79
Rafford. Mor 3E 159
Ragdale. Leics 4D 74
Ragdon. Shrp 1G 59
Ragged Appleshaw. Hants 2B 24
Raggra. High 4F 169
Raglan. Mon 5H 47
Ragnall. Notts 3F 87
Raigbeg. High 1C 150
Rainford. Mers 4C 90
Rainford Junction. Mers 4C 90
Rainham. G Lon 2G 39
Rainham. Medw 4C 40
Rainhill. Mers 1G 83
Rainow. Ches E 3D 84
Rainton. N Yor 2F 99
Rainworth. Notts 5C 86
Raisbeck. Cumb 4H 103
Raise. Cumb 5A 114
Rait. Per 1E 137
Raithby. Linc 2C 88
Raithby by Spilsby. Linc 4C 88
Raithwaite. N Yor 3F 107
Rake. W Sus 4G 25
Rake End. Staf 4E 73
Rakeway. Staf 1E 73
Rakewood. G Man 3H 91
Ralia. High 4B 150
Ram Alley. Wilts 5H 35
Ramasaig. High 4A 154
Rame. Corn
nr. Millbrook 4A 8
nr. Penryn 5B 6
Ram Lane. Kent 1D 28
Ramnageo. Shet 1H 173
Rampisham. Dors 2A 14
Rampside. Cumb 3B 96
Rampton. Cambs 4D 64
Rampton. Notts 3E 87
Ramsbottom. G Man 3F 91
Ramsburn. Mor 3C 160
Ramsbury. Wilts 4A 36
Ramscraigs. High 1H 165
Ramsdean. Hants 4F 25
Ramsdell. Hants 1D 24
Ramsden. Oxon 4B 50
Ramsden. Worc 1E 49
Ramsden Bellhouse. Essx 1B 40
Ramsden Heath. Essx 1B 40
Ramsey. Cambs 2B 64
Ramsey. Essx 2F 55
Ramsey. IOM 2D 108
Ramsey Forty Foot. Cambs 2C 64
Ramsey Heights. Cambs 2B 64
Ramsey Island. Essx 5C 54
Ramsey Mereside. Cambs 2B 64
Ramsey St Mary's. Cambs 2B 64
Ramsgate. Kent 4H 41
Ramsgill. N Yor 2D 98
Ramshaw. Dur 5C 114
Ramshorn. Staf 1E 73
Ramsley. Devn 3G 11
Ramsnest Common. Surr 2A 26
Ramstone. Abers 2D 152
Ranais. W Isl 5G 171
Ranby. Linc 3B 88
Ranby. Notts 2D 86
Rand. Linc 3A 88
Randalstown. Ant 3F 175
Randwick. Glos 5D 48
Ranfurly. Ren 3E 127
Rangag. High 4D 169
Rangemore. Staf 3F 73
Rangeworthy. S Glo 3B 34
Rankinston. E Ayr 3D 116
Rank's Green. Essx 4H 53
Ranmore Common. Surr 5C 38
Rannoch Station. Per 3B 142
Ranochan. High 5G 147
Ranskill. Notts 2D 86
Ranton. Staf 3C 72
Ranton Green. Staf 3C 72
Ranworth. Norf 4F 79
Raploch. Stir 4G 135
Rapness. Orkn 3E 172
Rapps. Som 1G 13
Rascal Moor. E Yor 1B 94
Rascarrel. Dum 5E 111
Rasharkin. Caus 2F 175
Rashfield. Arg 1C 126
Rashwood. Worc 4D 60
Raskelf. N Yor 2G 99
Rassau. Blae 4E 47
Rastrick. W Yor 2B 92
Ratagan. High 2B 148
Ratby. Leics 5C 74
Ratcliffe Culey. Leics 1H 61
Ratcliffe on Soar. Notts 3B 74
Ratcliffe on the Wreake
Leics 4D 74
Rathen. Abers 2H 161
Rathfriland. Arm 6G 175
Rathillet. Fife 1F 137
Rathmell. N Yor 3H 97
Ratho. Edin 2E 129
Ratho Station. Edin 2E 129
Rathven. Mor 2B 160
Ratley. Hants 4B 24
Ratley. Warw 1B 50
Ratlinghope. Shrp 1G 59
Rattar. High 1E 169
Ratten Row. Cumb 5E 113
Ratten Row. Lanc 5D 96
Rattery. Devn 2D 8
Rattlesden. Suff 5B 66
Ratton Village. E Sus 5G 27
Rattray. Abers 3H 161
Rattray. Per 4A 144
Raughton. Cumb 5E 113
Raughton Head. Cumb 5E 113
Raunds. Nptn 3G 63
Ravenfield. S Yor 1B 86
Ravenfield Common. S Yor 1B 86
Ravenglass. Cumb 5B 102
Ravenhills Green. Worc 5B 60
Raveningham. Norf 1F 67
Ravenscar. N Yor 4G 107
Ravensdale. IOM 2C 108
Ravensden. Bed 5H 63
Ravenseat. N Yor 4B 104
Ravenshead. Notts 5C 86
Ravensmoor. Ches E 5A 84
Ravensthorpe. Nptn 3D 62
Ravensthorpe. W Yor 2C 92
Ravenstone. Leics 4B 74
Ravenstone. Mil 5F 63
Ravenstonedale. Cumb 4A 104
Ravenstown. Cumb 2C 96
Ravenstruther. S Lan 5C 128
Ravensworth. N Yor 4E 105
Raw. N Yor 4G 107
Rawcliffe. E Yor 2G 93
Rawcliffe. York 4H 99
Rawcliffe Bridge. E Yor 2G 93
Rawdon. W Yor 1C 92
Rawgreen. Nmbd 4C 114
Rawmarsh. S Yor 1B 86
Rawnsley. Staf 4E 73
Rawreth. Essx 1B 40
Rawridge. Devn 2F 13
Rawson Green. Derbs 1A 74
Rawtenstall. Lanc 2G 91
Raydon. Suff 2D 54
Raylees. Nmbd 5D 120
Rayleigh. Essx 1C 40
Raymond's Hill. Devn 3G 13
Rayne. Essx 3H 53
Rayners Lane. G Lon 2C 38
Reach. Cambs 4E 65
Read. Lanc 1F 91
Reading. Read 4F 37
Reading Green. Suff 3D 66
Reading Street. Kent 2D 28
Readymoney. Corn 3F 7
Reagill. Cumb 3H 103
Rearquhar. High 4E 165
Rearsby. Leics 4D 74
Reasby. Linc 3H 87
Reaseheath. Ches E 5A 84
Reaster. High 2E 169
Reawick. Shet 7E 173
Reay. High 2B 168
Rechullin. High 3A 156
Reculver. Kent 4G 41
Redberth. Pemb 4E 43
Redbourn. Herts 4B 52
Redbourne. N Lin 4C 94
Redbrook. Glos 5A 48
Redbrook. Wrex 1H 71
Redburn. High 4D 158
Redburn. Nmbd 3A 114
Redcar. Red C 2D 106
Redcastle. High 4H 157
Redcliffe Bay. N Som 4H 33
Red Dial. Cumb 5D 112
Redding. Falk 2C 128
Reddingmuirhead. Falk 2C 128
The Reddings. Glos 3E 49
Reddish. G Man 1C 84
Redditch. Worc 4E 61
Rede. Suff 5H 65
Redenhall. Norf 2E 67
Redesdale Camp. Nmbd 5C 120
Redesmouth. Nmbd 1B 114
Redford. Ang 4E 145
Redford. Dur 1D 105
Redford. W Sus 4G 25
Redfordgreen. Bord 3F 119
Redgate. Corn 2G 7
Redgrave. Suff 3C 66
Red Hill. Warw 5F 61
Red Hill. W Yor 2E 93
Redhill. Abers 3E 153
Redhill. Herts 2C 52
Redhill. N Som 5A 34
Redhill. Shrp 4B 72
Redhill. Surr 5D 39
Redhouses. Arg 3B 124
Redisham. Suff 2G 67
Redland. Bris 4A 34
Redland. Orkn 5C 172
Redlingfield. Suff 3D 66
Red Lodge. Suff 3F 65
Redlynch. Som 3C 22
Redlynch. Wilts 4H 23
Redmain. Cumb 1C 102
Redmarley. Worc 4B 60
Redmarley D'Abitot. Glos 2C 48
Redmarshall. Stoc T 2A 106
Redmile. Leics 2E 75
Redmire. N Yor 5D 104
Rednal. Shrp 3F 71
Redpath. Bord 1H 119
Redpoint. High 2G 155
Red Post. Corn 2C 10
Red Rock. G Man 4D 90
Red Roses. Carm 3G 43
Red Row. Nmbd 5G 121
Redruth. Corn 4B 6
Red Street. Staf 5C 84
Redvales. G Man 4G 91
Red Wharf Bay. IOA 2E 81
Redwick. Newp 3H 33
Redwick. S Glo 3A 34
Redworth. Darl 2F 105
Reed. Herts 2D 52
Reed End. Herts 2D 52
Reedham. Linc 5B 88
Reedham. Norf 5G 79
Reedness. E Yor 2B 94
Reeds Beck. Linc 4B 88
Reemshill. Abers 4E 161
Reepham. Linc 3H 87
Reepham. Norf 3C 78
Reeth. N Yor 5D 104
Regaby. IOM 2D 108
Regil. N Som 5A 34
Regoul. High 3C 158
Reiff. High 2D 162
Reigate. Surr 5D 38
Reighton. N Yor 2F 101
Reilth. Shrp 2E 59
Reinigeadal. W Isl 7E 171
Reisque. Abers 2F 153
Reiss. High 3F 169
Rejerrah. Corn 3B 6
Releath. Corn 5A 6
Relubbus. Corn 3C 4
Relugas. Mor 4D 159
Remenham. Wok 3F 37
Remenham Hill. Wok 3F 37
Rempstone. Notts 3C 74
Rendcomb. Glos 5F 49
Rendham. Suff 4F 67
Rendlesham. Suff 5F 67
Renfrew. Ren 3G 127
Renhold. Bed 5H 63
Renishaw. Derbs 3B 86
Rennington. Nmbd 3G 121
Renton. W Dun 2E 127
Renwick. Cumb 5G 113
Repps. Norf 4G 79
Repton. Derbs 3H 73
Rescassa. Corn 4D 6
Rescobie. Ang 3E 145
Rescorla. Corn
nr. Penwithick 3E 7
nr. Sticker 4D 6
Resipole. High 2B 140
Resolfen. Neat 5B 46
Resolis. High 2A 158
Resolven. Neat 5B 46
Rest and be thankful. Arg 3B 134
Reston. Bord 3E 131
Restrop. Wilts 3F 35
Retford. Notts 2E 86
Retire. Corn 2E 6
Rettendon. Essx 1B 40
Revesby. Linc 4B 88
Rew. Devn 5D 8
Rewe. Devn 3C 12
Rew Street. IOW 3C 16
Rexon. Devn 4E 11
Reybridge. Wilts 5E 35
Reydon. Suff 3H 67
Reymerston. Norf 5C 78
Reynalton. Pemb 4E 43
Reynoldston. Swan 4D 31
Rezare. Corn 5D 10
Rhadyr. Mon 5G 47
Rhaeadr Gwy. Powy 4B 58
Rhandirmwyn. Carm 1A 46
Rhayader. Powy 4B 58
Rheindown. High 4H 157
Rhemore. High 3G 139
Rhenetra. High 3D 154
Rhewl. Den
nr. Llangollen 1D 70
nr. Ruthin 4D 82
Rhewl. Shrp 2F 71
Rhewl-Mostyn. Flin 2D 82
Rhian. High 2C 164
Rhian Breck. High 3C 164
Rhicarn. High 1E 163
Rhiconich. High 3C 166
Rhicullen. High 1A 158
Rhidorroch. High 4F 163
Rhifail. High 4H 167
Rhigos. Rhon 5C 46
Rhilochan. High 3E 165
Rhiroy. High 5F 163
Rhitongue. High 3G 167
Rhiw. Gwyn 3B 68
Rhiwabon. Wrex 1F 71
Rhiwbina. Card 3E 33
Rhiwbryfdir. Gwyn 1F 69
Rhiwderin. Newp 3F 33
Rhiwlas. Gwyn
nr. Bala 2B 70
nr. Bangor 4E 81
Rhiwlas. Powy 2D 70
Rhodes. G Man 4G 91
Rhodesia. Notts 2C 86
Rhodes Minnis. Kent 1F 29
Rhodiad-y-Brenin. Pemb 2B 42
Rhondda. Rhon 2C 32

St Mabyn – Scopwick

St Mabyn. *Corn* 5A 10
St Madoes. *Per* 1D 136
St Margaret's. *Herts* 4A 52
St Margaret's. *Wilts* 5H 35
St Margarets. *Here* 2G 47
St Margarets. *Herts* 4D 53
St Margaret's at Cliffe. *Kent* 1H 29
St Margaret's Hope. *Orkn* 8D 172
St Margaret South Elmham
 Suff 2F 67
St Mark's. *IOM* 4B 108
St Martin. *Corn*
 nr. Helston 4E 5
 nr. Looe 3G 7
St Martin's. *Shrp* 2F 71
St Martins. *Per* 5A 144
St Mary Bourne. *Hants* 1C 24
St Mary Church. *V Glam* 4D 32
St Marychurch. *Torb* 2F 9
St Mary Cray. *G Lon* 4F 39
St Mary Hill. *V Glam* 4C 32
St Mary Hoo. *Medw* 3C 40
St Mary in the Marsh. *Kent* 3E 29
St Mary's. *Orkn* 7D 172
St Mary's Airport. *IOS* 1B 4
St Mary's Bay. *Kent* 3E 29
St Marys Platt. *Kent* 5H 39
St Maughan's Green. *Mon* 4H 47
St Mawes. *Corn* 5C 6
St Mawgan. *Corn* 2C 6
St Mellion. *Corn* 2H 7
St Mellons. *Card* 3F 33
St Merryn. *Corn* 1C 6
St Mewan. *Corn* 3D 6
St Michael Caerhays. *Corn* 4D 6
St Michael Penkevil. *Corn* 4C 6
St Michaels. *Kent* 2C 28
St Michaels. *Torb* 3E 9
St Michaels. *Worc* 4H 59
St Michael's on Wyre. *Lanc* 5D 96
St Michael South Elmham
 Suff 2F 67
St Minver. *Corn* 1D 6
St Monans. *Fife* 3H 137
St Neot. *Corn* 2F 7
St Neots. *Cambs* 4A 64
St Newlyn East. *Corn* 3C 6
St Nicholas. *Pemb* 1C 42
St Nicholas. *V Glam* 4D 32
St Nicholas at Wade. *Kent* 4G 41
St Nicholas South Elmham
 Suff 2F 67
St Ninians. *Stir* 4G 135
St Olaves. *Norf* 1G 67
St Osyth. *Essx* 4E 54
St Osyth Heath. *Essx* 4E 55
St Owen's Cross. *Here* 3A 48
St Paul's Cray. *G Lon* 4F 39
St Paul's Walden. *Herts* 3B 52
St Peter's. *Kent* 4H 41
St Peter The Great. *Worc* 5C 60
St Petrox. *Pemb* 5D 42
St Pinnock. *Corn* 2G 7
St Quivox. *S Ayr* 2C 116
St Ruan. *Corn* 5E 5
St Stephen. *Corn* 3D 6
St Stephens. *Corn*
 nr. Launceston 4D 10
 nr. Saltash 3A 8
St Teath. *Corn* 4A 10
St Thomas. *Devn* 3C 12
St Thomas. *Swan* 3F 31
St Tudy. *Corn* 5A 10
St Twynnells. *Pemb* 5D 42
St Veep. *Corn* 3F 7
St Vigeans. *Ang* 4F 145
St Wenn. *Corn* 2D 6
St Weonards. *Here* 3H 47
St Winnolls. *Corn* 3H 7
St Winnow. *Corn* 3F 7
Salcombe. *Devn* 5D 8
Salcombe Regis. *Devn* 4E 13
Salcott. *Essx* 4C 54
Sale. *G Man* 1B 84
Saleby. *Linc* 3D 88
Sale Green. *Worc* 5D 60
Salehurst. *E Sus* 3B 28
Salem. *Carm* 3G 45
Salem. *Cdgn* 2F 57
Salen. *Arg* 4G 139
Salen. *High* 2A 140
Salesbury. *Lanc* 1E 91
Saleway. *Worc* 5D 60
Salford. *C Beds* 2H 51
Salford. *G Man* 1C 84
Salford. *Oxon* 3A 50
Salford Priors. *Warw* 5E 61
Salfords. *Surr* 1D 27
Salhouse. *Norf* 4F 79
Saligo. *Arg* 3A 124
Saline. *Fife* 4C 136
Salisbury. *Wilts* 3G 23
Salkeld Dykes. *Cumb* 1G 103
Sallachan. *High* 2D 141
Sallachy. *High*
 nr. Lairg 3C 164
 nr. Stromeferry 5B 156
Salle. *Norf* 3D 78
Salmonby. *Linc* 3C 88
Salmond's Muir. *Ang* 5E 145
Salperton. *Glos* 3F 49
Salph End. *Bed* 5H 63
Salsburgh. *N Lan* 3B 128
Salt. *Staf* 3D 72
Salta. *Cumb* 5B 112
Saltaire. *W Yor* 1B 92
Saltash. *Corn* 3A 8
Saltburn. *High* 2B 158
Saltburn-by-the-Sea. *Red C* 2D 106
Saltby. *Leics* 3F 75
Saltcoats. *Cumb* 5B 102
Saltcoats. *N Ayr* 5D 126
Saltdean. *Brig* 5E 27
Salt End. *E Yor* 2E 95
Salter. *Lanc* 3F 97
Salterforth. *Lanc* 5A 98
Salters Lode. *Norf* 5E 77
Salterswall. *Ches W* 4A 84
Salterton. *Wilts* 3G 23
Saltfleet. *Linc* 1D 88
Saltfleetby All Saints. *Linc* 1D 88
Saltfleetby St Clements. *Linc* 1D 88
Saltfleetby St Peter. *Linc* 2D 88
Saltford. *Bath* 5B 34
Salthouse. *Norf* 1C 78
Saltmarshe. *E Yor* 2A 94
Saltness. *Orkn* 9B 172
Saltness. *Shet* 7D 173
Saltney. *Flin* 4F 83
Salton. *N Yor* 2B 100
Saltrens. *Devn* 4E 19
Saltwick. *Nmbd* 2E 115
Saltwood. *Kent* 2F 29
Salum. *Arg* 4B 138
Salwarpe. *Worc* 4C 60
Salwayash. *Dors* 3H 13
Samalaman. *High* 1A 140
Sambourne. *Warw* 4E 61
Sambourne. *Wilts* 2D 22
Sambrook. *Telf* 3B 72
Samhia. *W Isl* 2C 170
Samlesbury. *Lanc* 1D 90
Samlesbury Bottoms. *Lanc* 2E 90
Sampford Arundel. *Som* 1E 12
Sampford Brett. *Som* 2D 20
Sampford Courtenay. *Devn* 2G 11
Sampford Peverell. *Devn* 1D 12
Sampford Spiney. *Devn* 5F 11
Samsonslane. *Orkn* 5F 172
Samuelston. *E Lot* 2A 130
Sanaigmore. *Arg* 2A 124
Sancreed. *Corn* 4B 4
Sancton. *E Yor* 1C 94
Sand. *High* 4D 162
Sand. *Shet* 7E 173
Sand. *Som* 2H 21
Sandaig. *Arg* 4A 138
Sandaig. *High* 3F 147
Sandale. *Cumb* 5D 112
Sandal Magna. *W Yor* 3D 92
Sandavore. *High* 5C 146
Sanday Airport. *Orkn* 3F 172
Sandbach. *Ches E* 4B 84
Sandbank. *Arg* 1C 126
Sandbanks. *Pool* 4F 15
Sandend. *Abers* 2C 160
Sanderstead. *G Lon* 4E 39
Sandfields. *Neat* 3G 31
Sandford. *Cumb* 3A 104
Sandford. *Devn* 2B 12
Sandford. *Dors* 4E 15
Sandford. *Hants* 2G 15
Sandford. *IOW* 4D 16
Sandford. *N Som* 1H 21
Sandford. *Shrp*
 nr. Oswestry 3F 71
 nr. Whitchurch 2H 71
Sandford. *S Lan* 5A 128
Sandfordhill. *Abers* 4H 161
Sandford-on-Thames. *Oxon* 5D 50
Sandford Orcas. *Dors* 4B 22
Sandford St Martin. *Oxon* 3C 50
Sandgate. *Kent* 2F 29
Sandgreen. *Dum* 4C 110
Sandhaven. *Abers* 2G 161
Sandhead. *Dum* 4F 109
Sandhill. *Cambs* 2E 65
Sandhills. *Dors* 1B 14
Sandhills. *Oxon* 5D 50
Sandhills. *Surr* 2A 26
Sandhoe. *Nmbd* 3C 114
Sand Hole. *E Yor* 1B 94
Sandholme. *E Yor* 1B 94
Sandholme. *Linc* 2C 76
Sandhurst. *Brac* 5G 37
Sandhurst. *Glos* 3D 48
Sandhurst. *Kent* 3B 28
Sandhurst Cross. *Kent* 3B 28
Sand Hutton. *N Yor* 4A 100
Sandhutton. *N Yor* 1F 99
Sandiacre. *Derbs* 2B 74
Sandilands. *Linc* 2E 89
Sandiway. *Ches W* 3A 84
Sandleheath. *Hants* 1G 15
Sandling. *Kent* 5B 40
Sandlow Green. *Ches E* 4B 84
Sandness. *Shet* 6C 173
Sandon. *Essx* 5H 53
Sandon. *Herts* 2D 52
Sandon. *Staf* 3D 72
Sandonbank. *Staf* 3D 72
Sandown. *IOW* 4D 16
Sandplace. *Corn* 3G 7
Sandridge. *Herts* 4B 52
Sandringham. *Norf* 3F 77
The Sands. *Surr* 2G 25
Sandsend. *N Yor* 3F 107
Sandside. *Cumb* 2C 96
Sandsound. *Shet* 7E 173
Sandtoft. *N Lin* 4H 93
Sandvoe. *Shet* 2E 173
Sandway. *Kent* 5C 40
Sandwich. *Kent* 5H 41
Sandwick. *Cumb* 3F 103
Sandwick. *Orkn*
 on Mainland 6B 172
 on South Ronaldsay 9D 172
Sandwick. *Shet*
 on Mainland 9F 173
 on Whalsay 5G 173
Sandwith. *Cumb* 3A 102
Sandy. *Carm* 5E 45
Sandy. *C Beds* 1B 52
Sandy Bank. *Linc* 5B 88
Sandycroft. *Flin* 4F 83
Sandy Cross. *Here* 5A 60
Sandygate. *Devn* 5B 12
Sandygate. *IOM* 2C 108
Sandy Haven. *Pemb* 4C 42
Sandyhills. *Dum* 4F 111
Sandylands. *Lanc* 3D 96
Sandy Lane. *Wilts* 5E 35
Sandylane. *Swan* 4E 31
Sandystones. *Bord* 2H 119
Sandyway. *Here* 3H 47
Sangobeg. *High* 2E 167
Sangomore. *High* 2E 166
Sankyn's Green. *Worc* 4B 60
Sanna. *High* 2F 139
Sanndabhaig. *W Isl*
 on Isle of Lewis 4G 171
 on South Uist 4D 170
Sannox. *N Ayr* 5B 126
Sanquhar. *Dum* 3G 117
Santon. *Cumb* 4B 102
Santon Bridge. *Cumb* 4C 102
Santon Downham. *Suff* 2H 65
Sapcote. *Leics* 1B 62
Sapey Common. *Here* 4B 60
Sapiston. *Suff* 3B 66
Sapley. *Cambs* 3B 64
Sapperton. *Derbs* 2F 73
Sapperton. *Glos* 5E 49
Sapperton. *Linc* 2H 75
Saracen's Head. *Linc* 3C 76
Sarclet. *High* 4F 169
Sardis. *Carm* 5F 45
Sardis. *Pemb*
 nr. Milford Haven 4D 42
 nr. Tenby 4F 43
Sarisbury Green. *Hants* 2D 16
Sarn. *B'end* 3C 32
Sarn. *Powy* 1E 58
Sarnau. *Carm* 3E 45
Sarnau. *Cdgn* 5C 56
Sarnau. *Gwyn* 2B 70
Sarnau. *Powy*
 nr. Brecon 2D 46
 nr. Welshpool 4E 71
Sarn Bach. *Gwyn* 3C 68
Sarnesfield. *Here* 5F 59
Sarn Meyllteyrn. *Gwyn* 2B 68
Saron. *Carm*
 nr. Ammanford 4G 45
 nr. Newcastle Emlyn 2D 45
Saron. *Gwyn*
 nr. Bethel 4E 81
 nr. Bontnewydd 5D 80
Sarratt. *Herts* 1B 38
Sarre. *Kent* 4G 41
Sarsden. *Oxon* 3A 50
Satley. *Dur* 5E 115
Satron. *N Yor* 5C 104
Satterleigh. *Devn* 4G 19
Satterthwaite. *Cumb* 5E 103
Satwell. *Oxon* 3F 37
Sauchen. *Abers* 2D 152
Saucher. *Per* 5A 144
Saughall. *Ches W* 3F 83
Saughtree. *Bord* 5H 119
Saul. *Glos* 5C 48
Saundby. *Notts* 2E 87
Saundersfoot. *Pemb* 4F 43
Saunderton. *Buck* 5F 51
Saunderton Lee. *Buck* 2G 37
Saunton. *Devn* 3E 19
Sausthorpe. *Linc* 4C 88
Saval. *High* 3C 164
Saverley Green. *Staf* 2D 72
Sawbridge. *Warw* 4C 62
Sawbridgeworth. *Herts* 4E 53
Sawdon. *N Yor* 1D 100
Sawley. *Derbs* 2B 74
Sawley. *Lanc* 5G 97
Sawley. *N Yor* 3E 99
Sawston. *Cambs* 1E 53
Sawtry. *Cambs* 2A 64
Saxby. *Leics* 3F 75
Saxby. *Linc* 2H 87
Saxby All Saints. *N Lin* 3C 94
Saxelby. *Leics* 3D 74
Saxelbye. *Leics* 3D 74
Saxham Street. *Suff* 4C 66
Saxilby. *Linc* 3F 87
Saxlingham. *Norf* 2C 78
Saxlingham Green. *Norf* 1E 67
Saxlingham Nethergate. *Norf* 1E 67
Saxlingham Thorpe. *Norf* 1E 66
Saxmundham. *Suff* 4F 67
Saxondale. *Notts* 1D 74
Saxon Street. *Cambs* 5F 65
Saxtead. *Suff* 4E 67
Saxtead Green. *Suff* 4E 67
Saxthorpe. *Norf* 2D 78
Saxton. *N Yor* 1E 93
Sayers Common. *W Sus* 4D 26
Scackleton. *N Yor* 2A 100
Scadabhagh. *W Isl* 8D 171
Scaftworth. *Notts* 1D 86
Scagglethorpe. *N Yor* 2C 100
Scaitcliffe. *Lanc* 2F 91
Scaladal. *W Isl* 6D 171
Scalasaig. *Arg* 4A 132
Scalby. *E Yor* 2B 94
Scalby. *N Yor* 5H 107
Scalby Mills. *N Yor* 5H 107
Scaldwell. *Nptn* 3E 63
Scaleby. *Cumb* 3F 113
Scaleby Hill. *Cumb* 3F 113
Scale Houses. *Cumb* 5G 113
Scales. *Cumb*
 nr. Barrow-in-Furness 2B 96
 nr. Keswick 2E 103
Scalford. *Leics* 3E 75
Scaling. *N Yor* 3E 107
Scaling Dam. *Red C* 3E 107
Scalloway. *Shet* 8F 173
Scalpaigh. *W Isl* 8E 171
Scalpay House. *High* 1E 147
Scamblesby. *Linc* 3B 88
Scamodale. *High* 1C 140
Scampston. *N Yor* 2C 100
Scampton. *Linc* 3G 87
Scaniport. *High* 5A 158
Scapa. *Orkn* 7D 172
Scapegoat Hill. *W Yor* 3A 92
Scar. *Orkn* 3F 172
Scarasta. *W Isl* 8C 171
Scarborough. *N Yor* 1E 101
Scarcliffe. *Derbs* 4B 86
Scarcroft. *W Yor* 5F 99
Scardroy. *High* 3E 156
Scarfskerry. *High* 1E 169
Scargill. *Dur* 3D 104
Scarinish. *Arg* 4B 138
Scarisbrick. *Lanc* 3B 90
Scarning. *Norf* 4B 78
Scarrington. *Notts* 1E 75
Scarth Hill. *Lanc* 4C 90
Scartho. *NE Lin* 4F 95
Scarvister. *Shet* 7E 173
Scatness. *Shet* 10E 173
Scatwell. *High* 3F 157
Scaur. *Dum* 4F 111
Scawby. *N Lin* 4C 94
Scawby Brook. *N Lin* 4C 94
Scawsby. *S Yor* 4F 93
Scawton. *N Yor* 1H 99
Scaynes Hill. *W Sus* 3E 27
Scethrog. *Powy* 3E 46
Scholar Green. *Ches E* 5C 84
Scholes. *G Man* 4D 90
Scholes. *W Yor*
 nr. Bradford 2B 92
 nr. Holmfirth 4B 92
 nr. Leeds 1D 93
Scholey Hill. *W Yor* 2D 93
School Aycliffe. *Darl* 2F 105
School Green. *Ches W* 4A 84
School Green. *Essx* 2H 53
Scissett. *W Yor* 3C 92
Scleddau. *Pemb* 1D 42
Scofton. *Notts* 2D 86
Scole. *Norf* 3D 66
Scolpaig. *W Isl* 1C 170
Scolton. *Pemb* 2D 43
Scone. *Per* 1D 136
Sconser. *High* 5E 155
Scoonie. *Fife* 3F 137
Scopwick. *Linc* 5H 87

Shieldmuir – Slimbridge

Shieldmuir. *N Lan* 4A 128
Shielfoot. *High* 1A 140
Shielhill. *Abers* 3H 161
Shielhill. *Ang* 3D 144
Shifnal. *Shrp* 5B 72
Shilbottle. *Nmbd* 4F 121
Shilbottle Grange. *Nmbd* 4G 121
Shildon. *Dur* 2F 105
Shillford. *E Ren* 4F 127
Shillingford. *Devn* 4C 20
Shillingford. *Oxon* 2D 36
Shillingford St George. *Devn* 4C 12
Shillingstone. *Dors* 1D 14
Shillington. *C Beds* 2B 52
Shillmoor. *Nmbd* 4C 120
Shilton. *Oxon* 5A 50
Shilton. *Warw* 2B 62
Shilvinghampton. *Dors* 4B 14
Shilvington. *Nmbd* 1E 115
Shimpling. *Norf* 2D 66
Shimpling. *Suff* 5A 66
Shimpling Street. *Suff* 5A 66
Shincliffe. *Dur* 5F 115
Shiney Row. *Tyne* 4G 115
Shinfield. *Wok* 5F 37
Shingay. *Cambs* 1D 52
Shingham. *Norf* 5G 77
Shingle Street. *Suff* 1G 55
Shinner's Bridge. *Devn* 2D 9
Shinness. *High* 2C 164
Shipbourne. *Kent* 5G 39
Shipdham. *Norf* 5B 78
Shipham. *Som* 1H 21
Shiphay. *Torb* 2E 9
Shiplake. *Oxon* 4F 37
Shipley. *Derbs* 1B 74
Shipley. *Nmbd* 3F 121
Shipley. *Shrp* 1C 60
Shipley. *W Sus* 3C 26
Shipley. *W Yor* 1B 92
Shipley Bridge. *Surr* 1E 27
Shipmeadow. *Suff* 2F 67
Shippon. *Oxon* 2C 36
Shipston-on-Stour. *Warw* 1A 50
Shipton. *Buck* 3F 51
Shipton. *Glos* 4F 49
Shipton. *N Yor* 4H 99
Shipton. *Shrp* 1H 59
Shipton Bellinger. *Hants* 2H 23
Shipton Gorge. *Dors* 3H 13
Shipton Green. *W Sus* 3G 17
Shipton Moyne. *Glos* 3D 35
Shipton-on-Cherwell. *Oxon* 4C 50
Shiptonthorpe. *E Yor* 5C 100
Shipton-under-Wychwood
Oxon 4A 50
Shirburn. *Oxon* 2E 37
Shirdley Hill. *Lanc* 3B 90
Shire. *Cumb* 1H 103
Shirebrook. *Derbs* 4C 86
Shiregreen. *S Yor* 1A 86
Shirehampton. *Bris* 4A 34
Shiremoor. *Tyne* 2G 115
Shirenewton. *Mon* 2H 33
Shireoaks. *Notts* 2C 86
Shires Mill. *Fife* 1D 128
Shirkoak. *Kent* 2D 28
Shirland. *Derbs* 5A 86
Shirley. *Derbs* 1G 73
Shirley. *Sotn* 1B 16
Shirley. *W Mid* 3F 61
Shirleywich. *Staf* 3D 73
Shirl Heath. *Here* 5G 59
Shirrell Heath. *Hants* 1D 16
Shirwell. *Devn* 3F 19
Shiskine. *N Ayr* 3D 122
Shobdon. *Here* 4F 59
Shobnall. *Staf* 3G 73
Shobrooke. *Devn* 2B 12
Shoby. *Leics* 3D 74
Shocklach. *Ches W* 1G 71
Shoeburyness. *S'end* 2D 40
Sholden. *Kent* 5H 41
Sholing. *Sotn* 1C 16
Sholver. *G Man* 4H 91
Shoot Hill. *Shrp* 4G 71
Shop. *Corn*
nr. Bude 1C 10
nr. Padstow 1C 6
Shop. *Devn* 1D 11
Shopford. *Cumb* 2G 113
Shoreditch. *G Lon* 2E 39
Shoreditch. *Som* 4F 21
Shoregill. *Cumb* 4A 104
Shoreham. *Kent* 4G 39
Shoreham-by-Sea. *W Sus* 5D 26
Shoresdean. *Nmbd* 5F 131
Shoreswood. *Nmbd* 5F 131
Shorncote. *Glos* 2F 35
Shorne. *Kent* 3A 40
Shorne Ridgeway. *Kent* 3A 40
Shortacombe. *Devn* 4F 11
Shortbridge. *E Sus* 3F 27
Shortgate. *E Sus* 4F 27
Short Green. *Norf* 2C 66
Shorthampton. *Oxon* 3B 50
Short Heath. *Derbs* 4H 73
Short Heath. *W Mid*
nr. Erdington 1E 61
nr. Wednesfield 5D 73
Shortlanesend. *Corn* 4C 6
Shorton. *Torb* 2E 9
Shortstown. *Bed* 1A 52
Shortwood. *S Glo* 4B 34
Shorwell. *IOW* 4C 16
Shoscombe. *Bath* 1C 22
Shotesham. *Norf* 1E 67
Shotgate. *Essx* 1B 40
Shotley. *Suff* 2F 55
Shotley Bridge. *Dur* 4D 115
Shotleyfield. *Nmbd* 4D 114
Shotley Gate. *Suff* 2F 55
Shottenden. *Kent* 5E 41
Shottermill. *Surr* 3G 25
Shottery. *Warw* 5F 61
Shotteswell. *Warw* 1C 50
Shottisham. *Suff* 1G 55
Shottle. *Derbs* 1H 73
Shotton. *Dur*
nr. Peterlee 1B 106
nr. Sedgefield 2A 106
Shotton. *Flin* 4F 83
Shotton. *Nmbd*
nr. Morpeth 2F 115
nr. Town Yetholm 1C 120
Shotton Colliery. *Dur* 5G 115
Shotts. *N Lan* 3B 128
Shotwick. *Ches W* 3F 83
Shouldham. *Norf* 5F 77
Shouldham Thorpe. *Norf* 5F 77
Shoulton. *Worc* 5C 60
Shrawardine. *Shrp* 4G 71
Shrawley. *Worc* 4C 60
Shreding Green. *Buck* 2B 38
Shrewley. *Warw* 4G 61
Shrewsbury. *Shrp* 4G 71
Shrewton. *Wilts* 2F 23
Shripney. *W Sus* 5A 26
Shrivenham. *Oxon* 3H 35
Shropham. *Norf* 1B 66
Shroton. *Dors* 1D 14
Shrub End. *Essx* 3C 54
Shucknall. *Here* 1A 48
Shudy Camps. *Cambs* 1G 53
Shulishadermor. *High* 4D 155
Shulista. *High* 1D 154
Shurdington. *Glos* 4E 49
Shurlock Row. *Wind* 4G 37
Shurrery. *High* 3C 168
Shurton. *Som* 2F 21
Shustoke. *Warw* 1G 61
Shute. *Devn*
nr. Axminster 3F 13
nr. Crediton 2B 12
Shutford. *Oxon* 1B 50
Shut Heath. *Staf* 3C 72
Shuthonger. *Glos* 2D 49
Shutlanehead. *Staf* 1C 72
Shutlanger. *Nptn* 1F 51
Shutt Green. *Staf* 5C 72
Shuttington. *Warw* 5G 73
Shuttlewood. *Derbs* 3B 86
Shuttleworth. *G Man* 3G 91
Siabost. *W Isl* 3E 171
Siabost bho Dheas. *W Isl* 3E 171
Siabost bho Thuath. *W Isl* 3E 171
Siadar. *W Isl* 2F 171
Siadar Uarach. *W Isl* 2F 171
Sibbaldbie. *Dum* 1C 112
Sibbertoft. *Nptn* 2D 62
Sibdon Carwood. *Shrp* 2G 59
Sibertswold. *Kent* 1G 29
Sibford Ferris. *Oxon* 2B 50
Sibford Gower. *Oxon* 2B 50
Sible Hedingham. *Essx* 2A 54
Sibsey. *Linc* 5C 88
Sibsey Fen Side. *Linc* 5C 88
Sibson. *Cambs* 1H 63
Sibson. *Leics* 5A 74
Sibster. *High* 3F 169
Sibthorpe. *Notts* 1E 75
Sibton. *Suff* 4F 67
Sicklesmere. *Suff* 4A 66
Sicklinghall. *N Yor* 5F 99
Sid. *Devn* 4E 13
Sidbury. *Devn* 3E 13
Sidbury. *Shrp* 2A 60
Sidcot. *N Som* 1H 21
Sidcup. *G Lon* 3F 39
Siddick. *Cumb* 1B 102
Siddington. *Ches E* 3C 84
Siddington. *Glos* 2F 35
Side of the Moor. *G Man* 3F 91
Sidestrand. *Norf* 2E 79
Sidford. *Devn* 3E 13
Sidlesham. *W Sus* 3G 17
Sidley. *E Sus* 5B 28
Sidlow. *Surr* 1D 26
Sidmouth. *Devn* 4E 13
Sigford. *Devn* 5A 12
Sigglesthorne. *E Yor* 5F 101
Sighthill. *Edin* 2E 129
Sigingstone. *V Glam* 4C 32
Signet. *Oxon* 4H 49
Silchester. *Hants* 5E 37
Sildinis. *W Isl* 6E 171
Sileby. *Leics* 4D 74
Silecroft. *Cumb* 1A 96
Silfield. *Norf* 1D 66
Silian. *Cdgn* 5E 57
Silkstone. *S Yor* 4C 92
Silkstone Common. *S Yor* 4C 92
Silksworth. *Tyne* 4G 115
Silk Willoughby. *Linc* 1H 75
Silloth. *Cumb* 4C 112
Sills. *Nmbd* 4C 120
Sillyearn. *Mor* 3C 160
Silpho. *N Yor* 5G 107
Silsden. *W Yor* 5C 98
Silsoe. *C Beds* 2A 52
Silverbank. *Abers* 4E 152
Silverburn. *Midl* 3F 129
Silverdale. *Lanc* 2D 96
Silverdale. *Staf* 1C 72
Silverdale Green. *Lanc* 2D 96
Silver End. *Essx* 4B 54
Silver End. *W Mid* 2D 60
Silvergate. *Norf* 3D 78
Silver Green. *Norf* 1E 67
Silverhillocks. *Abers* 2E 161
Silverley's Green. *Suff* 3E 67
Silverstone. *Nptn* 1E 51
Silverton. *Devn* 2C 12
Silverton. *W Dun* 2F 127
Silvington. *Shrp* 3A 60
Simm's Cross. *Hal* 2H 83
Simm's Lane End. *Mers* 4D 90
Simonburn. *Nmbd* 2B 114
Simonsbath. *Som* 3A 20
Simonstone. *Lanc* 1F 91
Simprim. *Bord* 5E 131
Simpson. *Pemb* 3C 42
Simpson Cross. *Pemb* 3C 42
Sinclairston. *E Ayr* 3D 116
Sinclairtown. *Fife* 4E 137
Sinderby. *N Yor* 1F 99
Sinderhope. *Nmbd* 4B 114
Sindlesham. *Wok* 5F 37
Sinfin. *Derb* 2H 73
Singleborough. *Buck* 2F 51
Singleton. *Kent* 1D 28
Singleton. *Lanc* 1B 90
Singleton. *W Sus* 1G 17
Singlewell. *Kent* 3A 40
Sinkhurst Green. *Kent* 1C 28
Sinnahard. *Abers* 2B 152
Sinnington. *N Yor* 1B 100
Sinton Green. *Worc* 4C 60
Sion Mills. *Derr* 3C 174
Sipson. *G Lon* 3B 38
Sirhowy. *Blae* 4E 47
Sisland. *Norf* 1F 67
Sissinghurst. *Kent* 2B 28
Siston. *S Glo* 4B 34
Sithney. *Corn* 4D 4
Sittingbourne. *Kent* 4D 40
Six Ashes. *Staf* 2B 60
Six Bells. *Blae* 5F 47
Six Hills. *Leics* 3D 74
Sixhills. *Linc* 2A 88
Six Mile Bottom. *Cambs* 5E 65
Sixpenny Handley. *Dors* 1E 15
Sizewell. *Suff* 4G 67
Skail. *High* 4H 167
Skaill. *Orkn* 6B 172
Skaills. *Orkn* 7E 172
Skares. *E Ayr* 3E 117
Skateraw. *E Lot* 2D 130
Skaw. *Shet* 5G 173
Skeabost. *High* 4D 154
Skeabrae. *Orkn* 5B 172
Skeeby. *N Yor* 4E 105
Skeffington. *Leics* 5E 75
Skeffling. *E Yor* 3G 95
Skegby. *Notts*
nr. Mansfield 4B 86
nr. Tuxford 3E 87
Skegness. *Linc* 4E 89
Skelberry. *Shet*
nr. Boddam 10E 173
nr. Housetter 3E 173
Skelbo. *High* 4E 165
Skelbo Street. *High* 4E 165
Skelbrooke. *S Yor* 3F 93
Skeldyke. *Linc* 2C 76
Skelfhill. *Bord* 4G 119
Skellingthorpe. *Linc* 3G 87
Skellister. *Shet* 6F 173
Skellorn Green. *Ches E* 2D 84
Skellow. *S Yor* 3F 93
Skelmanthorpe. *W Yor* 3C 92
Skelmersdale. *Lanc* 4C 90
Skelmorlie. *N Ayr* 3C 126
Skelpick. *High* 3H 167
Skelton. *Cumb* 1F 103
Skelton. *E Yor* 2A 94
Skelton. *N Yor*
nr. Richmond 4D 105
nr. Ripon 3F 99
Skelton. *Red C* 3D 106
Skelton. *York* 4H 99
Skelton Green. *Red C* 3D 106
Skelwick. *Orkn* 3D 172
Skelwith Bridge. *Cumb* 4E 103
Skendleby. *Linc* 4D 88
Skendleby Psalter. *Linc* 3D 88
Skenfrith. *Mon* 3H 47
Skerne. *E Yor* 4E 101
Skeroblingarry. *Arg* 3B 122
Skerray. *High* 2G 167
Skerricha. *High* 3C 166
Skerries Airport. *Shet* 4H 173
Skerton. *Lanc* 3D 97
Sketchley. *Leics* 1B 62
Sketty. *Swan* 3F 31
Skewen. *Neat* 3G 31
Skewsby. *N Yor* 2A 100
Skeyton. *Norf* 3E 79
Skeyton Corner. *Norf* 3E 79
Skiall. *High* 2C 168
Skidbrooke. *Linc* 1D 88
Skidbrooke North End. *Linc* 1D 88
Skidby. *E Yor* 1D 94
Skilgate. *Som* 4C 20
Skillington. *Linc* 3F 75
Skinburness. *Cumb* 4C 112
Skinflats. *Falk* 1C 128
Skinidin. *High* 4B 154
Skinnet. *High* 2F 167
Skinningrove. *Red C* 3E 107
Skipness. *Arg* 4G 125
Skippool. *Lanc* 5C 96
Skiprigg. *Cumb* 5E 113
Skipsea. *E Yor* 4F 101
Skipsea Brough. *E Yor* 4F 101
Skipton. *N Yor* 4B 98
Skipton-on-Swale. *N Yor* 2F 99
Skipwith. *N Yor* 1G 93
Skirbeck. *Linc* 1C 76
Skirbeck Quarter. *Linc* 1C 76
Skirlaugh. *E Yor* 1E 95
Skirling. *Bord* 1C 118
Skirmett. *Buck* 2F 37
Skirpenbeck. *E Yor* 4B 100
Skirwith. *Cumb* 1H 103
Skirwith. *N Yor* 2G 97
Skirza. *High* 2F 169
Skitby. *Cumb* 3F 113
Skitham. *Lanc* 5D 96
Skittle Green. *Buck* 5F 51
Skroo. *Shet* 1B 172
Skulamus. *High* 1E 147
Skullomie. *High* 2G 167
Skyborry Green. *Shrp* 3E 59
Skye Green. *Essx* 3B 54
Skye of Curr. *High* 1D 151
Slack. *W Yor* 2H 91
The Slack. *Dur* 2E 105
Slackhall. *Derbs* 2E 85
Slack Head. *Cumb* 2D 97
Slackhead. *Mor* 2B 160
Slackholme End. *Linc* 3E 89
Slacks of Cairnbanno
Abers 4F 161
Slad. *Glos* 5D 48
Slade. *Swan* 4D 31
The Slade. *W Ber* 5D 36
Slade End. *Oxon* 2D 36
Slade Field. *Cambs* 2C 64
Slade Green. *G Lon* 3G 39
Slade Heath. *Staf* 5D 72
Slade Hooton. *S Yor* 2C 86
Sladesbridge. *Corn* 5A 10
Slaggyford. *Nmbd* 4H 113
Slaidburn. *Lanc* 4G 97
Slaid Hill. *W Yor* 5F 99
Slaithwaite. *W Yor* 3A 92
Slaley. *Derbs* 5G 85
Slaley. *Nmbd* 4C 114
Slamannan. *Falk* 2B 128
Slapton. *Buck* 3H 51
Slapton. *Devn* 4E 9
Slapton. *Nptn* 1E 51
Slattocks. *G Man* 4G 91
Slaugham. *W Sus* 3D 26
Slaughterbridge. *Corn* 4B 10
Slaughterford. *Wilts* 4D 34
Slawston. *Leics* 1E 63
Sleaford. *Hants* 3G 25
Sleaford. *Linc* 1H 75
Sleagill. *Cumb* 3G 103
Sleap. *Shrp* 3G 71
Sledmere. *E Yor* 3D 100
Sleightholme. *Dur* 3C 104
Sleights. *N Yor* 4F 107
Slepe. *Dors* 3E 15
Slickly. *High* 2E 169
Sliddery. *N Ayr* 3D 122
Sligachan. *High* 1C 146
Slimbridge. *Glos* 5C 48

Soval Lodge – Steventon

Soval Lodge. *W Isl* 5F 171
Sowerby. *N Yor* 1G 99
Sowerby. *W Yor* 2A 92
Sowerby Bridge. *W Yor* 2A 92
Sowerby Row. *Cumb* 5E 113
Sower Carr. *Lanc* 5C 96
Sowley Green. *Suff* 5G 65
Sowood. *W Yor* 3A 92
Sowton. *Devn* 3C 12
Soyal. *High* 4C 164
Soyland Town. *W Yor* 2A 92
Spacey Houses. *N Yor* 4F 99
Spa Common. *Norf* 2E 79
Spalding. *Linc* 3B 76
Spaldington. *E Yor* 1A 94
Spaldwick. *Cambs* 3A 64
Spalford. *Notts* 4F 87
Spanby. *Linc* 2H 75
Sparham. *Norf* 4C 78
Sparhamhill. *Norf* 4C 78
Spark Bridge. *Cumb* 1C 96
Sparket. *Cumb* 2F 103
Sparkford. *Som* 4B 22
Sparkwell. *Devn* 3B 8
Sparrow Green. *Norf* 4B 78
Sparrowpit. *Derbs* 2E 85
Sparrow's Green. *E Sus* 2H 27
Sparsholt. *Hants* 3C 24
Sparsholt. *Oxon* 3B 36
Spartylea. *Nmbd* 5B 114
Spath. *Staf* 2E 73
Spaunton. *N Yor* 1B 100
Spaxton. *Som* 3F 21
Spean Bridge. *High* 5E 149
Spear Hill. *W Sus* 4C 26
Speen. *Buck* 2G 37
Speen. *W Ber* 5C 36
Speeton. *N Yor* 2F 101
Speke. *Mers* 2G 83
Speldhurst. *Kent* 1G 27
Spellbrook. *Herts* 4E 53
Spelsbury. *Oxon* 3B 50
Spencers Wood. *Wok* 5F 37
Spennithorne. *N Yor* 1D 98
Spennymoor. *Dur* 1F 105
Spernall. *Warw* 4E 61
Spetchley. *Worc* 5C 60
Spetisbury. *Dors* 2E 15
Spexhall. *Suff* 2F 67
Speybank. *High* 3C 150
Spey Bay. *Mor* 2A 160
Speybridge. *High* 1E 151
Speyview. *Mor* 4G 159
Spilsby. *Linc* 4D 88
Spindlestone. *Nmbd* 1F 121
Spinkhill. *Derbs* 3B 86
Spinney Hills. *Leic* 5D 74
Spinningdale. *High* 5D 164
Spital. *Mers* 2F 83
Spitalhill. *Derbs* 1F 73
Spital in the Street. *Linc* 1G 87
Spithurst. *E Sus* 4F 27
Spittal. *Dum* 4A 110
Spittal. *E Lot* 2A 130
Spittal. *High* 3D 168
Spittal. *Nmbd* 4G 131
Spittal. *Pemb* 2D 43
Spittalfield. *Per* 4A 144
Spittal of Glenmuick. *Abers* 5H 151
Spittal of Glenshee. *Per* 1A 144
Spittal-on-Rule. *Bord* 2H 119
Spixworth. *Norf* 4E 79
Splatt. *Corn* 4C 10
Spofforth. *N Yor* 4F 99
Spondon. *Derb* 2B 74
Spon End. *W Mid* 3H 61
Spooner Row. *Norf* 1C 66
Sporle. *Norf* 4H 77
Spott. *E Lot* 2C 130
Spratton. *Nptn* 3E 62
Spreakley. *Surr* 2G 25
Spreyton. *Devn* 3H 11
Spridlington. *Linc* 2H 87
Springburn. *Glas* 3H 127
Springfield. *Dum* 3E 113
Springfield. *Fife* 2F 137
Springfield. *High* 2A 158
Springfield. *W Mid* 2E 61
Spring Hill. *W Mid* 1C 60
Springhill. *Staf* 5D 73
Springholm. *Dum* 3F 111
Springside. *N Ayr* 1C 116
Springthorpe. *Linc* 2F 87
Spring Vale. *IOW* 3E 16
Spring Valley. *IOM* 4C 108
Springwell. *Tyne* 4F 115
Sproatley. *E Yor* 1E 95
Sproston Green. *Ches W* 4B 84
Sprotbrough. *S Yor* 4F 93
Sproughton. *Suff* 1E 54
Sprouston. *Bord* 1B 120
Sprowston. *Norf* 4E 79
Sproxton. *Leics* 3F 75
Sproxton. *N Yor* 1A 100
Sprunston. *Cumb* 5E 113
Spurstow. *Ches E* 5H 83
Squires Gate. *Bkpl* 1B 90
Sraid Ruadh. *Arg* 4A 138
Srannda. *W Isl* 9C 171
Sron an t-Sithein. *High* 2C 140
Sronphadruig Lodge. *Per* 1E 142
Sruth Mor. *W Isl* 2E 170
Stableford. *Shrp* 1B 60
Stackhouse. *N Yor* 3H 97
Stackpole. *Pemb* 5D 43
Stackpole Elidor. *Pemb* 5D 43
Stacksford. *Norf* 1C 66
Stacksteads. *Lanc* 2G 91
Staddiscombe. *Plym* 3B 8
Staddlethorpe. *E Yor* 2B 94
Staddon. *Devn* 2D 10
Stadhampton. *Oxon* 2E 36
Stadhlaigearraidh. *W Isl* 5C 170
Stafainn. *High* 2D 155
Staffield. *Cumb* 5G 113
Staffin. *High* 2D 155
Stafford. *Staf* 3D 72
Stafford Park. *Telf* 5B 72
Stagden Cross. *Essx* 4G 53
Stagsden. *Bed* 1H 51
Stag's Head. *Devn* 4G 19
Stainburn. *Cumb* 2B 102
Stainburn. *N Yor* 5E 99
Stainby. *Linc* 3G 75
Staincliffe. *W Yor* 2C 92
Staincross. *S Yor* 3D 92
Staindrop. *Dur* 2E 105
Staines-upon-Thames. *Surr* 3B 38
Stainfield. *Linc*
nr. Bourne 3H 75
nr. Lincoln 3A 88
Stainforth. *N Yor* 3H 97
Stainforth. *S Yor* 3G 93
Staining. *Lanc* 1B 90
Stainland. *W Yor* 3A 92
Stainsacre. *N Yor* 4G 107
Stainton. *Cumb*
nr. Carlisle 4E 113
nr. Kendal 1E 97
nr. Penrith 2F 103
Stainton. *Dur* 3D 104
Stainton. *Midd* 3B 106
Stainton. *N Yor* 5E 105
Stainton. *S Yor* 1C 86
Stainton by Langworth. *Linc* 3H 87
Staintondale. *N Yor* 5G 107
Stainton le Vale. *Linc* 1A 88
Stainton with Adgarley. *Cumb* 2B 96
Stair. *Cumb* 2D 102
Stair. *E Ayr* 2D 116
Stairhaven. *Dum* 4H 109
Staithes. *N Yor* 3E 107
Stakeford. *Nmbd* 1F 115
Stake Pool. *Lanc* 5D 96
Stakes. *Hants* 2E 17
Stalbridge. *Dors* 1C 14
Stalbridge Weston. *Dors* 1C 14
Stalham. *Norf* 3F 79
Stalham Green. *Norf* 3F 79
Stalisfield Green. *Kent* 5D 40
Stallen. *Dors* 1B 14
Stallingborough. *NE Lin* 3F 95
Stalling Busk. *N Yor* 1B 98
Stallington. *Staf* 2D 72
Stalmine. *Lanc* 5C 96
Stalybridge. *G Man* 1D 84
Stambourne. *Essx* 2H 53
Stamford. *Linc* 5H 75
Stamford. *Nmbd* 3G 121
Stamford Bridge. *Ches W* 4G 83
Stamford Bridge. *E Yor* 4B 100
Stamfordham. *Nmbd* 2D 115
Stamperland. *E Ren* 4G 127
Stanah. *Lanc* 5C 96
Stanborough. *Herts* 4C 52
Stanbridge. *C Beds* 3H 51
Stanbridge. *Dors* 2F 15
Stanbury. *W Yor* 1A 92
Stand. *N Lan* 3A 128
Standburn. *Falk* 2C 128
Standeford. *Staf* 5D 72
Standen. *Kent* 1C 28
Standen Street. *Kent* 2C 28
Standerwick. *Som* 1D 22
Standford. *Hants* 3G 25
Standford Bridge. *Telf* 3B 72
Standingstone. *Cumb* 5D 112
Standish. *Glos* 5D 48
Standish. *G Man* 3D 90
Standish Lower Ground
G Man 4D 90
Standlake. *Oxon* 5B 50
Standon. *Hants* 4C 24
Standon. *Herts* 3D 53
Standon. *Staf* 2C 72
Standon Green End. *Herts* 4D 52
Stane. *N Lan* 4B 128
Stanecastle. *N Ayr* 1C 116
Stanfield. *Norf* 3B 78
Stanfield. *Suff* 5G 65
Stanford. *C Beds* 1B 52
Stanford. *Kent* 2F 29
Stanford Bishop. *Here* 5A 60
Stanford Bridge. *Worc* 4B 60
Stanford Dingley. *W Ber* 4D 36
Stanford in the Vale. *Oxon* 2B 36
Stanford-le-Hope. *Thur* 2A 40
Stanford on Avon. *Nptn* 3C 62
Stanford on Soar. *Notts* 3C 74
Stanford on Teme. *Worc* 4B 60
Stanford Rivers. *Essx* 5F 53
Stanfree. *Derbs* 3B 86
Stanghow. *Red C* 3D 107
Stanground. *Pet* 1B 64
Stanhoe. *Norf* 2H 77
Stanhope. *Dur* 1C 104
Stanhope. *Bord* 2D 118
Stanion. *Nptn* 2G 63
Stanley. *Derbs* 1B 74
Stanley. *Dur* 4E 115
Stanley. *Per* 5A 144
Stanley. *Shrp* 2B 60
Stanley. *Staf* 5D 84
Stanley. *W Yor* 2D 92
Stanley Common. *Derbs* 1B 74
Stanley Crook. *Dur* 1E 105
Stanley Hill. *Here* 1B 48
Stanlow. *Ches W* 3G 83
Stanmer. *Brig* 5E 27
Stanmore. *G Lon* 1C 38
Stanmore. *Hants* 4C 24
Stanmore. *W Ber* 4C 36
Stannersburn. *Nmbd* 1A 114
Stanningfield. *Suff* 5A 66
Stannington. *Nmbd* 2F 115
Stannington. *S Yor* 2H 85
Stansbatch. *Here* 4F 59
Stanshope. *Staf* 5F 85
Stanstead. *Suff* 1B 54
Stanstead Abbotts. *Herts* 4D 53
Stansted. *Kent* 4H 39
Stansted Airport. *Essx* 3F 53
Stansted Mountfitchet. *Essx* 3F 53
Stanthorne. *Ches W* 4A 84
Stanton. *Derbs* 4G 73
Stanton. *Glos* 2F 49
Stanton. *Nmbd* 5F 121
Stanton. *Staf* 1F 73
Stanton. *Suff* 3B 66
Stanton by Bridge. *Derbs* 3A 74
Stanton-by-Dale. *Derbs* 2B 74
Stanton Chare. *Suff* 3B 66
Stanton Drew. *Bath* 5A 34
Stanton Fitzwarren. *Swin* 2G 35
Stanton Harcourt. *Oxon* 5C 50
Stanton Hill. *Notts* 4B 86
Stanton in Peak. *Derbs* 4G 85
Stanton Lacy. *Shrp* 3G 59
Stanton Long. *Shrp* 1H 59
Stanton-on-the-Wolds. *Notts* 2D 74
Stanton Prior. *Bath* 5B 34
Stanton St Bernard. *Wilts* 5F 35
Stanton St John. *Oxon* 5D 50
Stanton St Quintin. *Wilts* 4E 35
Stanton Street. *Suff* 4B 66
Stanton under Bardon. *Leics* 4B 74
Stanton upon Hine Heath
Shrp 3H 71
Stanton Wick. *Bath* 5B 34
Stanwardine in the Fields
Shrp 3G 71
Stanwardine in the Wood
Shrp 3G 71
Stanway. *Essx* 3C 54
Stanway. *Glos* 2F 49
Stanwell. *Surr* 3B 38
Stanwell Green. *Suff* 3D 66
Stanwell Moor. *Surr* 3B 38
Stanwick. *Nptn* 3G 63
Stanydale. *Shet* 6D 173
Staoinebrig. *W Isl* 5C 170
Stape. *N Yor* 5E 107
Stapehill. *Dors* 2F 15
Stapeley. *Ches E* 1A 72
Stapenhill. *Staf* 3G 73
Staple. *Kent* 5G 41
Staple Cross. *Devn* 4D 20
Staplecross. *E Sus* 3B 28
Staplefield. *W Sus* 3D 27
Staple Fitzpaine. *Som* 1F 13
Stapleford. *Cambs* 5D 64
Stapleford. *Herts* 4D 52
Stapleford. *Leics* 4F 75
Stapleford. *Linc* 5F 87
Stapleford. *Notts* 2B 74
Stapleford. *Wilts* 3F 23
Stapleford Abbotts. *Essx* 1G 39
Stapleford Tawney. *Essx* 1G 39
Staplegrove. *Som* 4F 21
Staplehay. *Som* 4F 21
Staple Hill. *S Glo* 4B 34
Staplehurst. *Kent* 1B 28
Staplers. *IOW* 4D 16
Stapleton. *Bris* 4B 34
Stapleton. *Cumb* 2G 113
Stapleton. *Here* 4F 59
Stapleton. *Leics* 1B 62
Stapleton. *N Yor* 3F 105
Stapleton. *Shrp* 5G 71
Stapleton. *Som* 4H 21
Stapley. *Som* 1E 13
Staploe. *Bed* 4A 64
Staplow. *Here* 1B 48
Star. *Fife* 3F 137
Star. *Pemb* 1G 43
Starbeck. *N Yor* 4F 99
Starbotton. *N Yor* 2B 98
Starcross. *Devn* 4C 12
Stareton. *Warw* 3H 61
Starkholmes. *Derbs* 5H 85
Starling. *G Man* 3F 91
Starling's Green. *Essx* 2E 53
Starston. *Norf* 2E 67
Start. *Devn* 4E 9
Startforth. *Dur* 3D 104
Start Hill. *Essx* 3F 53
Startley. *Wilts* 3E 35
Stathe. *Som* 4G 21
Stathern. *Leics* 2E 75
Station Town. *Dur* 1B 106
Staughton Green. *Cambs* 4A 64
Staughton Highway. *Cambs* 4A 64
Staunton. *Glos*
nr. Cheltenham 3C 48
nr. Monmouth 4A 48
Staunton in the Vale. *Notts* 1F 75
Staunton on Arrow. *Here* 4F 59
Staunton on Wye. *Here* 1G 47
Staveley. *Cumb* 5F 103
Staveley. *Derbs* 3B 86
Staveley. *N Yor* 3F 99
Staveley-in-Cartmel. *Cumb* 1C 96
Staverton. *Devn* 2D 9
Staverton. *Glos* 3D 49
Staverton. *Nptn* 4C 62
Staverton. *Wilts* 5D 34
Stawell. *Som* 3G 21
Stawley. *Som* 4D 20
Staxigoe. *High* 3F 169
Staxton. *N Yor* 2E 101
Staylittle. *Powy* 1A 58
Staynall. *Lanc* 5C 96
Staythorpe. *Notts* 5E 87
Stean. *N Yor* 2C 98
Stearsby. *N Yor* 2A 100
Steart. *Som* 2F 21
Stebbing. *Essx* 3G 53
Stebbing Green. *Essx* 3G 53
Stedham. *W Sus* 4G 25
Steel. *Nmbd* 4C 114
Steel Cross. *E Sus* 2G 27
Steelend. *Fife* 4C 136
Steele Road. *Bord* 5H 119
Steel Heath. *Shrp* 2H 71
Steen's Bridge. *Here* 5H 59
Steep. *Hants* 4F 25
Steep Lane. *W Yor* 2A 92
Steeple. *Dors* 4E 15
Steeple. *Essx* 5C 54
Steeple Ashton. *Wilts* 1E 23
Steeple Aston. *Oxon* 3C 50
Steeple Barton. *Oxon* 3C 50
Steeple Bumpstead. *Essx* 1G 53
Steeple Claydon. *Buck* 3E 51
Steeple Gidding. *Cambs* 2A 64
Steeple Langford. *Wilts* 3F 23
Steeple Morden. *Cambs* 1C 52
Steeton. *W Yor* 5C 98
Stein. *High* 3B 154
Steinmanhill. *Abers* 4E 161
Stelling Minnis. *Kent* 1F 29
Stembridge. *Som* 4H 21
Stemster. *High*
nr. Halkirk 2D 169
nr. Westfield 2C 168
Stenalees. *Corn* 3E 6
Stenhill. *Devn* 1D 12
Stenhouse. *Edin* 2F 129
Stenhousemuir. *Falk* 1B 128
Stenigot. *Linc* 2B 88
Stenscholl. *High* 2D 155
Stenso. *Orkn* 5C 172
Stenson. *Derbs* 3H 73
Stenson Fields. *Derbs* 2H 73
Stenton. *E Lot* 2C 130
Stenwith. *Linc* 2F 75
Steòrnabhagh. *W Isl* 4G 171
Stepaside. *Pemb* 4F 43
Stepford. *Dum* 1F 111
Stepney. *G Lon* 2E 39
Steppingley. *C Beds* 2A 52
Stepps. *N Lan* 3H 127
Sterndale Moor. *Derbs* 4F 85
Sternfield. *Suff* 4F 67
Stert. *Wilts* 1F 23
Stetchworth. *Cambs* 5F 65
Stevenage. *Herts* 3C 52
Stevenston. *N Ayr* 5D 126
Stevenstone. *Devn* 1F 11
Steventon. *Hants* 2D 24

Talog – Thorpe Hamlet

Talog. Carm 2H 43
Talsarn. Carm 3A 46
Talsarn. Cdgn 5E 57
Talsarnau. Gwyn 2F 69
Talskiddy. Corn 2D 6
Talwrn. IOA 3D 81
Talwrn. Wrex 1E 71
Tal-y-Bont. Cnwy 4G 81
Tal-y-bont. Cdgn 2F 57
Tal-y-bont. Gwyn
nr. Bangor 3F 81
nr. Barmouth 3E 69
Talybont-on-Usk. Powy 3E 46
Tal-y-cafn. Cnwy 3G 81
Tal-y-coed. Mon 4H 47
Tal-y-llyn. Gwyn 5G 69
Talyllyn. Powy 3E 46
Talysarn. Gwyn 5D 81
Tal-y-waenydd. Gwyn 1F 69
Talywain. Torf 5F 47
Tal-y-Wern. Powy 5H 69
Tamerton Foliot. Plym 2A 8
Tamworth. Staf 5G 73
Tamworth Green. Linc 1C 76
Tandlehill. Ren 3F 127
Tandragee. Arm 5F 175
Tandridge. Surr 5E 39
Tanerdy. Carm 3E 45
Tanfield. Dur 4E 115
Tanfield Lea. Dur 4E 115
Tangasdal. W Isl 8B 170
Tang Hall. York 4A 100
Tangiers. Pemb 3D 42
Tangley. Hants 1B 24
Tangmere. W Sus 5A 26
Tangwick. Shet 4D 173
Tankerness. Orkn 7E 172
Tankersley. S Yor 1H 85
Tankerton. Kent 4F 41
Tan-lan. Cnwy 4G 81
Tan-lan. Gwyn 1F 69
Tannach. High 4F 169
Tannadice. Ang 3D 145
Tanner's Green. Worc 3E 61
Tannington. Suff 4E 67
Tannochside. N Lan 3A 128
Tan Office Green. Suff 5G 65
Tansley. Derbs 5H 85
Tansley Knoll. Derbs 4H 85
Tansor. Nptn 1H 63
Tantobie. Dur 4E 115
Tanton. N Yor 3C 106
Tanvats. Linc 4A 88
Tanworth-in-Arden. Warw 3F 61
Tan-y-bwlch. Gwyn 1F 69
Tan-y-fron. Cnwy 4B 82
Tanyfron. Wrex 5E 83
Tanygrisiau. Gwyn 1F 69
Tan-y-groes. Cdgn 1C 44
Tan-y-pistyll. Powy 3C 70
Tan-yr-allt. Den 2C 82
Taobh a Chaolais. W Isl 7C 170
Taobh a Deas Loch Aineort
W Isl 6C 170
Taobh a Ghlinne. W Isl 6F 171
Taobh a Tuath Loch Aineort
W Isl 6C 170
Taplow. Buck 2A 38
Tapton. Derbs 3A 86
Tarbert. Arg
on Jura 1E 125
on Kintyre 3G 125
Tarbert. W Isl 8D 171
Tarbet. Arg 3C 134
Tarbet. High
nr. Mallaig 4F 147
nr. Scourie 4B 166
Tarbock Green. Mers 2G 83
Tarbolton. S Ayr 2D 116
Tarbrax. S Lan 4D 128
Tardebigge. Worc 4D 61
Tarfside. Ang 1D 145
Tarland. Abers 3B 152
Tarleton. Lanc 2C 90
Tarlogie. High 5E 165
Tarlscough. Lanc 3C 90
Tarlton. Glos 2E 35
Tarnbrook. Lanc 4E 97
Tarnock. Som 1G 21
Tarns. Cumb 5C 112
Tarporley. Ches W 4H 83
Tarpots. Essx 2B 40
Tarr. Som 3E 20
Tarrant Crawford. Dors 2E 15
Tarrant Gunville. Dors 1E 15
Tarrant Hinton. Dors 1E 15
Tarrant Keyneston. Dors 2E 15
Tarrant Launceston. Dors 2E 15
Tarrant Monkton. Dors 2E 15
Tarrant Rawston. Dors 2E 15
Tarrant Rushton. Dors 2E 15
Tarrel. High 5F 165
Tarring Neville. E Sus 5F 27
Tarrington. Here 1B 48
Tarsappie. Per 1D 136
Tarscabhaig. High 3D 147
Tarskavaig. High 3D 147
Tarves. Abers 5F 161
Tarvie. High 3G 157
Tarvin. Ches W 4G 83
Tasburgh. Norf 1E 66
Tasley. Shrp 1A 60
Taston. Oxon 3B 50
Tatenhill. Staf 3G 73
Tathall End. Mil 1G 51
Tatham. Lanc 3F 97
Tathwell. Linc 2C 88
Tatling End. Buck 2B 38
Tatsfield. Surr 5F 39
Tattenhall. Ches W 5G 83
Tatterford. Norf 3A 78
Tattersett. Norf 2H 77
Tattershall. Linc 5B 88
Tattershall Bridge. Linc 5A 88
Tattershall Thorpe. Linc 5B 88
Tattingstone. Suff 2E 55
Tattingstone White Horse
Suff 2E 55
Tattle Bank. Warw 4F 61
Tatworth. Som 2G 13
Taunton. Som 4F 21
Taverham. Norf 4D 78
Taverners Green. Essx 4F 53
Tavernspite. Pemb 3F 43
Tavistock. Devn 5E 11
Tavool House. Arg 1B 132
Taw Green. Devn 3G 11
Tawstock. Devn 4F 19
Taxal. Derbs 2E 85
Tayinloan. Arg 5E 125
Taynish. Arg 1F 125
Taynton. Glos 3C 48
Taynton. Oxon 4H 49
Taynuilt. Arg 5E 141
Tayport. Fife 1G 137
Tay Road Bridge. D'dee 1G 137
Tayvallich. Arg 1F 125
Tealby. Linc 1A 88
Tealing. Ang 5D 144
Teams. Tyne 3F 115
Teangue. High 3E 147
Teanna Mhachair. W Isl 2C 170
Tebay. Cumb 4H 103
Tebworth. C Beds 3H 51
Tedburn St Mary. Devn 3B 12
Teddington. Glos 2E 49
Teddington. G Lon 3C 38
Tedsmore. Shrp 3F 71
Tedstone Delamere. Here 5A 60
Tedstone Wafer. Here 5A 60
Teesport. Red C 2C 106
Teesside. Stoc T 2C 106
Teeton. Nptn 3D 62
Teffont Evias. Wilts 3E 23
Teffont Magna. Wilts 3E 23
Tegryn. Pemb 1G 43
Teigh. Rut 4F 75
Teigncombe. Devn 4G 11
Teigngrace. Devn 5B 12
Teignmouth. Devn 5C 12
Telford. Telf 4A 72
Telham. E Sus 4B 28
Tellisford. Som 1D 22
Telscombe. E Sus 5F 27
Telscombe Cliffs. E Sus 5E 27
Tempar. Per 3D 142
Templand. Dum 1B 112
Temple. Corn 5B 10
Temple. Glas 3G 127
Temple. Midl 4G 129
Temple Balsall. W Mid 3G 61
Temple Bar. Carm 4F 45
Temple Bar. Cdgn 5E 57
Temple Cloud. Bath 1B 22
Templecombe. Som 4C 22
Temple Ewell. Kent 1G 29
Temple Grafton. Warw 5F 61
Temple Guiting. Glos 3F 49
Templehall. Fife 4E 137
Temple Hirst. N Yor 2G 93
Temple Normanton. Derbs 4B 86
Templepatrick. Ant 3G 175
Temple Sowerby. Cumb 2H 103
Templeton. Devn 1B 12
Templeton. Pemb 3F 43
Templeton. W Ber 5B 36
Templetown. Dur 5E 115
Tempsford. C Beds 5A 64
Tenandry. Per 2G 143
Tenbury Wells. Worc 4H 59
Tenby. Pemb 4F 43
Tendring. Essx 3E 55
Tendring Green. Essx 3E 55
Tenga. Arg 4G 139
Ten Mile Bank. Norf 1F 65
Tenterden. Kent 2C 28
Terfyn. Cnwy 3B 82
Terhill. Som 3E 21
Terling. Essx 4A 54
Ternhill. Shrp 2A 72
Terregles. Dum 2G 111
Terrick. Buck 5G 51
Terrington. N Yor 2A 100
Terrington St Clement. Norf 3E 77
Terrington St John. Norf 4E 77
Terry's Green. Warw 3F 61
Teston. Kent 5B 40
Testwood. Hants 1B 16
Tetbury. Glos 2D 35
Tetbury Upton. Glos 2D 35
Tetchill. Shrp 2F 71
Tetcott. Devn 3D 10
Tetford. Linc 3C 88
Tetney. Linc 4G 95
Tetney Lock. Linc 4G 95
Tetsworth. Oxon 5E 51
Tettenhall. W Mid 5C 72
Teversal. Notts 4B 86
Teversham. Cambs 5D 65
Teviothead. Bord 4G 119
Tewel. Abers 5F 153
Tewin. Herts 4C 52
Tewkesbury. Glos 2D 49
Teynham. Kent 4D 40
Teynham Street. Kent 4D 40
Thackthwaite. Cumb 2F 103
Thakeham. W Sus 4C 26
Thame. Oxon 5F 51
Thames Ditton. Surr 4C 38
Thames Haven. Thur 2B 40
Thamesmead. G Lon 2F 39
Thamesport. Medw 3C 40
Thanington Without. Kent 5F 41
Thankerton. S Lan 1B 118
Tharston. Norf 1D 66
Thatcham. W Ber 5D 36
Thatto Heath. Mers 1H 83
Thaxted. Essx 2G 53
Theakston. N Yor 1F 99
Thealby. N Lin 3B 94
Theale. Som 2H 21
Theale. W Ber 4E 37
Thearne. E Yor 1D 94
Theberton. Suff 4G 67
Theddingworth. Leics 2D 62
Theddlethorpe All Saints
Linc 2D 88
Theddlethorpe St Helen
Linc 2D 89
Thelbridge Barton. Devn 1A 12
Thelnetham. Suff 3C 66
Thelveton. Norf 2D 66
Thelwall. Warr 2A 84
Themelthorpe. Norf 3C 78
Thenford. Nptn 1D 50
Therfield. Herts 2D 52
Thetford. Linc 4A 76
Thetford. Norf 2A 66
Thethwaite. Cumb 5E 113
Theydon Bois. Essx 1F 39
Thick Hollins. W Yor 3B 92
Thickwood. Wilts 4D 34
Thimbleby. Linc 4B 88
Thimbleby. N Yor 5B 106
Thingwall. Mers 2E 83
Thirlby. N Yor 1G 99
Thirlestane. Bord 5B 130
Thirn. N Yor 1E 98
Thirsk. N Yor 1G 99
Thirtleby. E Yor 1E 95
Thistleton. Lanc 1C 90
Thistleton. Rut 4G 75
Thistley Green. Suff 3F 65
Thixendale. N Yor 3C 100
Thockrington. Nmbd 2C 114
Tholomas Drove. Cambs 5D 76
Tholthorpe. N Yor 3G 99
Thomas Chapel. Pemb 4F 43
Thomas Close. Cumb 5F 113
Thomastown. Abers 4E 160
Thomastown. Rhon 3D 32
Thompson. Norf 1B 66
Thomshill. Mor 3G 159
Thong. Kent 3A 40
Thongsbridge. W Yor 4B 92
Thoralby. N Yor 1C 98
Thoresby. Notts 3D 86
Thoresway. Linc 1A 88
Thorganby. Linc 1B 88
Thorganby. N Yor 5A 100
Thorgill. N Yor 5E 107
Thorington. Suff 3G 67
Thorington Street. Suff 2D 54
Thorlby. N Yor 4B 98
Thorley. Herts 4E 53
Thorley Street. Herts 4E 53
Thorley Street. IOW 4B 16
Thormanby. N Yor 2G 99
Thorn. Powy 4E 59
Thornaby-on-Tees. Stoc T 3B 106
Thornage. Norf 2C 78
Thornborough. Buck 2F 51
Thornborough. N Yor 2E 99
Thornbury. Devn 2E 11
Thornbury. Here 5A 60
Thornbury. S Glo 2B 34
Thornby. Cumb 4D 112
Thornby. Nptn 3D 62
Thorncliffe. Staf 5E 85
Thorncombe. Dors 2G 13
Thorncombe Street. Surr 1A 26
Thorncote Green. C Beds 1B 52
Thorndon. Suff 4D 66
Thorndon Cross. Devn 3F 11
Thorne. S Yor 3G 93
Thornehillhead. Devn 1E 11
Thorner. W Yor 5F 99
Thorne St Margaret. Som 4D 20
Thorney. Notts 3F 87
Thorney. Pet 5B 76
Thorney. Som 4H 21
Thorney Hill. Hants 3G 15
Thorney Toll. Cambs 5C 76
Thornfalcon. Som 4F 21
Thornford. Dors 1B 14
Thorngrafton. Nmbd 3A 114
Thorngrove. Som 3G 21
Thorngumbald. E Yor 2F 95
Thornham. Norf 1G 77
Thornham Magna. Suff 3D 66
Thornham Parva. Suff 3D 66
Thornhaugh. Pet 5H 75
Thornhill. Cphy 3E 33
Thornhill. Cumb 4B 102
Thornhill. Derbs 2F 85
Thornhill. Dum 5A 118
Thornhill. Sotn 1C 16
Thornhill. Stir 4F 135
Thornhill. W Yor 3C 92
Thornhill Lees. W Yor 3C 92
Thornhills. W Yor 2B 92
Thornholme. E Yor 3F 101
Thornicombe. Dors 2D 14
Thornington. Nmbd 1C 120
Thornley. Dur
nr. Durham 1A 106
nr. Tow Law 1E 105
Thornley Gate. Nmbd 4B 114
Thornliebank. E Ren 3G 127
Thornroan. Abers 5F 161
Thorns. Suff 5G 65
Thornsett. Derbs 2E 85
Thornthwaite. Cumb 2D 102
Thornthwaite. N Yor 4D 98
Thornton. Ang 4C 144
Thornton. Buck 2F 51
Thornton. E Yor 5B 100
Thornton. Fife 4E 137
Thornton. Lanc 5C 96
Thornton. Leics 5B 74
Thornton. Linc 4B 88
Thornton. Mers 4B 90
Thornton. Midd 3B 106
Thornton. Nmbd 5F 131
Thornton. Pemb 4D 42
Thornton. W Yor 1A 92
Thornton Curtis. N Lin 3D 94
Thorntonhall. S Lan 4G 127
Thornton Heath. G Lon 4E 39
Thornton Hough. Mers 2F 83
Thornton-in-Craven. N Yor 5B 98
Thornton in Lonsdale. N Yor 2F 97
Thornton-le-Beans. N Yor 5A 106
Thornton-le-Clay. N Yor 3A 100
Thornton-le-Dale. N Yor 1C 100
Thornton le Moor. Linc 1H 87
Thornton-le-Moor. N Yor 1F 99
Thornton-le-Moors. Ches W 3G 83
Thornton-le-Street. N Yor 1G 99
Thorntonloch. E Lot 2D 130
Thornton Rust. N Yor 1B 98
Thornton Steward. N Yor 1D 98
Thornton Watlass. N Yor 1E 99
Thornwood Common. Essx 5E 53
Thornythwaite. Cumb 2E 103
Thoroton. Notts 1E 75
Thorp Arch. W Yor 5G 99
Thorpe. Derbs 5F 85
Thorpe. E Yor 5D 101
Thorpe. Linc 2D 89
Thorpe. Norf 1G 67
Thorpe. N Yor 3C 98
Thorpe. Notts 1E 75
Thorpe. Surr 4B 38
Thorpe Abbotts. Norf 3D 66
Thorpe Acre. Leics 3C 74
Thorpe Arnold. Leics 3E 75
Thorpe Audlin. W Yor 3E 93
Thorpe Bassett. N Yor 2C 100
Thorpe Bay. S'end 2D 40
Thorpe by Water. Rut 1F 63
Thorpe Common. S Yor 1A 86
Thorpe Common. Suff 2F 55
Thorpe Constantine. Staf 5G 73
Thorpe End. Norf 4E 79
Thorpe Fendike. Linc 4D 88
Thorpe Green. Essx 3E 55
Thorpe Green. Suff 5B 66
Thorpe Hall. N Yor 2H 99
Thorpe Hamlet. Norf 5E 79

Thorpe Hesley – Torwood

Thorpe Hesley. *S Yor* 1A **86**
Thorpe in Balne. *S Yor* 3F **93**
Thorpe in the Fallows. *Linc* 2G **87**
Thorpe Langton. *Leics* 1E **63**
Thorpe Larches. *Dur* 2A **106**
Thorpe Latimer. *Linc* 1A **76**
Thorpe-le-Soken. *Essx* 3E **55**
Thorpe le Street. *E Yor* 5C **100**
Thorpe Malsor. *Nptn* 3F **63**
Thorpe Mandeville. *Nptn* 1D **50**
Thorpe Market. *Norf* 2E **79**
Thorpe Marriott. *Norf* 4D **78**
Thorpe Morieux. *Suff* 5B **66**
Thorpeness. *Suff* 5G **67**
Thorpe on the Hill. *Linc* 4G **87**
Thorpe on the Hill. *W Yor* 2D **92**
Thorpe St Andrew. *Norf* 5E **79**
Thorpe St Peter. *Linc* 4D **89**
Thorpe Salvin. *S Yor* 2C **86**
Thorpe Satchville. *Leics* 4E **75**
Thorpe Thewles. *Stoc T* 2A **106**
Thorpe Tilney. *Linc* 5A **88**
Thorpe Underwood. *N Yor* 4G **99**
Thorpe Waterville. *Nptn* 2H **63**
Thorpe Willoughby. *N Yor* 1F **93**
Thorpland. *Norf* 5F **77**
Thorrington. *Essx* 3D **54**
Thorverton. *Devn* 2C **12**
Thrandeston. *Suff* 3D **66**
Thrapston. *Nptn* 3G **63**
Thrashbush. *N Lan* 3A **128**
Threapland. *Cumb* 1C **102**
Threapland. *N Yor* 3B **98**
Threapwood. *Ches W* 1G **71**
Threapwood. *Staf* 1E **73**
Three Ashes. *Here* 3A **48**
Three Bridges. *Linc* 2D **88**
Three Bridges. *W Sus* 2D **27**
Three Burrows. *Corn* 4B **6**
Three Chimneys. *Kent* 2C **28**
Three Cocks. *Powy* 2E **47**
Three Crosses. *Swan* 3E **31**
Three Cups Corner. *E Sus* 3H **27**
Threehammer Common
Norf 3F **79**
Three Holes. *Norf* 5E **77**
Threekingham. *Linc* 2H **75**
Three Leg Cross. *E Sus* 2A **28**
Three Legged Cross. *Dors* 2F **15**
Three Mile Cross. *Wok* 5F **37**
Threemilestone. *Corn* 4B **6**
Three Oaks. *E Sus* 4C **28**
Threlkeld. *Cumb* 2E **102**
Threshfield. *N Yor* 3B **98**
Thrigby. *Norf* 4G **79**
Thringarth. *Dur* 2C **104**
Thringstone. *Leics* 4B **74**
Thrintoft. *N Yor* 5A **106**
Thriplow. *Cambs* 1E **53**
Throckenholt. *Linc* 5C **76**
Throcking. *Herts* 2D **52**
Throckley. *Tyne* 3E **115**
Throckmorton. *Worc* 1E **49**
Throop. *Bour* 3G **15**
Throphill. *Nmbd* 1E **115**
Thropton. *Nmbd* 4E **121**
Throsk. *Stir* 4A **136**
Througham. *Glos* 5E **49**
Throughgate. *Dum* 1F **111**
Throwleigh. *Devn* 3G **11**
Throwley. *Kent* 5D **40**
Throwley Forstal. *Kent* 5D **40**
Throxenby. *N Yor* 1E **101**
Thrumpton. *Notts* 2C **74**
Thrumster. *High* 4F **169**
Thrunton. *Nmbd* 3E **121**
Thrupp. *Glos* 5D **48**
Thrupp. *Oxon* 4C **50**
Thrushelton. *Devn* 4E **11**
Thrushgill. *Lanc* 3F **97**
Thrussington. *Leics* 4D **74**
Thruxton. *Hants* 2A **24**
Thruxton. *Here* 2H **47**
Thrybergh. *S Yor* 1B **86**
Thulston. *Derbs* 2B **74**
Thundergay. *N Ayr* 5G **125**
Thundersley. *Essx* 2B **40**
Thundridge. *Herts* 4D **52**
Thurcaston. *Leics* 4C **74**
Thurcroft. *S Yor* 2B **86**
Thurdon. *Corn* 1C **10**
Thurgarton. *Norf* 2D **78**
Thurgarton. *Notts* 1D **74**
Thurgoland. *S Yor* 4C **92**
Thurlaston. *Leics* 1C **62**
Thurlaston. *Warw* 3B **62**
Thurlbear. *Som* 4F **21**
Thurlby. *Linc*
nr. Alford 3D **89**
nr. Baston 4A **76**
nr. Lincoln 4G **87**
Thurleigh. *Bed* 5H **63**
Thurlestone. *Devn* 4C **8**
Thurloxton. *Som* 3F **21**
Thurlstone. *S Yor* 4C **92**
Thurlton. *Norf* 1G **67**
Thurmaston. *Leics* 5D **74**
Thurnby. *Leics* 5D **74**
Thurne. *Norf* 4G **79**
Thurnham. *Kent* 5C **40**
Thurning. *Norf* 3C **78**
Thurning. *Nptn* 2H **63**
Thurnscoe. *S Yor* 4E **93**
Thursby. *Cumb* 4E **113**
Thursford. *Norf* 2B **78**
Thursford Green. *Norf* 2B **78**
Thursley. *Surr* 2A **26**
Thurso. *High* 2D **168**
Thurso East. *High* 2D **168**
Thurstaston. *Mers* 2E **83**
Thurston. *Suff* 4B **66**
Thurston End. *Suff* 5G **65**
Thurstonfield. *Cumb* 4E **112**
Thurstonland. *W Yor* 3B **92**
Thurton. *Norf* 5F **79**
Thurvaston. *Derbs*
nr. Ashbourne 2F **73**
nr. Derby 2G **73**
Thuxton. *Norf* 5C **78**
Thwaite. *Dur* 3D **104**
Thwaite. *N Yor* 5B **104**
Thwaite. *Suff* 4D **66**
Thwaite Head. *Cumb* 5E **103**
Thwaites. *W Yor* 5C **98**
Thwaite St Mary. *Norf* 1F **67**
Thwing. *E Yor* 2E **101**
Tibbermore. *Per* 1C **136**
Tibberton. *Glos* 3C **48**
Tibberton. *Telf* 3A **72**
Tibberton. *Worc* 5D **60**
Tibenham. *Norf* 2D **66**
Tibshelf. *Derbs* 4B **86**
Tibthorpe. *E Yor* 4D **100**
Ticehurst. *E Sus* 2A **28**
Tichborne. *Hants* 3D **24**
Tickencote. *Rut* 5G **75**
Tickenham. *N Som* 4H **33**
Tickhill. *S Yor* 1C **86**
Ticklerton. *Shrp* 1G **59**
Ticknall. *Derbs* 3A **74**
Tickton. *E Yor* 5E **101**
Tidbury Green. *W Mid* 3F **61**
Tidcombe. *Wilts* 1A **24**
Tiddington. *Oxon* 5E **51**
Tiddington. *Warw* 5G **61**
Tiddleywink. *Wilts* 4D **34**
Tidebrook. *E Sus* 3H **27**
Tideford. *Corn* 3H **7**
Tideford Cross. *Corn* 2H **7**
Tidenham. *Glos* 2A **34**
Tideswell. *Derbs* 3F **85**
Tidmarsh. *W Ber* 4E **37**
Tidmington. *Warw* 2A **50**
Tidpit. *Hants* 1F **15**
Tidworth. *Wilts* 2H **23**
Tidworth Camp. *Wilts* 2H **23**
Tiers Cross. *Pemb* 3D **42**
Tiffield. *Nptn* 5D **62**
Tifty. *Abers* 4E **161**
Tigerton. *Ang* 2E **145**
Tighnabruaich. *Arg* 2A **126**
Tigley. *Devn* 2D **8**
Tilbrook. *Cambs* 4H **63**
Tilbury. *Thur* 3H **39**
Tilbury Green. *Essx* 1H **53**
Tilbury Juxta Clare. *Essx* 1A **54**
Tile Hill. *W Mid* 3G **61**
Tilehurst. *Read* 4E **37**
Tilford. *Surr* 2G **25**
Tilgate Forest Row. *W Sus* 2D **26**
Tillathrowie. *Abers* 5B **160**
Tillers Green. *Glos* 2B **48**
Tillery. *Abers* 1G **153**
Tilley. *Shrp* 3H **71**
Tillicoultry. *Clac* 4B **136**
Tillingham. *Essx* 5C **54**
Tillington. *Here* 1H **47**
Tillington. *W Sus* 3A **26**
Tillington Common. *Here* 1H **47**
Tillybirloch. *Abers* 3D **152**
Tillyfourie. *Abers* 2D **152**
Tilmanstone. *Kent* 5H **41**
Tilney All Saints. *Norf* 4E **77**
Tilney Fen End. *Norf* 4E **77**
Tilney High End. *Norf* 4E **77**
Tilney St Lawrence. *Norf* 4E **77**
Tilshead. *Wilts* 2F **23**
Tilstock. *Shrp* 2H **71**
Tilston. *Ches W* 5G **83**
Tilstone Fearnall. *Ches W* 4H **83**
Tilsworth. *C Beds* 3H **51**
Tilton on the Hill. *Leics* 5E **75**
Tiltups End. *Glos* 2D **34**
Timberland. *Linc* 5A **88**
Timbersbrook. *Ches E* 4C **84**
Timberscombe. *Som* 2C **20**
Timble. *N Yor* 4D **98**
Timperley. *G Man* 2B **84**
Timsbury. *Bath* 1B **22**
Timsbury. *Hants* 4B **24**
Timsgearraidh. *W Isl* 4C **171**
Timworth Green. *Suff* 4A **66**
Tincleton. *Dors* 3C **14**
Tindale. *Cumb* 4H **113**
Tindale Crescent. *Dur* 2F **105**
Tingewick. *Buck* 2E **51**
Tingrith. *C Beds* 2A **52**
Tingwall. *Orkn* 5D **172**
Tinhay. *Devn* 4D **11**
Tinshill. *W Yor* 1C **92**
Tinsley. *S Yor* 1B **86**
Tinsley Green. *W Sus* 2D **27**
Tintagel. *Corn* 4A **10**
Tintern. *Mon* 5A **48**
Tintinhull. *Som* 1H **13**
Tintwistle. *Derbs* 1E **85**
Tinwald. *Dum* 1B **112**
Tinwell. *Rut* 5H **75**
Tippacott. *Devn* 2A **20**
Tipperty. *Abers* 1G **153**
Tipps End. *Cambs* 1E **65**
Tiptoe. *Hants* 3A **16**
Tipton. *W Mid* 1D **60**
Tipton St John. *Devn* 3D **12**
Tiptree. *Essx* 4B **54**
Tiptree Heath. *Essx* 4B **54**
Tirabad. *Powy* 1B **46**
Tircoed Forest Village. *Swan* 5G **45**
Tiree Airport. *Arg* 4B **138**
Tirinie. *Per* 2F **143**
Tirley. *Glos* 3D **48**
Tiroran. *Arg* 1B **132**
Tir-Phil. *Cphy* 5E **47**
Tirril. *Cumb* 2G **103**
Tirryside. *High* 2C **164**
Tir-y-dail. *Carm* 4G **45**
Tisbury. *Wilts* 4E **23**
Tisman's Common. *W Sus* 2B **26**
Tissington. *Derbs* 5F **85**
Titchberry. *Devn* 4C **18**
Titchfield. *Hants* 2D **16**
Titchmarsh. *Nptn* 3H **63**
Titchwell. *Norf* 1G **77**
Tithby. *Notts* 2D **74**
Titley. *Here* 5F **59**
Titlington. *Nmbd* 3E **121**
Titsey. *Surr* 5F **39**
Titson. *Corn* 2C **10**
Tittensor. *Staf* 2C **72**
Tittleshall. *Norf* 3A **78**
Titton. *Worc* 4C **60**
Tiverton. *Ches W* 4H **83**
Tiverton. *Devn* 1C **12**
Tivetshall St Margaret. *Norf* 2D **66**
Tivetshall St Mary. *Norf* 2D **66**
Tivington. *Som* 2C **20**
Tixall. *Staf* 3D **73**
Tixover. *Rut* 5G **75**
Toab. *Orkn* 7E **172**
Toab. *Shet* 10E **173**
Toadmoor. *Derbs* 5A **86**
Tobermory. *Arg* 3G **139**
Toberonochy. *Arg* 3E **133**
Tobha Beag. *W Isl* 5C **170**
Tobha-Beag. *W Isl* 1E **170**
Tobha Mor. *W Isl* 5C **170**
Tobhtarol. *W Isl* 4D **171**
Tobson. *W Isl* 4D **171**
Tocabhaig. *High* 2E **147**
Tocher. *Abers* 5D **160**
Tockenham. *Wilts* 4F **35**
Tockenham Wick. *Wilts* 3F **35**
Tockholes. *Bkbn* 2E **91**
Tockington. *S Glo* 3B **34**
Tockwith. *N Yor* 4G **99**
Todber. *Dors* 4D **22**
Todding. *Here* 3G **59**
Toddington. *C Beds* 3A **52**
Toddington. *Glos* 2F **49**
Todenham. *Glos* 2H **49**
Todhills. *Cumb* 3E **113**
Todmorden. *W Yor* 2H **91**
Todwick. *S Yor* 2B **86**
Toft. *Cambs* 5C **64**
Toft. *Linc* 4H **75**
Toft Hill. *Dur* 2E **105**
Toft Monks. *Norf* 1G **67**
Toft next Newton. *Linc* 2H **87**
Toftrees. *Norf* 3A **78**
Tofts. *High* 2F **169**
Toftwood. *Norf* 4B **78**
Togston. *Nmbd* 4G **121**
Tokavaig. *High* 2E **147**
Tokers Green. *Oxon* 4F **37**
Tolastadh a Chaolais
W Isl 4D **171**
Tolladine. *Worc* 5C **60**
Tolland. *Som* 3E **20**
Tollard Farnham. *Dors* 1E **15**
Tollard Royal. *Wilts* 1E **15**
Toll Bar. *S Yor* 4F **93**
Toller Fratrum. *Dors* 3A **14**
Toller Porcorum. *Dors* 3A **14**
Tollerton. *N Yor* 3H **99**
Tollerton. *Notts* 2D **74**
Toller Whelme. *Dors* 2A **14**
Tollesbury. *Essx* 4C **54**
Tolleshunt D'Arcy. *Essx* 4C **54**
Tolleshunt Knights. *Essx* 4C **54**
Tolleshunt Major. *Essx* 4C **54**
Tollie. *High* 3H **157**
Tollie Farm. *High* 1A **156**
Tolm. *W Isl* 4G **171**
Tolpuddle. *Dors* 3C **14**
Tolstadh bho Thuath
W Isl 3H **171**
Tolworth. *G Lon* 4C **38**
Tomachlaggan. *Mor* 1F **151**
Tomaknock. *Per* 1A **136**
Tomatin. *High* 1C **150**
Tombuidhe. *Arg* 3H **133**
Tomdoun. *High* 3D **148**
Tomich. *High*
nr. Cannich 1F **149**
nr. Invergordon 1B **158**
nr. Lairg 3D **164**
Tomintoul. *Mor* 2F **151**
Tomnavoulin. *Mor* 1G **151**
Tomsléibhe. *Arg* 5A **140**
Ton. *Mon* 2G **33**
Tonbridge. *Kent* 1G **27**
Tondu. *B'end* 3B **32**
Tonedale. *Som* 4E **21**
Tonfanau. *Gwyn* 5E **69**
Tong. *Shrp* 5B **72**
Tonge. *Leics* 3B **74**
Tong Forge. *Shrp* 5B **72**
Tongham. *Surr* 2G **25**
Tongland. *Dum* 4D **111**
Tong Norton. *Shrp* 5B **72**
Tongue. *High* 3F **167**
Tongue End. *Linc* 4A **76**
Tongwynlais. *Card* 3E **33**
Tonmawr. *Neat* 2B **32**
Tonna. *Neat* 2A **32**
Tonnau. *Neat* 2A **32**
Ton Pentre. *Rhon* 2C **32**
Ton-Teg. *Rhon* 3D **32**
Tonwell. *Herts* 4D **52**
Tonypandy. *Rhon* 2C **32**
Tonyrefail. *Rhon* 3D **32**
Toot Baldon. *Oxon* 5D **50**
Toot Hill. *Essx* 5F **53**
Toothill. *Hants* 1B **16**
Topcliffe. *N Yor* 2G **99**
Topcliffe. *W Yor* 2C **92**
Topcroft. *Norf* 1E **67**
Topcroft Street. *Norf* 1E **67**
Toppesfield. *Essx* 2H **53**
Toppings. *G Man* 3F **91**
Toprow. *Norf* 1D **66**
Topsham. *Devn* 4C **12**
Torbay. *Torb* 2F **9**
Torbeg. *N Ayr* 3C **122**
Torbothie. *N Lan* 4B **128**
Torbryan. *Devn* 2E **9**
Torcross. *Devn* 4E **9**
Tore. *High* 3A **158**
Torgyle. *High* 2F **149**
Torinturk. *Arg* 3G **125**
Torksey. *Linc* 3F **87**
Torlum. *W Isl* 3C **170**
Torlundy. *High* 1F **141**
Tormarton. *S Glo* 4C **34**
Tormitchell. *S Ayr* 5B **116**
Tormore. *High* 3E **147**
Tormore. *N Ayr* 2C **122**
Tornagrain. *High* 4B **158**
Tornaveen. *Abers* 3D **152**
Torness. *High* 1H **149**
Toronto. *Dur* 1E **105**
Torpenhow. *Cumb* 1D **102**
Torphichen. *W Lot* 2C **128**
Torphins. *Abers* 3D **152**
Torpoint. *Corn* 3A **8**
Torquay. *Torb* 2F **9**
Torr. *Devn* 3B **8**
Torra. *Arg* 4B **124**
Torran. *High* 4E **155**
Torrance. *E Dun* 2H **127**
Torrans. *Arg* 1B **132**
Torranyard. *N Ayr* 5E **127**
Torre. *Som* 3D **20**
Torre. *Torb* 2F **9**
Torridon. *High* 3B **156**
Torrin. *High* 1D **147**
Torrisdale. *Arg* 2B **122**
Torrisdale. *High* 2G **167**
Torrish. *High* 2G **165**
Torrisholme. *Lanc* 3D **96**
Torroble. *High* 3C **164**
Torroy. *High* 4C **164**
Torry. *Aber* 3G **153**
Torryburn. *Fife* 1D **128**
Torthorwald. *Dum* 2B **112**
Tortington. *W Sus* 5B **26**
Tortworth. *S Glo* 2C **34**
Torvaig. *High* 4D **155**
Torver. *Cumb* 5D **102**
Torwood. *Falk* 1B **128**

Tumbler's Green – Upper Sanday

Tumbler's Green. *Essx* 3B **54**
Tumby. *Linc* 4B **88**
Tumby Woodside. *Linc* 5B **88**
Tummel Bridge. *Per* 3E **143**
Tunbridge Wells, Royal *Kent* 2G **27**
Tunga. *W Isl* 4G **171**
Tungate. *Norf* 3E **79**
Tunley. *Bath* 1B **22**
Tunstall. *E Yor* 1G **95**
Tunstall. *Kent* 4C **40**
Tunstall. *Lanc* 2F **97**
Tunstall. *Norf* 5G **79**
Tunstall. *N Yor* 5F **105**
Tunstall. *Staf* 3B **72**
Tunstall. *Stoke* 5C **84**
Tunstall. *Suff* 5F **67**
Tunstall. *Tyne* 4G **115**
Tunstead. *Derbs* 3F **85**
Tunstead. *Norf* 3E **79**
Tunstead Milton. *Derbs* 2E **85**
Tunworth. *Hants* 2E **25**
Tupsley. *Here* 1A **48**
Tupton. *Derbs* 4A **86**
Turfholm. *S Lan* 1H **117**
Turfmoor. *Devn* 2F **13**
Turgis Green. *Hants* 1E **25**
Turkdean. *Glos* 4G **49**
Turkey Island. *Hants* 1D **16**
Tur Langton. *Leics* 1E **62**
Turleigh. *Wilts* 5D **34**
Turlin Moor. *Pool* 3E **15**
Turnastone. *Here* 2G **47**
Turnberry. *S Ayr* 4B **116**
Turnchapel. *Plym* 3A **8**
Turnditch. *Derbs* 1G **73**
Turners Hill. *W Sus* 2E **27**
Turners Puddle. *Dors* 3D **14**
Turnford. *Herts* 5D **52**
Turnhouse. *Edin* 2E **129**
Turnworth. *Dors* 2D **14**
Turriff. *Abers* 4E **161**
Tursdale. *Dur* 1A **106**
Turton Bottoms. *Bkbn* 3F **91**
Turtory. *Mor* 4C **160**
Turves Green. *W Mid* 3E **61**
Turvey. *Bed* 5G **63**
Turville. *Buck* 2F **37**
Turville Heath. *Buck* 2F **37**
Turweston. *Buck* 2E **50**
Tushielaw. *Bord* 3F **119**
Tutbury. *Staf* 3G **73**
Tutnall. *Worc* 3D **61**
Tutshill. *Glos* 2A **34**
Tuttington. *Norf* 3E **79**
Tutts Clump. *W Ber* 4D **36**
Tutwell. *Corn* 5D **11**
Tuxford. *Notts* 3E **87**
Twatt. *Orkn* 5B **172**
Twatt. *Shet* 6E **173**
Twechar. *E Dun* 2H **127**
Tweedale. *Telf* 5B **72**
Tweedbank. *Bord* 1H **119**
Tweedmouth. *Nmbd* 4F **131**
Tweedsmuir. *Bord* 2C **118**
Twelveheads. *Corn* 4B **6**
Twemlow Green. *Ches E* 4B **84**
Twenty. *Linc* 3A **76**
Twerton. *Bath* 5C **34**
Twickenham. *G Lon* 3C **38**
Twigworth. *Glos* 3D **48**
Twineham. *W Sus* 4D **26**
Twinhoe. *Bath* 1C **22**
Twinstead. *Essx* 2B **54**
Twinstead Green. *Essx* 2B **54**
Twiss Green. *Warr* 1A **84**
Twiston. *Lanc* 5H **97**
Twitchen. *Devn* 3A **20**
Twitchen. *Shrp* 3F **59**
Two Bridges. *Devn* 5G **11**
Two Bridges. *Glos* 5B **48**
Two Dales. *Derbs* 4G **85**
Two Gates. *Staf* 5G **73**
Two Mile Oak. *Devn* 2E **9**
Twycross. *Leics* 5H **73**
Twyford. *Buck* 3E **51**
Twyford. *Derbs* 3H **73**
Twyford. *Dors* 1D **14**
Twyford. *Hants* 4C **24**
Twyford. *Leics* 4E **75**
Twyford. *Norf* 3C **78**
Twyford. *Wok* 4F **37**
Twyford Common. *Here* 2A **48**
Twynholm. *Dum* 4D **110**
Twyning. *Glos* 2D **49**
Twyning Green. *Glos* 2E **49**
Twynllanan. *Carm* 3A **46**
Twyn-y-Sheriff. *Mon* 5H **47**
Twywell. *Nptn* 3G **63**
Tyberton. *Here* 2G **47**
Tyburn. *W Mid* 1F **61**
Tyby. *Norf* 3C **78**
Tycroes. *Carm* 4G **45**
Tycrwyn. *Powy* 4D **70**
Tyddewi. *Pemb* 2B **42**
Tydd Gote. *Linc* 4D **76**
Tydd St Giles. *Cambs* 4D **76**
Tydd St Mary. *Linc* 4D **76**
Tye. *Hants* 2F **17**
Tye Green. *Essx*
nr. Bishop's Stortford 3F **53**
nr. Braintree 3A **54**
nr. Saffron Walden 2F **53**
Tyersal. *W Yor* 1B **92**
Ty Issa. *Powy* 2D **70**
Tyldesley. *G Man* 4E **91**
Tyler Hill. *Kent* 4F **41**
Tyler's Green. *Essx* 5F **53**
Tylers Green. *Buck* 2G **37**
Tylorstown. *Rhon* 2D **32**
Tylwch. *Powy* 2B **58**
Y Tymbl. *Carm* 4F **45**
Ty-nant. *Cnwy* 1B **70**
Tyndrum. *Stir* 5H **141**
Tyneham. *Dors* 4D **15**
Tynehead. *Midl* 4G **129**
Tynemouth. *Tyne* 3G **115**
Tyneside. *Tyne* 3F **115**
Tyne Tunnel. *Tyne* 3G **115**
Tynewydd. *Rhon* 2C **32**
Tyninghame. *E Lot* 2C **130**
Tynron. *Dum* 5H **117**
Ty'n-y-bryn. *Rhon* 3D **32**
Tyn-y-celyn. *Wrex* 2D **70**
Tyn-y-cwm. *Swan* 5G **45**
Tyn-y-ffridd. *Powy* 2D **70**
Tynygongl. *IOA* 2E **81**
Tynygraig. *Cdgn* 4F **57**
Ty'n-y-groes. *Cnwy* 3G **81**
Ty'n-yr-eithin. *Cdgn* 4F **57**
Tyn-y-rhyd. *Powy* 4C **70**
Tyn-y-wern. *Powy* 3C **70**
Tyrie. *Abers* 2G **161**
Tyringham. *Mil* 1G **51**
Tythecott. *Devn* 1E **11**
Tythegston. *B'end* 4B **32**
Tytherington. *Ches E* 3D **84**
Tytherington. *Som* 2C **22**
Tytherington. *S Glo* 3B **34**
Tytherington. *Wilts* 2E **23**
Tytherleigh. *Devn* 2G **13**
Tywardreath. *Corn* 3E **7**
Tywardreath Highway. *Corn* 3E **7**
Tywyn. *Cnwy* 3G **81**
Tywyn. *Gwyn* 5E **69**

U

Uachdar. *W Isl* 3D **170**
Uags. *High* 5G **155**
Ubbeston Green. *Suff* 3F **67**
Ubley. *Bath* 1A **22**
Uckerby. *N Yor* 4F **105**
Uckfield. *E Sus* 3F **27**
Uckinghall. *Worc* 2D **48**
Uckington. *Glos* 3E **49**
Uckington. *Shrp* 5H **71**
Uddingston. *S Lan* 3H **127**
Uddington. *S Lan* 1A **118**
Udimore. *E Sus* 4C **28**
Udny Green. *Abers* 1F **153**
Udny Station. *Abers* 1G **153**
Udston. *S Lan* 4H **127**
Udstonhead. *S Lan* 5A **128**
Uffcott. *Wilts* 4G **35**
Uffculme. *Devn* 1D **12**
Uffington. *Linc* 5H **75**
Uffington. *Oxon* 3B **36**
Uffington. *Shrp* 4H **71**
Ufford. *Pet* 5H **75**
Ufford. *Suff* 5E **67**
Ufton. *Warw* 4A **62**
Ufton Nervet. *W Ber* 5E **37**
Ugadale. *Arg* 3B **122**
Ugborough. *Devn* 3C **8**
Ugford. *Wilts* 3F **23**
Uggeshall. *Suff* 2G **67**
Ugglebarnby. *N Yor* 4F **107**
Ugley. *Essx* 3F **53**
Ugley Green. *Essx* 3F **53**
Ugthorpe. *N Yor* 3E **107**
Uidh. *W Isl* 9B **170**
Uig. *Arg* 3C **138**
Uig. *High*
nr. Balgown 2C **154**
nr. Dunvegan 3A **154**
Uigshader. *High* 4D **154**
Uisken. *Arg* 2A **132**
Ulbster. *High* 4F **169**
Ulcat Row. *Cumb* 2F **103**
Ulceby. *Linc* 3D **88**
Ulceby. *N Lin* 3E **94**
Ulceby Skitter. *N Lin* 3E **94**
Ulcombe. *Kent* 1C **28**
Uldale. *Cumb* 1D **102**
Uley. *Glos* 2C **34**
Ulgham. *Nmbd* 5G **121**
Ullapool. *High* 4F **163**
Ullenhall. *Warw* 4F **61**
Ulleskelf. *N Yor* 1F **93**
Ullesthorpe. *Leics* 2C **62**
Ulley. *S Yor* 2B **86**
Ullingswick. *Here* 5H **59**
Ullinish. *High* 5C **154**
Ullock. *Cumb* 2B **102**
Ulpha. *Cumb* 5C **102**
Ulrome. *E Yor* 4F **101**
Ulsta. *Shet* 3F **173**
Ulting. *Essx* 5B **54**
Ulva House. *Arg* 5F **139**
Ulverston. *Cumb* 2B **96**
Ulwell. *Dors* 4F **15**
Umberleigh. *Devn* 4G **19**
Unapool. *High* 5C **166**
Underbarrow. *Cumb* 5F **103**
Undercliffe. *W Yor* 1B **92**
Underdale. *Shrp* 4H **71**
Underhoull. *Shet* 1G **173**
Underriver. *Kent* 5G **39**
Under Tofts. *S Yor* 2H **85**
Underton. *Shrp* 1A **60**
Underwood. *Newp* 3G **33**
Underwood. *Notts* 5B **86**
Underwood. *Plym* 3B **8**
Undley. *Suff* 2F **65**
Undy. *Mon* 3H **33**
Union Mills. *IOM* 4C **108**
Union Street. *E Sus* 2B **28**
Unstone. *Derbs* 3A **86**
Unstone Green. *Derbs* 3A **86**
Unthank. *Cumb*
nr. Carlisle 5E **113**
nr. Gamblesby 5H **113**
nr. Penrith 1F **103**
Unthank End. *Cumb* 1F **103**
Upavon. *Wilts* 1G **23**
Up Cerne. *Dors* 2B **14**
Upchurch. *Kent* 4C **40**
Upcott. *Devn* 2F **11**
Upcott. *Here* 5F **59**
Upend. *Cambs* 5F **65**
Up Exe. *Devn* 2C **12**
Upgate. *Norf* 4D **78**
Upgate Street. *Norf* 1C **66**
Uphall. *Dors* 2A **14**
Uphall. *W Lot* 2D **128**
Uphall Station. *W Lot* 2D **128**
Upham. *Devn* 2B **12**
Upham. *Hants* 4D **24**
Uphampton. *Here* 4F **59**
Uphampton. *Worc* 4C **60**
Up Hatherley. *Glos* 3E **49**
Uphill. *N Som* 1G **21**
Up Holland. *Lanc* 4D **90**
Uplawmoor. *E Ren* 4F **127**
Upleadon. *Glos* 3C **48**
Upleatham. *Red C* 3D **106**
Uplees. *Kent* 4D **40**
Uploders. *Dors* 3A **14**
Uplowman. *Devn* 1D **12**
Uplyme. *Devn* 3G **13**
Up Marden. *W Sus* 1F **17**
Upminster. *G Lon* 2G **39**
Up Nately. *Hants* 1E **25**
Upottery. *Devn* 2F **13**
Uppat. *High* 3F **165**
Upper Affcot. *Shrp* 2G **59**
Upper Arley. *Worc* 2B **60**
Upper Armley. *W Yor* 1C **92**
Upper Arncott. *Oxon* 4E **50**
Upper Astrop. *Nptn* 2D **50**
Upper Badcall. *High* 4B **166**
Upper Bangor. *Gwyn* 3E **81**
Upper Basildon. *W Ber* 4D **36**
Upper Batley. *W Yor* 2C **92**
Upper Beeding. *W Sus* 4C **26**
Upper Benefield. *Nptn* 2G **63**
Upper Bentley. *Worc* 4D **61**
Upper Bighouse. *High* 3A **168**
Upper Boddam. *Abers* 5D **160**
Upper Boddington. *Nptn* 5B **62**
Upper Bogside. *Mor* 3G **159**
Upper Booth. *Derbs* 2F **85**
Upper Borth. *Cdgn* 2F **57**
Upper Boyndlie. *Abers* 2G **161**
Upper Brailes. *Warw* 1B **50**
Upper Breinton. *Here* 1H **47**
Upper Broughton. *Notts* 3D **74**
Upper Brynamman. *Carm* 4H **45**
Upper Bucklebury. *W Ber* 5D **36**
Upper Bullington. *Hants* 2C **24**
Upper Burgate. *Hants* 1G **15**
Upper Caldecote. *C Beds* 1B **52**
Upper Canterton. *Hants* 1A **16**
Upper Catesby. *Nptn* 5C **62**
Upper Chapel. *Powy* 1D **46**
Upper Cheddon. *Som* 4F **21**
Upper Chicksgrove. *Wilts* 4E **23**
Upper Church Village *Rhon* 3D **32**
Upper Chute. *Wilts* 1A **24**
Upper Clatford. *Hants* 2B **24**
Upper Coberley. *Glos* 4E **49**
Upper Coedcae. *Torf* 5F **47**
Upper Cound. *Shrp* 5H **71**
Upper Cudworth. *S Yor* 4D **93**
Upper Cumberworth. *W Yor* 4C **92**
Upper Cuttlehill. *Abers* 4B **160**
Upper Cwmbran. *Torf* 2F **33**
Upper Dallachy. *Mor* 2A **160**
Upper Dean. *Bed* 4H **63**
Upper Denby. *W Yor* 4C **92**
Upper Derraid. *High* 5E **159**
Upper Diabaig. *High* 2H **155**
Upper Dicker. *E Sus* 5G **27**
Upper Dinchope. *Shrp* 2G **59**
Upper Dochcarty. *High* 2H **157**
Upper Dounreay. *High* 2B **168**
Upper Dovercourt. *Essx* 2F **55**
Upper Dunsforth. *N Yor* 3G **99**
Upper Dunsley. *Herts* 4H **51**
Upper Eastern Green. *W Mid* 2G **61**
Upper Elkstone. *Staf* 5E **85**
Upper Ellastone. *Staf* 1F **73**
Upper End. *Derbs* 3E **85**
Upper Enham. *Hants* 2B **24**
Upper Farmcote. *Shrp* 1B **60**
Upper Farringdon. *Hants* 3F **25**
Upper Framilode. *Glos* 4C **48**
Upper Froyle. *Hants* 2F **25**
Upper Gills. *High* 1F **169**
Upper Glenfintaig. *High* 5E **149**
Upper Godney. *Som* 2H **21**
Upper Gravenhurst. *C Beds* 2B **52**
Upper Green. *Essx* 2E **53**
Upper Green. *W Ber* 5B **36**
Upper Green. *W Yor* 2C **92**
Upper Grove Common *Here* 3A **48**
Upper Hackney. *Derbs* 4G **85**
Upper Hale. *Surr* 2G **25**
Upper Halliford. *Surr* 4B **38**
Upper Halling. *Medw* 4A **40**
Upper Hambleton. *Rut* 5G **75**
Upper Hardres Court. *Kent* 5F **41**
Upper Hardwick. *Here* 5G **59**
Upper Hartfield. *E Sus* 2F **27**
Upper Haugh. *S Yor* 1B **86**
Upper Hayton. *Shrp* 2H **59**
Upper Heath. *Shrp* 2H **59**
Upper Hellesdon. *Norf* 4E **78**
Upper Helmsley. *N Yor* 4A **100**
Upper Hengoed. *Shrp* 2E **71**
Upper Hergest. *Here* 5E **59**
Upper Heyford. *Nptn* 5D **62**
Upper Heyford. *Oxon* 3C **50**
Upper Hill. *Here* 5G **59**
Upper Hindhope. *Bord* 4B **120**
Upper Hopton. *W Yor* 3B **92**
Upper Howsell. *Worc* 1C **48**
Upper Hulme. *Staf* 4E **85**
Upper Inglesham. *Swin* 2H **35**
Upper Kilcott. *S Glo* 3C **34**
Upper Killay. *Swan* 3E **31**
Upper Kirkton. *Abers* 5E **161**
Upper Kirkton. *N Ayr* 4C **126**
Upper Knockando. *Mor* 4F **159**
Upper Knockchoilum *High* 2G **149**
Upper Lambourn. *W Ber* 3B **36**
Upper Langford. *N Som* 1H **21**
Upper Langwith. *Derbs* 4C **86**
Upper Largo. *Fife* 3G **137**
Upper Latheron. *High* 5D **169**
Upper Layham. *Suff* 1D **54**
Upper Leigh. *Staf* 2E **73**
Upper Lenie. *High* 1H **149**
Upper Lochton. *Abers* 4D **152**
Upper Longdon. *Staf* 4E **73**
Upper Longwood. *Shrp* 5A **72**
Upper Lybster. *High* 5E **169**
Upper Lydbrook. *Glos* 4B **48**
Upper Lye. *Here* 4F **59**
Upper Maes-coed. *Here* 2G **47**
Upper Midway. *Derbs* 3G **73**
Uppermill. *G Man* 4H **91**
Upper Millichope. *Shrp* 2H **59**
Upper Milovaig. *High* 4A **154**
Upper Minety. *Wilts* 2F **35**
Upper Mitton. *Worc* 3C **60**
Upper Nash. *Pemb* 4E **43**
Upper Neepaback. *Shet* 3G **173**
Upper Netchwood. *Shrp* 1A **60**
Upper Nobut. *Staf* 2E **73**
Upper North Dean. *Buck* 2G **37**
Upper Norwood. *W Sus* 4A **26**
Upper Nyland. *Dors* 4C **22**
Upper Oddington. *Glos* 3H **49**
Upper Ollach. *High* 5E **155**
Upper Outwoods. *Staf* 3G **73**
Upper Padley. *Derbs* 3G **85**
Upper Pennington. *Hants* 3B **16**
Upper Poppleton. *York* 4H **99**
Upper Quinton. *Warw* 1G **49**
Upper Rissington. *Glos* 4H **49**
Upper Rochford. *Worc* 4A **60**
Upper Rusko. *Dum* 3C **110**
Upper Sandaig. *High* 2F **147**
Upper Sanday. *Orkn* 7E **172**

Upper Sapey – Wanswell

Upper Sapey. Here 4A 60
Upper Seagry. Wilts 3E 35
Upper Shelton. C Beds 1H 51
Upper Sheringham. Norf 1D 78
Upper Skelmorlie. N Ayr 3C 126
Upper Slaughter. Glos 3G 49
Upper Sonachan. Arg 1H 133
Upper Soudley. Glos 4B 48
Upper Staploe. Bed 5A 64
Upper Stoke. Norf 5E 79
Upper Stondon. C Beds 2B 52
Upper Stowe. Nptn 5D 62
Upper Street. Hants 1G 15
Upper Street. Norf
nr. Horning 4F 79
nr. Hoveton 4F 79
Upper Street. Suff 2E 55
Upper Strensham. Worc 2E 49
Upper Studley. Wilts 1D 22
Upper Sundon. C Beds 3A 52
Upper Swell. Glos 3G 49
Upper Tankersley. S Yor 1H 85
Upper Tean. Staf 2E 73
Upperthong. W Yor 4B 92
Upperthorpe. N Lin 4A 94
Upper Thurnham. Lanc 4D 96
Upper Tillyrie. Per 3D 136
Upperton. W Sus 3A 26
Upper Tooting. G Lon 3D 39
Upper Town. Derbs
nr. Bonsall 5G 85
nr. Hognaston 5G 85
Upper Town. Here 1A 48
Upper Town. N Som 5A 34
Uppertown. Derbs 4H 85
Uppertown. High 1F 169
Uppertown. Nmbd 2B 114
Uppertown. Orkn 8D 172
Upper Tysoe. Warw 1B 50
Upper Upham. Wilts 4H 35
Upper Upnor. Medw 3B 40
Upper Urquhart. Fife 3D 136
Upper Wardington. Oxon 1C 50
Upper Weald. Mil 2F 51
Upper Weedon. Nptn 5D 62
Upper Wellingham. E Sus 4F 27
Upper Whiston. S Yor 2B 86
Upper Wield. Hants 3E 25
Upper Winchendon. Buck 4F 51
Upperwood. Derbs 5G 85
Upper Woodford. Wilts 3G 23
Upper Wootton. Hants 1D 24
Upper Wraxall. Wilts 4D 34
Upper Wyche. Worc 1C 48
Uppincott. Devn 2B 12
Uppingham. Rut 1F 63
Uppington. Shrp 5A 72
Upsall. N Yor 1G 99
Upsettlington. Bord 5E 131
Upshire. Essx 5E 53
Up Somborne. Hants 3B 24
Upstreet. Kent 4G 41
Up Sydling. Dors 2B 14
Upthorpe. Suff 3B 66
Upton. Buck 4F 51
Upton. Cambs 3A 64
Upton. Ches W 4G 83
Upton. Corn
nr. Bude 2C 10
nr. Liskeard 5C 10
Upton. Cumb 1E 102
Upton. Devn
nr. Honiton 2D 12
nr. Kingsbridge 4D 8
Upton. Dors
nr. Poole 3E 15
nr. Weymouth 4C 14
Upton. E Yor 4F 101
Upton. Hants
nr. Andover 1B 24
nr. Southampton 1B 16
Upton. IOW 3D 16
Upton. Leics 1A 62
Upton. Linc 2F 87
Upton. Mers 2E 83
Upton. Norf 4F 79
Upton. Nptn 4E 62
Upton. Notts
nr. Retford 3E 87
nr. Southwell 5E 87
Upton. Oxon 3D 36
Upton. Pemb 4E 43
Upton. Pet 5A 76
Upton. Slo 3A 38
Upton. Som
nr. Somerton 4H 21
nr. Wiveliscombe 4C 20
Upton. Warw 5F 61
Upton. W Yor 3E 93
Upton. Wilts 3D 22
Upton Bishop. Here 3B 48
Upton Cheyney. S Glo 5B 34
Upton Cressett. Shrp 1A 60
Upton Crews. Here 3B 48
Upton Cross. Corn 5C 10
Upton End. C Beds 2B 52
Upton Grey. Hants 2E 25
Upton Heath. Ches W 4G 83
Upton Hellions. Devn 2B 12
Upton Lovell. Wilts 2E 23
Upton Magna. Shrp 4H 71
Upton Noble. Som 3C 22
Upton Pyne. Devn 3C 12
Upton St Leonards. Glos 4D 48
Upton Scudamore. Wilts 2D 22
Upton Snodsbury. Worc 5D 60
Upton upon Severn. Worc 1D 48
Upton Warren. Worc 4D 60
Upwaltham. W Sus 4A 26
Upware. Cambs 3E 65
Upwell. Norf 5E 77
Upwey. Dors 4B 14
Upwick Green. Herts 3E 53
Upwood. Cambs 2B 64
Urafirth. Shet 4E 173
Uragaig. Arg 4A 132
Urchany. High 4C 158
Urchfont. Wilts 1F 23
Urdimarsh. Here 1A 48
Ure. Shet 4D 173
Ure Bank. N Yor 2F 99
Urgha. W Isl 8D 171
Urlay Nook. Stoc T 3B 106
Urmston. G Man 1B 84
Urquhart. Mor 2G 159
Urra. N Yor 4C 106
Urray. High 3H 157
Usan. Ang 3G 145
Ushaw Moor. Dur 5F 115
Usk. Mon 5G 47
Usselby. Linc 1H 87
Usworth. Tyne 4G 115
Utkinton. Ches W 4H 83
Uton. Devn 3B 12
Utterby. Linc 1C 88
Uttoxeter. Staf 2E 73
Uwchmynydd. Gwyn 3A 68
Uxbridge. G Lon 2B 38
Uyeasound. Shet 1G 173
Uzmaston. Pemb 3D 42

V

Valley. IOA 3B 80
Valley End. Surr 4A 38
Valley Truckle. Corn 4B 10
Valsgarth. Shet 1H 173
Valtos. High 2E 155
Van. Powy 2B 58
Vange. Essx 2B 40
Varteg. Torf 5F 47
Vatsetter. Shet 3G 173
Vatten. High 4B 154
Vaul. Arg 4B 138
The Vauld. Here 1A 48
Vaynor. Mer T 4D 46
Veensgarth. Shet 7F 173
Velindre. Powy 2E 47
Vellow. Som 3D 20
Velly. Devn 4C 18
Veness. Orkn 5E 172
Venhay. Devn 1A 12
Venn. Devn 4D 8
Venngreen. Devn 1D 11
Vennington. Shrp 5F 71
Venn Ottery. Devn 3D 12
Venn's Green. Here 1A 48
Venny Tedburn. Devn 3B 12
Venterdon. Corn 5D 10
Ventnor. IOW 5D 16
Vernham Dean. Hants 1B 24
Vernham Street. Hants 1B 24
Vernolds Common. Shrp 2G 59
Verwood. Dors 2F 15
Veryan. Corn 5D 6
Veryan Green. Corn 5D 6
Vicarage. Devn 4F 13
Vickerstown. Cumb 3A 96
Victoria. Corn 2D 6
Vidlin. Shet 5F 173
Viewpark. N Lan 3A 128
Vigo. W Mid 5E 73
Vigo Village. Kent 4H 39
Vinehall Street. E Sus 3B 28
Vine's Cross. E Sus 4G 27
Viney Hill. Glos 5B 48
Virginia Water. Surr 4A 38
Virginstow. Devn 3D 11
Vobster. Som 2C 22
Voe. Shet
nr. Hillside 5F 173
nr. Swinister 3E 173
Vole. Som 2G 21
Vowchurch. Here 2G 47
Voxter. Shet 4E 173
Voy. Orkn 6B 172
Vulcan Village. Mers 1H 83

W

Waberthwaite. Cumb 5C 102
Wackerfield. Dur 2E 105
Wacton. Norf 1D 66
Wadbister. Shet 7F 173
Wadborough. Worc 1E 49
Wadbrook. Devn 2G 13
Waddesdon. Buck 4F 51
Waddeton. Devn 3E 9
Waddicar. Mers 1F 83
Waddingham. Linc 1G 87
Waddington. Lanc 5G 97
Waddington. Linc 4G 87
Waddon. Devn 5B 12
Wadebridge. Corn 1D 6
Wadeford. Som 1G 13
Wadenhoe. Nptn 2H 63
Wadesmill. Herts 4D 52
Wadhurst. E Sus 2H 27
Wadshelf. Derbs 3H 85
Wadsley. S Yor 1H 85
Wadsley Bridge. S Yor 1H 85
Wadswick. Wilts 5D 34
Wadwick. Hants 1C 24
Wadworth. S Yor 1C 86
Waen. Den
nr. Llandymog 4D 82
nr. Nantglyn 4B 82
Waen. Powy 1B 58
Waen Fach. Powy 4E 70
Waen Goleugoed. Den 3C 82
Wag. High 1H 165
Wainfleet All Saints. Linc 5D 89
Wainfleet Bank. Linc 5D 88
Wainfleet St Mary. Linc 5D 89
Wainhouse Corner. Corn 3B 10
Wainscott. Medw 3B 40
Wainstalls. W Yor 2A 92
Waitby. Cumb 4A 104
Waithe. Linc 4F 95
Wakefield. W Yor 2D 92
Wakerley. Nptn 1G 63
Wakes Colne. Essx 3B 54
Walberswick. Suff 3G 67
Walberton. W Sus 5A 26
Walbottle. Tyne 3E 115
Walby. Cumb 3F 113
Walcombe. Som 2A 22
Walcot. Linc 2H 75
Walcot. N Lin 2B 94
Walcot. Swin 3G 35
Walcot. Telf 4H 71
Walcot. Warw 5F 61
Walcote. Leics 2C 62
Walcot Green. Norf 2D 66
Walcott. Linc 5A 88
Walcott. Norf 2F 79
Walden. N Yor 1C 98
Walden Head. N Yor 1B 98
Walden Stubbs. N Yor 3F 93
Walderslade. Medw 4B 40
Walderton. W Sus 1F 17
Walditch. Dors 3H 13
Waldley. Derbs 2F 73
Waldridge. Dur 4F 115
Waldringfield. Suff 1F 55
Waldron. E Sus 4G 27
Wales. S Yor 2B 86
Walesby. Linc 1A 88
Walesby. Notts 3D 86
Walford. Here
nr. Leintwardine 3F 59
nr. Ross-on-Wye 3A 48
Walford. Shrp 3G 71
Walford. Staf 2C 72
Walford Heath. Shrp 4G 71
Walgherton. Ches E 1A 72
Walgrave. Nptn 3F 63
Walhampton. Hants 3B 16
Walkden. G Man 4F 91
Walker. Tyne 3F 115
Walkerburn. Bord 1F 119
Walker Fold. Lanc 5F 97
Walkeringham. Notts 1E 87
Walkerith. Linc 1E 87
Walkern. Herts 3C 52
Walker's Green. Here 1A 48
Walkerton. Fife 3E 137
Walkerville. N Yor 5F 105
Walkford. Dors 3H 15
Walkhampton. Devn 2B 8
Walkington. E Yor 1C 94
Walkley. S Yor 2H 85
Walk Mill. Lanc 1G 91
Wall. Corn 3D 4
Wall. Nmbd 3C 114
Wall. Staf 5F 73
Wallaceton. Dum 1F 111
Wallacetown. Shet 6E 173
Wallacetown. S Aymr. Ayr 2C 116
nr. Dailly 4B 116
Wallands Park. E Sus 4F 27
Wallasey. Mers 1E 83
Wallaston Green. Pemb 4D 42
Wallbrook. W Mid 1D 60
Wallcrouch. E Sus 2A 28
Wall End. Cumb 1B 96
Wallend. Medw 3C 40
Wall Heath. W Mid 2C 60
Wallingford. Oxon 3E 36
Wallington. G Lon 4D 39
Wallington. Hants 2D 16
Wallington. Herts 2C 52
Wallis. Pemb 2E 43
Wallisdown. Bour 3F 15
Walliswood. Surr 2C 26
Wall Nook. Dur 5F 115
Walls. Shet 7D 173
Wallsend. Tyne 3G 115
Wallsworth. Glos 3D 48
Wall under Heywood. Shrp 1H 59
Wallyford. E Lot 2G 129
Walmer. Kent 5H 41
Walmer Bridge. Lanc 2C 90
Walmersley. G Man 3G 91
Walmley. W Mid 1F 61
Walnut Grove. Per 1D 136
Walpole. Suff 3F 67
Walpole Cross Keys. Norf 4E 77
Walpole Gate. Norf 4E 77
Walpole Highway. Norf 4E 77
Walpole Marsh. Norf 4D 77
Walpole St Andrew. Norf 4E 77
Walpole St Peter. Norf 4E 77
Walsall. W Mid 1E 61
Walsall Wood. W Mid 5E 73
Walsden. W Yor 2H 91
Walsgrave on Sowe
W Mid 2A 62
Walsham le Willows. Suff 3C 66
Walshaw. G Man 3F 91
Walshford. N Yor 4G 99
Walsoken. Norf 4D 76
Walston. S Lan 5D 128
Walsworth. Herts 2B 52
Walter's Ash. Buck 2G 37
Walterston. V Glam 4D 32
Walterstone. Here 3G 47
Waltham. Kent 1F 29
Waltham. NE Lin 4F 95
Waltham Abbey. Essx 5D 53
Waltham Chase. Hants 1D 16
Waltham Cross. Herts 5D 52
Waltham on the Wolds. Leics 3F 75
Waltham St Lawrence. Wind 4G 37
Waltham's Cross. Essx 2G 53
Walthamstow. G Lon 2E 39
Walton. Cumb 3G 113
Walton. Derbs 4A 86
Walton. Leics 2C 62
Walton. Mers 1F 83
Walton. Mil 2G 51
Walton. Pet 5A 76
Walton. Powy 5E 59
Walton. Som 3H 21
Walton. Staf
nr. Eccleshall 3C 72
nr. Stone 2C 72
Walton. Suff 2F 55
Walton. Telf 4H 71
Walton. Warw 5G 61
Walton. W Yor
nr. Wakefield 3D 92
nr. Wetherby 5G 99
Walton Cardiff. Glos 2E 49
Walton East. Pemb 2E 43
Walton Elm. Dors 1C 14
Walton Highway. Norf 4D 77
Walton in Gordano. N Som 4H 33
Walton-lè-Dale. Lanc 2D 90
Walton-on-Thames. Surr 4C 38
Walton on the Hill. Surr 5D 38
Walton-on-the-Hill. Staf 3D 72
Walton-on-the-Naze. Essx 3F 55
Walton on the Wolds. Leics 4C 74
Walton-on-Trent. Derbs 4G 73
Walton West. Pemb 3C 42
Walwick. Nmbd 2C 114
Walworth. Darl 3F 105
Walworth Gate. Darl 2F 105
Walwyn's Castle. Pemb 3C 42
Wambrook. Som 2F 13
Wampool. Cumb 4D 112
Wanborough. Surr 1A 26
Wanborough. Swin 3H 35
Wandel. S Lan 2B 118
Wandsworth. G Lon 3D 38
Wangford. Suff
nr. Lakenheath 2G 65
nr. Southwold 3G 67
Wanlip. Leics 4C 74
Wanlockhead. Dum 3A 118
Wannock. E Sus 5G 27
Wansford. E Yor 4E 101
Wansford. Pet 1H 63
Wanshurst Green. Kent 1B 28
Wanstead. G Lon 2F 39
Wanstrow. Som 2C 22
Wanswell. Glos 5B 48

West Tytherley – Wigbeth

West Tytherley. *Hants* 4A 24
West Tytherton. *Wilts* 4E 35
West View. *Hart* 1B 106
Westville. *Notts* 1C 74
West Walton. *Norf* 4D 76
Westward. *Cumb* 5D 112
Westward Ho!. *Devn* 4E 19
Westwell. *Kent* 1D 28
Westwell. *Oxon* 5H 49
Westwell Leacon. *Kent* 1D 28
West Wellow. *Hants* 1A 16
West Wemyss. *Fife* 4F 137
West Wick. *N Som* 5G 33
Westwick. *Cambs* 4D 64
Westwick. *Dur* 3D 104
Westwick. *Norf* 3E 79
West Wickham. *Cambs* 1G 53
West Wickham. *G Lon* 4E 39
West Williamston. *Pemb* 4E 43
West Willoughby. *Linc* 1G 75
West Winch. *Norf* 4F 77
West Winterslow. *Wilts* 3H 23
West Wittering. *W Sus* 3F 17
West Witton. *N Yor* 1C 98
Westwood. *Devn* 3D 12
Westwood. *Kent* 4H 41
Westwood. *Pet* 5A 76
Westwood. *S Lan* 4H 127
Westwood. *Wilts* 1D 22
West Woodburn. *Nmbd* 1B 114
West Woodhay. *W Ber* 5B 36
West Woodlands. *Som* 2C 22
West Woodside. *Cumb* 5E 112
Westwoodside. *N Lin* 1E 87
West Worldham. *Hants* 3F 25
West Worlington. *Devn* 1A 12
West Worthing. *W Sus* 5C 26
West Wratting. *Cambs* 5F 65
West Wycombe. *Buck* 2G 37
West Wylam. *Nmbd* 3E 115
West Yatton. *Wilts* 4D 34
West Yell. *Shet* 3F 173
West Youlstone. *Corn* 1C 10
Wetheral. *Cumb* 4F 113
Wetherby. *W Yor* 5G 99
Wetherden. *Suff* 4C 66
Wetheringsett. *Suff* 4D 66
Wethersfield. *Essx* 2H 53
Wethersta. *Shet* 5E 173
Wetherup Street. *Suff* 4D 66
Wetley Rocks. *Staf* 1D 72
Wettenhall. *Ches E* 4A 84
Wetton. *Staf* 5F 85
Wetwang. *E Yor* 4D 100
Wetwood. *Staf* 2B 72
Wexcombe. *Wilts* 1A 24
Wexham Street. *Buck* 2A 38
Weybourne. *Norf* 1D 78
Weybourne. *Surr* 2G 25
Weybread. *Suff* 2E 67
Weybridge. *Surr* 4B 38
Weycroft. *Devn* 3G 13
Weydale. *High* 2D 168
Weyhill. *Hants* 2B 24
Weymouth. *Dors* 5B 14
Weythel. *Powy* 5E 59
Whaddon. *Buck* 2G 51
Whaddon. *Cambs* 1D 52
Whaddon. *Glos* 4D 48
Whaddon. *Wilts* 4G 23
Whale. *Cumb* 2G 103
Whaley. *Derbs* 3C 86
Whaley Bridge. *Derbs* 2E 85
Whaley Thorns. *Derbs* 3C 86
Whalley. *Lanc* 1F 91
Whalton. *Nmbd* 1E 115
Whaplode. *Linc* 3C 76
Whaplode Drove. *Linc* 4C 76
Whaplode St Catherine *Linc* 3C 76
Wharfe. *N Yor* 3G 97
Wharles. *Lanc* 1C 90
Wharley End. *C Beds* 1H 51
Wharncliffe Side. *S Yor* 1G 85
Wharram-le-Street. *N Yor* 3C 100
Wharton. *Ches W* 4A 84
Wharton. *Here* 5H 59
Whashton. *N Yor* 4E 105
Whasset. *Cumb* 1E 97
Whatcote. *Warw* 1B 50
Whateley. *Warw* 1G 61
Whatfield. *Suff* 1D 54
Whatley. *Som*
nr. Chard 2G 13
nr. Frome 2C 22
Whatlington. *E Sus* 4B 28
Whatmore. *Shrp* 3A 60
Whatstandwell. *Derbs* 5H 85
Whatton. *Notts* 2E 75
Whauphill. *Dum* 5B 110
Whaw. *N Yor* 4C 104
Wheatacre. *Norf* 1G 67
Wheatcroft. *Derbs* 5A 86
Wheathampstead. *Herts* 4B 52
Wheathill. *Shrp* 2A 60
Wheatley. *Devn* 3B 12
Wheatley. *Hants* 2F 25
Wheatley. *Oxon* 5E 50
Wheatley. *S Yor* 4F 93
Wheatley. *W Yor* 2A 92
Wheatley Hill. *Dur* 1A 106
Wheatley Lane. *Lanc* 1G 91
Wheatley Park. *S Yor* 4F 93
Wheaton Aston. *Staf* 4C 72
Wheatstone Park. *Staf* 5C 72
Wheddon Cross. *Som* 3C 20
Wheelerstreet. *Surr* 1A 26
Wheelock. *Ches E* 5B 84
Wheelock Heath. *Ches E* 5B 84
Wheelton. *Lanc* 2E 90
Wheldrake. *York* 5A 100
Whelford. *Glos* 2G 35
Whelpley Hill. *Buck* 5H 51
Whelpo. *Cumb* 1E 102
Whelston. *Flin* 3E 82
Whenby. *N Yor* 3A 100
Whepstead. *Suff* 5H 65
Wherstead. *Suff* 1E 55
Wherwell. *Hants* 2B 24
Wheston. *Derbs* 3F 85
Whetsted. *Kent* 1A 28
Whetstone. *G Lon* 1D 38
Whetstone. *Leics* 1C 62
Whicham. *Cumb* 1A 96
Whichford. *Warw* 2B 50
Whickham. *Tyne* 3F 115
Whiddon. *Devn* 2E 11
Whiddon Down. *Devn* 3G 11
Whigstreet. *Ang* 4D 145
Whilton. *Nptn* 4D 62
Whimble. *Devn* 2D 10
Whimple. *Devn* 3D 12
Whimpwell Green. *Norf* 3F 79
Whinburgh. *Norf* 5C 78
Whin Lane End. *Lanc* 5C 96
Whinney Hill. *Stoc T* 3A 106
Whinnyfold. *Abers* 5H 161
Whippingham. *IOW* 3D 16
Whipsnade. *C Beds* 4A 52
Whipton. *Devn* 3C 12
Whirlow. *S Yor* 2H 85
Whisby. *Linc* 4G 87
Whissendine. *Rut* 4F 75
Whissonsett. *Norf* 3B 78
Whisterfield. *Ches E* 3C 84
Whistley Green. *Wok* 4F 37
Whiston. *Mers* 1G 83
Whiston. *Nptn* 4F 63
Whiston. *S Yor* 1B 86
Whiston. *Staf*
nr. Cheadle 1E 73
nr. Penkridge 4C 72
Whiston Cross. *Shrp* 5B 72
Whiston Eaves. *Staf* 1E 73
Whitacre Heath. *Warw* 1G 61
Whitbeck. *Cumb* 1A 96
Whitbourne. *Here* 5B 60
Whitburn. *Tyne* 3H 115
Whitburn. *W Lot* 3C 128
Whitburn Colliery. *Tyne* 3H 115
Whitby. *Ches W* 3F 83
Whitby. *N Yor* 3F 107
Whitbyheath. *Ches W* 3F 83
Whitchester. *Bord* 4D 130
Whitchurch. *Bath* 5B 34
Whitchurch. *Buck* 3F 51
Whitchurch. *Card* 4E 33
Whitchurch. *Devn* 5E 11
Whitchurch. *Hants* 2C 24
Whitchurch. *Here* 4A 48
Whitchurch. *Pemb* 2B 42
Whitchurch. *Shrp* 1H 71
Whitchurch Canonicorum *Dors* 3G 13
Whitchurch Hill. *Oxon* 4E 37
Whitchurch-on-Thames *Oxon* 4E 37
Whitcombe. *Dors* 4C 14
Whitcot. *Shrp* 1F 59
Whitcott Keysett. *Shrp* 2E 59
Whiteash Green. *Essx* 2A 54
Whitebog. *High* 2B 158
Whitebridge. *High* 2G 149
Whitebrook. *Mon* 5A 48
Whitecairns. *Abers* 2G 153
Whitechapel. *Lanc* 5E 97
Whitechurch. *Pemb* 1F 43
White Colne. *Essx* 3B 54
White Coppice. *Lanc* 3E 90
White Corries. *High* 3G 141
Whitecraig. *E Lot* 2G 129
Whitecroft. *Glos* 5B 48
White Cross. *Corn* 4D 5
Whitecross. *Corn* 1D 6
Whitecross. *Falk* 2C 128
White End. *Worc* 2C 48
Whiteface. *High* 5E 164
Whitefarland. *N Ayr* 5G 125
Whitefaulds. *S Ayr* 4B 116
Whitefield. *Dors* 3E 15
Whitefield. *G Man* 4G 91
Whitefield. *Som* 4D 20
Whiteford. *Abers* 1E 152
Whitegate. *Ches W* 4A 84
Whitehall. *Devn* 1E 12
Whitehall. *Hants* 1F 25
Whitehall. *Orkn* 5F 172
Whitehall. *W Sus* 3C 26
Whitehaven. *Cumb* 3A 102
Whitehaven. *Shrp* 3E 71
Whitehill. *Hants* 3F 25
Whitehill. *N Ayr* 4D 126
Whitehills. *Abers* 2D 160
Whitehills. *Ang* 3D 144
White Horse Common *Norf* 3F 79
Whitehough. *Derbs* 2E 85
Whitehouse. *Abers* 2D 152
Whitehouse. *Arg* 3G 125
Whiteinch. *Glas* 3G 127
Whitekirk. *E Lot* 1B 130
White Kirkley. *Dur* 1D 104
White Lackington. *Dors* 3C 14
Whitelackington. *Som* 1G 13
White Ladies Aston. *Worc* 5D 60
White Lee. *W Yor* 2C 92
Whiteley. *Hants* 2D 16
Whiteley Bank. *IOW* 4D 16
Whiteley Village. *Surr* 4B 38
Whitemans Green. *W Sus* 3E 27
White Mill. *Carm* 3E 45
Whitemire. *Mor* 3D 159
Whitemoor. *Corn* 3D 6
Whitenap. *Hants* 4B 24
Whiteness. *Shet* 7F 173
White Notley. *Essx* 4A 54
Whiteoak Green. *Oxon* 4B 50
Whiteparish. *Wilts* 4H 23
White Pit. *Linc* 3C 88
Whiterashes. *Abers* 1F 153
White Rocks. *Here* 3H 47
White Roding. *Essx* 4F 53
Whiterow. *High* 4F 169
Whiterow. *Mor* 3E 159
Whiteshill. *Glos* 5D 48
Whiteside. *Nmbd* 3A 114
Whiteside. *W Lot* 3C 128
Whitesmith. *E Sus* 4G 27
Whitestaunton. *Som* 1F 13
White Stone. *Here* 1A 48
Whitestone. *Abers* 4D 152
Whitestone. *Devn* 3B 12
Whitestones. *Abers* 3F 161
Whitestreet Green. *Suff* 2C 54
Whitewall Corner. *N Yor* 2B 100
White Waltham. *Wind* 4G 37
Whiteway. *Glos* 4E 49
Whitewell. *Lanc* 5F 97
Whitewell Bottom. *Lanc* 2G 91
Whiteworks. *Devn* 5G 11
Whitewreath. *Mor* 3G 159
Whitfield. *D'dee* 5D 144
Whitfield. *Kent* 1H 29
Whitfield. *Nptn* 2E 50
Whitfield. *Nmbd* 4A 114
Whitfield. *S Glo* 2B 34
Whitford. *Devn* 3F 13
Whitford. *Flin* 3D 82
Whitgift. *E Yor* 2B 94
Whitgreave. *Staf* 3C 72
Whithorn. *Dum* 5B 110
Whiting Bay. *N Ayr* 3E 123
Whitkirk. *W Yor* 1D 92
Whitland. *Carm* 3G 43
Whitleigh. *Plym* 3A 8
Whitletts. *S Ayr* 2C 116
Whitley. *N Yor* 2F 93
Whitley. *Wilts* 5D 35
Whitley Bay. *Tyne* 2G 115
Whitley Chapel. *Nmbd* 4C 114
Whitley Heath. *Staf* 3C 72
Whitley Lower. *W Yor* 3C 92
Whitley Thorpe. *N Yor* 2F 93
Whitlock's End. *W Mid* 3F 61
Whitminster. *Glos* 5C 48
Whitmore. *Dors* 2F 15
Whitmore. *Staf* 1C 72
Whitnage. *Devn* 1D 12
Whitnash. *Warw* 4H 61
Whitney. *Here* 1F 47
Whitrigg. *Cumb*
nr. Kirkbride 4D 112
nr. Torpenhow 1D 102
Whitsbury. *Hants* 1G 15
Whitsome. *Bord* 4E 131
Whitson. *Newp* 3G 33
Whitstable. *Kent* 4F 41
Whitstone. *Corn* 3C 10
Whittingham. *Nmbd* 3E 121
Whittingslow. *Shrp* 2G 59
Whittington. *Derbs* 3B 86
Whittington. *Glos* 3F 49
Whittington. *Lanc* 2F 97
Whittington. *Norf* 1G 65
Whittington. *Shrp* 2F 71
Whittington. *Staf*
nr. Kinver 2C 60
nr. Lichfield 5F 73
Whittington. *Warw* 1G 61
Whittington. *Worc* 5C 60
Whittington Barracks. *Staf* 5F 73
Whittlebury. *Nptn* 1E 51
Whittleford. *Warw* 1H 61
Whittle-le-Woods. *Lanc* 2D 90
Whittlesey. *Cambs* 1B 64
Whittlesford. *Cambs* 1E 53
Whittlestone Head. *Bkbn* 3F 91
Whitton. *N Lin* 2C 94
Whitton. *Nmbd* 4E 121
Whitton. *Powy* 4E 59
Whitton. *Bord* 2B 120
Whitton. *Shrp* 3H 59
Whitton. *Stoc T* 2A 106
Whittonditch. *Wilts* 4A 36
Whittonstall. *Nmbd* 4D 114
Whitway. *Hants* 1C 24
Whitwell. *Derbs* 3C 86
Whitwell. *Herts* 3B 52
Whitwell. *IOW* 5D 16
Whitwell. *N Yor* 5F 105
Whitwell. *Rut* 5G 75
Whitwell-on-the-Hill *N Yor* 3B 100
Whitwick. *Leics* 4B 74
Whitwood. *W Yor* 2E 93
Whitworth. *Lanc* 3G 91
Whixall. *Shrp* 2H 71
Whixley. *N Yor* 4G 99
Whoberley. *W Mid* 3H 61
Whorlton. *Dur* 3E 105
Whorlton. *N Yor* 4B 106
Whygate. *Nmbd* 2A 114
Whyle. *Here* 4H 59
Whyteleafe. *Surr* 5E 39
Wibdon. *Glos* 2A 34
Wibtoft. *Warw* 2B 62
Wichenford. *Worc* 4B 60
Wichling. *Kent* 5D 40
Wick. *Bour* 3G 15
Wick. *Devn* 2E 13
Wick. *High* 3F 169
Wick. *Shet*
on Mainland 8F 173
on Unst 1G 173
Wick. *Som*
nr. Bridgwater 2F 21
nr. Burnham-on-Sea 1G 21
nr. Somerton 4H 21
Wick. *S Glo* 4C 34
Wick. *V Glam* 4C 32
Wick. *W Sus* 5B 26
Wick. *Wilts* 4G 23
Wick. *Worc* 1E 49
Wick Airport. *High* 3F 169
Wicken. *Cambs* 3E 65
Wicken. *Nptn* 2F 51
Wicken Bonhunt. *Essx* 2E 53
Wickenby. *Linc* 2H 87
Wicken Green Village *Norf* 2H 77
Wickersley. *S Yor* 1B 86
Wicker Street Green. *Suff* 1C 54
Wickford. *Essx* 1B 40
Wickham. *Hants* 1D 16
Wickham. *W Ber* 4B 36
Wickham Bishops. *Essx* 4B 54
Wickhambreaux. *Kent* 5G 41
Wickhambrook. *Suff* 5G 65
Wickhamford. *Worc* 1F 49
Wickham Green. *Suff* 4C 66
Wickham Heath. *W Ber* 5C 36
Wickham Market. *Suff* 5F 67
Wickhampton. *Norf* 5G 79
Wickham St Paul. *Essx* 2B 54
Wickham Skeith. *Suff* 4C 66
Wickham Street. *Suff* 4C 66
Wick Hill. *Wok* 5F 37
Wicklewood. *Norf* 5C 78
Wickmere. *Norf* 2D 78
Wick St Lawrence. *N Som* 5G 33
Wickwar. *S Glo* 3C 34
Widdington. *Essx* 2F 53
Widdrington. *Nmbd* 5G 121
Widdrington Station *Nmbd* 5G 121
Widecombe in the Moor *Devn* 5H 11
Widegates. *Corn* 3G 7
Widemouth Bay. *Corn* 2C 10
Wide Open. *Tyne* 2F 115
Widewall. *Orkn* 8D 172
Widford. *Essx* 5G 53
Widford. *Herts* 4E 53
Widham. *Wilts* 3F 35
Widmer End. *Buck* 2G 37
Widmerpool. *Notts* 3D 74
Widnes. *Hal* 2H 83
Widworthy. *Devn* 3F 13
Wigan. *G Man* 4D 90
Wigbeth. *Dors* 2F 15

Woodborough. Wilts......1G 23
Woodborough. Devn......3E 13
Woodbridge. Devn......1C 14
Woodbridge. Suff......1F 55
Wood Burcote. Nptn......1E 51
Woodbury. Devn......4D 12
Woodbury Salterton. Devn......4D 12
Woodchester. Glos......5D 48
Woodchurch. Kent......2D 28
Woodchurch. Mers......2E 83
Woodcock Heath. Staf......3E 73
Woodcombe. Som......2C 20
Woodcote. Oxon......3E 37
Woodcote Green. Worc......3D 60
Woodcott. Hants......1C 24
Woodcroft. Glos......2A 34
Woodcutts. Dors......1E 15
Wood Dalling. Norf......3C 78
Woodditton. Cambs......5F 65
Wood Eaton. Staf......4C 72
Woodeaton. Oxon......4D 50
Wood End. Bed......4H 63
Wood End. Herts......3D 52
Wood End. Warw
 nr. Bedworth......2G 61
 nr. Dordon......1G 61
 nr. Tanworth-in-Arden......3F 61
Woodend. Cumb......5C 102
Woodend. Nptn......1E 50
Woodend. Staf......3F 73
Woodend. W Sus......2G 17
Wood Enderby. Linc......4B 88
Woodend Green. Essx......3F 53
Woodfalls. Wilts......4G 23
Woodfield. Oxon......3D 50
Woodfields. Lanc......1E 91
Woodford. Corn......1C 10
Woodford. Devn......3D 9
Woodford. Glos......2B 34
Woodford. G Lon......1E 39
Woodford. G Man......2C 84
Woodford. Nptn......3G 63
Woodford. Plym......3B 8
Woodford Green. G Lon......1F 39
Woodford Halse. Nptn......5C 62
Woodgate. Norf......4C 78
Woodgate. W Mid......2D 61
Woodgate. W Sus......5A 26
Woodgate. Worc......4D 60
Wood Green. G Lon......1D 39
Woodgreen. Hants......1G 15
Woodgreen. Oxon......4B 50
Woodhall. Inv......2E 127
Woodhall. Linc......4B 88
Woodhall. N Yor......5C 104
Woodhall Spa. Linc......4A 88
Woodham. Surr......4B 38
Woodham Ferrers. Essx......1B 40
Woodham Mortimer. Essx......5B 54
Woodham Walter. Essx......5B 54
Woodhaven. Fife......1G 137
Wood Hayes. W Mid......5D 72
Woodhead. Abers
 nr. Fraserburgh......2G 161
 nr. Fyvie......5E 161
Woodhill. N Som......4H 33
Woodhill. Shrp......2B 60
Woodhill. Som......4G 21
Woodhorn. Nmbd......1F 115
Woodhouse. Leics......4C 74
Woodhouse. S Yor......2B 86
Woodhouse. W Yom. Leeds......1C 92
 nr. Normanton......2D 93
Woodhouse Eaves. Leics......4C 74
Woodhouses. Ches W......3H 83
Woodhouses. G Man
 nr. Failsworth......4H 91
 nr. Sale......1B 84
Woodhouses. Staf......4F 73
Woodhuish. Devn......3F 9
Woodhurst. Cambs......3C 64
Woodingdean. Brig......5E 27
Woodland. Devn......2D 9
Woodland. Dur......2D 104

Woodland Head. Devn......3A 12
Woodlands. Abers......4E 153
Woodlands. Dors......2F 15
Woodlands. Hants......1B 16
Woodlands. Kent......4G 39
Woodlands. N Yor......4F 99
Woodlands. S Yor......4F 93
Woodlands Park. Wind......4G 37
Woodlands St Mary. W Ber......4B 36
Woodlane. Shrp......3A 72
Woodlane. Staf......3F 73
Woodleigh. Devn......4D 8
Woodlesford. W Yor......2D 92
Woodley. G Man......1D 84
Woodley. Wok......4F 37
Woodmancote. Glos
 nr. Cheltenham......3E 49
 nr. Cirencester......5F 49
Woodmancote. W Sus
 nr. Chichester......2F 17
 nr. Henfield......4D 26
Woodmancote. Worc......1E 49
Woodmancott. Hants......2D 24
Woodmansey. E Yor......1D 94
Woodmansgreen. W Sus......4G 25
Woodmansterne. Scot......5D 38
Woodmanton. Devn......4D 12
Woodmill. Staf......3F 73
Woodminton. Wilts......4F 23
Woodnesborough. Kent......5H 41
Woodnewton. Nptn......1H 63
Wood Norton. Norf......3C 78
Woodplumpton. Lanc......1D 90
Woodrising. Norf......5B 78
Wood Row. W Yor......2D 93
Woodrow. Cumb......5D 112
Woodrow. Dors
 nr. Fifehead Neville......1C 14
 nr. Hazelbury Bryan......2C 14
Woods Eaves. Here......1F 47
Woodseaves. Shrp......2A 72
Woodseaves. Staf......3C 72
Woodsend. Wilts......4H 35
Woodsetts. S Yor......2C 86
Woodsford. Dors......3C 14
Wood's Green. E Sus......2H 27
Woodshaw. Wilts......3F 35
Woodside. Aber......3G 153
Woodside. Brac......3A 38
Woodside. Derbs......1A 74
Woodside. Dum......2B 112
Woodside. Dur......2E 105
Woodside. Fife......3G 137
Woodside. Herts......5C 52
Woodside. Per......5B 144
Woodstock. Oxon......4C 50
Woodstock Slop. Pemb......2E 43
Woodston. Pet......1A 64
Wood Street. Norf......3F 79
Wood Street Village. Surr......5A 38
Woodthorpe. Derbs......3B 86
Woodthorpe. Leics......4C 74
Woodthorpe. Linc......2D 88
Woodthorpe. Notts......1C 74
Woodthorpe. York......5H 99
Woodton. Norf......1E 67
Woodtown. Devn
 nr. Bideford......4E 19
 nr. Littleham......4E 19
Woodvale. Mers......3B 90
Woodville. Derbs......4H 73
Woodwalton. Cambs......2B 64
Woodwick. Orkn......5C 172
Woodyates. Dors......1F 15
Woody Bay. Devn......2G 19
Woofferton. Shrp......4H 59
Wookey. Som......2A 22
Wookey Hole. Som......2A 22
Wool. Dors......4D 14
Woolacombe. Devn......2E 19
Woolage Green. Kent......1G 29
Woolage Village. Kent......5G 41

Woolaston. Glos......2A 34
Woolavington. Som......2G 21
Woolbeding. W Sus......4G 25
Woolcotts. Som......3C 20
Wooldale. W Yor......4B 92
Wooler. Nmbd......2D 121
Woolfardisworthy. Devn
 nr. Bideford......4D 18
 nr. Crediton......2B 12
Woolfords. S Lan......4D 128
Woolgarston. Dors......4E 15
Woolhampton. W Ber......5D 36
Woolhope. Here......2B 48
Woolland. Dors......2C 14
Woollard. Bath......5B 34
Woolley. Bath......5C 34
Woolley. Cambs......3A 64
Woolley. Corn......1C 10
Woolley. Derbs......4A 86
Woolley. W Yor......3D 92
Woolley Green. Wilts......5D 34
Woolmer Green. Worc......4D 60
Woolmer Green. Herts......4C 52
Woolminstone. Som......2H 13
Woolpit. Suff......4B 66
Woolridge. Glos......3D 48
Woolscott. Warw......4B 62
Woolsery. Devn......4D 18
Woolsington. Tyne......3E 115
Woolstaston. Shrp......1G 59
Woolsthorpe By Belvoir. Linc......2F 75
Woolsthorpe-by-
 Colsterworth. Linc......3G 75
Woolston. Devn......4D 8
Woolston. Shrp
 nr. Church Stretton......2G 59
 nr. Oswestry......3F 71
Woolston. Som......4B 22
Woolston. Sotn......1C 16
Woolston. Warr......2A 84
Woolstone. Glos......2E 49
Woolstone. Oxon......3A 36
Woolston Green. Devn......2D 9
Woolton. Mers......2G 83
Woolton Hill. Hants......5C 36
Woolverstone. Suff......2E 55
Woolverton. Som......1C 22
Woolwell. Devn......2B 8
Woolwich. G Lon......3F 39
Woonton. Here
 nr. Kington......5F 59
 nr. Leominster......4H 59
Wooperton. Nmbd......2E 121
Woore. Shrp......1B 72
Wooth. Dors......3H 13
Wootton. Bed......1A 52
Wootton. Hants......3H 15
Wootton. IOW......3D 16
Wootton. Kent......1G 29
Wootton. Nptn......5E 63
Wootton. N Lin......3D 94
Wootton. Oxon
 nr. Abingdon......5C 50
 nr. Woodstock......4C 50
Wootton. Shrp
 nr. Ludlow......3G 59
 nr. Oswestry......3F 71
Wootton. Staf
 nr. Eccleshall......3C 72
 nr. Ellastone......1F 73
Wootton Bassett, Royal
 Wilts......3F 35
Wootton Bridge. IOW......3D 16
Wootton Common. IOW......3D 16
Wootton Courtenay. Som......2C 20
Wootton Fitzpaine. Dors......3G 13
Wootton Rivers. Wilts......5G 35
Wootton St Lawrence
 Hants......1D 24
Wootton Wawen. Warw......4F 61
Worcester. Worc......5C 60
Worcester Park. G Lon......4D 38
Wordsley. W Mid......2C 60

Worfield. Shrp......1B 60
Work. Orkn......6D 172
Workhouse Green. Suff......2C 54
Workington. Cumb......2A 102
Worksop. Notts......3C 86
Worlaby. N Lin......3D 94
World's End. W Ber......4C 36
World's End. W Sus......4E 27
Worlds End. Hants......1E 17
Worlds End. W Mid......2F 61
Worldsend. Shrp......1G 59
Worle. N Som......5G 33
Worleston. Ches E......5A 84
Worlingham. Suff......2G 67
Worlington. Suff......3F 65
Worlingworth. Suff......4E 67
Wormbridge. Here......2H 47
Wormegay. Norf......4F 77
Wormelow Tump. Here......2H 47
Wormhill. Derbs......3F 85
Wormingford. Essx......2C 54
Worminghall. Buck......5E 51
Wormington. Glos......2F 49
Worminster. Som......2A 22
Wormit. Fife......1F 137
Wormleighton. Warw......5B 62
Wormley. Herts......5D 52
Wormley. Surr......2A 26
Wormshill. Kent......5C 40
Wormsley. Here......1H 47
Worplesdon. Surr......5A 38
Worrall. S Yor......1H 85
Worsbrough. S Yor......4D 92
Worsley. G Man......4F 91
Worstead. Norf......3F 79
Worsthorne. Lanc......1G 91
Worston. Lanc......5G 97
Worth. Kent......5H 41
Worth. W Sus......2D 27
Wortham. Suff......3C 66
Worthen. Shrp......5F 71
Worthenbury. Wrex......1G 71
Worthing. Norf......4B 78
Worthing. W Sus......5C 26
Worthington. Leics......3B 74
Worth Matravers. Dors......5E 15
Worting. Hants......1E 24
Wortley. Glos......2C 34
Wortley. S Yor......1H 85
Wortley. W Yor......1C 92
Worton. N Yor......1B 98
Worton. Wilts......1E 23
Wortwell. Norf......2E 67
Wotherton. Shrp......5E 71
Wothorpe. Pet......5H 75
Wotter. Devn......2B 8
Wotton. Glos......4D 48
Wotton. Surr......1C 26
Wotton-under-Edge. Glos......2C 34
Wotton Underwood. Buck......4E 51
Wouldham. Kent......4B 40
Wrabness. Essx......2E 55
Wrafton. Devn......3E 19
Wragby. Linc......3A 88
Wragby. W Yor......3E 93
Wramplingham. Norf......5D 78
Wrangbrook. W Yor......3E 93
Wrangle. Linc......5D 88
Wrangle Lowgate. Linc......5D 88
Wrangway. Som......1E 13
Wrantage. Som......4G 21
Wrawby. N Lin......4D 94
Wraxall. N Som......4H 33
Wraxall. Som......3B 22
Wray. Lanc......3F 97
Wraysbury. Wind......3B 38
Wrayton. Lanc......2F 97
Wrea Green. Lanc......1B 90
Wreay. Cumb
 nr. Carlisle......5F 113
 nr. Penrith......2F 103
Wrecclesham. Surr......2G 25
Wrecsam. Wrex......5F 83
Wrekenton. Tyne......4F 115

Wrelton. N Yor......1B 100
Wrenbury. Ches E......1H 71
Wreningham. Norf......1D 66
Wrentham. Suff......2G 67
Wrenthorpe. W Yor......2D 92
Wrentnall. Shrp......5G 71
Wressle. E Yor......1H 93
Wressle. N Lin......4C 94
Wrestlingworth. C Beds......1C 52
Wretton. Norf......1F 65
Wrexham. Wrex......5F 83
Wreyland. Devn......4A 12
Wrickton. Shrp......2A 60
Wrightington Bar. Lanc......3D 90
Wright's Green. Essx......4F 53
Wrinehill. Staf......1B 72
Wrington. N Som......5H 33
Writtle. Essx......5G 53
Wrockwardine. Telf......4A 72
Wroot. N Lin......4H 93
Wrotham. Kent......5H 39
Wrotham Heath. Kent......5H 39
Wroughton. Swin......3G 35
Wroxall. IOW......4D 16
Wroxall. Warw......3G 61
Wroxeter. Shrp......5H 71
Wroxham. Norf......4F 79
Wroxton. Oxon......1C 50
Wyaston. Derbs......1F 73
Wyatt's Green. Essx......1G 39
Wybers Wood. NE Lin......4F 95
Wyberton. Linc......1C 76
Wyboston. Bed......5A 64
Wybunbury. Ches E......1A 72
Wychbold. Worc......4D 60
Wyck Cross. E Sus......2F 27
Wychnor. Staf......4F 73
Wychnor Bridges. Staf......4F 73
Wyck. Hants......3F 25
Wyck Hill. Glos......3G 49
Wyck Rissington. Glos......3G 49
Wycliffe. Dur......3E 105
Wycombe Marsh. Buck......2G 37
Yr Wyddgrug. Flin......4E 83
Wyddial. Herts......2D 52
Wye. Kent......1E 29
Wyesham. Mon......4A 48
Wyfold. Oxon......3E 37
Wyfordby. Leics......4E 75
The Wyke. Shrp......5B 72
Wyke. Devn......3B 12
Wyke. Dors......4C 22
Wyke. Surr......5A 72
Wyke. Surr......5A 38
Wyke. W Yor......2B 92
Wyke Champflower. Som......3B 22
Wykeham. Linc......3B 76
Wykeham. N Yor
 nr. Malton......2C 100
 nr. Scarborough......1D 100
Wyken. Shrp......1B 60
Wyken. W Mid......2A 62
Wyke Regis. Dors......5B 14
Wykey. Shrp......3F 71
Wykin. Leics......1B 62
Wylam. Nmbd......3E 115
Wylde Green. W Mid......1F 61
Wylye. Wilts......3F 23
Wymering. Port......2E 17
Wymeswold. Leics......3D 74
Wymington. Bed......4G 63
Wymondham. Leics......4F 75
Wymondham. Norf......5D 78
Wyndham. B'end......2C 32
Wynford Eagle. Dors......3A 14
Wyng. Orkn......8C 172
Wynyard Village. Stoc T......2B 106
Wyre Piddle. Worc......1E 49
Wysall. Notts......3D 74
Wyson. Here......4H 59
Wythall. Worc......3E 61
Wytham. Oxon......5C 50
Wythenshawe. G Man......2C 84
Wythop Mill. Cumb......2C 102

Published by Geographers' A-Z Map Company Limited
An imprint of HarperCollins Publishers
Westerhill Road
Bishopbriggs
Glasgow
G64 2QT

www.az.co.uk
a-z.maps@harpercollins.co.uk

HarperCollinsPublishers
1st Floor, Watermarque Building, Ringsend Road, Dublin 4, Ireland

31st edition 2022

© Collins Bartholomew Ltd 2022

A catalogue record for this book is available from the British Library.

ISBN 978-0-00-852871-3

10 9 8 7 6 5 4 3 2 1

Printed in Poland